P9-BYQ-465

The Journals of

ANDRÉ GIDE

Published by VINTAGE BOOKS, INC.
Reprinted by arrangement with ALFRED A. KNOPF, INC.

THE JOURNALS OF ANDRÉ GIDE *were originally*
published in English as follows:
VOLUME I, 1889–1913: *September 15, 1947;*
VOLUME II, 1914–1927: *May 24, 1948;*
VOLUME III, 1928–1939: *March 21, 1949;*
VOLUME IV, 1939–1949: *April 16, 1951.*

Copyright 1947, 1948, 1949, 1951, 1956 by ALFRED A. KNOPF,
INC. *All rights reserved. No part of this book may be reproduced
in any form without permission in writing from the publisher,
except by a reviewer who may quote brief passages in a review
to be printed in a magazine or newspaper. Manufactured in the
United States of America. Published simultaneously in Canada
by McClelland and Stewart Limited.*

FIRST VINTAGE EDITION

The Journals of

ANDRÉ GIDE

1889–1949

EDITED, TRANSLATED, ABRIDGED, AND
WITH AN INTRODUCTION BY
Justin O'Brien

VOLUME II: 1924–1949

---

1 9 5 6
Vintage Books: New York

The Journals of

ANDRÉ GIDE

Dates in brackets have been supplied by the editor.

1924

[CONTINUED]

26 October

In the train began *The Egoist*,[5] which I continue with an increasing irritation.

A letter from Gosse informs me that I have been "unanimously" named an honorary member of the Royal Academy to replace Anatole France.[6]

Some people head toward an objective. Others simply go straight ahead.

As for me, I do not know where I am going; but I am making progress.

I am perhaps merely an adventurer.

It is only in adventure that some people succeed in knowing themselves—in finding themselves.

It is true of my *Faux-Monnayeurs* as it is of piano-practice: it is not always by plugging away at a difficulty and sticking at it that one overcomes it; but, rather, often by working on the one next to it. Certain people and certain things require to be approached on an angle.

[November]

For *Les Faux-Monnayeurs*:

There is what you know and what you don't know. Between the two what you suppose. I wonder at certain novelists who are never at a loss. As for me, rather than to invent, I prefer to confess: I don't know.

I listen to my characters; I hear what they say; but what they think and what they feel? As soon as I infer, I draw them my way. As soon as a person differentiates himself, he does so much more than one supposes. Only the masses understand the masses; community of thoughts and feelings belongs to ordinary people.

So long as Bernard kept talking I had only to listen to him; but as soon as he falls silent he eludes me; I don't know where I am.

. . .

[5] This is George Meredith's novel.
[6] Anatole France had died on 12 October 1924.

It is certain that if *I*, the novelist, have in me the character of the novelist Édouard, I must have also the novel he is writing.

(Scene of the interception of the counterfeit coin.)

P.'s "sublime remarks";

"It is by dint of praying that you come to believe."

Make the minister say in his prayer:

"My Lord, my Lord, my Lord . . . why do you withdraw from me? Are you deaf to my prayer because I am not calling you by the proper name? Must I cease believing in you, or must I believe that you are acting against me? Nothing of what I have put under your charge has prospered. I loathe thinking that when I rely on your promise I am wrong. I have put my whole family under your protection and you ignored them. I had entrusted my children to you; they grew up to curse you, and all my fidelity could not restrain their blasphemy. If I have not deceived myself, You have deceived me."

3 December

New attacks by the little Gourmont in this month's *Mercure* (apropos of the reprinting of Rivière's *Études*).[7] He blames my writings for being "full of tears and moonlight," to which, he claims, I owe my success among society people. Which is more worthy of wonder: his silliness or his bad faith? If he is convinced, how stupid he is! If he is intelligent, how false he is!

I hope that some critic, later on, will gather together these attacks and some of the perfidious shafts that certain reviews shoot at me the first of every month. Since no friend steps up to protest, any more than I do, the legend is gaining credit little by little. The public knows nothing of me but the caricature, and since it does not invite anyone to know me better, people don't go any further. What am I saying? If some people have enough curiosity to read me, they do so with such a prejudiced mind that the real meaning of my writings eludes them. They will eventually see in them what they have been told was there, and not see anything else. My sincerity is taken for a grimace, and for affectation everything that

[7] The little Gourmont is Remy's younger and less distinguished brother, Jean de Gourmont. Rivière's *Studies*, containing essays on Claudel, Gide, etc., had originally appeared in 1911.

contradicts the monster they have been persuaded I am.

The essential thing is not to write anything that one wouldn't have written without these attacks, nor to write it differently; it is to go on being what one is, just as simply as if this weren't being questioned. It would be a miracle if a singer who constantly heard that he didn't have a strong voice did not get to forcing a strong voice. Furthermore, I tell myself that after all there is a greater danger for talent in praises; as Blake would have said, they relax one; in attacks there is something "bracing" that I do not mind. The trying part of it is that they are so awkward that I have trouble recognizing that they are aimed at me. People don't strike me; they strike the artificial hump they had first rigged me up with.

To be pursued by a little simpleton who is dominated by his late brother and to whom no one listens doesn't matter. But Massis, but Béraud especially, kick up a devil of a row. . . . Their attacks have made me more famous in three months than my books had done in thirty years.

13 December

He (the demon) creates in us a sort of reverse repentance of an abominable sort, a regret not for having sinned, but for not having sinned more, for having let some opportunity for sinning slip by unused. And just as the regret for one's missteps and tears of repentance wash away earlier impurities, it sometimes happens that the soul's present corruption spreads out and overflows onto spotless pages, and that the demon wins back what had eluded him.

Kept at the Villa by grippe. Physical and moral numbness. Apathy.

Read Conrad's *Falk* and much Diderot. When he is good, he is bewitching.

20 December

Kept to my room the last few days. Not too painful confinement, thanks to M., who came to keep me company in the Villa. But my soul was wrapped in a fog that his good humor, good grace, and fancy barely succeeded in piercing. Visit from Martin du Gard every second day. He has just telephoned me for the sole purpose of asking if I have noted down our conversation of yesterday. He did not hang up until I had promised to do so at once. I wanted to convince him that *he* should do so, but he is too busy. One is more inclined to note someone else's remarks than one's own. Still, it is not so much the expression that matters here as the very substance of the conversation.

I believe what brought us to it was what I told Martin du Gard of my difficulty in recognizing people, of which I gave him a few fresh examples. . . . (In particular, I told him the story of a certain substitution of persons that I should not have noticed if Ghéon, who was present, had not warned me.)

"No," I went on, "this cannot be attributed to any lack of attention or of interest. My interest for each individual remains very great. . . . I believe it comes rather from my lack of a certain *sense of reality.* I can be extremely sensitive to the outer world, but I never succeed completely in believing in it. What I am saying has nothing theoretical about it. . . . I can imagine that a very learned doctor would be able to discover that some 'internally secreting gland,' some 'adrenal capsule' is atrophied in me. And furthermore I believe that that gland, if it exists, functions very unequally according to the individual. I even believe that this sense of the exterior world varies greatly according to the animal species. A cat is accustomed to an apartment; but were he, upon leaving this dining-room, to find next to it, instead of the long room, a virgin forest, he would not be too much surprised. I have seen my animals on certain days after a fall of snow; the landscape, even the ground, was unrecognizable; they seemed to find this quite natural and entered into that new world as if nothing had happened. It seems to me that I too. . . . If upon opening that door I were suddenly to find myself facing—well, the sea. . . . Why yes, I should say; that's odd! because I know that it ought not to be there; but that is a rationalization. I can never get over a certain amazement that things are as they are, and if they were suddenly different, it seems to me that that would hardly amaze me any more. The physical world always seems to me a little fantastic. I began to be aware of this a long time ago. It was during a trip in Brittany that I took at the age of eighteen. I had hired, at

Douarnenez I believe, a little one-seater carriage, a sort of strange gig driven by a little old coachman who was thrown from his seat by a bump; he began to slip, to slide down, beside the seat, without saying a word and without dropping the reins; he hung on for a few moments, dangling in the void I don't know just how. I had not noticed the accident at once, absorbed as I was in my reading. When I raised my eyes from my book, there was no more coachman. I leaned forward; he was on the point of falling under the wheels. I seized the reins, though this was not very easy, pulled on them, and managed to stop the horse. It was just in time. . . . But if I tell you this, it is because I recall the strange state in which I found myself. It was a sort of sudden revelation about myself. I did not feel the slightest emotion; simply I was extraordinarily interested (*amused* would be more exact), very ready moreover to avert an accident, capable of the proper reflexes, etc. But taking part in all that as if at a show *outside of reality*. And if the accident had occurred to me, it would have been exactly the same; for I don't want you to see in this a mark of insensitivity. It has happened to me . . . why, in the gondola in Venice when the gondolier who had taken me into a deserted canal at midnight put out his lantern and, standing in front of me, asked for my wallet, I experienced quite clearly the feeling that my life was in danger. Well, I could not manage to take it all 'seriously.' I acted as if I did, with complete presence of mind and in a state of extreme nervous tension and hypersensitivity . . . but I was as if at the theater, amused, simply amused. For naturally fear, real fear, becomes impossible at such moments. This is a fact: I can no longer manage to be afraid. . . . You were worried the other day to see me living in the Villa alone."

"At least, you lock your door at night?"

"No, not even when the cellar door remains open. Why, the other evening I tried to frighten myself; I was alone in the Villa; it was very late; I was seated at my table and, opposite me, behind the large glass door through which I could see only a black abyss, I made an effort to imagine the head of a burglar. I managed to make my heart beat a little faster; but it was mere amusement, nothing more. Yet I have known what fear was; when I

was a child I was extremely funky; I used to have frightful nightmares from which I would wake bathed in sweat.
. . . And suddenly the gland ceased to function. At present I can have horrible dreams, see myself pursued by
monsters, knifed, cut in bits . . . but it never becomes a
nightmare. Ah! German philosophy found in me a favorable soil. When I read Schopenhauer's *The World as Will
and Idea*, I thought at once: so that's it! But already a
certain remark of Flaubert's had given me the cue. It is, I
believe, in the preface to the poems of Bouilhet. I recall
the revelation it was for me when Pierre Louÿs read it to
me (we were still in our next to last year). It is 'advice'
that Flaubert is giving to a young man who is planning to
write. He says (I do not take responsibility for quoting it
exactly): 'If the external world has ceased to appear to
you as anything but an illusion to be described . . .' And
I do not indulge in metaphysics. I forbid myself to be a
mystic, and my intelligence does not give complete assent
either to Kant or to Plato. It's something else. I am not
worried to know whether or not I believe in the external
world: it is the *feeling of reality* that I haven't got. It
seems to me that we are all moving about in a fantastic
show and that what others call reality, that their external
world, has not much more existence than the world of
Les Faux-Monnayeurs or of *Les Thibault*."

1925

January

Some of those young men make great and somewhat ridiculous efforts to stifle the contradictions they have felt rising within them or before them, without understanding that the spark of life can flash only between two contrary poles, and that it is larger and more beautiful the greater the distance between them and the richer the opposition with which each pole is charged.

God's effort to produce the triangle from Himself.

15 May

Yesterday evening, call on Claudel. He had asked me to come and was waiting for me. At number 80 rue de Passy, an apartment set back and not giving onto the street. I go through two rooms, the second of which is rather large, and find myself in a third one, still larger, which he uses as a bedroom and workroom. Open army couch in a corner; a low book-case goes around two sides of the room; many objects, brought back from the Far East, decorate it.

At my ring, Claudel came to meet me and holds out his hand. He seems to have shrunk. A short, swansdown-lined jacket of coffee-colored silk makes him look still thicker. He is enormous and short; he looks like Ubu.[1] We sit down in two armchairs. He completely fills his. Mine, a sort of chaise-longue, has such a low back that to be comfortable in it I should have to get too far away from Claudel. I give up and lean forward.

In the presence of Claudel I am aware only of what I lack; he dominates me; he overhangs me; he has more base and surface, more health, money, genius, power, children, faith, etc., than I. I think only of obeying without a word.

Cuverville, end of May

Visit from Paul Valéry. Cleaning up and typing of five chapters of *Les Faux-Monnayeurs*. A deadly chore, which,

---

[1] The grotesque hero of Alfred Jarry's farce *King Ubu*.

however, fits my apathy. I have given up counting on anything but the Congo to get me out of it. Preparations for
this trip and the expectation of new landscapes have disenchanted the present; I am experiencing how true it was
to say that happiness lies in the moment. Nothing seems
to me anything but provisional now. (The hope of eternal
life likewise excels in this.)

My sight has weakened considerably of late. Spectacles
relieve this deficiency. Would that the brain could wear
them too! Difficulty my mind has in "focusing" the idea it
is examining; analogous to my eye's difficulty today. The
outlines remain fuzzy.

8 June

Finished *Les Faux-Monnayeurs.*

14 July

Departure for the Congo.[2]

---

[2] From July 1925 to June 1926, Le Voyage au Congo and Le
Retour du Tchad (combined in English in Travels in the Congo) take
the place of the Journal.

1926

[*Cuverville,*] *14 June*

I feel again that odd numbness of the mind, of the will, of my whole being, which I rarely experience except at Cuverville. Writing the least note takes an hour; the least letter, a whole morning.

. . . .

I was still full of fervor just a few days ago; it seemed to me that I could move mountains; today I am crushed.

The difficulty comes from this, that Christianity (Christian orthodoxy) is exclusive and that belief in *its* truth excludes belief in any other truth. It does not absorb; it repulses.

And humanism, on the contrary, or whatever other name you give to it, tends to understand and absorb all forms of life, to explain to itself if not to assimilate all beliefs, even those that repulse it, even those that deny it, even the Christian belief.

Culture must understand that by trying to absorb Christianity it is absorbing something that is mortal for it. It is trying to admit something that cannot admit it; something that denies it.

15 June

With great effort I succeed in turning out a few letters —to *Le Progrès civique,* to a minister who, in *Le Christianisme social,* had gone to some length to maltreat me, to Claudel, etc.

I have put order into my papers and tried, but in vain, to start my report to the Minister.[1] Went over a part of my travel notes. If I produce my *Journal* in continuous form, the tragic parts, which it is important to bring out, will be drowned under the abundance of descriptions, etc. I do not know what decision to make.

Strange state of mind. No desire to open any book.

[1] In 1925 André Gide and Marc Allégret spent several months in the Congo on a mission for the Ministry of Colonies: Gide returned with two volumes of travel-diaries and Allégret with a film and many still photographs.

Could this be the result of the trip? My library is disenchanted.

13 August

J. Renard: The sentence strangles the thought. He produces the right note, but always as a pizzicato.

15 August

The poor old woman who is called "Grandma" here is
eighty-six. So humpbacked, or at least so bent double
(for her back is straight) by constant gardening that she
cannot straighten up and walks with her rear higher than
her head, very slowly, leaning on a cane. She has always
worked, always labored. From Hyères she went to Saint-
Clair, whence Mme Théo brought her here out of pity and
rather than let her enter the poorhouse. Her hands are
completely deformed by rheumatism; it seems that her
feet are worse. At night she suffers so that she cannot
sleep. From morning till night she is working in the
garden, for she is always afraid of being dependent and
insists on earning her living. She pulls up the weeds—and
sometimes the flowers too, but with such zeal that no one
dares correct her. She is told: "Grandma, take a rest. It's
Sunday." But when she is not working, she is bored. She
envies those who know how to read. She remains seated
on the canal embankment, her eyes half-closed, turning
over old memories in her mind. I approach her, for she
claims that she is bored and that she enjoys chatting. But
when she complains, says that she would like to die, that
life is nothing but one long suffering for her, and "yet I
can't kill myself . . ." and then adds: "I'd like to, though"
—I don't know what to say.

It is for such creatures, to help them endure their suffering, to put up with life, that rosaries exist, and prayers,
and belief in a better life, in the reward for one's labors.
Skepticism, incredulity, are all right for the rich, the
happy, the favored, those who don't need hope and for
whom the present is enough. And that is just the saddest
part of it: poor Grandma does not believe in God, or that
anything beyond death will make up for her sorry life.

She says: "Do you want me to tell you? If there is a
God, well, he's an idiot—or a bad one. . . . He takes
away young Madame Flé, who wanted nothing better
than to go on living and whom everyone liked. And I

want nothing better than to die, but he prolongs me.
. . ." All this said with the accent of the Midi.

22 August

We reached Auxerre by auto from Brignoles. Spent the
first night at Grenoble. Modernized city; nothing left of
the charm of the Place Grenette in 1890, when André
Walter was looking for an inn where he could settle down
and write his *Cahiers*.[2] The square was full of life, but not
noisy as it is today. As far as I can remember, it was surrounded with old houses. There were blossoming orange
trees in tubs. A heady perfume floated in the air in front
of the café terrace where I sipped a coffee ice, white with
milk (such as I have never tasted since). I did not yet
know Stendhal.[3] I did not yet smoke. My glance was
chaste and did not disturb, or but rarely, my peace of
mind. The hotel was dear and I was afraid of not having
enough money.

Exhausting landscape of the Grenoble environs. We
stopped at Les Mées to have a close view of the very odd
alignments of rocks with unexplainable erosions.

The second day, spent the night at Bourg. The tame
fox belonging to the hotelkeepers. His amorous play with
the dogs. The following day was market day (Wednes-
day). Amazing produce of the farms; each farmer's wife,
well dressed, in line with her hand placed on the basket
in front of her, which was full of butter, eggs, vegetables,
and sometimes a little bouquet of centauries or garden
flowers.

Church of Brou. Overloading: useless and cosmopolitan
luxury. Bought, imported art, come from a distance. The
marvel of Florence is that the art is born of the very soil.
The only really Christian art is that which, like St.
Francis, does not fear being wedded to poverty. This
rises far above art as adornment. Nothing is less Christian,
less spiritual than the ornamentation of Brou. Very beautiful, however, but profane. Preciosity begins with useless
expense.

All our writers of today (I am speaking of the best)

[2] Gide's first published work was entitled *The Notebooks of André
Walter*.
[3] Born in Grenoble, on the Place Grenette, Henri Beyle (Stendhal)
spent his childhood there.

are *precious*. I hope to acquire ever more poverty. (Paradox.) In destitution lies salvation.

Cluny. One has not the right to be consoled for this crime. The church sold, becoming a quarry for ready-cut stones. The exploitation of others' work.

Amazing Cluny stud-farm. Wonderful neck and withers of the work-horses. Those in the Renaissance drawings were not at all exaggerated, then. The animal—a work of art. Between the bars of their stalls we twice see stallions rub their noses together, knock their teeth together, one of them seize and suck the other's tongue, all with delight and undeniable signs of sexual pleasure. I stay rather long watching them. The stable-master as he passes says: "They are trying to bite each other. When they are too vicious they sometimes have to be separated." Is he deceived? or, out of propriety, is he trying to deceive us?

Spent the night at Beaune, at the hotel where I had dined with Copeau two years ago. Rather early the next day, visit to the Copeaus at Pernand. Jacques Copeau in very good form, but no time to talk. I regret seeing Copeau enjoy and encourage his son's shortcomings. He shows me with indulgence a sheaf of large brown sheets on which Pascal has pasted photographs of political figures cut out of periodicals—and carefully, cleverly chosen to throw the most unfavorable light on the "government." With such a device one could make Christ himself ridiculous.

When I ask Jacques if it wouldn't be painful to him to see such a *treatment* inflicted on us, and if he is quite sure that we would come off any better, he replies: "We would always have more nobility." But I do not believe this. I have just seen, among M.'s photos, certain portraits of me back from the Chad that would delight Béraud and Massis; and Copeau himself doesn't always look like a "great man."

Spent the night at Semur.

Auxerre—then Chablis, where I am writing this.

23 August

The London Royal Society of Literature, of which I was elected a member, eighteen months ago, to take the place of France (or Loti?), asks me today what titles and

decorations are to follow my name in the list of Honorary
Fellows that is "about to appear."

I reply: "Honors began by fleeing me. Later I fled
honors. On the list of Honorary Fellows of the Royal Society my name is not to be followed by any title. The
F.R.S.L. will only stand out the better."

The most important things to say are those which often
I did not think necessary for me to say—because they
seemed to me too obvious.

[Pontigny,] 26 August

Finished correcting the proofs of *Les Nourritures* (Aveline edition).[4] Fear of self-indulgence leads me to take a
severe view of that book. The constant use of dashes (I
am suppressing more than three quarters of them) annoys
me, and even more of certain words, particularly the
"après," of which I make an improper and excessive use.[5]
But, despite myself, I must recognize the importance of
this book. And, after all, it is such as it had to be, and
successful. It is even well composed, and all the disag-
gregation of the middle was inevitable and necessary. The
last part brings this out and, in its very dissatisfaction,
announces something different and leads farther. I read
there the permission of becoming—and almost the announcement of my subsequent books, of what I have become. For anyone who is willing to read carefully and
without prejudice, there is the criticism of the book in the
book itself, as is fitting.

It does not seem to me possible that, some day, a critic
shall not come along and notice all this on his own. And
that it would have been madness to write this book with
more wisdom.

I understand moreover what Lebey disliked here. "It is
from this point onward that you must write." But it so

[4] A new edition of *Les Nourritures terrestres* (*The Fruits of the
Earth*) was brought out in 1927 by Claude Aveline, Éditeur, with an
important new preface by Gide dated July 1926 and two appendices:
one containing an enthusiastic letter from Albert Samain dated 1897
and the other reproducing the original publisher's inventories, which
show that exactly five hundred copies were sold during the first ten
years (1897–1908).

[5] Gide must be referring to the independent use of *"après"* in the
sense of "later on."

happens that this book (the middle of this book at least)
had to be stammered. And the least precious epithet, the
least attempt at an effect, all effort toward literature, had
to be banished from it. It went against everything that
"symbolism" liked. It was with this book that I was to
begin to get myself reviled.

29 August

Dreadful fatigue. The Pontigny discussions are getting
more and more specialized.[6] Only professional philoso-
phers can take part in them. I wonder at the outlay of
subtlety on the part of those who, without any creative
power, exhaust the unrest of their strong minds in the
examination and critical analysis of others' works. Just because, in a few words, I tried to bring Montaigne a little
closer to reality, to *his* reality, just because I tried to de-
scend a bit from those abstract regions in which the air
was becoming almost unbreathable for many among us, I
am now looked upon as an enemy of philosophy.

16 October

Paris again. Tumult. I feel myself becoming unsociable.
No desire to chat any more. And more absolutely: no
desires. Conversation with Adrienne Monnier, who does
not like *Les Faux-Monnayeurs*. In general there is taking
place with this latest book what has already taken place
so many times with the preceding ones. The most recent
one is liked only by those who hadn't yet liked the others,
and all the readers who had been won over by the preceding books declare they like "this one much less." I am
accustomed to it and know that it is enough to wait.

Adrienne Monnier talks to me for some time and rather
eloquently of the coldness and fundamental *unkindness*
that this book reveals and that must be my hidden nature.
I don't know what to say, what to think. Whatever criticism is made of me, I always acquiesce. But I know that
Stendhal likewise was long accused of insensibility and
coldness. . . .

---

[6] In 1910 Paul Desjardins organized summer discussion groups in
the abandoned Abbey of Pontigny, which gathered writers and artists
from all over Europe. Each *décade*, or ten-day session, was devoted to
a specific topic. With an interruption during the first World War,
those meetings, at which Gide was one of the most regular attendants,
continued until 1939.

1927

There is not a single declaration of this type (profession of fidelity in the preface to *Les Nourritures*[1]) that does not seem to me to ring a little false when I reread it a short time afterward. What is the good of saying one was sincere when writing it? There is no character so simple that it does not involve complicated byways. The peculiarity that seems to win out is the one on which attention centers; the mere beholding eye already distorts and enlarges. One loses sight of the whole physiognomy, and a certain feature that one causes to dominate is not perhaps the dominant feature.

Because it has always been easier for me to choose and to reject in the name of someone else than in my own name, and because I always feel I am impoverishing myself when I limit myself, I am quite willing to have no well-defined existence if the individuals I create and draw from myself have one.

Saint-Clair, 8 February

Everything I might write to explain, exonerate, or defend myself I must refuse myself. I often imagine such a preface for *L'Immoraliste,* for *Les Faux-Monnayeurs,* for *La Symphonie pastorale*—one, above all, that would set forth what I mean by fictional objectivity, that would establish two sorts of novels, or at least two ways of looking at and depicting life, which in certain novels (*Wuthering Heights,* Dostoyevsky's novels) are joined. The first, exterior and commonly called objective, which begins by visualizing others' acts and events and then

---

[1] "I am commonly judged on the basis of this youthful book, as if the ethics of *Les Nourritures* had been mine throughout life, as if I had not been the very first to follow the advice I give to my young reader: 'Throw my book away and leave me.' Yes, I immediately left the man I was when I wrote *Les Nourritures;* to such a point that, when I examine my life, the dominant feature I find in it—far from being inconstancy—is fidelity. That profound fidelity of heart and mind I believe to be infinitely rare. Those who, before dying, can see accomplished what they had planned to accomplish, I ask you to name them, and I take my place among them."

interprets them. The second, which begins by paying attention to emotions and thoughts and runs the risk of being powerless to depict anything that the author has not first felt himself. The resources of the author, his complexity, the antagonism of his too diverse possibilities, will permit the greatest diversity of his creations. But everything derives from him. He is the only one to vouch for the truth he reveals, and the only judge. All the heaven and hell of his characters is in him. It is not himself that he depicts, but he could have become what he depicts if he had not become everything himself. It was in order to be able to write *Hamlet* that Shakespeare did not let himself become Othello.

. . . Yes, I could set forth all this. But haven't I already said it or let it be sufficiently understood when speaking of Dostoyevsky? What is the good of repeating? It is better to say to the reader: read me more carefully; reread me; and go on to something else.

One of the great rules of art: do not linger.

Nothing is accomplished if I have not truly been able to become, to the point of deceiving myself, this character that I am assuming and to depersonalize myself in him to the extent of being blamed for never having managed to portray anyone but myself—however different from one another may be Saul, Candaules, Lafcadio, the minister of my *Symphonie pastorale,* or La Pérouse or Armand. It is returning to myself that embarrasses me, for, in truth, I no longer really know who I am; or, if you prefer: I never *am;* I am *becoming.*

Paris, 11 February

All that Hirsch found to quote in the account of my travels in the Congo was the paragraph having to do with elephantiasis of the genital organs, so frequent among the natives—a juicy morsel for the readers of the *Mercure;* and in the commentary preceding and following the quotation Hirsch went to great lengths to ridicule me— and this is always easy when speaking of someone you don't know. Now, I am known to the readers of the *Mercure* only by Jean de Gourmont's invectives and by Hirsch's silences. I warned Vallette that more than I was involved; that it was inadmissible for the *Mercure* to pass over in silence so legitimate a claim; that Hirsch ought for a time to declare a truce, even if he is to resume his silence and hostility right afterward. And this month Hirsch disarms, quotes me at length, and even claims to "regret" his irony of the preceding month. It is so disagreeable to me to hear my "humanity" praised by him that it makes me, too, "regret" his irony and silence. The only praise that touches me comes from those I can esteem.

But I am writing all this only for the sake of writing something and of getting back into the habit of chatting with this notebook.

5 *March*

They insist on seeing in *Les Faux-Monnayeurs* an abortive book. The same thing was said of Flaubert's *Éducation sentimentale* and of Dostoyevsky's *The Possessed*. (I remember that what made me read *The Possessed* and *The Brothers Karamazov* was the retreat of that great ninny Melchior before these "apocalyptical and sinister" books.[2]) Before twenty years are up it will be recognized that what people now hold against my book is precisely its qualities. I am sure of this.

[*Zurich,*] 6 *May*

Lunched with Strohl, whom I had gone to pick up at the university, where he shows me various collections of shells, shellfish, corals, insects—of the greatest interest; visit somewhat spoiled, in my memory, by my need of showing off my knowledge—but it was also to encourage Strohl, whose conversation can become most exalting. He always says exactly what can be most valuable to me, and I listen to him tirelessly. A pity that his study of me is so awkward in expression![3] He takes me to lunch in a little restaurant in old Zurich made precious by the memory of Gottfried Keller. I insist on paying for the meal; but, through awkwardness, "modesty," stinginess, I leave an insufficient tip, the memory of which is enough to poison the rest of the day for me.

[2] Gide is referring to Eugène-Melchior de Vogüé in *Le Roman russe* (1886), which introduced Russian fiction to France.
[3] Jean Strohl's study of Gide entitled "Reflections on the Relations between Art and Science" appeared in the volume of homage called *André Gide* and published by Éditions du Capitole in 1928.

Yesterday Strohl had taken me on a wonderful auto ride, in a landscape extraordinarily full of flowers: unbroken conversation that teaches me more than the reading of a pile of books.

7 May

What annoys me is not being able to understand why I left an insufficient tip.—Could it be because I felt that Strohl was watching me?

Yes, perhaps.

(See Ubu's admirable remark to Mme Ubu: "You are very ugly today. Is it because we have guests?" [4])

Basel, 11 May

Retrospective exhibit of Böcklin. Enough to make one think that there is no real school or tradition of painting (in our day and for some time now) except in France. Today all the foreign painters of value come to Paris to be informed. Böcklin is worth nothing save by his intentions. The hell of art is paved with them. Nothing distinguishes some of his canvases from the most vulgar daubs, except a certain assurance that impresses and that apes *maestria*. What vulgarity! What presumptuousness! Poverty of draftsmanship. Bumptiousness of the color.

Heidelberg, 12 May

The game is lost, which I could win only with her. Lack of confidence on her part, and great assumption on mine. It is no good to recriminate, or even to regret. What *is not* is what *could not be*. Whoever starts out toward the unknown must consent to venture alone. Creusa, Eurydice, Ariadne, always a woman tarries, worries, fears to let go and to see the thread break that ties her to her past. She pulls Theseus back and makes Orpheus look back. She is afraid.

One by one I recapture each thought of my youth.

The want of logic annoys. Too much logic bores. Life eludes logic, and everything that logic alone constructs remains artificial and forced. *Therefore* is a word the poet must not know, which exists only in the mind.

"Infinite" conversations with Ernst-Robert Curtius. I often feel closer to him than perhaps to anyone else; and

---

[4] In Alfred Jarry's farce *Ubu Roi* (*King Ubu*).

not only am I not embarrassed by our diversity of origin, but my thought finds an encouragement in that very diversity. It seems to me more authentic, more valid, when, in contact with his, I become aware that there was no need for this or that particular culture to produce it and that, having both set out from such different places, we meet on so many points. Finally, I find in him, in his eyes, in the tone of his voice, in his gestures, a gentleness, amenity, and kindness that are as if evangelical and to which my confidence responds more and more.

To win one's joy through struggle is better than to yield to melancholy.

Need of asserting this, after reading some *"Notes en marge des Voyageurs traqués"* by Montherlant[5]—who, as it just happens, informs me of his return and says he wishes to see me:

Arrogance and boredom are the two most authentic products of hell. I have done everything to defend myself against them and have not always succeeded in keeping them at a distance. They are the two great provinces of romanticism. It is always easier to yield to them than to overcome them, and it is impossible to achieve this without some deceit. It is important to know when to prefer being a dupe, lending oneself to delusion, and the cleverest man, in this regard, is surely not the one "who cannot be imposed on," but who on the contrary enters into the game, above all anxious to maintain his joy.

No, I do not want anything to do with a felicity that can spoil clairvoyance. It is essential to be able to find happiness beyond. Acceptation; confidence; serenity. Virtues of an old man. The age of struggling with the angel is over.

Cuverville, June

They talk of constructing a system. Artificial construction from which all life immediately withdraws. I let *my* system grow up slowly and naturally. What eludes logic is the most precious element in us, and one can draw

[5] The issue of the *Nouvelle Revue Française* (N.R.F.) for January 1927 carried some reflections by Henry de Montherlant entitled *"Les Voyageurs traqués"* ("The Hunted Travelers"), and the June issue some "Supplementary Notes to 'The Hunted Travelers'" to which Gide is alluding here.

nothing from a syllogism that the mind has not put there in advance. I let the most antagonistic proposals of my nature gradually come to agreement without violence. Suppressing the dialogue in oneself really amounts to stopping the development of life. Everything leads to harmony. The fiercer and more persistent the discord had been, the broader the reconciliation blossoms.

It is as natural for him who borrows his thought from another to hide the source as it is for him who recognizes his thought in another to proclaim that meeting of minds.

The most original artists are not necessarily the most uncultivated.

However rare and bold a thought may be, it is impossible that it should not be related to some other; and the greater an artist's solitude in his own epoch, the greater and more fecund his joy at finding relatives in the past.

Youth attracts me, and even more than beauty. A certain freshness, an innocence, one would like to recapture. . . .

3 July

This morning, as soon as I awake (much too early) my brain, despite me, begins to construct sentences. Some of them are quite well turned out, but mean nothing. There are some that I should like not to lose, that I try to learn by heart, to remember; and it is all up with sleep.

Good God, how complicated everything is becoming! Lines in all directions; and no guidance. No way of knowing what to believe, what to think! . . .

Cuverville

Unhealthy torpor. The constrictions and pains in the esophagus (?) are becoming almost continuous and unbearable. I take refuge in sleep like a sulky child withdrawing from the game.

Reread *La Jeune Parque.*[6] Despite some charming movements that artifice alone could not invent and in which Valéry shows himself to be truly a musician, I cannot prefer this long poem to certain other ones, more recent and shorter, of *Charmes.* Not yet sufficiently de-

[6] Paul Valéry's long poem, *The Young Fate*, which marked his return to literature. The title *Charmes* contains a play on the Latin *Carmina* and the word *Charms* in the sense of *spells*.

tached from Mallarmé; marking time; abuse of the return to oneself, of the meander. . . .

11 August

It is a mistake to intend to write only very important things in a *Journal*. That is not its justification. I want to write in it this evening what I should write if I had kept it up the last few days.

Great fatigue of the heart, yesterday and especially to-day. Done nothing that matters.

In the morning wrote some letters; read with Élisabeth Van Rysselberghe the beginning of the twelfth canto of the *Purgatorio*, which I finish alone a little later. How have I been able to abandon Dante for so long?—(I like Élisabeth's application, and her patience, and her horror of the approximate.) In the evening a chapter of the *Grüne Heinrich*. But I feel devoid of vigor, devoid of virtue.

13 August

I drag myself around all day long.—How many times have I already written that sentence! Yet, this morning, rather good work. M. helps me considerably; and I am cowardly about letting myself be helped, ready to accept any idea, any sentence that is offered me. I am astonished that I can differ from myself to this extent.

I cannot cease thinking of this work on the big Concessionary Companies, and so long as I have not finished it, I shall not feel as if I belong to myself.[7] How difficult everything seems to me! I progress step by step, laboring, out of breath, of joy, of fervor. Can anything good come out of such an exertion of all the faculties? But I will not, I cannot, let go. It seems to me that I shall never see the end of it. And all day long I keep repeating to myself: *It must be done,* and it will not be done by anyone else.

1 October

Maurois speaks of Wilde with elegance; the witticisms he quotes are well chosen; but this little study—very much a "lecture before a ladies' club"—leaves me dissatisfied.[8] One feels that he does not *possess* his subject. The "figure in the carpet" eludes him; or is he pretending not

[7] A reference to an article for the *Revue de Paris*, in which he reveals the abuses of those companies in exploiting the African natives.
[8] The study appeared in *Études anglaises* (*English Studies*).

to see it? [9] I believe to be utterly false what he repeats
after so many others, or what he lets be assumed: that
Wilde's way of life was a dependence of his æstheticism
and that he merely carried over into his habits his love of
the artificial. I believe quite on the contrary that this
affected æstheticism was for him merely an ingenious
cloak to hide, while half revealing, what he could not let
be seen openly; to excuse, provide a pretext, and even apparently motivate; but that that very motivation is but a
pretense. Here, as almost always, and often even without
the artist's knowing it, it is the secret of the depths of his
flesh that prompts, inspires, and decides.

Lighted in this way and, as it were, from beneath,
Wilde's plays reveal, beside the surface witticisms, sparkling like false jewels, many oddly revelatory sentences of
great psychological interest. And it is for them that Wilde
wrote the whole play—let there be no doubt about it.

Try to let some understand what one has an interest in
hiding from all. As for me, I have always preferred frankness. But Wilde made up his mind to make of falsehood a
work of art. Nothing is more precious, more tempting,
more flattering than to see in the work of art a falsehood
and, reciprocally, to look upon falsehood as a work of art.
That is what made him say: "Never use *I*." The *I* belongs
to the very face, and Wilde's art had something of the
mask about it, insisted on the mask. But never did he
mean to say thereby: be "objective." Always he managed
in such a way that the informed reader could raise the
mask and glimpse, under it, the true visage (which Wilde
had such good reasons to hide). This artistic hypocrisy
was imposed on him by respect, which was very keen in
him, for the proprieties; and by the need of self-protec-
tion. Likewise, moreover, for Proust, that great master of
dissimulation.

How much more flattering it is to see a critic, out of
malice or spite, force himself to disparagement than, out
of cliquishness, to indulgence!

5 October

How to get into a novel that impression felt as I entered the D.'s the other evening? First it would take the

[9] Gide uses Henry James's title in English.

gradual portrayal of a young, good, intelligent person, often capable of the best, but clumsy when it comes to getting someone to love him, or rather hardly even aiming for this, out of misanthropy, disdain, pride; courageous, but timid in the face of life; full of withdrawals, and seeming, even in broad daylight, covered with shadow; capable of resolve, but without enough enthusiasm to make his way; already crushed by petty cares.

When, after dinner, I enter their little living-room, he is smoking his pipe beside a gramophone that he is playing probably not so much for his sake as to amuse his young wife and his sister-in-law; she lives with them to help in the housekeeping; the three of them are there in that little room to which he returns after the day's work. This is the only time he has to himself. And this time even, when he could catch hold of himself, is completely taken up by the family. In order to live on the same level as "his family," he comes down from his level, sets himself on that modest plane. Could he, with greater financial resources, spend more time by himself? I don't believe so. I believe he would not try to. These evening hours he owes to his young wife, whom he has not seen all day. He feels mediocrity sweeping over him. But what can he do about it? He has ceased struggling; sacrifices himself, hiding within him his ambitions, his dreams, his hopes, everything that would compromise that domestic felicity. —The chapter would be entitled:

CONJUGAL HAPPINESS
Et tibi magna satis . . .[10]

And no possible way out; no escape that does not appear cowardly, egotistical, impious . . . to the weak person.

9 October

At Cuverville again. Arrived yesterday on the evening train after a very reassuring visit to Dr. A., who informs me of the result of the X-rays I had taken four days ago. Those spasms of the esophagus, from which I suffered during my last stay in Cuverville, do not have the terrible organic cause I had feared. Due probably to ill-regulated

[10] "And large enough for you . . ." from Virgil: *Bucolics*, I, 47

reflexes caused by hypertrophy of the liver. And most likely
my recent spells of insomnia have no other cause either.

A rather good night and this morning, at my awakening, radiant weather. A sky such as we have not seen all
summer.

I took care to leave in Paris all the files relative to the
Congo, to get rid of it, at last.[11] (My article on the Concessionary Companies is to appear in a few days in the
Revue de Paris.) More loaded down with projects than
ever.

Finished learning the Prelude in F-sharp major from
the second book.

These last few days in Paris, I should have written excellent pages if only I had had the time. To what a degree
I can be upset by "others," they will never know.

Do not pose in your own presence. *Id est:* do not affect
the qualities and virtues you would like to have but have
not.

But the human being is so extraordinarily perfectible
(Amiel would first have written: malleable, alterable,
etc.)—that often you become what you want to be, and
you eventually really experience the feeling that you began by pretending to experience; that is, if you are not
playing that comedy for others. And how many people,
just because they thought themselves devout or in love,
soon became sincerely devout or in love! How many, on
the other hand, by doubting their sentiments, prevented
them from developing! It is not bad, on occasion, to trust
yourself. It is almost always good to trust another, for the
credit he sees extended to this or that virtue binds him
and encourages him to take on what he would not have
been able to maintain if left to himself. Certain persons
keep themselves in the path of virtue only in order to
resemble the opinion they know, or hope, that others have
of them. Nothing can be more harmful, for certain
people, than trying to achieve sincerity, which inclines
them to doubt of what are often their best sentiments, to
consider themselves sure only of the worst. I never *am;*
I am *becoming.* I am becoming the person that I believe

---

[11] The last seven words appear in English.

(or that *you* believe) I am. There is in every human being a little bit of the irresistible and a great deal of as you will. And even the share of irresistible can be reduced.

(It is easier to think this at the age of fifty-eight than at twenty.)

If it is still fanciful at the age of sixty to think you know yourself thoroughly; it is dangerous at twenty to try to know yourself thoroughly.

My desire, doubtless, is sincere; but my desire to overcome it is no less so. But that is not the important thing, and it matters little to me to weigh the authenticity of one or the other. The important thing is to know whether I am right to try to overcome that desire, whether I am struggling out of fear or virtue, out of fear of others or of myself, etc., etc. Questions, moreover, that I never ask myself any more. The novelist who makes his hero ask himself these things one after another is not following truth; or else his hero is a mere hypocrite. One begins instinctively by solving all these questions; one asks them of oneself only later on and only if one is a quibbler. They do not so often precede action as they substitute for it.

The sentence that begins with: "I know myself . . ." always ends with a negative. "I know myself: I . . . not. . . ."

11 October

Radiant weather, projection of my inner serenity. Read the sermon on "the rich man"—or "final impenitence." [12] Some Herrick.

Made a bit more progress in my new novel, for which I have not yet found a title.

12 October

Everything is ready for work; I cleared up everything yesterday in order to get at it as soon as I get up; but here is the mail: no less than fifteen letters; and in addition I have left four on my mantel that have been awaiting a reply since my return here.

From Paris I write that I am leaving for Cuverville; from Cuverville, that I am soon to return to Paris. . . .

---

[12] Bossuet's *Sermon on the Evil Rich Man* or on *Final Impenitence,* inspired by Luke xvi, was preached before the court during Lent of 1662.

20 October

My grandmother Rondeaux, likewise, had saved up for
the end the best of what she had to say, the last instruc-
tions and recommendations she wished to leave with her
children. When she felt that the solemn hour was approaching, she gathered them all round her, but at that
moment was seized with a paralysis of the tongue and,
instead of a sublime speech, could only utter a tremendous
scream. Such a loud scream, Albert told me as he related
this recollection, that it was heard all the way to the end
of the garden. This took place at La Mivoie.

That is perhaps what lies in store for me if I delay too
much.

I cannot be satisfied with Roger Martin du Gard's absolute nihilism. I do not sidestep it, nor repulse it, but
intend to go beyond, to pass through it. It is beyond,
that I want to rebuild. It strikes me as monstrous that
man should need the idea of God in order to feel steady
on earth; that he should be forced to accept absurdities
in order to construct something solid; that he should
recognize himself incapable of demanding of himself
what religious convictions obtained from him artificially,
so that he lets himself go to nothing as soon as his heaven
is empty.

The best thing Sisyphus can do is to leave his rock
alone and to climb up on it in order to "dominate the
situation." But, for this, it is still essential that the rock
should be of good quality. How many of these young
writers, who make so much of their writhings, are pushing
only a cardboard rock, or have nothing to lift but a book-
case.

This image of Sisyphus is very good, but I believe I
have already used it. It's a pity. But it is better to use it
twice than to let it be lost.

23 October

All the thoughts that desire once nourished, all the
anxieties it provoked, ah, how difficult it becomes to understand them when the source of lust dries up! And how
can one be surprised by the intransigence of those who
have never been led by desire? . . . It seems, with the
coming of age, that one had somewhat exaggerated its

demands and one is astonished to see younger men letting themselves still be tormented. The waves subside when the wind drops; the whole ocean falls asleep and reflects the sky. Knowing how to wish for the inevitable, this is all wisdom. All the wisdom of the aged.

28 October

I do not believe the future will be grateful to us for all the care we take with our books; quite the contrary, too much care might well cool them off sooner than others.

The habit of reading, for past centuries, only the books that deserved to survive does not give us much idea of why the others perished. Without going very far back, there is something to be learned from reading, for instance, Feydeau's *Fanny,* which many contemporaries of Flaubert considered a masterpiece. I believe that, later on, *Le Nègre* by Soupault—which I have just read in the train taking me to Carcassonne—will not encounter any more indulgence, and that the very virtues of the book will seem, above all, examples of self-satisfaction, a sort of assent to oneself and to the epoch. . . . But nothing is harder than to get outside one's epoch enough to perceive the shortcomings common to a whole generation.

I am writing this very badly, tired out by a sleepless night. Arriving in Carcassonne before six o'clock, I had nevertheless been sleeping since Toulouse and got out of my compartment in such haste that I left in it a hat that was as dear to me as Lafcadio's beaver to him.[13]

Carcassonne, 30 October

How charming Alibert was yesterday when he exclaimed: "I would give all the symphonies of Beethoven, yoo all the symphonies for a single ballade by Chopin!"

Never younger, more intelligent, more lively, more delightful. One of the very rare people who have not let themselves be misled, or intimidated. Much more intelligent than his work suggests; there is no psychological, ethical, social, literary question on which you cannot talk with him endlessly and in the most amusing way, for he knows how to laugh and make others laugh, and knows how not to laugh when it is appropriate to be sad or anxious. I haven't a single friend with whom I feel more

[13] In *Les Caves du Vatican (Lafcadio's Adventures)* the hero loses his new beaver hat in sensational circumstances on a train.

perfectly at ease; that is to say, with whom I have to be less wary in talking. Conversation, under such circumstances, far from being a strain and an acrobatic feat, is restful, and one lets oneself go as to a natural impulse.

He is surprised to see me like Chardin so much. It was natural that, but little gifted to like painting naturally, I should attach myself particularly to a painter whom I could like only quite specifically for the qualities of which I had been most peculiarly deprived. In the beginning I may have had to apply myself, but, certain of liking him for the right reason, there are few painters who more authentically taught me to enjoy painting.

4 November

Daniel Simond, from Lausanne, whom I meet the day before yesterday on the boulevards and invite to lunch this noon, tells me that his professor has suggested to him as a thesis-subject: the influence of Nietzsche on my work. It is flattering; but to what can it lead? To seeking out, in my *Immoraliste* for example, everything that might recall Zarathustra and paying no attention to what life itself taught me.

The book was entirely composed in my head and I had begun to write it when I made my encounter with Nietzsche, who at first got in my way. I found in him, not an instigation, but rather on the contrary a hindrance. If Nietzsche stood me in good stead in this case, it was subsequently by purging my book of a whole theoretical side that could not but have overweighted it.

I have reflected considerably about this question of "influences" and believe that very gross errors are committed in this regard. The only thing that is worth anything in literature is what life teaches us. Everything we learn only from books remains abstract, a dead letter. Had I not encountered Dostoyevsky, Nietzsche, Blake, or Browning, I cannot believe that my work would have been any different. At the most they helped me to disentangle my thought. And even then? I took pleasure in hailing those in whom I recognized my thought. But that thought was mine, and it is not to them that I owe it. Otherwise it would be valueless. The great influence perhaps that I have really *undergone* is that of Goethe, and even then I am not sure whether or not my admiration for Greek literature and Hellenism would not have sufficed to counterbalance my original Christian formation.

Furthermore, I feel rich enough never to have tried to pass off as mine the thoughts that belonged to someone else.

Alibert told me that he wondered if one ought not to see precaution, prudence on the part of Racine's wife, much rather than the indifference that is generally imputed to her, in her refusal to read or see any play by her husband. Shouldn't one see in it respect for the work and a need of giving assurance wholeheartedly in a domain that escaped her competence?[14]

This is about what Alibert told me; but I have just re-read in the biographical notice (at the head of the Grands Écrivains de la France edition) what Paul Mesnard wrote on this subject, which does not contribute, it must be admitted, to these suppositions. Perhaps Alibert outlined that thesis to me only because he was thinking more of Cuverville and of me than of Racine, and perhaps he was attempting, under this pretext, to show me discreetly how capable he was of understanding the modesty and secret wisdom of such a feminine reserve. In Racine's household it accompanied Racine's renunciation and almost the disavowal of his thought.

6 November

I am an unbeliever. I shall never be an ungodly man.

Those who claim to act according to rules of life (however beautiful those rules may be) strike me as idiots, or at least blunderers, incapable of taking advantage of life —I mean: of learning from life. In any case unbearable people.

9 November

One must resign oneself to it: rather than to remain sullen, deign to say a few banalities, a few stupidities. Moreover, this puts the other at ease.

Under whatever form it appears, there is no worse enemy than mysticism. I have reason to know. And I should like my deep knowledge of the subject, through

[14] I believe today that one must see in it a quite Christian horror of what belongs to the demon, and that Mme Racine had much to do with her husband's silence. (Added in 1929.) [A.]

repeated personal experience and through sympathy (for theoretical, or philosophical, or historical, or scientific knowledge of the mystical state scarcely informs one at all), to give some weight to my evidence. It is too easy to jump with Souday to the conclusion that every swerve in that direction implies a certain lack of gray matter. Sympathy—yes, sympathy, detachment and diffidence, and modesty can intervene. I claim to be much better qualified to denounce or accuse mysticism than someone who has never had to deal with it.

"But what do you mean by 'mystical'?"

"Whatever presupposes and demands the abdication of the reason."

24 November

B. sends me a series of American newspaper and magazine articles on the translation of *Les Faux-Monnayeurs*.

Sad to note that there is not one of them that is not better than the best of the articles that appeared in France.

With one or two exceptions, when a French critic wants to write an article about me, he strives not to explain or understand me, but to take up and maintain a position against me.

25 November

Noting the progressive decay of age requires the most difficult form of sincerity to obtain from oneself. A journal that kept track of it would be vastly interesting. Moreover I do not believe that that decay is unavoidable, and, were it not for a slight weakening of my senses (sight especially), I should barely feel touched by age; if I did not see it in the mirror and if I did not constantly repeat it to myself, nothing in me would remind me that three days ago I entered my fifty-ninth year. But perhaps it is one of the privileges of age not to be too conscious itself of what is a glaring fact to everyone else.

DETACHED PAGES

If the book had not already appeared,[15] I should take care to add to the appendix several considerations that the excessive zeal of some may arouse.

[15] *Voyage au Congo* and *Retour du Tchad* (*Travels in the Congo*).

Nothing more prejudicial to a cause, however excellent it may be, than certain exaggerations on the part of its defenders. The adversaries of that cause easily turn this into a weapon, which they turn against the cause, retaining and presenting to the public only the very exaggeration of certain claims, in themselves, however, thoroughly justified.

In the almost total ignorance of the public in regard to colonial questions, it is only too easy to mislead opinion in one direction or the other. No possible check. In case of a conflict, the victory most often goes to the one who speaks loudest, or longest, or last.

I should merely like to indicate here the few reflections I have had as a result of the polemics opened up concerning the abuses my book denounced.

It seems to me, to begin with, that the famous question of portage, which has been especially brought up, has not been examined calmly. Were I to astonish or even to inspire indignation in some people, I must confess, to be frank, that I cannot denounce the custom of portage. Its abuses are frightful. In itself I cannot consider it an evil. Besides, it seems to me inevitable. Some people write, rather thoughtlessly: the railway, trucks, and boats must everywhere take the place of portage. That is easy to say. But for the railway tremendous construction work is required; for trucks, motor roads are needed; and as for the boats themselves, since the Congo becomes navigable again only at a great distance from its mouth, it is necessary—it was long necessary at least (see *The Heart of Darkness*[16])—to transport through the jungle, on human backs, the heavy dismantled parts of any boat whatever.

Portage will therefore be, for a long time at least, necessary. The African native, moreover, submits to it without any protest, if the load that is imposed on him is not too heavy, and especially *if he is not taken too far from his village—and if it is a time of year when the cultivation of his crops, which must assure his family's life, do not require his presence.*

But one cannot go through a village in those equatorial regions without noticing the habit of the natives, from

---

[16] A powerful story by Joseph Conrad (1902), which is laid in the Congo. Gide cites it frequently in his *Travels in the Congo*.

their earliest age, of carrying loads. . . . I dare not say for their amusement or pleasure, but quite naturally. Just think that they have neither wheelbarrows nor hand-carts, nor yet any beast of burden. I am willing to believe, even, that it is to that habit of carrying rather heavy weights on their heads that the natives—men as well as women— often owe the nobility of their bearing and posture. At least, I remember that the remark was made about the ancient canephori. But it goes without saying that it is not æsthetic reasons that I should like to have prevail. Children when still very young (the little girls especially) carry on their back, on their hip, a brother or sister just a little younger. This on the other hand, it will be said, runs the risk of deforming them. Not at all. I add this, in reply to exaggerated and unseasonable commiserations: the load we impose on our soldiers in the field is considerably higher than that which it is customary to impose on bearers. That load must not normally exceed forty-four pounds. So it is not exactly there that the abuse lies. And, once more, one runs the risk of compromising the most just cause by protesting at random.

Everywhere where the administration has been able sufficiently to regulate the functioning of the halting-places, they are properly spaced, and the relays are organized in such a way as not to take the native more than four, five, or six days at most from his home point. The administration, in addition, sees that the natives are paid, rather little to be sure, but, after all, sufficiently. If there is some abuse, the conscientious administrator can and must clear it up. So it is not there that the evil lies.

But, it cannot be too often repeated, in order to persuade those who are left unmoved by a question of mere humaneness, that all the abuses in our equatorial colonies have in common this particularly deplorable aspect, that, to make a greater profit, the Companies are ruining the colony. The natives die or desert in great numbers, and labor cannot be found for the most useful, most urgent undertakings. This consideration ought to touch the most obstinate, since it is addressed to their most sensitive part: the purse.

Care has been taken to shout aloud that my attacks were directed against our colonial administration; and this is utterly false. It was hoped, thereby, to ruin the value of my evidence. I met down there many remarkable administrators, accomplishing an extraordinarily difficult task with intelligence, patience, and courage; and, as for the others, they were chiefly lacking in help. Many abuses and exactions would be made impossible if only the supervision were better conducted, if the administrators were more numerous. Often overwhelmed by an amount of work he cannot handle, a minor official loses courage, isolated in the jungle and not feeling himself to be part of an organization.

1928

Cuverville, 2 January

I had hoped to finish out this notebook with the year. Two days behind. The cold dismays and knots me up. Have been out only twice in the last week: visit to the unfortunate Déhais, who is never free of the most frightful pain; then, the next day, a more distant call on the Malendins to see again the three little orphans who had spoken to me so nicely on the road as I was coming back from the Déhaises' and to whom I wanted to take something to help them celebrate New Year's Day a bit more gaily. Immensity of human poverty. In contrast to which the indifference of certain rich people or their egotism is becoming more and more incomprehensible to me. Concern with oneself, one's comfort, one's ease, one's salvation, denotes an absence of charity that is ever becoming more disgusting to me.

Each one of these young writers analyzing his suffering from the *"mal du siècle,"* [1] or from mystic aspirations, or from unrest, or from boredom, would be cured at once if he strove to cure or to relieve the *real* sufferings of those around him. We who have been favored have no right to complain. If, with all we have, we still don't know how to be happy, this is because we have a false idea of happiness. When we understand that the secret of happiness lies not in possessing but in giving, by making others happy we shall be happier ourselves.—Why and how have not those who call themselves Christians better understood this initial truth of the Gospel?

Cuverville, 3 January

Despite every resolution of optimism, melancholy occasionally wins out: man has decidedly botched up the planet.

• • •

---

[1] The term, meaning "world-weariness" and corresponding closely to the German *Weltschmerz*, was coined by Musset during the romantic period and revived in 1924 by the young essayist Marcel Arland as typical of the postwar unrest.

At Beuzeville. I am waiting on the platform with other third-class passengers. An employee is holding back the crowd: "Don't get in; the train is going to move up."

A well-dressed gentleman disregards him in order to get into the car ahead of the others:

"Never mind, never mind," he says to the employee trying to hold him back; "I have the habit."

"The habit of what?" asks the employee, somewhat abashed by the other's assurance and cheek. As he gets in, the other shouts:

"The habit of sitting down."

And he reappears a moment later at the window, smiling and looking very pleased with himself. He has found a corner seat. He is one of those who know their way around.

13 February

Preface to *Lucien Leuwen* by Valéry—in the very beautiful Schiffrin edition that I received yesterday evening.[2] I recognize in it, for the first time in Valéry, a certain desire to conciliate, a certain fear of displeasing. Would Valéry dare write today his wonderful pages on Pascal that appeared in the *Revue hebdomadaire*?[3]

Later on, through a desire to clarify the question (for despite everything these pages struck me as very beautiful), I read a few pages of *L'Esprit des lois* . . . marvellous.[4] How does it happen that no one has ever compared Valéry (I am speaking of Valéry as a prose writer) to Montesquieu?

I plunge with rapture into Hölderlin's *Hyperion*,[5] happy to understand it so well.

But these calm hours, which for one were paradise, tired the patience of the other who tolerated them only when provisional. He used them as a springboard, stretching himself taut, with but one anxiety, but one restraint: to hide from his companion that he was getting ready to leap.

[2] *Lucien Leuwen* is one of Stendhal's less famous novels. Valéry's preface can be found in his *Variété II* (1929).

[3] This essay was republished in Valéry's *Variété* (1924).

[4] *The Spirit of Laws* by Montesquieu is one of the great works of the Enlightenment.

[5] *Hyperion* (1797–9) is a novel concerning the Greek uprising against the Turks in 1770.

24 February[6]

It happens that in various associations, whether conjugal or friendly, involving life in common, the common sense of the couple or team is, as it were, joint, and that the excess of one of the pair involves, as a sort of counterpoise, a contrary excess on the part of the other. Thus the wife's excessive piety can hurl the husband into atheism; one becomes more negligent the more finicky becomes the other, who in the beginning simply had a sense of order; one becomes more avaricious the more prodigal the other. If one locks up everything, this is because the other leaves everything lying about. Likewise, in the jaws of rodents, we see a tooth of the lower maxilla lengthen if the one opposite it in the upper maxilla is missing.

Tuesday, 28 February[7]

There is a certain relationship between the third and the fifth that is repeated from octave to octave, giving, by reversal, the sixth, and whose ensemble forms the common chord. Yes, from octave to octave the number of vibrations (which number I do not know) must remain in a constant relationship. And this in all keys.

And most likely I should find them, with an infinitely higher number of vibrations, in the visual domain, in the perception of colors. The ear and the eye permit an immediate intuition of these relationships. And I wonder at the fact that both these senses, through a gradual familiarization, a sort of taming process, come to enjoy other relationships, whose effect they first considered as disagreeable to the ear and the eye, as *dissonant*. (Perhaps, or probably, those that haven't between them any important "common denominators.")

Yes, the interval of the minor seventh, and, consequently, that of the major second, of which it is the reversal, must at first and for a long time have seemed painful to the ear and to be avoided. Later on, people took pleasure in it, as in the augmented fourth, each of these intervals permitting the passage from one key to another, the modulation, which soon became a delight to the ear.

Today these oversimple, too familiar relationships have no charm for our blunted senses. The ear accepts aug-

[6] Dictated. [A.]   [7] Dictated. [A.]

mented and diminished intervals which pained it in the beginning. Neither the major seventh nor the minor second is outlawed. And that the ear should enjoy these dissonances, just as, in another domain, the eye should enjoy more subtle pictorial disharmonies, goes without saying.

I cannot think that our senses have acquired a greater acuteness; but perhaps they are more capable of enjoying any relationship of numbers whatever.

No longer aiming toward consonance and harmony, toward what is music heading? Toward a sort of barbarism. Sound itself, so gradually and exquisitely liberated from noise, is returning to it. At first only the lords, the nobles, are allowed to appear on the stage; then the bourgeoisie; then the masses. Once the stage is overrun, nothing distinguishes it from the street. But what can be done about it? What madness it is to strive to oppose that fatal progress! In modern music the consonant intervals of the past seem to us like the "ci-devant" aristocrats during the French Revolution.

Saint-Clair, 3 March

Sudden departure for the Midi. I convinced myself that I needed a change of air to cure my grippe. Central heating makes Élisabeth's new house very comfortable; but today, the day after my arrival, I stay in bed all day. Driving rain outside. Tremendous appetite for rest. Yet brain very active, at once receptive and creative. Ah, to be able to begin a new career; start out anew and under another name! How little satisfies those who are succeeding today! Launching a tone of voice, a gait, a bearing, is enough for them. No maturation of thought; no composition. (If ever, later on, someone reads these lines, he will wonder whom I am getting at. . . . I am none too sure of it myself.)

9 March

X. splits hairs in order to know more about their nature. Y., to show off his subtlety.

How often have I directed my attention, my study, to this or that fugue of Bach, for instance, precisely because in the beginning it discouraged me; through a need of doing myself violence and guided by that obscure feeling

that what thwarts us and demands of us the greatest
effort is also what can teach us most.

Read with the greatest interest *Une Fille d'Ève* and
Une Double Famille, which I did not yet know and which
seem to me, if not among the best, at least among the
most revelatory.[8] Completely gripped by Balzac again.

29 March

Seated in front of a Cointreau at the wine-shop opposite
the Gare d'Auteuil. I planned to go home and practice
the piano and work right after dinner, but T. V. is arriving this evening, at ten fifteen, It is raining; it is cold. I
can imagine such an arrival in Paris as so lugubrious that
I cannot keep from going and meeting her train. I am
writing these lines to keep myself busy while waiting for
the train. I am leaving tomorrow for Cuverville, where I
hope to get ahead with *L'École des femmes*.[9] Worked
rather well these last few days; after enormous efforts at
Saint-Clair, where I had spent ten days, I had managed
to get the book into movement again, after having been
stalled for more than six months (I believe). The wine-
shop's pen is too bad. . . . Impossible to go on. . . .

Cuverville, 30 March

T. V. would like love; I can only give her friendship.
However great this may be, her expectation of a more
affectionate state falsifies all my acts and leads me to the
edge of insincerity. I explain myself this evening in a
letter, which will perhaps hurt her and which it is hard
for me to write; but the fear of hurting is one of the forms
of cowardice, and my whole being revolts against it.

17 April

Back from Le Tertre, where I could tarry only two
days.[10] Very full and profitable conversations, as always
with Roger. Reciprocal (I was about to say: mutual)
readings of *L'École des femmes* and of two long chapters
of *Les Thibault*, those that are to frame in the death of
old Thibault, to wit: the dialogue of Oscar Thibault with
the Abbé Vécard, and Abbé Vécard's dialogue with

---

[8] *A Daughter of Eve* and *A Double Family* are both novels by Balzac.

[9] His tale *The School for Wives* was first published in 1929.

[10] Le Tertre is the name of Roger Martin du Gard's home at
Bellême.

Antoine. Both of them seem excellent to me. What a joy to be able to tell him so with complete sincerity! But we are both rather vexed by the fact that in each of these dialogues the Abbé triumphs, after all; he has the best role and the final word. Though Roger puts himself into Antoine much more than I ever did into Édouard,[11] he does, despite himself and through a sort of professional honesty, let the Abbé get the advantage over him and dominate the discussion from a lofty position.

Roger is deeply concerned by the "idiotic" role I make him play in *Si le grain ne meurt* . . . and in *Le Journal des Faux-Monnayeurs;* I bring him in, he says, only to prove him wrong, and offer on his behalf only a few absurd objections, with the sole purpose of defending myself against him and showing that I am right to pay no attention to them, etc. It will be none the less clear that he was the only one I consulted and whose advice I sought: I noted down only those against which I balked, but this is because I followed the others—beginning with the advice to gather together the various plots of *Les Faux-Monnayeurs,* which, had it not been for him, would have formed so many separate "tales." [12] And this is why I dedicated the volume to him. Likewise, why note down his few criticisms of *L'École des femmes* since I am paying attention to every one of them?—they will lead me to retouch a few spots and especially to make a few additions, which now, in fact, seem to me indispensable.

And reciprocally, according to my suggestions, he will fuse certain parts of the dialogue between Abbé Vécard and Antoine.

Bennett is amazed that we should thus seek each other's advice; yet nothing is more advantageous.

18 April

My writings are comparable to Achilles' spear, with which a second contact cured those it had first wounded. If one of my books disconcerts you, reread it; under the

[11] The novelist character of *The Counterfeiters.*

[12] Until *The Counterfeiters,* Gide had been unwilling to call any of his fictions "novels," intentionally limiting them by the designation "tales."

apparent poison, I took care to hide the antidote; each one of them does not so much disturb as it warns.

9 *June*

Lassitude and computation of death.

For a long time now, no further enjoyment in writing in this notebook. Aged considerably. Pottered away at chores rather than really worked.

After a trip to Belgium (lecture and showing of the film in Brussels) and to Holland (The Hague and Amsterdam) in order to prepare our trip to New Guinea, we give up the project.

When I think that I am barely beginning to shake off the Congo (I am still involved in correcting proofs for the big edition), I am somewhat terrified by the possible results of this new trip, even more than by the trip itself. Since our return Marc has done almost nothing; or at least has not really worked. I fear that, *for greater facility,* he may give up the best in him.

I fear, if I take him to New Guinea, doing him a disservice and getting him definitely out of the habit of work. It is the pleasure, the happiness of being with him, that leads me there, even more than any curiosity for distant places. That felicity, to which I surrender, seriously falsifies my thought. It was for him, to win his attention, his esteem, that I wrote *Les Faux-Monnayeurs,* just as I wrote all my preceding books under the influence of Em.[13] or in the vain hope of convincing her. Urgent need of solitude and of recovering myself. It is no longer a matter of charming someone else—which can never be done without concessions and a certain self-deception. I must accept the fact that my path takes me away from those toward whom my heart inclines; and even recognize that it is my path from this: that it isolates me. If I were truly capable of prayer, I should cry out to God: Permit me to need only You. Seductions of the flesh are less distracting than those of the heart and mind. (And perhaps I am writing this because I know that for a long time now I have found it good not to resist the former. Useless to close my parenthesis. . . .

[13] One of Gide's names for his wife, Madeleine Rondeaux Gide.

12 June[14]

I greatly enjoyed dining the other evening with Julien Green. It had been promised for some time. With a really charming deference, and very rare in the new generation, he had made it clear that he insisted on my considering myself as his guest. I therefore had to let myself be taken by him to Prunier's, avenue Victor-Hugo, less ostentatious on the inside than the outside, which until now had frightened me off, had filled me with fear. In regard to luxury I remain insurmountably shy, though this had per- haps somewhat decreased, but now it seems to revive and become more intense with age. I remember the time when Vielé-Griffin and Jacques Blanche having asked me to meet them for lunch at the Terminus Saint-Lazare, I could not get myself, however unlikely this may seem, to go into the restaurant, but remained waiting for them in the lounge of the hotel, where they finally came to look for me after having waited for a very long time.

Green is probably extraordinarily like what I was at his age. More anxious, still, to understand and to agree than to assert his personality by resisting. I should have liked to be able to talk better with him. He was eager to show his confidence in me, and mine was very great toward him; but I have ever greater difficulty in opening up freely in a conversation. I fear to have disappointed him dreadfully, for I managed to say almost nothing but banal things to him; nothing of what he had a right to expect and hope for from me. Furthermore, I was ex- tremely tired; anxious not to show it too much.

After having tarried at Prunier's, we reached the avenue des Champs-Élysées. The night was beautiful and both of us enjoyed walking. I offered to take him to the Lido, where neither one of us had ever been.[15] We had no need of being in ordinary clothes, among so many people dressed for the evening, to feel utterly out of place in this haunt of pleasure and luxury. Once seated at a table near the pool, we wanted to wait for the show, which was not

[14] Dictated. [A.]
[15] The Lido is a well-known cabaret halfway down the avenue des Champs-Élysées.

to begin until after midnight. Had it been one of my good days, nothing would have been more charming; but the conversation dragged on and on. Yet I heard with great interest what he told me of his next book. I like the fact that he does not know too well in advance where his characters are going to lead him, but I am not at all sure he did not say that just to please me, and remembering what I said of mine in my *Journal des Faux-Monnayeurs*. He has the good luck not to know insomnia, waking up every morning, he says, in exactly the position he took the night before to go to sleep. This doubtless assures him an evenness in his work, an almost excessive evenness in him: every day, at the same time and in the same number of hours he writes the same number of pages and of the same quality. His intellectual curiosity and his appetite for reading delight me. I should like him not to have too bad a recollection of that evening in which he showed himself to be so charming and in which I revealed myself as so ordinary; in which I deplore not having been able to talk to him better.

Marseille, 1 July

In Paris I at least can fall back on blaming others for making me waste my time. Here I can only hold it against myself. And I don't know when that pursuit is more degrading and more empty—when one encounters pleasure or when one seeks it without finding it? I am writing this now that I am getting old, and this evening when I feel tired. And tomorrow I shall begin again.

Hammamet, 6 July

Later on, that moderation, that forbearance, that tolerance we have shown toward Catholicism will be hard to forgive; our sympathy will seem weakness, and our indulgence will be judged without indulgence. Still fortunate if it is not said that we were afraid. And perhaps, after all, it would be justifiable to say so; but what frightens us is not the enemy, nor the forces he has at his disposition, so much as our own thought. I am afraid of my intransigence.

Tunis, 19 July

Does it occur to anyone to wonder: "What would Christ have done, what wouldn't he have done, if he had been allowed to live?" So deep is the habit of considering his suffering and death as forming part of his life and less as an end than as an accomplishment.

Paris, 22

Not only does M. not know what it is to love—but he does not even know that he doesn't know it. He knows affection and desire—not love.

Someone who can never take the "daily special"; or else he has to have the vegetable changed.

There is not one of my friends of whom, if I drew his portrait, I should not seem to be "saying ill." Love can be blind; friendship cannot; it owes it to itself not to be; and one can even go as far as to like a friend's short-comings; but in order to help him know them. What have I to do with a friendship devoid of perspicacity? I intend to carry my hatred of indulgence to that extent.

Cuverville, 30 July

At times it seems to me, alas! that I have passed the best time for writing. I feel painfully in arrears with my-self. And if you wish me to say: in arrears with God, I don't mind doing so, all the same. This simply means that I sometimes fear having waited too long, that I fear not only lacking time, but also fervor and that unsubdued exigence of thought that urges it to manifest itself. You resign yourself to silence, and nothing is more to be feared from old age than a sort of taciturn resignation. Even of those we most admire and know best, who can claim that we know the best and that they were permitted to say what mattered most to them? Just when one would like to speak, voice fails one and, when it returns, one expresses but memories of thoughts. Montaigne's strength comes from the fact that he always writes on the spur of the moment, and that his great lack of confidence in his memory, which he believes to be bad, dissuades him from putting off anything that comes to mind with a view to a more skillful and better-ordered presentation. I have al-ways counted too much on the future and had recourse to too much rhetoric.

Paris, 19 September

Mme Théo's remark about Charles Du Bos is excellent (after reading his long study on, or indictment of, me):

"He is assuring his salvation at your expense." [16]

5 *October*

My greed contained much curiosity. Nothing displeases me and makes my conscience so ill at ease as too much expenditure at table. Yesterday young Gabriel B., whom I am lodging, took me to a little restaurant on the boulevard Saint-Germain, where it cost the two of us together sixteen francs. He was delighted; I too. "And admit that we aren't hungry any more," he kept saying gaily. I recall the period of the Foyer, when Mme Théo and I, busy together from morning till night aiding refugees, made it a point of honor, when ordering our lunch, never to go beyond two francs. (We took our dinners at her house.) In that time of shortages it always seemed to me that I was taking away from others hungrier than I everything that went beyond the strictly necessary. This feeling has never left me, and I never enjoy a definite pleasure when I feel how much it costs. It is not that I am not interested in eating and I even pride myself on being a connoisseur in matters of cooking: I know what the dishes I am served are made of and can say what they need; but can never forget that if I take the white meat, the next person will have to take the drumstick. Consequently, when I serve myself first, I always take the drumstick; and all the more willingly since I really prefer it. I should like to settle in here in such a way as to be able to sup every evening on a plate of porridge and a fruit.

I should be glad to write an *essay* on gluttony.

It is hard for me to believe that the healthiest, wisest, and most sensible thought is not also the one which, when expressed in writing, produces the most harmonious and most beautiful lines.

Roquebrune, 22 October

My fear, formerly, of letting myself be misled by laziness, while thinking I was paying attention to my fatigue. . . . Now, on the contrary, I force myself to rest and keep constantly saying to myself: No, poor old boy, this is not laziness; you are really very tired.

. . .

[16] *Le Dialogue avec André Gide* (*Dialogue with André Gide*) by Charles Du Bos appeared in 1929.

Nothing good is achieved unless the balance happens to be upset between the real world and the mind's creation, the latter appearing, for a time, more real than the other. As for that voluntary illusion, with age the mind becomes less and less capable of it—at least spontaneously; but more and more skillful, on the other hand, at getting the best out of its luck and at considering all the cards in its hand, even the most insignificant ones, as trumps.

Self-indulgence. Advantageous postures.

I have written (in *Les Nourritures* or *L'Immoraliste*, I believe):
"The day will come when, even to lift to my lips merely the water for which I have the greatest thirst, I shall no longer have enough strength"—or something close to this. . . . No, that is not the way it happens: along with one's strength, one's desires decrease also. If the glass no longer reaches the lips, this is also because the water seems less cool and because one is less thirsty.

The type of thoughts that it is probably inopportune to write. Or else find in oneself the strength to think that it is good for things to be thus. Such thoughts ape sincerity rather than being truly sincere.

Whoever would note down simply, from day to day, the cracks, the crumbling of his person, the gradual effect of age . . .

At one time, to accompany that sudden sensation of falling off to sleep, I used to dream that I was falling into an abyss; now, simply that I am stepping out on a stairway that isn't there.

Good heavens! Dostoyevsky likewise yields to reasons of art (just as Valéry claims that Racine did, who, he said, would have changed the character of Phèdre rather than write a bad line), but this is because he understood, just like Racine, that reasons of art are the least misleading. It was perhaps purely æsthetic necessities and exigencies that led him to his most daring and truest psychological notations. And vice versa. Academic form, conventional beauty, etc. are often responsible, in psychology, for the

most monstrous mistakes. There are certain outlines that
nothing but falsehood can fill.

A sort of strange moodiness inclines me to give up suddenly what would be most agreeable to me and what occasionally I have most consistently longed for; for the advantage of some indefinable superior satisfaction, it must
be supposed, of an almost mystical nature . . . ? I don't
really know.—Isn't it this that already, in the pilgrimage
I made to the Grande-Chartreuse at the age of twenty,
turned me away at the last moment by some secret dissua-
sion, so that, on the point of reaching my objective, I
turned about and started off intoxicated with a different
satisfaction and as if enriched by that privation. That sort
of maceration plunged me at that time into a state of ineffable lyricism.

Is not unrelated, I believe, with solitary practices,
which invite dream to dominate reality, so that one comes
to prefer imaginary possession to real possession.

Cuverville, 21 November[17]

What the notion of time can become in a dream;—nothing is more mysterious. Generally a dream represents
merely a succession of images, but it sometimes happens
that the emotion aroused by certain ones among them presupposes the existence and recognition of a past. . . .

I dreamed last night that I met my brother-in-law
Marcel at some exhibit or other of sculpture. Together we
were admiring some architectural decorations copied
from some Versailles or Trianon. At that moment I said
to my brother-in-law that they were the exact reproduction of those I had admired at the Louvre Museum that
very morning, and, at once, it seemed to me that I had
previously dreamed that visit to the Louvre of which I
was speaking. I say "dreamed," for that visit, which
I truthfully said I had made and which was suddenly
represented in my mind *in the form of a recollection,*
remained exactly in the very atmosphere in which I then
was; that is to say, in the atmosphere of dream. And
can one remember a dream in a dream? Perhaps the sensation of a recollection implied no preceding image. But

[17] Dictated. [A.]

then what could that very precise sensation of a *recollection* be made of? Did it involve at that very moment a more distant and somewhat blurred image like those of memory? For at that very moment when, in that dream, I spoke of it to my brother-in-law, I saw again precisely (but in the form of a recollection) that previous visit to the Louvre. I saw again those same ornaments, or, at least, experienced that odd sensation of merely being in the act of seeing them again, of having already seen them a short time before; and I even remembered exactly that, on that visit to the Louvre, another person who was with me (I don't know who) had told me the name of the artist—which I was now striving in vain to recall, finding in its place only the name of Pigalle, which I knew was not the right one. So that, fearing to be corrected by my brother-in-law, I kept from mentioning it.

Upon waking I remembered this dream in rather great detail; the second part at least, for it was impossible for me to be sure whether I had really first dreamed that original visit to the Louvre or simply dreamed that I remembered it; and, as I said above, that is just where the mystery lies.

I find that mystery just about the same—although based on quite different elements—in the impression of *surprise* that certain dreams provide, though we ourselves are the sole, unconscious artisans of all the elements that combine with a view to provoking that emotion of surprise. I shall not be understood without an example. Here is one: this is a dream that goes back more than ten years; it must therefore have made a deep impression for me to remember it. I was traveling with X. (a feminine character; I don't remember who, but that doesn't matter), and this took place at Rouen or Amiens, where we had just (probably) visited the cathedral. We go into, or more exactly: we happen to be in a pastry-shop where I am choosing cakes or candies for X., which we are planning to take with us. A salesgirl takes them, wraps them in paper, then, picking up a very delicate pair of scissors, begins to use them to finish the package in an amazing manner that I watch out of the corner of my eye while I approach the cashier to pay. Whether candies or cakes,

I knew that I had chosen about five francs' worth. "That will be twenty francs," said the cashier; and when I showed my astonishment: "Oh!" she exclaimed, "monsieur, it's because of the *Gothic package*." My surprise at these words was so great that it woke me up (or, if you prefer, a sudden awakening immediately emphasized my surprise), and that is what allowed me to remember that dream so well. My amazement on awaking, my wonder as I thought it over, was that I had so carefully favored that surprise. It seemed to me that everything had been invented with the sole purpose of leading up to that word, just as it would have happened in real life; but how could it be explained then that I so little expected it? It was *I* who had prepared it and I knew nothing of it.

I had told this dream to Mme Théo, who at once told me another dream which again involved that same inexplicable feeling of surprise. In the afternoon she had received a certain rather beautiful piece of cloth from which she thought she could have a bodice made, and, with this in mind, had taken the cloth to a dressmaker. The following night she dreamed that she was going to see the dressmaker; I was with her; and as soon as we entered the fitting-room, we both saw, laid out on an armchair, the bodice in question. It was obvious that the cloth had been irretrievably spoiled, that the bodice was hideous, unwearable. It gave her a great shock. And, seeing how upset she was, I approached her and exclaimed, as I patted her back in friendly fashion:

"Don't be upset, dear, you will find a way to fix it up."

Turning around toward me, she then exclaimed in stupefaction:

"So you are calling me 'dear' now!"

And I replied at once:

"My dear friend, I always do on such occasions."

Obviously there was in this dream too an inexplicable displacement. She had given herself an unconsciously prepared surprise, for which, immediately afterward, she had given herself an explanation that, however preposterous it was, had none the less been foreseen by her, without her knowing it.

DETACHED PAGES

When intelligent people pride themselves on not understanding, it is quite natural that they should succeed better than fools. The camel has been discussed, the eye has been discussed, the needle has been discussed, and people have above all discussed to find out to what degree the rich man could or could not approach the kingdom of heaven. Yet what is more luminous than the word of the Gospel? It should be clear to the blindest that for "a camel to pass through the eye of a needle" is the Oriental equivalent of "jumping over the moon" or some other image of which the utter absurdity tends to exaggerate the *impossible.*

It simply means: it is *impossible,* forever impossible, and among impossible things there is none more completely impossible than this: a rich man in the kingdom of heaven. The kingdom of heaven is formed of the surrender of riches.

Nothing is heavier, more important than this: necessity of option between the temporal and the spiritual. The possession of the other world is based on the renunciation of this world.

Consequently, even the Gospel according to Mark, the oldest, had already felt the influence of Paul. It is essential above all to explain that influence.

Certainly Christ and his disciples on their way to Jerusalem were marching toward triumph—Christ with the certainty of his divine vocation. There was, in the eyes of the world at least, complete failure. This is the first thing that it was important to save. It was essential to work for the justification of the cross, of the torment, of the ignominy to which that career seemed to lead. It was essential to show that that end had been foreseen, show that it was necessary to the accomplishment of the Scriptures and likewise to the salvation of humanity. And that Christ died *because of* sinners, or *for* sinners . . . the distinction was mystically so delicate that it was easy to pass from one to the other and that a happy confusion

grew up in favor of St. Paul's preaching. People ceased
to see Christ anywhere save on the cross; the cross became the indispensable symbol. It was the mark of ignominy that it was important to glorify most. Only thus
could appear as triumphant, in spite of everything, the
work of the one who had called himself the Son of God.

That was indispensable in the beginning; for the official
recognition and propagation of the doctrine.

But, after all, that ignominious end, though it became
indispensable to the dogma, was in no wise a part of the
very teaching of Christ. It was on the contrary its check,
or rather the supreme obstacle over which the lesson of
happiness (see the words spoken on the cross) was likewise to triumph.

No matter: once that doctrine had mastered minds and
hearts—that is to say, when people felt they had a right
to seek out Christ *before* the torment, and in the fullness
of his *joy*—it was too late: the cross had overcome Christ
himself; it was Christ crucified that people continued to
see and to teach.

And thus it is that that religion came to plunge the
world into gloom.

✳

The following pages were written between 1922 and
1928 (?). I thought then, I don't know just why, that I
did not have much longer to live and was inclined to look
upon *Les Nouvelles Nourritures,* of which these pages
were to be a part, as a sort of testament which, in my
plan, was to form a tardy counterpart for my *Nourritures
terrestres.*[18] These pages that I wrote from day to day, I
was to distribute them throughout the volume in certain
places that I had assigned to them in advance; many
other pages, interpolated among them, were to support
and motivate them, but I shall probably never write
them. And I fear very much that this book may remain
unfinished. It is not so much that my thoughts have
changed direction, but events have allowed them to take
a more definite orientation.

.   .   .

[18] *The Fruits of the Earth* appeared in 1897 and *New Fruits of the
Earth* did not come out until 1935, though a few pages had been included in the *Selections from André Gide* of 1921.

Few sentences have vexed me as much as this one: "What is everything that is not eternal?" What an absurd conception of the world and of life manages to cause three quarters of our unhappiness! Through loyalty to the past, our mind refuses to realize that tomorrow's joy is possible only if today's makes way for it; that each wave owes the beauty of its line only to the withdrawal of the preceding one; that each flower owes it to itself to fade for the sake of its fruit; that the fruit, unless it falls and dies, cannot assure new blooms, so that spring itself rests on winter's grief.

I cannot believe in Nietzsche's "eternal return," but I like that need of optimism which makes him invent it, in order to balance regrets with *insouciance*.

For a long time, for too long a time (yes, until these very last years) I have gone to great efforts to believe that I was wrong; to accuse myself, to contradict myself; to bend my way of seeing, feeling, and thinking to the way of others, etc. I noticed that the most obstinate in their own direction are ordinarily stupid; and I did not set much store by stupidity. But one would have said that my own thought frightened me, and this is the source of the need I felt of attributing it to the heroes of my books in order the better to separate it from me. Some who refuse to see a novelist in me are perhaps right, for it is that that recommends the novel to me, rather than telling stories.

Paul Laurens told me of having met by chance an old classmate of the studios he had not seen in twenty-five years. In the beginning they feign great delight at seeing each other again, as is fitting, then they soon realize they have nothing in common but a few vague memories; the conversation wanes rapidly; but suddenly X. says:

"Oh! I was about to forget . . . something very important . . . last year, old man, I got converted. Yes indeed!"

"Well," asks Paul Laurens, "are you satisfied?"

"Oh! you know, old man, Catholicism . . . is corking."

A few moments of silence. They decide to separate. But at the moment of shaking hands the other one repeats again:

"Besides, you know, old man . . . ab-so-lute-ly cork-ing!"

Paul told this in a charming way, just as I think Fromentin would have done.

✳

For a long time people blamed me for what they called my unrest; then, when they began to realize that that unrest belonged not to me but to the creatures I depicted and that I could not depict them as restless without having ceased to be restless myself, they blamed me for having found calm and that very serenity which allowed me to produce. This is because they did not suppose, would not admit that unrest could lead elsewhere than to that harbor where they themselves have dropped anchor, and because, so long as they thought me adrift, they could still hope that I would come and seek refuge among them.

✳

Are so many words necessary? and the concentration of the mind, the effort to construct a plot, in order to stretch before the reader that motley embroidery which, for a time, shimmers before him and veils reality. On the other hand, it is to that reality that I want to recall him constantly, to reveal it to him in a better light, to present it to him as even more real than he has been able to see it hitherto.

✳

Do not turn away, through cowardice, from despair. Go through it. It is *beyond* that it is fitting to find a motive for hope. Go straight ahead. Pass beyond. On the other side of the tunnel you will find light again.

✳

The odd thing, when speaking of *influence,* is that one almost never considers any but direct influences. Influence through protest is, in certain natures, at least as important; sometimes it is much more so, though most often very hard to recognize. It is by no means always through affection, weakness, and need of imitation that our characters are bent. A somewhat strong nature yields more to reaction than to direct action. Those who oppose interest me more than those who follow; but I am still more interested in the very rare ones who neither follow nor oppose and yet are no more deaf than stupid.

✳

That lack of curiosity of the flesh which precedes by far impotence and even the dying-out of desires, which makes the latter compromise and even ease their dominion, no, it is not apathy; but, the mind resuming the upper hand, it leaves the way open for moralizing.

1929

13 *January*

A sea so calm as to make one sometimes wonder whether or not we are making any progress. A deserted sea; as uninhabited this morning as my brain. One wonders where the flying fish, porpoises, and dolphins have gone. If Arion fell overboard, he would go straight to the bottom. (Manner of speaking, for it is known that drowned men float, when their soul is not too heavily laden with sins.)

Very painful coughing spells last night again; it lasted about an hour, then yielded to a double dose of neonal.

This morning the passengers, the appearance of the sea and sky, everything seems to me so unappetizing that I go back down to my cabin to read a bit of *Oblomov*[1] and sleep, for I myself feel as uninteresting and unlikable as the others, as "the rest," as everything.

Low physical condition due to fatigue, doubtless. Stretched out on the deck, rather comfortably wrapped in my green shawl, I lie patiently in wait and watch (amused as at the age of fifteen when, calmly seated on the edge of the woods of La Roque, I used to see squirrels and rabbits make up their mind to reappear and shake themselves, nature on all sides become animate and give up its hypocritical and forced immobility)—my thoughts, somewhat timidly at first, come out of their burrows, scan the near horizon, risk a few jumps at first, and then set out inconsiderately in seach of adventure.

Trace the itinerary and the topography.

Influence (to be reworked); positions already taken, deeds already done; responsibilities already assumed—disregard them.

And always the question of humanity's listed value (very much exaggerated)—humanity at least such as it is, not such as it might be. From what direction can hope come?

[1] The novel *Oblomov* by Ivan Goncharov depicts the decay of the Russian gentry before the Revolution of 1917.

Atheism. There is not a single exalting and emancipatory influence that does not in turn become inhibitory. Of the need of changing guides.

Around noon my mind finally freed from the neonal and the codeine I had to take last night, liberated also from a lot of annoying preoccupations, becomes marvelously active. If I were not at the common table, a bit curbed after all by my neighbors' looks, I should note down at once the main lines that I see becoming clear, with greater sharpness and vigor than ever—of the antagonism between Christ and God—of Christ's *error* (wonderful to explain why that error was intentional and necessary) of claiming that he was closely associated with God—leading to the cry, at last revelatory: "My God, why hast thou forsaken me?"

God = nature; Christ = supernature.

Algiers, 13. six thirty

With the aid of Jupiter and Neptune, we had docked by two o'clock. Algiers seems to have changed so little that it is really not worth feeling so much older since the last time I saw it.

The moment when I feel most violently like leaving a town is when I have just arrived there. What squalor! What poverty! What approximations! What piddling "promises of happiness"! or rather: how few promises, and of what piddling happiness!

It would perhaps be sufficient to say that I feel very tired, with a somewhat painful spot at the base of my left lung which makes me fear severe coughing spells again tonight.

17

Another walk, yesterday evening, above the town; I return by way of the Kasbah and recover, if not my intoxication of the first visit, at least the elements of that intoxication. Had I lived less chaste at the age of twenty, I should give up with less difficulty, it seems to me.

This little apartment, where I have moved in, is frigid; I can keep somewhat warm only in bed under a pile of coats and blankets. And this morning, not an aspiration, not a desire. The sky is gray like my heart. I make up my mind to take a room at the hotel again. I buy a hat that will make me less noticeable than the one Marc was

right to advise me not to take. Is it merely the cold that
reduces me thus? If I didn't have the means of paying
for a good meal, what should I become? I set down here
shamelessly and at length my lamentation, in order to
blush for it, I think, a little later on, and in the hope of
at least learning something from it.

When I think of all that is spared me: tooth- and
stomach-aches, heart-aches, and money troubles, I wonder
that there are not more people to jump into the river, and
judge that humanity, all in all, shows remarkable guts. It
is perhaps also because humanity lacks that little bit of
courage that is necessary to end it all.

21 January

What I call "fatigue" is old age, and nothing can rest
one from it, but death.

Of all this "bad because contrary to nature" what is the
worse? To refuse oneself to pleasures as a young man or,
as an old man, to still seek them? There is a certain
felicity of the flesh that the aging body pursues, and ever
more uselessly, if it has not been sated with them in
youth. Too chaste an adolescence makes for a dissolute
old age. It is doubtless easier to give up something one
has known than something one imagines. It is not what
one has done that one regrets here; but rather what one
has not done and might have done. And one's regret even
takes on the somber color of repentance.

It seems to me that here too what most induces me to
renunciation are æsthetic reasons. Old hands soil, it seems,
what they caress; but they too have their beauty when
they are joined in prayer. Young hands are made for
caresses and the sheathing of love; it is a pity to make
them join too soon. Yes, that gesture of prayer simulates
the mystic embrace of the impalpable after loving arms
have closed on the flight of reality and on absence.

Paris, 24

Very good late afternoon yesterday in Marseille at
Auguste Bréal's. Almost finished *Pride and Prejudice,*
begun in Algiers, in which Jane Austen achieves perfection, but in which one realizes rather readily (as in
Marivaux) that she will never risk herself on heights
exposed to too strong winds. An exquisite mastery of

what can be mastered. Charming differentiation of the secondary characters. Perfect achievement and easy triumph of decorum. What a charming woman she must have been! Incapable of any intoxication, but almost forcing one to think: it is better thus.

In Paris again. I come back rested; feel alive again. Did I do right to return? No more empty question, and to which the reply matters less. Whatever one does, do not ask oneself whether or not one was right to do it, but rather get the best out of it, and from the situation in which one has put oneself.

25

Returned to the piano, which I had not opened since . . . (?) Went over the *Caprice in B minor* by Paganini-Schumann.

Yesterday evening got myself to go to a good restaurant and to dine without considering the expense, a thing that had happened to me, so far as I can remember, but once, very long ago (I mean when I am alone and have no one to treat). Went to Marius's, rue de Bourgogne; ordered oysters, a sole, peas, and stewed pears. Everything was excellent and cost only three times as much as my ordinary meals. It always seems to me that egotism is most shamelessly manifested in gluttony. The other memorable solitary meal was at the Hotel Saint-Georges of Mustapha, where I had stopped after a frightful crossing and which I left the following day moreover. A heavy sea had made us eight hours late; I had been horribly sick; it seemed to me that nothing would be good enough to cure me. I had chosen the best room in the best hotel; had a meal sent up that I washed down with champagne. All this more foreign to me than Algiers itself, where I believe that I had landed for the first time. . . .

30 January

You know very well that I was not free to write other books except out of cowardice and by avoiding what I considered my duty.

31

A certain melancholy in connection with the *Volpone* that Zweig and Romains have just put on the stage.[2]

---

[2] Jules Romains translated Stefan Zweig's adaptation of Jonson's *Volpone*, which Dullin staged at the Atelier.

There are few plays that I should have so much wished
to translate and that I felt more appropriate to my hand.
I spoke to Copeau of it a long time ago, almost announced
it; and, probably, if the Vieux-Colombier had lived. . . .
But I believe that, out of respect for the text, I should not
have dared to *adapt* it, as Zweig and Romains have done;
and very happily, I believe. At least I have the consolation of knowing that that admirable play is perfectly
reclaimed. The real sorrow would have been seeing it
ruined. But the theatre bores me so that I cannot make
up my mind to go and see it.

6 February[3]

Whether works of art or people, we judge everything
according to a certain bias, and the judgment of others
predisposes us. A certain book strikes us as the less good
the more we have heard it praised to excess, or all the
better since a certain critic has spoken ill of it. La Fontaine would have enjoyed Baruch less if he had not discovered him himself. And how much my admiration for
Jane Austen is embarrassed to hear her compared to
Shakespeare! A critic very rarely opens a book without
being well or badly disposed to it in advance, and this
prejudgment, which the English call "prejudice," disposes
us, often without our knowing it, to being particularly sensitive to the qualities or shortcomings of the author. According to the nature of minds, some will praise with the
crowd and even exaggerate; others will stand in opposition who are inclined to express the reverse of the
common opinion.

Originality is perhaps never so rare as in matters of
judgment; and never less noticeable, for an opinion,
though it is original, does not necessarily differ from the
accepted opinion; the important thing is that it does not
try to conform to it. I can admire Bossuet, La Fontaine,
or Voltaire for the same reasons as the most banal literary
handbook and not suffer at all from this. But I can perceive later that some of my admirations were not altogether sincere and that my judgment on that point was
merely conforming.

A revision of values is useful at a certain age; but it
takes a singular liberty of mind to get away from the

[3] Dictated. [A.]

accepted. I know subtle intelligences, profoundly capable of appreciating fully and delicately in a work the qualities that are pointed out to them, but just as incapable of discovering new ones as of inventing reasons for admiring less works that have long been extolled.

5 March

I would not swear that at a certain period of my life I was not very close to being converted. Thank God, a few converts among my friends took care of this, however. Jammes, or Claudel, or Ghéon, or Charlie Du Bos will never know how instructive their example was for me. I repeat this to myself as I read in that monument of immodesty and unconscious self-indulgence, Charlie's journal.[4] Throughout, it breathes an amazing need for self-admiration, joined to a naïveté such that it both provokes and disarms laughter.

10 April

I wonder if one of the greatest marks of strength in an artist is not resolutely going ahead without granting too much importance to something that will not reveal his superiority.

I write this without too much believing in it, being inclined, on the contrary, to "neglect nothing" and to devote the most care to just what most discourages me: the transitions, the welding of joints, everything in which Flaubert recognized the master writer.

But this is the only excuse I find for the bad parts of Green's latest novel[5]—and they are numerous: impossible dialogues (in particular the one between Grosgeorges and Guéret), artificially constructed characters (Mme Londe), impossible situation. . . . It would seem that it matters little to him, he is so eager to go ahead, to go on, to reach the parts where his power is clearly marked and that sort of somber genius which relates him to the greatest. A certain evenness of flow in the course of the narrative bothers me more; I should prefer it more like a torrent, with pauses, windings, disappearances, cascades. Doubtless he conforms a little too closely, for my taste at least, to the tradition of the well-made novel. But otherwise he would have to be willing often to dissatisfy his

---

[4] *Extracts from a Journal* by Charles Du Bos appeared in 1931.
[5] *Léviathan.*

public, and this calls for a sort of courage of which very few are capable.

11 *or* 12 *April*

Yesterday spent almost three hours with Green. How I should have been attached to him if I had met him in my youth! I like everything in him; he is one of those for whom one would demand the best of oneself. Without beating about the bush I was able to tell him everything I have written above regarding *Léviathan;* but adding at once that I considered as a proof of value the very short-comings of his book, and not having spent time or effort in trying to correct them.

He told me again that he had begun this book without a plan, without a definite outline, without at all knowing how his characters were going to act; that they surprised him and that, as soon as they began to live in him, he ceased to feel himself their master and could not foresee the outcome of the drama into which their passions hurled them. For instance, he had no idea of the importance that Mme Grosgeorges was going to assume, of the role that she was going to play. He speaks of all this with simplicity and one feels him to be utterly sincere. That sub-conscious logic on which the automatism of his characters depends eludes him, and I believe that it is better so. But, from the point of view of Freud, here is something of the greatest interest. The characters of *Léviathan,* the plot of the novel, everything is of the same stuff as our dreams and the projection on a black background of everything that does not come to light in life.

That evenness of flow of which I spoke to Green is explained by his method of work and the fear he has, if he drops his characters for a moment, of not being able to find them very readily. He dares not and cannot leave them. But that is why the reader cannot leave them either.

A really powerful artist is he who knows how to turn even his shortcomings to advantage and to transform all the cards in his hand into trumps. (I believe I have already said this somewhere.)

Close and niggardly . . . yes, I know that I am; and I admit that I am to excess. But this is because I prefer

with all my heart being able to give what they who call
me a miser are so willing to spend on themselves.

26 April

Yesterday, after a meeting at rue Visconti where there
were only five of us (Desjardins, Jean Schlumberger, Du
Bos, Fernandez, and I) to make decisions about the
décade of this summer[6]—Charlie walks back with me to
the *N.R.F.* Constrained conversation, in which one shelters
from shock everything one used to talk of, everything
dear to one—and the end of which is marked by Charlie's
tipping his hat ceremoniously. I do not know what I am
to see in it: contempt? scorn? need of emphasizing the
distance that Charlie's conversion sets between us? And
Charlie, seeing me keep my hat on (for such an attempt
at ceremony between us seems to me ridiculous), did he
imagine on my behalf contempt, coldness, need of emphasizing a feeling of superiority which is utterly foreign
to me? . . . Had I in turn tipped my hat to him, it seems
to me that he could have seen in this salutation nothing
but irony. . . . No, I see in that ridiculous gesture only
an instinctive and irresistible need of assigning himself
the best part, and what he takes for the desire for *perfection;* the need of being able to say to himself: "With Gide,
again, as with everyone, as always and everywhere, I was
perfect." So that I, on the other hand, I looked like a
boor. And since, moreover, I felt him to be tormented
and anguished, that meeting left me very ill at ease.

28 July

And constantly (nothing so absurd as) this thought:
Not worth while settling in for the little time that is left
me to live.

Big article by the L. brothers on *L'École des femmes.*
Those "two imbeciles," as Charles-Louis Philippe used to
call them, protest grandiloquently that I am wronging
men of letters and that not all in France are as vile as I
depicted my hero. I write them:

"My dear brothers,

"No, calm yourselves: it is not you that I portrayed in

---

[6] This meeting was held at the *Union pour la vérité* to discuss the
program for the next session at Pontigny.

the hero of my *École des femmes*. And, moreover, where
the devil did you get the idea that my Robert was a man
of letters? Aside from the little letter at the beginning in
which he announces the death of his mother, when do you
see him writing? I specify that he wants to indulge in
politics, at least so his fiancée believes, and that he assumes the political editorship of a literary review. . . .
Let me add at once, to reassure you completely, that I do
not at all claim that all politicians in France are like
him. . . .

"I have said somewhere: 'It is with fine sentiments that
bad literature is made'; bad criticism also. But those sentiments honor you, and I remain most cordially yours. . . ."

I do not send the letter. That would be doing too much
honor to those two fools.

Article by Crémieux on *Les Thibault*, in which he
quotes this passage from *La Mort du père*[7] (passage that
I had already noticed, on which I stumbled):

". . . One does not succeed in understanding a man
until after his death. As long as a person is alive, all the
things he might still accomplish, and which one cannot
know, constitute unknowns that upset all computations.
Death finally fixes the outlines. . . ."

Obviously. But, good heavens! those things he might
still accomplish can remain unaccomplished; and it is a
cruel error to believe them less important when they
become, irremediably through death, those that he can
no longer accomplish. Because one is forced to *cease
taking them into account*, one can fancy one knows the
dead man better, but the really loving soul cannot allow
itself to be taken in; it knows that the undeveloped, the
unrevealed elements of a person can remain much more
important than what he succeeded (or what events au-
thorized him) in bringing to completion.

Were it not for the war, how many poor fellows would
themselves never have known their courage, and even
those closest to them never have known that they had it
in them to force one's admiration and appear as heroes.

At most that assertion is true for the novel. (That is to

[7] *The Father's Death* is Part VI of Roger Martin du Gard's long
novel, *The World of the Thibaults.*

say that the art of the novel tends to make us take this lie for the truth.)

And yet what a wonderful novel could be written that would make us realize this is false!

That original Christian upbringing, irremediably, *detached* me from this world, inculcating in me, not so much a disgust for this earth, as rather a disbelief in its reality. I have known subsequently many converts who could not manage, despite the most constant effort, to maintain themselves in that position of the soul which had become natural to me and from which, subsequently, I made an effort to get away. I have never managed to take this life quite seriously; by no means because I have ever been able to believe (in so far as I remember) in eternal life (I mean in an after-life), but rather in another facet of this life which escapes our senses and of which we can have but a very imperfect knowledge. . . . Indefinable impression of being "on tour" and of playing, in makeshift sets, with cardboard daggers.

Met Valéry the eve of my departure for Le Tertre; that is, Saturday, the last day of July (?). In the back of the *N.R.F.* shop he was autographing some copies of the reprint of *Teste*.[8] He took me by the arm and accompanied me to the corner of the rue de Bellechasse and the boulevard Saint-Germain. We even walked up and down in front of the Ministry of War until the stroke of twelve thirty reminded him that he was expected for lunch. More intelligent, more charming, more affectionate than over. Yet I leave that meeting rather depressed, as from almost all other meetings with Valéry. But this time it is not so much feeling an intelligence so incomparably superior to mine attach no value to the commodities I can supply, accept only the coin of which I am most bereft; no, it was not that frightful feeling of insolvency (which used to drive me to despair), but a much more subtle feeling, a close relative of the one I tried to note yes-

[8] The famous *Soirée avec M. Teste* (*An Evening with M. Teste*) appeared first in 1896 and, with the addition of seven other brief essays on the same subject, eventually became simply *Monsieur Teste*. The *N.R.F.* publishing house maintains a bookshop on the boulevard Raspail.

terday. Valéry, on the contrary, is closely attached to life. He relates to me his conversations with Marshals Foch and Pétain; he always says exactly what is appropriate to say, which is always a bit more and a bit different from what one expects. He tells of Barthou's petty intrigues to take away from him the speech of welcome for Pétain, which Valéry is to pronounce, but which Barthou would be glad to pronounce in his place "if it just happened that it bored you or that you felt tired." [9] He is playing his life like a game of chess that it is important to win, and as he writes his poems, placing just the right word, as one moves up a pawn, in just the right place. He has managed his life so well that mine, in comparison, seems to me but a sorry succession of blunders. I remember that, still quite young, Valéry said to me: "If I wanted to be rich, it would be in order to be able, always and in any society or circumstance whatever, to wear the appropriate costume. . . ."

I show him the letter I have just written to Poincaré, in gratitude for his very kind letter thanking me for my *Voyage au Congo*. I just happened to be on my way to take the letter to the hospital in rue de la Chaise, where Poincaré has just been operated on; I therefore take it out of my pocket to show it to Valéry. He finds almost nothing in it that does not need to be changed, to be rewritten; almost nothing that is appropriate. And he is right. His remarks, his suggestions are excellent. As soon as I get home, rewriting my letter, I take them into account, very glad to have met him, but shocked to the bottom of my heart by the *inappropriateness* of my mind and all its manifestations.

6 October

Quickly a few lines before going to bed and solely in order not to let go; and because tomorrow, leaving for Cuverville, I shall not find a moment.

Back to the piano for the last four days. Returned to the third and fifth *Barcarolles* of Fauré. Fugue in A major (first book of the *Well-Tempered Clavichord*).

[9] When a new member is received into the French Academy he must make a formal speech, which is traditionally devoted to the career of the Immortal he is replacing; in reply to this an older member makes a speech of welcome in which he treats the career of the new member.

Long visit from Green the day before yesterday; I introduce him to Curtius, come to take tea. Green stays after him, talks to me about his next book, which he wants to be quite different from the preceding ones, and for which he is inaugurating an entirely new method of work. I let myself be led into reading him almost all I have written of *Œdipe* through a desire to show him my confidence and through a need to try out my sentences on a mind so different from mine. I do not believe he is very sensitive to qualities of style; but it just happens to be something else that I am aiming for. I let myself be led into reading him likewise some already old pages on mythology, and am angry with myself afterward, fearing to have tired him. These pages seemed to me overwritten and lacking in spontaneity. I do not think he could have liked them; and, as a result, I ceased to like them myself.

7 October

Exhausted by a very bad night. The fate of X. and of Y., which is at stake, torments me so that I cannot get more than four hours' sleep. I have very serious conversations with one and then with the other; do not know what to fear, what to wish for. . . .

I cannot write in this notebook anything of what is most dear to me; thus it is that not a trace will be found here of the Constantinople adventure, which, during the last three months, has so filled my mind and which I am not yet willing to believe closed. I think of it every day and never pass in front of the concierge's door without looking anxiously to see if perhaps at last a letter . . . I cannot believe that Émile D. will accept being forbidden to write me. . . . It is better to say nothing of it than to say too little.

Cuverville, 8 October

It is certain that I change my opinions with a facility that disconcerts even me. P., with whom I dined yesterday, told us (Marc and me) what ready ground anxiety found in her, and her disposition to imagine the worst at once, as soon as, for instance, Marc left her without news or the auto that was to bring little Michel back to her was late. I too, I told her, I always imagine the worst; but quite calmly. Not a day goes by without my imagining my death and that of all my friends. And, for example: every

night when I used to return alone to Auteuil, I expected
to find the Villa burned down or robbed, an assassin
behind the door, which I nevertheless would open without
trembling; none of all this (which on certain evenings,
however, I visualized with an impressive preciseness)
managed to get any real anguish out of me. In my childhood I was subject to frequent nightmares, which left
me terrorized; I used to wake up screaming or in tears
and would be afraid to go back to sleep. At a certain age,
around sixteen, I don't know just what happened . . .
the anguish left me. I would sometimes happen to dream
the same things; yes, the very ones that a short time before would have filled me with terror; but interest and
curiosity took the place of the fear, horror, or distress of
the past.

It is the same today; gray, leaden, dark feelings are the
ones I find hardest to produce; I am almost inclined to
say they are trumped up and that I feel them only because of telling myself that I ought to feel them. Most
likely this derives in part from the fact that I no longer
authentically value anything much, anything at all, since
I lost what I most valued. (But this is true only of the
last twelve years.)

How can it be that I am not more saddened by little
Émile D.'s sudden silence, even though not an hour passes
without my thinking of it? It is partly because I am not
willing to yield to sadness, for I see in that very surrender
a sort of self-indulgence that I deplore, against which I
protest and balk just as, when very young, I did against
the state of sin. A certain element of resolve enters into
this, to be sure, but the state of joy (which I should like
always to maintain in me) is the most natural to me and
also the state in which I am most happily stretched to
my fullest capacity, in which I feel that I am at my best.
If I do not succeed in achieving it, the reason is almost
always physical.

I should nevertheless like to be sure that the little
fellow did not kill himself. In the state of exaltation he
had reached he was capable of doing so if he suddenly
met a blind, absurd opposition from his parents, who, in
case he should kill himself, after being driven to despair

by them, would certainly consider me responsible for that death . . . just as they already considered me responsible for everything that upset them, for everything they did not understand in their child, for everything in him that escaped them and in which they could no longer recognize themselves. They were terrified to see their son "become too fond of me." Even if he were, as the mother wrote me, "in distress," no one was more capable of understanding him, of holding out a helping hand, of saving him . . . than I. But Metaneira reappears in almost every mother, just as in this case Ceres relives in me.[10]

9 October

"You say you *believe*" (said Count de X., an extreme Catholic, to the good Protestant minister). "You people believe, but we *know*."

12 October

What is he doing? Where is he? Is he thinking of me? Is he telling himself perhaps that I am forgetting him? . . . This constant interrogation plays a muffled accompaniment to all my thoughts.

13 October

Sweating, puffing, exhausted, and exasperated by my cold. Incapable of a sustained effort. I am waiting for it to get over, but know that I am in for a fortnight more of it.

Mme Théo is to return this evening. Everything tires and bores me. With that youngster has left me all the youth that remained to me.

15 October

The feelings I noted down the last few days strike me as exaggerated to the very edge of insincerity. It is true that the thought of that child concerns me greatly and that at every moment of the day I feel it breaking through . . . but without any great sorrow. I cannot say either that I am resigned to this silence; but *what is* always seems to me *what had to be;* the dominant feature of my character is perhaps an extraordinary, untranslatable "buoyancy." [11]

[10] Ceres or Demeter horrified Metaneira by holding the latter's child in the fire to purge away its mortality and make it immortal.
[11] This last word appears in English.

17 October

Went to have my throat thermo-cauterized by Luc Durtain. Lunch at Mme Théo's with Jean Schlumberger, to whom I had read, the evening before, my *Suite à l'École des femmes*. He, and Mme Théo likewise, made some very sensible remarks that I shall have to take into account. Day particularly broken up by unwelcome visitors. Received a visit from Crès about the reprinting of *André Walter;*[12] from J., who begs me to come and see his new home; from young C., whom I had met in Algiers (very likable and charming, but entangled in a lot of insoluble and vital problems . . .), etc. Go to the Review, where I find Benda, Malraux, and Groethuysen with Paulhan.[13] Corrected in a hurry the proofs of Pierre Louÿs's letters, which are to appear in the November issue, and those of the supplement to *L'École des femmes*.

As I pass the concierge's door he gives me a letter from Émile. At last! I cannot read it at once, but keep on fingering it in my pocket until the blow it contains strikes my heart. Certainly he had no idea how cruel his letter would be to me. The abominable calumnies he has been told about me have touched him and since he believes, according to what he has been told, that I am a two-faced, heartless person, he has no fear of hurting me. He is in Paris; went by near the rue Vaneau a few days ago, almost came up to see me; congratulates himself on not having done so; tells me at one and the same time that he still loves me and has made up his mind not to love me any more. He talks as if all the feeling were on his side. Finally he asks me to make no attempt to reach him, to forget him as he is going to forget me; and, to be sure of my silence, he refuses to give me his address.

To pull myself together I read Massis's two scathing articles in the *Revue universelle*. They are entitled "The Bankruptcy of André Gide" and are inspired by the book

[12] André Gide's first two works, *The Notebooks of André Walter* and *The Poems of André Walter*, which had both appeared anonymously in 1891 and 1892 respectively, were reissued together for the first time in 1930 by Editions des Œuvres Représentatives under the direction of George Célestin Crès.

[13] Jean Paulhan was by now editor-in-chief of *La Nouvelle Revue Française*.

by Du Bos, who has so masterfully and pertinently distinguished and exposed in his former friend a case of
"generalized inversion." Etc., etc.

It seems to me that in the whole affair of little Émile
I let myself be taken in most absurdly. This is just because
I was unwilling to look upon it as a game (which is the
surest means of all of letting oneself be taken in)—and
this is why it is all so painful to me today. We should be
half cured of a love-affair if we could convince ourself
that the person with whom we are in love is, after all,
but a rather ordinary creature. The strength of the attachment comes from the gnawing conviction that there is
something exceptional, unique, irreplaceable in the beloved, which we shall never again find.

22 October

Ghéon's book seems to me made up of the devotion of
a simpleton and an art more rudimentary than unaffected
. . . but he has just written in *Latinité* an article on
Ducoté and the role played by his *Ermitage* which is full
of intelligence, ponderation, tact, and sympathy; and
which makes me think sadly of the gesture of gratitude
and piety that I could have, and should have, made—and
which I did not make.[14]

But how difficult it is for me to be timely! All my
thoughts, all my feelings, all my acts come too late or too
early, and I feel always and everywhere *unseasonable*.

I remember my surprise when Ducoté asked me to
open the first issue of that new *Ermitage* of which he had
assumed the editorship. I do not think that anything, in
my whole career, ever flattered me more, for Ducoté did
not yet know me. I was on my wedding-trip in the
Engadine; I received his letter at Saint-Moritz. I was
working on my *Nourritures terrestres*. It was Ménalque's
tale (from that work) that I sent him at once. It would
have been hard for me today to write an article on Ducoté
without relating all this and without talking a bit too
much of myself. I tell myself this as a sort of excuse; but
it scarcely convinces me and does not console me much.

[14] Édouard Ducoté, who edited the monthly *Ermitage* from 1897
until 1906 with the collaboration of Gide, Gourmont, Copeau, Ghéon,
Claudel, Vielé-Griffin, etc., had just died.

23 October

I knew someone who was plunged into black melancholy at the mere thought of having to replace, soon and from time to time, the pair of shoes he was wearing; and likewise his clothing, his hat, his linen, his necktie. This was not an evidence of avarice, but a sort of anguish at not being able to rely on anything durable, definitive, anything *absolute*.

25 October

Few things annoy me more than seeing famous remarks repeated awkwardly.

In today's *Nouvelles littéraires* I encounter a remark of Barbey d'Aurevilly that Jules Lemaître had quoted years ago in one of his "Morning Notes" in *Le Temps*. I recall it well enough to be able to guarantee its exactitude.

"My word, Monsieur d'Aurevilly," Jules Lemaître said to him as he met him in the avenue des Champs-Élysées, "that is certainly a wonderfully fitted frock-coat!"

Whereupon d'Aurevilly let drop in his lofty manner this simple and marvelous little sentence:

"Were I to take communion, I should burst."

Now this is what becomes of this charming remark under the pen of M. Nicolas Ségur:

"Sir, it would be enough for me to take communion to burst utterly."

Such remarks, often so typical, which Heredia was ever ready to quote, I fear that they may be deformed or lost if everyone were as lazy as I about noting them down. Let me quickly quote this other one, in which Aurevilly relives completely:

This takes place rue Royale. It is very late. No one left in the streets; Aurevilly, who this evening has drunk a quantity of local white wine together with his friend X., is relieving himself. A gendarme passes by: "At least, sir, you might get a little closer to the wall." For Barbey has not abandoned his customary aloofness. Thereupon he turns round and:

"Would you want me to skin myself?" [15]

[15] The use of the imperfect subjunctive makes this even better in the original: "*Voudriez-vous que je m'écorchasse?*"

28 October

In bed since Friday evening. A sort of colonial diarrhea; that is, bleeding. Starvation diet. A few griping pains, but bearable after all. Impression of a crossing (with possible shipwreck), having broken off all connections with the outer world, or at least with society. An excellent excuse for refusing invitations and failing to receive any but a few intimate friends. No worry about going out even to get my meals. A very long and unbroken succession of hours, of undifferentiated hours. I hardly dare confess how delighted I am, for fear of seeming affected. The conventional is the only thing that never looks like "pose." I shall finally be able to finish *Der Zauberberg*! [16]

But before getting back to it; for I am still a bit too weak for that effort (in two days I have lost almost a quart of blood and eaten nothing since Friday morning), I am reading *Maxime* by Duvernois—much less good than *Edgar* and a few others—then launch into *Le Soulier de satin*.[17]

Yesterday visit from Valéry. He repeats to me the fact that, for many years now, he has written only on order and urged on by a need for money.

"That is to say that, for some time, you have written nothing for your own pleasure?"

"For my own pleasure?!" he continues. "But my pleasure consists precisely in writing *nothing*. I should have done something other than writing, for my own pleasure. No, no; I have never written anything, and I never write anything, save under compulsion, forced to, and cursing against it."

He tells me with admiration (or at least with an astonishment full of consideration) about Dr. de Martel, who has just saved his wife; about the tremendous amount of work that he succeeds in getting through every day and about the sort of pleasure, of intoxication even, that he can get from a successful operation and even from the mere fact of operating.

"It is also the intoxication of abnegation," I say. At this

[16] Thomas Mann's novel, *The Magic Mountain*, first appeared in German in 1924.

[17] *The Satin Slipper* is a long drama in verse by Paul Claudel laid in Renaissance Spain and first published in 1929.

word *abnegation* Valéry pricks up his ears, leaps very amusingly from his chair to my bedside, runs to the hall door, and, leaning out, shouts:

"Bring some ice! Boy, bring some ice! The patient is raving. . . . He is 'abnegating'!"

At many a point in the conversation I am aware that he thinks me quite entangled in pietism and sentimentality.

29 October

"I have never been able to invent anything." It is by means of such a sentence in the *Journal d'Édouard* [18] that I thought to separate myself from Édouard, to distinguish him. . . . And it is this sentence on the contrary that is used to prove that, "incapable of invention," I have depicted myself in Édouard and that I am not a novelist.

30 October

Finished *Le Soulier de satin*. Staggering. It is hard to imagine that in another religion Claudel's shortcomings could have developed as unimpeded as in Catholicism. What a warning! And yet:

I am in no way inclined to consider myself better than Claudel, and for certain aspects of his character I maintain a great esteem. But I note with curiosity that not one of my shortcomings would find encouragement in Catholicism; quite the contrary, only my good qualities would, and doubtless the best ones (or so it seems to me this evening)—so that from the effect of Catholicism on Claudel I am quite unable to deduce the effect Catholicism would have on me.

16 November

It seems to me that I should now write masterpieces— if only the time were not lacking. This revision of the Prinzhorn translation of the *Nourritures*, however interesting it may be, wears me out. Every day we work at it until past eleven o'clock. At times the difficulties and our desire for perfection are such that we spend more than two hours on a page.

. . .

[18] The "Journal of Édouard" is a part of *The Counterfeiters*, being the diary kept by the novelist character who stands at the center of the action.

I should like, in reply to all the requests from bores, to send a printed card which would read, under my name: "is working and urgently begs you to leave him alone for a while"; this joined to the usual formulas of salutation.

Yet I managed to give two hours to the piano today and the last few days. I have picked up again Chopin's *Études*, which I had long neglected, particularly the third, fifth, and eleventh of the second book. Moreover, there are very few that I do not know by heart.

20 November

This morning, visit from Jean Cassou accompanied by a would-be[19] publisher who, I am told, is going to publish that Anglo-French or Franco-English review a representative of which recently came to ask permission to publish my translation of the first act of *Hamlet*.[20] Cassou having asked me what I think of Pourtalès's translation, I am led to speak to him of that odd misinterpretation (?) that almost all translators make and which I wish to note here, for it is most significant.

The ghost, speaking to Hamlet in Scene v of Act I, expresses himself thus:

> *But virtue, as it never will be moved,*
> *Though lewdness court it in a shape of heaven,*
> *So lust, though to a radiant angel link'd,*
> *Will sate itself in a celestial bed,*
> *And prey on garbage.*

Pourtalès (like many others) translates this:

". . . thus lust, though linked to a radiant angel, will grow tired of a celestial bed to go and prey on garbage . . ."[21] dropping out, it seems to me, the best and most important part of the image and the thought, which he makes banal: it is not a question here of turning away from the celestial bed but rather of bringing the garbage to it. I believe the true meaning is:

[19] The expression *would-be* appears in English.

[20] The Franco-American review *Échanges* published Gide's version of the first act of *Hamlet* in December 1929. Not until 1942 did he continue his translation of Shakespeare's tragedy, which first appeared in New York in 1945.

[21] ". . . *ainsi la luxure, bien qu'accouplée à un ange radieux, se dégoûtera d'un lit céleste pour s'aller gorger d'ordure* . . ."

"So lust, even though married to an angel, will glut itself on a celestial bed and there will prey on garbage (will bring garbage there)." [22]

"Perhaps your mind was especially bent toward this interpretation after you had translated *The Marriage of Heaven and Hell,*" Cassou said to me.

25 November

Strohl, always most charmingly thoughtful, sends me, together with two bits of amber containing almost invisible insects, a little paper by Maurice Trembley read in 1902 before the Société Helvétique des Sciences Naturelles. This little study recounts the observations of his grandfather Abraham Trembley on fresh-water polyps and quotes several letters from the latter to Réaumur. From Maurice Trembley's conclusions I pick out this sentence, which delights me:

"He (the good observer) recognizes the necessity and the advantage there is in knowing how to doubt at the right moment and is able to doubt his own conclusions.

"He constantly makes an effort to see facts as they are in reality and not as he would like to see them."

I should have preferred: "as he would like them to be."

But this doesn't matter: his remark is perfect.

And he adds:

"It is in this regard that Réaumur (since he is concerned here) served the cause of science better than Buffon."

30 November

Élisabeth V. R., who is amazed to see little Catherine so disinclined to miss La Bastide, tries to question her on this subject. Is it a lack of memory? No, she remembers everything.

"You didn't like La Bastide, then?"

"Oh, yes! Very much."

"But tell me . . . where do you most like to be?"

The question seems so odd to the child that at first she appears to be disconcerted.

---

[22] "Ainsi la luxure, encore que mariée à un ange, se soûlera sur une couche céleste et s'y repaîtra d'immondices (y apportera l'immondice)."

In the 1945 version this has become ". . . ainsi la luxure, qu'on la marie avec un ange, si céleste que soit la couche elle saura s'y satisfaire, et s'y repaître d'immondices." The sense is the same.

Then, in her most natural voice, and as if it couldn't be otherwise:

"Why . . . *wherever I am.*"

This morning Élisabeth and Catherine took to Bormes, to give it to the little daughter of the Mayrisches' gardener, a puppy, the son of Nyska. Catherine was crazy about him; she never let him out of her sight. It seemed that she must have been very sorry to give him away.

Yesterday Élisabeth told her of her plan:

"Oh, what a good idea!" Catherine exclaimed at once. "How happy she will be!"

Regret is an emotion that is not natural to her, that she cannot "produce" *naturally*.

Later on, this spontaneous optimism may seem affected to others and to herself, and yet nothing is more sincere. But one comes to suspect the sincerity of a feeling that is too rare.

2 December

Radiant morning. Managed to devote four to five hours to the piano all these recent days; perfected (and really succeeded in bringing to perfection) several Études and Preludes.

Saw come out of their chrysalis two laurel hawk-moths. I am reading *L'Abbesse de Jouarre*,[23] with no admiration.

I have discovered quite by chance and without much believing in astrology that it just happens that on the 21st of November, my birthday, our earth leaves the influence of Scorpio to enter that of Sagittarius.

Is it my fault if your God took such great care to have me born between two stars, the fruit of two races, of two provinces, and of two faiths? [24]

3 December

L'Abbesse de Jouarre strikes me as beneath the ordinary, childish.—Real repulsion for this flabby style: "Fate does not grant two such delights as the one I enjoyed last night. . . ." And Renan is still considered a master of the French language!

[23] A novel by Ernest Renan.
[24] André Gide's father came from a Protestant family of the Gard *département* in the south, whereas his mother issued from a traditionally Catholic family of Normandy.

8 December

There remain too many things that I should have liked to say, and should have said, and have not said, and which clutter up my mind.

I was like unto those creatures which cannot grow without successive metamorphoses.

That violence, that impetuosity of our desires does not seem to us to lie in us, but rather in the very object of our desires, whose attraction it constitutes. An attraction that therefore strikes us as irresistible; so that we are incapable of understanding that someone else can endow another type of object with the same irresistible attraction toward which a like impetuosity will impel him with an equal violence. Whoever is not first convinced of this would do better to remain silent in regard to sexual questions. For a mind to which a question appears in advance in the form of a reply, it can be said that the question has not even been posed. And will it not be permitted me to say that it is the same in matters of mystic adoration and that all those attractions of God (which they call attributes) which make him so essentially adorable are but a projection of their own inner fervor?

X. and Y. go about repeating that they are fed up with pretense, that they have made up their mind to speak frankly henceforth, to brave opinion, to burn their bridges behind them, etc. But they are not burning anything at all; they are very careful not to. The courage of which they boast costs them nothing of what they continue to cling to. And in the new book they have just produced they have taken great care that their confessions should be of such a sort and so speciously hidden that only the most alert readers can read them between the lines; of such a sort that they will have nothing to retract if later on they become converted or aim at the Academy; of such a sort that their future apologists will have no trouble sweeping it all away and can brand as slanderers those who, reading the truth between the lines, attempt to reassert that truth. Thus sham is accredited.

Today, when the risk of moral discredit is not so great

as it once was and the penalty is less severe, pretenses and camouflages are frequent in literature, I know. I tell myself that people have always lied when customs have forced people to lie, and, nothing authorizing me to believe Sodom more populated today than it was yesterday, I become somewhat suspicious in regard to some of our ancient authors.

Marseille, 27 December

The newspapers have related:

that a friend saw me, contrary to my custom, give fifty centimes to a beggar and heard me whisper, as I leaned toward him: "Yes, but when will you pay them back?"

that a fellow writer (another paper that relates the same absurdity said: an Italian prince), invited to dinner by me, waited in vain for me to call for the bill and was obliged to pay in my stead and to give a tip to the checkroom, while with clenched teeth, I said: "I can't help it; I am a miser."

that, going to cash a check at the bank and seeing people ahead of me at the cashier's window, I said: "I am André Gide and do not like waiting," in such a tone that I was served first.

that, caught by the rain at Luna Park, I exclaimed: "Gosh, it stinks!" assuming a roughneck manner that decidedly did not suit me. Etc.[25]

When I am feeling well, this kind of thing has no effect on me; but as soon as I am weak, such hateful tales rise up within me and I suffer to feel such stupidity and hatred aroused against me. I also fear that such details may cling to my image, since I know so well that falsehood is more readily credited than truth.

---

[25] The first two bits of gossip are invented out of whole cloth. Not the two others. It is true that, going to the Société Générale, not with a check to cash but with an American banknote, I first inquired and was told that the currency exchange was not handled at the same window. This is why the anonymous witness saw me taken care of before the others, and, since I deposited the amount instead of taking it at once, I was able to leave the bank without having had to stand in line. If this malicious witness had had the slightest acquaintance with me, he would have known that I detest illegitimate favors and privileges and make it a point of honor never to get out of turn.

As for the episode of Luna Park, it is absurd; if I said to M.: "Ça chelingue," it was because we were passing through a smelly area. [A.] *Chelingue* is a vulgar expression.

La Souco-Roquebrune, 30 December

Radiant weather. Oh, to set sail, and for anywhere whatever! Why and how did I allow myself to be so long held in check, during my youth? At present I feel more desires in me than can be satisfied in the time that remains to me to live. Why did I not meet, at twenty, him who would have led me off! and whom I should have accompanied to the very ends of the earth. But at that time no one spoke of traveling; and it was already considerable to have gone as far as Algeria. What would my *Nourritures* have been like if I had known enough to take my hunger to the very tropics? But the strength of the bonds to be broken constitutes the beauty of the liberation, and my first care was to forge the bonds. I should like to regret nothing and to convince myself that, more obviously vagabond, my life would have been less significant; and that I should never have written *La Porte étroite*.

"Suffer me first to go and bury my father and mother," says to Christ he who refuses to understand that it is essential to follow Him *at once*.—Not knowing how to drop everything at once.

The morning hours are the best. If I let them be taken up by conversation, correspondence, and bustle, my whole day reflects this and is lost.

1930

No good work without a long succession of hours, of quite empty days, before me. My hosts are willing, in friendly fashion, for me to escape them every morning. Yesterday I withdrew in this manner likewise for the whole afternoon. I *worked* a bit, something that I have not been able to do for months past. That is, I forced myself to write a whole scene of *Œdipe,* which this morning strikes me as very ordinary. I shall not be able to keep a single word of it. But, thanks to that work, I glimpse now what that scene ought to be: abrupt, extraordinarily clear and simplified. I always take great joy in suppressing everything useless. My waste-baskets fill up with "changes" that would have seemed mere stuffing; but what good is that false wealth to me? A writer is said to be rich and fertile who, often, is merely avaricious and does not know how, or dare, to suppress anything. (Strange example of Péguy, who, among all the lines that lead his thought from one point to another, unwilling to . . . choose, sets them all down, one after the other. I always long to draw the narrowest line, the most sudden and least expected.)

3 January

At Hyères, at the Noailleses', where I find Marc, together with Cocteau and Auric, I had come merely for lunch; I gladly let myself be detained for dinner, then for the night. Extreme and charming kindness of our hosts; amazing ingenuity in comfort; such perfect functioning of everything that contributes to one's ease that this morning, when after my bath the English butler brings my breakfast, I butter my toast with a spoon, for fear that the absence of a knife, on the tray loaded with delicacies and fruits, might look like catastrophe.

Gymnastics, swimming in a rather large pool, new games, the names of which I do not know, with shuttle-cocks and balls of all sizes—one especially that four of us played (the very pleasant gym teacher, Noailles, Marc, and I) with a medium-sized ball that one must keep from falling on this side of a high net that separates the two sides. We play almost naked, then, damp all over, run and plunge into the warm water of the pool. This game amused me more than I should have thought it still possible, amused me like a child and a god, and especially since I was not bad at it. What absurd things Pascal has said about games! And how the very gratuitousness of that struggle, of that effort, seems to me beautiful! Yes indeed, I cannot remember having had, even in my youth or childhood, more ardent, purer, and more complete pleasure.

I recall that Charlie Du Bos, after reading *Si le grain ne meurt* . . . , excusing himself for the little interest he took in the account of my childhood games, said: "But what do you expect, my friend? *I never played.*" This is the secret of a tremendous lack, which remains invisible to *whoever has never played.* As for me, on the other hand, I am always inclined to look upon art itself as a game, and upon the Cosmos as God's game.

9 *January*

"*Classic impersonality,*" says the critic who signs himself Robert le Diable in *L'Action française* when speaking of Lacretelle's latest book, so easily to be compared with my *Immoraliste.* "Classic impersonality that M. Gide might well envy his disciple."—But I don't envy that quality at all! And I have never considered impersonality as a particularly classical virtue. On the contrary, I have always striven to give to each of my books the least impersonal character possible, the least objective, the most *penetrating.* It is just in regard to this matter that Chardonne's remark strikes me as so correct (try to find it again).

Returned from the south on the 7th with Lacretelle; seats reserved by him in the Pullman; meeting as the train went through Toulon, Lacretelle coming from Cap-Ferrat. I confess that I rather feared that long *confrontation* (for our two seats faced each other across a small table over which we had to lean to talk) and the effort of a conversation with someone a bit hard of hearing. No, the time passed most pleasantly, and Lacretelle, as it often happens, hears better when speech has a background of uninterrupted sound.

At the table directly opposite us was a rather attractive young couple. Probably a wedding-trip, for the table is covered with flowers. The young man was reading *Les Caves du Vatican*. This is the first time I have ever happened to meet someone actually reading *me*. (The scene: "Oh! Monsieur Duhamel!!") Occasionally he turned toward me and, when I was not looking at him, I felt him staring at me. Most likely he recognized me. Lacretelle kept telling me: "Go ahead! Tell him who you are. Sign his book for him. . . ." In order to do this I should have had to be more certain that he liked the book, in which he remained absorbed even during the meal. But suddenly I saw him take a little knife out of his pocket. . . . Lacretelle was seized with uncontrollable laughter on seeing him slash *Les Caves du Vatican*. Was he doing so out of exasperation? For a moment I thought so. But no: carefully he cut the binding threads, took out the first few sheets, and handed a whole part of the book that he had already read to his young wife, who immediately plunged into her reading.

[*Roquebrune*] *4 February*

No doubt of it: what Charlie Du Bos likes in Nietzsche is that he is at the point of death. He would turn away from him if Nietzsche were cured. What cajoleries he had for me so long as he thought me anguished, disturbed, and he could play the advantageous role of comforter! He used to caress himself against me like a cat.

One evening (at P.'s) we were stunned to hear him declare that he felt really capable of friendship only for women. He likes to bend over . . . and to pity, and to sympathize with. And everything would be all right if he were motivated by the need to make others happy. But let there be no mistake about it: what he likes is suffering itself, sorrow; this is what makes him feel Christian. He looks upon happiness as a *despiritualization* and this is what, by a secret intuition, warns him against Mozart. The very spiritualization of that exquisite art does not so much elude as embarrass him, that sovereign penetration and domination of suffering and joy by intelligence, by

the mind, which purifies suffering itself of its injurious element (what Charlie considers its absolving virtue), so
that, for Mozart, it becomes simply a deep purple in that
rainbow which his genius serenely spreads before us.

13 February

Saddened, the last few days, by the fear that little
Guido may be avoiding me. Nothing of the sort. I managed to find out last night. He went by on the road; I
accompanied him to the village, where he was going to
mail a letter and where he remained for some time playing with four other children, first in the streets, then on
the terrace in front of the school. Bright moonlight. I rather
unwisely tarried with them and even thought that I had
caught cold again; but the attraction was so great that I
abandoned all prudence. Besides, the hope of going back
down with Guido kept me there. Utterly chilled, I dragged
myself away from them and returned home on the run;
then, somewhat warmed up, went back up to the village
and found them still there, unable to resign myself to
leaving Guido. He was in a grocery, whence he came out
with a package and a bottle of bleaching water, and at
last I was able to go back down with him as far as La
Souco.

There is hardly any desire in this; or it is so confused,
so drowned in a general liking, that it becomes indistin-
guishable. But the joy that I feel throughout my whole
being is so great that it makes me forget my age, dominates all other preoccupations, all regard for the conventions.

29 February

The pernicious and deplorable influence of Barrès.
There has been no more baneful educator, and everything
that remains marked by his influence is already dying, already dead. His qualities as an artist were monstrously
exaggerated; is not all the best in him already found in
Chateaubriand? Nothing better marks his limits than his
Cahiers, which, in this regard, are powerfully interesting.
His taste for death, for the beyond, his Asiaticism; his desire for popularity and applause, which he takes for a love
of fame; his lack of curiosity, his ignorance, his scorn; the
choice of his gods; but what I dislike most of all: the

finicky affectation, the soft prettiness of certain sentences, in which breathes the soul of Mimi Pinson. . . .[1]

9 March

Back to Paris, yesterday at noon. Notable improvement, though my throat is still irritated. I ought to give up smoking. And as I write these words I light another cigarette.

My mind is waking up somewhat from this long hibernation. Some progress in English. I now succeed in understanding currently Dorothy Bussy's conversation and reading. Read with delight, enthusiasm, the two *Henry IV*'s and the *Henry V* of Shakespeare.

Ceased thinking, for a time, of my *Œdipe* (which nevertheless has been greatly enriched by the reflections arising from Mauriac's article on *Molière* in that monument of boredom, the first issue of *Vigile*)[2]—in favor of a book that I now glimpse and which is already taking shape: *Geneviève* or *La Nouvelle École des femmes*—in which I shall boldly tackle the whole question of feminism.[3] I long to get to Cuverville to work on it.

14 March

Visit from Charlie Du Bos; together we lunch at Mme Théo's. I always have great pleasure in seeing him, but can no longer be natural and sincere with him; and I do not really know what goes into his friendship, since I have taken away from him all reason to pity me and the hope of converting me.

To what a degree the confessional warps his tastes, his admirations, his thoughts, I realized yesterday in unexpected fashion:

[1] This influence is marked in Montherlant's pages, very beautiful as they are, which I read in the latest *Nouvelles littéraires*. It could lead only to despair as soon as one refused to take seriously the role and attitude that Barrès himself had at first assumed only to escape boredom. [A.] Mimi Pinson is the central character in a story of the same name by Alfred de Musset. The typical *grisette*, or Paris working girl, she has come to be a symbol of naïve sentimentality.

[2] *Vigil* was a short-lived Catholic literary quarterly founded in 1930 and edited by Charles Du Bos.

[3] *Geneviève*, published in 1939, forms indeed with *The School for Wives* and *Robert* the third panel of the triptych: after the wife and the husband have told their tales in turn, the daughter now recounts the story as she saw it.

I do not know how, having begun to talk of Keats,
Charlie read me a long passage of *The Fall of Hyperion*,
which I told him I did not yet know. Somewhat indulgently, I followed him in expressing my admiration for
those lines which he read with a charming voice. During
the night following our conversation, unable to sleep, I
picked up the little volume and reread from the beginning
The Fall of Hyperion, which seemed to me, I must say,
less good Keats. I came to the long passage read by
Charlie, in which I see only too well what can please and
flatter him. . . . Eventually, continuing my reading, a succession of admirable lines that, suddenly, *I recognize*.
These are the lines that Keats took over into the other
Hyperion, as I note the next morning. I read attentively
the note to *The Fall of Hyperion*. . . . Either Keats returned to this first version, dropping the least good; or
else on the other hand this *Fall of Hyperion* is posterior
and one must see in it, with Charles Brown, an effort on
the part of Keats "of remodelling the fragment of H. into
the form of a Vision" which, says the note, "perhaps
affords the most astounding instance on record of the loss
of artistic power and perception under physical decay and
mental agony"—whether it is "a re-cast or a draft"—I
wonder at the way Charlie becomes enthusiastic about
just those least good passages and prefers them simply
because he finds in them traces of that "spirituality"
which will perhaps allow him to annex to Catholicism a
poet he admires above all and whom he felt about to
escape him.

"Annex to Catholicism" is perhaps going too far, and
probably is an insult to Charlie's perfect integrity. But is
it not already too much that he should admire a weakness
and that it should be that weakness that awakens the
most echo in him?

I was still in the next to last year in school when I read
Hyperion for the first time. It was Louÿs who, informed
by his brother, introduced me to it. Neither one of us
knew English and we had to look up word after word in
the dictionary.

Cuverville, 31 March
I thought this was the 24th of March and here it is al-

ready the end of the month. What have I done all these recent days? Wrote some thirty pages of that *Geneviève*, but do not know whether or not I shall be able to complete it successfully. I keep repeating to myself that this book must be written without any care for style and that any effort toward formal perfection I might evidence in it would reveal my hand too obviously; my heroine cannot have these qualities and I should betray her character by attributing them to her. I easily escape from myself and, letting a very different personality substitute itself for mine, only through complete self-effacement and an utter lack of application can I let it express itself appropriately through me. But I feel no satisfaction in writing, as women do, with rapid ease, and I dislike everything I write this way. I begin to doubt that this style lacking in density can have any value and sometimes fear I am hazarding a desperate undertaking, unworthy of all the other projects which I then reproach myself with having forsaken for this one. I must admit to myself that this book does not touch me very deeply and does not reply to any profound exigency like that which dictated to me my *Nouvelles Nourritures* and my *Œdipe*. Yet I should not give it up without cowardice, and the inclination that urges me to write it is great enough to nourish the book. With each of my books have I not managed, on my bad days, to give myself good reasons for *not* writing it? And as for everything I think of this book today, is not mere laziness prompting me?

I have returned to the piano, which I had not opened in the last three months; delight at finding my memory so good, better perhaps than on my best days. It was enough for me to work over them for a few hours in order to bring back to memory all the preludes and fugues of the *Well-Tempered Clavichord* I had learned, and even some I had not seen in a long time, and which I certainly play better than I used to.

Read a great deal of English with an extraordinary pleasure, and more and more easily. I do not think that my faculties are diminishing, but a secret, morose resignation makes me apply them with less hope and ardor. I aspire less to vanquish what strikes me as less impregnable or less indispensable to my happiness. The satisfaction it would give me seems to me more empty, and the time too short that is left me to enjoy it. It is not without self-directed irony that I am still striving to learn, and not without smiling at my vain curiosity. Everything I learn today could have been of some advantage to me twenty years earlier; this is what I constantly tell myself, and that the heavier the baggage is, the harder it is to move on when the hour comes. Then I tell myself, immediately afterward, that of all fruitless anxieties there is none more fruitless than that of death (though it constantly pursues me) and that the part of wisdom is to go on living without thinking too much that one must die. That constant idea of death, moreover, does not exactly sadden me; on the contrary, I am unwilling to admit that it should darken my thoughts. But, looking back over my life, what saddens me rather is the thought of the little I have done, the thought of all I might have and should have done. All the books I should have written, so many countries I might have known, so much happiness I might have caused. An unaccountable diffidence, modesty, shyness, reticence, laziness, excessive understanding of the *other side*, etc., have constantly held me back, unfailingly checked me in mid-course. I have always been paralyzed by scruples and by fear of hurting whomever I loved; and nothing is more ruinous when one loves what differs from oneself.

It goes without saying that I feel all this especially at Cuverville and when with Em. He whose heart is free can go far; I have never been able to keep myself from taking into account everything that kept me from advancing, never resigning myself to going alone and ever more anxious to lead others than to venture forth alone. Real pioneers do not care whether or not they are followed; they go forward without looking back.

In the Congo what joy could I take in gathering unknown flowers with no one to whom to give them?

Cuverville, 8 April

French literature, much more anxious to know and to depict man in general than men in particular. Ah, if only Bacon rather than Descartes! But Cartesianism was not concerned with *Every man in his humour;*[4] no great de-

---

[4] The expression in italics appears in English.

sire for experience and, all in all, insufficient curiosity. The so-called pure sciences preferred to the so-called *natural* sciences. Buffon himself is not a good observer.

The idea that one must start from the simple to reach the compound and that one can compound through deduction; that deceptive belief that the compound created by the mind corresponds to nature's complexity, that the concrete can be derived from the abstract. . . .

Lanson, in his very good study of the influence of Cartesianism (p. 89),[5] quotes Montesquieu's amazing declaration:

"I established principles and saw particular cases conform to them as if automatically. . . . When I discovered those principles, everything I was seeking came to me. . . ."

This is because he was seeking only what he had found in advance. Frightful limitation! And how much I admire, by contrast, Claude Bernard's remark, which I have noted somewhere or other and which I am probably quoting inexactly and amplifying:

"The true scholar (?) is he who is able to find in experience perhaps a reply to what he was seeking, but also to listen to the reply to what he was not asking"; who accepts considering even what he did not expect to see, were it to surprise and embarrass him considerably. The Cartesian does not accept ever being surprised. In short, he does not accept being taught.

Paris, 14 April

I was able to stay at Cuverville only four days; the first three poisoned by an article promised to a German review (*Die Koralle*) to go with some photos by Marc Allégret. Nothing to say about the Congo that I have not already served up. Horror of working on order. I constantly tell myself: all the time left me is not too much for . . .

From a letter from Marcel Drouin:

"Last night I read in Michelet's *La Montagne:*[6] *They*

[5] Gustave Lanson's scholarly essay, *L'Influence de la philosophie cartésienne sur la littérature française* was included in his *Études d'histoire littéraire* (*Studies in Literary History*) in 1929.
[6] *The Mountain.*

laugh to see Xerxes in love with a plane tree; a quarter of
an hour later, in Donne:

> *Xerxes strange Lydian love, the platane tree.*

"It is especially odd," adds Marcel, "since the idea of
love does not figure in Herodotus' text."

And on the other hand Michelet probably did not know
Donne. What can be the source from which both drew?

Berlin, May

To cease to take oneself into consideration for days,
weeks, months. Lose sight of oneself. It amounts to going
through a long tunnel beyond which one can hope to find
a new landscape. . . . I have often feared that an uninterrupted consciousness might attach our future too
logically to our past, might prevent becoming. Night and
sleep alone permit metamorphoses; without oblivion in
the chrysalis, the caterpillar could not become a butterfly.
The hope of awaking someone else urges me to let the
man I am sink into sleep.

It is not going to paradise myself, but leading you there
that matters to me. What unbearable happiness if one had
to enjoy it alone. . . .

And what can be said of a happiness that is achieved
only at the expense of another!

Berlin

It is fashionable to admire Vermeer above all others.
The Vermeer of the Berlin Museum does not strike me as
superior to the Pieter de Hoogh that flanks it, which, as
far as I am concerned, I even believe I prefer.

By Govaert Flinck, a very delectable female nude. Very
different qualities from those I used to admire in that
extraordinary *Goldsmith's Family* in the Brussels Museum,
which was long attributed to him.

Wonderful landscape filled with ponds, by Ruysdael.
How slight and frail the Hobbemas appear by comparison!

The most beaten paths are certainly the surest; but do
not hope to scare up much game on them.

Berlin, 18 May

It was Barrès who made it fashionable. That need of
looking for a lesson, a "message" everywhere and constantly is intolerable to me. Vassalage that debases the

mind. Great works do not so much teach us as they plunge us into a sort of almost loving bewilderment. I compare those who are everywhere seeking their advantage to those prostitutes who, before giving themselves, ask: "How much is your little gift?"

At once my only desire is to get away.

I should like to enjoy this summer flower by flower, as if it were to be the last one for me.

Fish die belly-upward and rise to the surface; it is their way of falling.

Cuverville, Thursday, 30 May

Read *La Prisonnière*[7] in the train. I write this morning to Bourdet, whose *Sexe faible* I had seen with considerable amusement last Monday.

Found at the Librairie Gallimard the little pamphlet (*Nouveaux Cahiers de la quinzaine*) that is devoted to me, and which had not been sent me. If I had been at that meeting, I should not have kept from replying to Maxence's attack.[8]

Nothing is more intolerable to me than false quotations. With them one can make an author say whatever one wants. M. Maxence, by attributing to me the anecdote of *Les Faux-Monnayeurs* (which moreover he completely falsifies; when he says: "a Russian writer quoted the anecdote to me," is not this tantamount to confessing that he has not read the book and that his opinion is based merely on secondhand information?), reminds me of Lombroso, who concluded from Baudelaire's prose poem *Le Mauvais Vitrier* that the poet was very cruel.[9]

---

[7] Édouard Bourdet's play, *The Captive*, deals with the problem of a Lesbian wife. *Le Sexe faible* was entitled *The Sex Fable* in New York.

[8] In the debate on André Gide that took place at the Studio Franco-Russe on 25 March 1930, Louis Martin-Chauffier and Georges Adamovitch spoke at length. Jean Maxence accused Gide of cruelty and of a humanism that excludes God. The debate was published by the *Cahiers de la quinzaine*, series 20, cahier 6.

[9] In "The Bad Glazier," one of the *Little Poems in Prose*, Baudelaire relates the experience of forcing a glazier, with his heavy load of glass, to climb five flights of stairs only to be told his services were not needed and then have a flowerpot dropped on him as he issued from the front door. A glorification of the satisfaction to be derived from yielding to a momentary impulse, the poem is more likely inspired by Poe's *Imp of the Perverse* than by actual experience.

But I note this in his declaration: "Nietzsche is an adversary who touches me deeply because, in his very refusal, he is suffering." Yes, that is it; and Charlie Du Bos likewise; what they blame me for is not being unhappy. In their eyes happiness is the greatest crime, or at least the greatest misfortune of a soul, when that happiness is not achieved through their means.

Let us remember the name of Georges Adamovitch. No one has spoken more intelligently of my books than he (at the Franco-Russian meeting of 25 March 1930, which was reported in the *Cahiers de la quinzaine* of 5 April).

A great confusion came from the fact that people wanted to find a personal profession of faith in every statement of my heroes, however diverse and contradictory those heroes might be. And this was all the more tempting since originally I had been denied all creative talent. I was incapable of getting away, of detaching myself, from myself, it was said, and in each creature I animated my resemblance was looked for. This also allowed people to think that fundamentally I was never very sincere. I came to understand that *objective depiction* often means a superficial representation; but, for a profound depiction, the poet must experiment in himself what is to be the subject of his picture. And Browning does not exactly confess himself in *Bishop Blougram*, in *Sludge*, in *Andrea del Sarto*, to be sure—yet in order to discover the form of those characters, his elastic soul deigns to identify itself in turn with each of them for a time. And since one cannot really understand a feeling without experiencing it oneself, I submit that he depicts himself, if one admits that he becomes in turn each of them.

Not that I have not taken my stand on many points; or rather that I was forced to take that stand. But as soon as I am inhabited by a character to whom "my noble poetic faculty" (as Mallarmé said) obliges me to give life, I owe myself to him and have no opinion of my own. I am with him. I am him. I let myself be led by him where I should not have gone by myself—whether this character be the Immoralist, or Alissa, or Candaules, or Saul, or the minister of my *Symphonie pastorale*, or the Édouard of *Les Faux-Monnayeurs*, or Éveline, or Lafcadio.

Of the incestuous character of Barrès's theories: according to him, you should not, you could not, really love anyone who was not of your own blood.

Barrès (the second volume of whose *Mes Cahiers* I am reading at this moment with an assiduous exasperation) seems to have been worried by Chopin's Nancy origins on the paternal side of the family. (I have written a few pages on this subject that I must find and develop.) He points out the fact (p. 182), then immediately drops it. What a wonderful contradiction of all his theories! And likewise Claude Gelée, called *le Lorrain*!

This is perhaps the most touching, most moving thing in all Barrès: his obstinate perseverance in the absurd.

But perhaps his liana-like thought needed that vine trellis to climb upward:

". . . laws of human production. We *know* notably that the individual's energy is the sum of the souls of the dead behind him and that that sum can be achieved only through the permanence of the earthly influence." (Page 93).

And he is naïve enough to add:

"This is one of those fundamental ideas which are almost enough to establish the fecundity of a mind, *so rich are they in applications*."

And, in fact, his whole intellectual effort consisted in applying that theory to individual cases.

It cannot exactly be said that that theory is false; but, like all theories, after a short time and once they have accomplished the little progress they were capable of allowing the mind, it ceases to invite the mind to anything but indolence and soon works toward preventing its development.

And suddenly this surprising confession (p. 192):

"Can I sincerely say that I love Lorraine? . . ."[10]

". . . But my life that does not belong to her is penetrated, perhaps confiscated by her. I do not know whether or not I love her; having entered me through suffering,

[10] What he really loves is Toledo, Venice, Constantinople, Astiné Aravian, Asia. [A.] Astiné Aravian is an Armenian woman who figures prominently in *Les Déracinés* (*The Uprooted*) by Barrès.

she has become one of the means of my development."

It cannot be better expressed; he reveals himself here to be oddly perspicacious. And further on (p. 215):

"I did not come to love Lorraine easily. (The customs in Lorraine are always *shabby* [page 190].) At the age of ten, at twenty, at thirty, I looked upon myself as an exile. . . . I did not cease to desire the Orient. With experience I came to see that *in those countries I loved only the land of the dead,* cemeteries, reveries, the place of dreams and of mystery, etc. . . ."

And again:

"In the beginning I did not love her. I began to like her when I began to realize that she had her dead" (p. 237).

As if every country did not have them!

"And moreover this is a reply to: *what is the good of it"* (p. 238).

The need of creating that factitious interest and of artificially establishing his pose is born in Barrès of the profound awareness of his poverty. No real, essential problem in him; no "figure in the carpet." [11] He must invent it; otherwise he would have nothing to say. Whence that keen sense of the abyss, of emptiness, of death, that need of "withdrawing to his minima" (p. 236).

At Cuverville I had read rather much, and with great appetite: the latest Mauriac (in installments in the *Revue de Paris*), *Demian* by Hesse (in translation), Jouhandeau's remarkable *Parricide imaginaire;* unable to get interested in *Babbitt;* then everything concerning Delphi in the *Greek History* of Curtius (Vol. II). Reread with very great joy the first book of *Dichtung und Wahrheit* in German. For the seventh or eighth time (at least), attempted *Also sprach Zarathustra.*[12] IMPOSSIBLE. The tone of this book is unbearable to me. And all my admiration for Nietzsche cannot succeed in making me put up with it. Finally, it seems to me slightly supererogatory in his work; it would assume importance only if all the other books

[11] Gide uses Henry James's title in English.
[12] Mauriac's "latest" was probably the novel *Ce qui était perdu* (*What was Lost*), which, like Jouhandeau's *Imaginary Parricide*, came out in 1930; *Babbitt* is of course Sinclair Lewis's novel; *Truth and Poetry* is by Goethe, and *Thus Spake Zarathustra* by Nietzsche.

did not exist. I constantly feel him here to be jealous of Christ, anxious to give the world a book that can be read *as the Gospel is read*. If this book has become more famous than all the others of Nietzsche, it is because, basically, it is a *novel*. But, for this very reason, he addresses himself to the lowest class of his readers: those who still need a myth. And what I especially like in Nietzsche is his hatred of fiction.

23 June

The *Scènes de la vie future* by the excellent Duhamel, which I am finishing, leaves me very dissatisfied.[13] A few lines in his preface had made me hope for more. If Americanism triumphs and if, later on, when Americanism has triumphed, his book is consulted, I fear it will appear childish. A higher individualism must wish for the standardization of the masses. What is to be deplored is that America is stopping at the first stage. But is she stopping? Thanks to her, humanity is beginning to glimpse new problems, to develop under a new sky.—A sky *devoid of stars?* . . . No, but whose stars we have not yet managed to discover.

Jean Prévost; cantankerous. Bad, for a novelist who flatters himself that he knows men, always to make them, at one's first approach, withdraw and close up.

As for me, I am well aware that I run the risk of being considered flattering and obsequious since my first care, in the company of almost anyone, is to say what will put him most at ease and invite him to unfold, one after the other, all his petals.

Often very disappointing!

29 June

It is certain that my love for Em. has greatly withheld my thought; but, forcing it constantly to consider what it left behind and yet would have wished to follow along, I believe that thought gained in depth and breadth what it lost in sharpness and impetus. Moreover, I am not even sure that I should have felt a sufficient need to write such works as *Corydon*[14] or the second part of *Si le grain ne*

---

[13] *America the Menace*, as this harsh judgment of American mechanized civilization was called in English, originally came out in 1930.

[14] *Corydon* is formed of four Socratic dialogues on homosexuality; *If It Die* . . . is Gide's memoirs, often touching on the same subject.

meurt . . . unless I had been pushed on by so vexing a clash. There is hardly a day on which I do not feel checked by *my* love, by *her* thought.

30 June

Twenty minutes of inhalation, twice a day. Mortal!

"What do you think of while you are under the steam?"

"Of all sorts of things; of death, of my brother Joseph. . . ."

"But I thought you didn't have a brother."

"Oh, that doesn't keep me from thinking of him!"

To abstain through virtue is perfect; but too often fear also held her back; as soon as the grass was a bit deep, she dared not venture onto the lawn. *"Latet anguis in herba."* [15]

2 July

Finished a very interesting and convincing study on *J.-J. Rousseau's Malady* that I had sent for. The author reduces everything to the fact that he did not pass his urine, whence slow poisoning of the blood, etc.

I recall that after the birth of R. P. the nurse came to tell the father that the baby "pissed awry."

"I don't give a damn, if only he thinks straight," exclaimed the father with perhaps more humor than wisdom.

3 July

The only drama that really interests me and that I should always be willing to depict anew is the debate of the individual with whatever keeps him from being authentic, with whatever is opposed to his integrity, to his integration. Most often the obstacle is within him. And all the rest is merely accidental.

6 July

Pin, who cannot be suspected of any lack of understanding in regard to my writings, but rather of indulgence, told me of his indignation on reading in my *Retour du Tchad* the disrespectful way in which I speak of *La Mort du loup*.[16] He told me that all domestic animals bellow when killed and that, if I had been a hunter, I should have been struck by the silent agony of wild

---

[15] "A snake lies hidden in the grass," from Virgil: *Bucolics,* III, 93.

[16] In Vigny's famous poem *The Death of the Wolf,* men are urged to suffer and die in silence as the wolf does. Gide had argued that wild animals are not necessarily silent at the moment of death.

animals. He went so far as to make me regret having
written those lines.[17]

13 July

The closer I approach death, the weaker becomes fear
of death. I hold that fear in great scorn as soon as I feel
it being played up, as soon as the artist yields to it and
delights in it. It has always seemed to me that the first
virtue of man was knowing how to face death; and it is
a lamentable thing to see it less feared by very young
men than by those who ought to be, if not tired of life,
at least, having lived, resigned to death.

"Let the dead bury their dead." There is not a single
word of Christ to which the so-called Christian religion
has paid less attention.

In the train

While I am skimming through Maurois's disappointing
Relativisme, a young Finnish girl beside me is reading his
Aspects de la biographie[18] with pencil in hand. At in-
tervals the pencil descends: the Finnish girl has probably
recognized one of her own thoughts, one of those to which
I long ago said farewell.

No, I do not like disorder; but I am exasperated by
those who shout: "Don't move," when no one is yet in
place.

14 July

Never have I been able to settle in life. Always seated
askew, as if on the arm of a chair; ready to get up, to
leave.

---

[17] In regard to this paragraph Marcel de Coppet, then Governor of
the Chad, wrote me:

Paris, 20 June 1932

DEAR FRIEND,

Many wild animals do not die in silence: the lion and the leopard
roar; many antelopes, and particularly gazelles, bleat plaintively; the
rhinoceros squeaks (a faint mouse's squeak, extraordinary from such a
big carcass); our African hares cry out too; jackals, bush-dogs bark and
howl. Is it from pain? Is it from fear of a new wound or of death?
That is another question; but they do not keep silent in their agony.

Nor the buffalo (which I was forgetting) either.

I have never killed any wolves.

Yours,

COPPET [A.]

[18] *Relativism* (1930) and *Aspects of Biography* (1928) are both
essays.

21 July

At Cuverville two days now. Frightful weather.

Piano completely out of tune as a result of replacing some strings.

In the whole region not a single young and handsome creature to smile at, to look upon. Languor. Torpor. I am smoking too much. I should read all day long if my eyes did not become tired readily and if I were not trying to give to *Œdipe* the hours in which I feel most lucid; but without fervor.

I enjoy chatting with Edmond, our gardener; but he is getting old; he complains of pains, of itchings, of sleeplessness.

"What about your appetite?"

"Oh, my appetite's still good. That's what I said to the doctor: 'When I am dead, I'll still eat.'—'You old rascal!' he said to me."

I have just finished the wonderful *Moby Dick*.

22 July

X. told me he had recently met Franz Blei in Berlin. The old bohemian still seems extraordinarily hale and hearty; and when X. congratulated him on this, Blei, leaning toward him, whispered:

"I'll tell you my secret: *No sports!*"

24 July

Rather hasty reading (but it is not worth more) of Zola's *Lourdes*. A book constructed in this way calls for the method of *"Nulla dies sine linea."* [19]

Immediately afterward I plunge back into Walter Pater's *Greek Studies* and *Dichtung und Wahrheit*, taking up, at Goethe's invitation, the wonderful story of *Genesis*, of which he gives such a remarkable summary.

Finished the dialogue between Eteocles and Polynices for the second act of my *Œdipe*, but do not yet know whether I can consider myself satisfied with it.

25 July

I believe that illnesses are the keys that can open certain doors for us. I believe that there are certain doors that only illness can open. There is a certain state of

[19] "Not a day without a line."

health that does not allow us to understand everything; and perhaps illness shuts us off from certain truths; but health shuts us off just as effectively from others, or turns us away from them so that we are not concerned with them.

I have never met one of those who boast of never having been ill who was not, in some way or other, a bit stupid; like those who have never traveled; and I remember that Charles-Louis Philippe very prettily called illnesses the poor man's travels.

Those who have never been ill are incapable of real sympathy for a great many misfortunes.

1 August

I go to buy some cigarettes at Criquetot.

The sight of that ordinary little village (moreover so exactly similar to many others in the region), each time I return to it, saddens me. What insufficient regard for hygiene, for comfort, for well-being, for gaiety! (Skillful gradation in the choice of words.) A sort of sordid economy seems to have dictated the placing and the contracting of the houses, in which no one but equally sordid people could achieve a semblance of happiness, in which any aspiration toward betterment is condemned to languish miserably. Everything there is ugly, shabby, set. No public garden, no place except the café to gather in on Sunday; no song, no game, show, or music; no invitation to get away for a minute from one's work and one's most selfish interests. There are few towns in which one feels less happy to be alive, despite its relative prosperity. And I think with melancholy of those new villages that I saw in Germany, where everything seems attractive, houses and people. . . .

Little François D., whom I question about what he is going to do now that he has received his school diploma, tells me that he wanted to continue studying to become a school-teacher (his mother wanted to hire him out as a farm-hand). Immense desire to help him, which immediately filled my heart and made tears come to my eyes. . . . How can I express that urge in a way that will not immediately seem ridiculous to me? I think that those who in their writings readily voice "good sentiments" are not really moved by them in a very pathetic and profound way. Most often the charity they express is but a superficial philanthropy. They would fail to find words to express it if they were completely upset by it.

It was also because I foresaw the superhuman difficulties the little fellow would encounter when trying to rise a bit above his original condition. . . .

Out of eight children in that family only one seems to have "gone bad." The father, who had long been a laborer and with whom I used to go frequently to chat since he had been laid up by illness, died last year of cancer, after months of frightful suffering. He was a sort of muzhik, a rebellious fellow greatly tormented by a persecution-mania, who poisoned his existence whenever he judged that he had not got his due from his neighbor or from the government. Day and night he ruminated on the injustices he claimed to have suffered, and all the help one could give him meant less to him than the least centime of which he thought he had been cheated. Illness had cast a considerable gloom over his mind. I had for him the sort of friendship that, in the whole township, I now feel only for our old Edmond, who, moreover, liked him very much and endured listening tirelessly to all his complaints, realizing full well that D. was not always in possession of his wits. The other people hereabouts scarcely liked him; he had a touchy character and was ill inclined to mingle.

Edmond, our gardener, has for some time now slept badly. His rheumatism gives him pain, and some nervous worry, almost moral in nature, keeps him awake. His numerous children are nevertheless all healthy and happy; their new families are prospering; he has always done his best; but this simple, honest soul always fears falling beneath his task, having forgotten something, being in arrears. And when he goes to sleep at once, worn out by his day's work, he wakes up well before dawn, much too early, gets up, goes back to bed, and tosses.

"It's partly the birds that wake me up when they begin to squawk," he says to his wife. She protests:

"But, Edmond, birds don't *squawk*, they sing." Then

she adds: "And don't you think it's wonderful that they are always happy?" Whereupon he, grumpily:

"Well, there's no denying that *they* are lucky, at least!"

3 August

In the latest *Candide*,[20] which Jacques brought us yesterday from Paris, a diverting article by Montfort (it is a long time since I had read anything by him) on Catulle Mendès. Montfort is of the opinion that people "do not do justice" to that sorry poet, so happily forgotten (happily for us and for him). It is hard to understand today the extraordinary celebrity he achieved in his lifetime.[21] Then he spread out everywhere; he reigned supreme; he debased everything his pen touched, and it claimed to touch everything. Fortunately I encountered him but very rarely; yet the last glimpse I had of him remains unforgettable. It was in a theater lobby during an intermission. He had on his arm an enormous tart, wearing a frightfully low-necked gown (for the epoch), who was simpering and manipulating her fan; he himself, in evening dress, was strutting, thrusting out his pot belly, throwing back his head, which suggested a Christ for brothels. He was wearing a low, wide-winged collar, from which cascaded a soft white silk tie; his long blond hair made a dull halo; his languishing and insipid eyes glanced from under heavy, half-closed lids. The couple was so large, so voluminous, that it blocked the passage. Not being known to him, I was able to stand there looking at him. Both of them seemed boneless, soft, and as if covered with Vaseline. They gave off an extraordinary scent of eau de Cologne or Lubin water, of toilet water, of library paste, of the bed, and of cigarette butts. Young men kept rushing up and bowing before this Moloch. It is impossible to see, or to fancy, anything more shameful.

Montfort quotes one of his remarks which bears witness, he claims, "to an extraordinary humility": "If I had not been a Jew, I would have had genius." "It would require many pages," Montfort adds, "to examine this opinion, and probably to refute it." I reread twelve times over

[20] A weekly newspaper devoted chiefly to literature and the arts.

[21] Or rather it is very easy to understand when one knows the important position he occupied in "journalism." [A.]

Mendès's statement, then Montfort's, without succeeding in understanding them. Obviously Montfort intends to imply that, Jew though he was, Mendès still had genius. I believe rather that Mendès meant: "If I were not known to be a Jew, I should be granted genius."

Not worth mentioning.[22]

It was most appropriate for Mendès to be praised by Montfort.

4 August

Some of my judgments, when they are at variance with the accepted opinion, I do not consider so assured as not to re-examine them from time to time. Most often the result is only to go further in my own direction (as with Tolstoy, or Gautier, whom I pick up again almost every year).

Every year I reread Coleridge's *Kubla Khan* with the greatest effort of poetic attention (which has almost no connection with mere intellectual attention). Very unhappy at first to remain almost insensitive to the charm of that poem, which is considered by the best judges to be incantatory. The incantation did not work. I go back to it again, sharpening my taste on those lines as on a gun-flint; really "whetting" it, convinced that there is no better way to give it a delicate edge. . . .

Very happy, yesterday evening, to understand *Kubla Khan* much better at last. I am well aware that one eventually finds beauty in what one has decided to consider beautiful. But in this case I do not think I am taken in, however subtle may be the debate between my will and my sincerity. Obviously nothing comes up to that immediate and irresistible emotion that makes you kneel panting before certain works of which the echo was latent in you; but there are acquired admirations, sometimes slowly and patiently acquired, which have their value too, and I am not quite sure if they are not even of greater advantage and better educative value for our whole being than the former.

François D., who comes to recite to us the little comedy he was learning for the commencement exercises, is all upset by his brother Paul's opposition. The latter cannot admit François's spending so much time, by entering the

[22] This line appears in English in the original.

Montivilliers school, without contributing to the support of their mother. It is his turn to help her (he is now twelve). In short, he has made it a matter of scruple, and the little fellow, without support, without example, without advice, frightened by his "egotism," gives up, with a broken heart.

I write to the school-teacher to inform him of the situation. François D. has promised me that he will go and see him on his return to Criquetot. The teacher can give him good advice. Em. has already talked with him in the best possible way. I was too deeply stirred to find anything to say, and as much by Em.'s words as by the child's distress.

The thing I am most aware of is my limits. And this is natural; for I never, or almost never, occupy the middle of my cage; my whole being surges toward the bars.

Calvi, 21 August

Ah, how wise little Henri B. was not to come and how mad I should have been to bring him! How well off I am to be alone! For such a long time I have not traveled alone; however free I am with Marc, still my thought is influenced by him and cannot follow its natural course.

Left Marseille at three p.m.; disembarked this morning before six o'clock at Bastia, where I immediately took an auto for Calvi. Calmest possible crossing, but sleepless night. Cloudy at the moment of sailing, the sky quickly cleared. After some hesitation, I have taken a room in the best hotel; the price of the *pension* obliges me to stay at least seven days.

I was finishing lunch when B., whom I had met in Berlin, came over to my table. I am waiting for him, as I write this, to take coffee with him. A young athlete with bare arms, whom I had greatly admired, was seated at his table. B. tells me that O. G. is here. I notify the hotel office and beg them not to give my name.

22 August

How could complete frankness with you have been possible, since it implied the confession of what I knew you to consider abominable, and I not? since you considered abominable a part of me that I neither could nor would sacrifice?

. . .

Wonderful flight of the palm trees, in the night, along the quay of Calvi; wonderful outpouring of their palms. Wonderful façades of the tall houses behind them; balconies, terraces above the narrow street, which is already dark. On the quays a half-naked people walk about, the high society of several pleasure yachts mingling with the fishermen of the little harbor; all redolent of thoughtlessness and pleasure-making. The atmosphere invites one to summary physical pleasures, to games, to debaucheries, and remains quite inappropriate for meditation.

That self-indulgence to which love invites us, drawing from us not the best but what is most likely to please the other; you do not so much raise him as he debases you. The leveling process is of necessity effected at the expense of the superior one.

What a masterpiece I should write on this subject if only I were thirty and with the experience of my sixty years! But a whole lifetime is not too much to realize, once awakened from that deception, that you have been tricked. And, naturally, the noblest ones make the best dupes.[23]

Noon, 1 September

Col d'Allos.

I do not believe my joy has ever been deeper or keener. The air has never been softer and I have never breathed it more lovingly. My subtly active mind, beclouded by no worry, smiles at the humblest and pleasantest thought, as my flesh does at the azure, at the sun, and my heart at everything that lives. I did not feel any younger at twenty; and I am better aware of the value of the moment. I was more tormented by desires, by imperious demands. To my excesses at Calvi I owe a great calm. My glances are disinterested and the mirror of my mind is comparable to the surface of an unruffled lake on which all the reflections round about come voluptuously, but very purely, to take their place.

Probably some catastrophe is awaiting me in Paris in return for all this happiness.

My greatest emotion of this day, and one that will remain very green in my memory: at the last turn in the road before going through the Col d'Allos, suddenly, a

[23] See entry of 4 December 1938. [A.]

tremendous flock of sheep grazing the short grass of those heights. The evening sun was casting its last rays on those slopes, and the russet-green grass, the russet-white of the sheep, spread out like a frieze, made a powerful and perfect harmony under the sky. It seemed to me that it had been a long time since I had seen anything so beautiful.

When the bus stopped, almost immediately afterward, beyond the col, I went to talk with the old shepherd. As I had thought, those sheep (about a thousand, he said, but divided among various parts of the mountains) come from near Arles. They are the ones that pass through Manosque and that Giono told me about so enthusiastically. They take between eight and twelve days to come this far. All this seems to leave rather indifferent my traveling companions, to whom I tried to communicate some of my emotion. But no; looking later on, at Barcelonnette, for some postcards as a reminder of those admirable grassy summits we had just left, I found nothing but dry photographic records as unattractive as affidavits. And I thought sadly: but that is what they see; such is the world's appearance to them: clear, sharp, precise, stripped, with nothing left of that poetic halo which enchants it: a world without overtones, which awakens no echo in their hearts, incapable of intoxication.

The stupidity of my neighbors' remarks last night at the movies in Nice! Yet rich and "distinguished." But it is for just such people that films are made. Success depends on them. They are the great number. They are humanity. Where Flaubert shook with laughter, I feel only an immense sadness.

20 October

Back in Cuverville for several days now, I shall leave again tomorrow evening, having much improved but not completely finished my *Œdipe*. Long and patient piano-practice; made undeniable progress. I suffered not to have begun some important reading, but it might perhaps have distracted me too much from *Œdipe*. The *Memories of an Infantry Officer* by Siegfried Sassoon, which I had got on Bennett's recommendation, has an exquisite tone and I should like it very much if I could understand it completely, but many slang terms and popular expressions escape me and I look for them in vain in the dictionaries. I should like to return here with *Clarissa Harlowe*.

Certainly I am no longer tormented by an imperious desire to write. The feeling that "the most important remains to be said" has ceased to inhabit me as it once did, and I convince myself on the contrary that perhaps I no longer have much to add to what a perspicacious reader can glimpse in my writings.

But these are a lazy man's reasons that I invent *a posteriori* and that a bit of fervor would melt. By now, moreover, I am too well aware that I am being observed, and writing is like the piano: I play better when I know I am not being listened to. Besides, just now, I am quite taken up with *Œdipe*.

Saint-Clair, 7 November

After several days of violent *mistral*, radiant weather. Read between Paris and Marseille *The Virgin and the Gipsy*, which Bennett had sent me; the most recent book by D. H. Lawrence, by whom I had not yet read anything. The discovery of Lawrence, Ruyters told me, was the great event of his life. I fear that there may be much resentment in his present predilection for contemporary English literature. I think, and hope, that the other books by Lawrence are better. This one struck me as so empty and so crude in its brutality that its cynicism, which I might otherwise like, becomes quite inoffensive. There are few books that I have disliked as much.

9 November

Radiant weather. I should like to be gone. Oh, I should like to put to better use the time that is left me to live!

I really believe that I have finished *Œdipe*, and I believe that I have really finished it properly. That is, that I got into it almost everything I had planned to put into it. But I do not much like this work of fitting together. I am eager to get to something else, where I can let myself go.

14 November

No pleasure in being in Tunis again save that of showing to Élisabeth a country that is new to her. As far as I am concerned, I return here as in a rut and am angry with myself for falling back into it. My brain, moreover, is still numbed by all the Mothersills I absorbed yesterday, thanks to which, doubtless, I avoided being seasick. Rather bad crossing; remained in bed almost all the time. Reached Tunis in the rain. (On approaching the coast, wonderful color of the sea, first green, then gradually yellowing, under a lavender sky; beauty of the waves, etc. . . . Very Delacroix.)

This morning frightful weather. No desire, except to read and to work. The mail brings me the proofs of *Œdipe*.

Tunis, 15 November

Saw last night a film by René Clair: *Sous les toits de Paris*.[24] Probably one of the best French films; perhaps the best.

Got home at midnight; *crapette*[25] until one o'clock, which I am furious to have lost.

Rose early to pick up Tournier, who is called to court by jury duty. We go there with him. A little room lacking the solemnity of the great Assize Courts. Everything takes place as if in the bosom of the family. Six jurors sit on the right and left of the three judges. Since the accused is an Italian, three of the jurors are Italians. The case has no great intrinsic interest: an attempted robbery, which would be handled in a mere police court were it not for the apparent housebreaking that accompanies it. But it is in no wise certain that the accused is the guilty person. And I feel again the atrocious anguish that used to seize me at the Rouen Assize Court. The public prosecutor's implacable charge, speaking in the name of society, appealing to the jury's instincts of conservation, defense of private property . . . "how far would we go if . . ." etc. would be enough to make me an anarchist. The lawyer for the defense, extremely young and most likable, was addressing a jury for the first time. He had succeeded in convincing me of his client's innocence, so that the sentence to five years in prison without benefit of reprieve really flabbergasted me.

[24] *Under the Roofs of Paris* was filmed in 1929.
[25] An ancient French game of cards, a sort of "patience" for two hands.

16 November

With all information in hand, it is clear that the condemned is certainly the guilty man (though he did not
deserve such a heavy sentence). No doubt would have
been possible had it not been for fear of compromising
an important personage—which prevented bringing all
the details out into the open.

Gabès, 21 November

The oasis of Gabès, which I did not yet know, seems
to me one of the most beautiful I have known. The
abundance of the waters (warm). . . . I did not think
myself any longer capable of such admiration. If I had
encountered Gabès at twenty, it seems to me that I might
have turned it to richer account than Biskra. The extraordinary indentations of the rocks above the oasis.

A few kilometers from Sfax, a little owl, perched on
the point of an aloe leaf, alongside the road. We back
up to see him better, but he flies away at our approach.
Two days before, we had already seen one shortly beyond
Zaghouan on a telegraph wire, and we spent a long time
observing each other. He preened himself and made faces,
turning sidewise to look at us over his shoulder.

First night at Kairouan. (The guide, in the square, after
a night walk through the Arab town.) The second at Sfax.
From Sousse to Sfax, followed the coast, as I had never
done. Monastir and Malidia, marvelous.

Between Sfax and Gabès we leave the direct road to
reach "la Skéra" on the edge of the sea, where we lunch
in the shade of a palm tree (foie-gras and orange marma-
lade). Extraordinary landscape, abandoned beach: an ass,
a palm tree, the clay cliff; an ineffably soft sky. Rarely
seen a more stirring landscape.

19 December

Back to France.

Our judgments about things vary according to the
time left us to live—that we think is left us to live.

1931

S talled at Saint-Clair; cold caught on the way back, during the crossing, then the automobile ride from Marseille here. I should like to be at Cuverville. . . .

2 January

Finished going over (with Élisabeth) the translation of *The Old Wives' Tale*. Sent back to Roger Martin du Gard the second volume of proofs with corrections written in. Enormous work that we had the constancy to continue throughout our trip in Tunisia, at a rate of about two hours every day.

Meanwhile read Bennett's *Imperial Palace* with very great interest and Marie Delcourt's *Vie d'Euripide*.[1]

At Saint-Clair reread *Honorine* and *Un Début dans la vie*.[2]

X. reproaches me with so many hours devoted to piano-practice, lost, he says, to literary production. . . . But I am not quite persuaded that, even with more time, I should have been able to produce more, or especially (for I am not quite sincere in writing the lines I have just written: very often I have wept over the number of projected works that I could have, should have, written) that my work would have gained much by being more abundant. Probably I would have won greater notoriety and my thought would have imposed itself more; but it seems to me that, most often, people write too much, that the thought of many authors would gain by being less diluted, and that by exposing itself too diffusely it makes itself more vulnerable to time, to ruin. Most often the most prolix are those who have the least to say.

La Rochefoucauld would doubtless have been very ill-advised to spin out his *Maximes* into novels. How often I am seized by the desire to write, then stopped by the question: is this worth saying? I like feeling in an author

---

[1] *Life of Euripides. Imperial Palace* (1930) was then a recent book, whereas *The Old Wives' Tale* by the same author had appeared in 1908.

[2] *Honorine* and *A Start in Life* are both short novels by Balzac.

an inner, unexploited wealth, which only rises to the surface in the rare writings he gives us. But perhaps I have come to think thus only to excuse in my own eyes an excessive continence, with which I am occasionally able to reproach myself bitterly. What I want above all to avoid is remorse, regret, sorrow; I will not allow them to darken the end of my life.

4 January

For Em. Dare to tell her:

"Have you not understood that I prefer to die anywhere rather than in Paris, and that if I cannot have you beside my bed at my last moment, I prefer not to have anyone?"

Every evening, before going to sleep, and often besides during the day, X. (that is, I) would ask himself this question:

"Am I really ready to die?"

He took it upon himself to reply: "Yes."

15 January

Lecture by Copeau at the Vieux-Colombier (the second, but I had grippe too badly to be able to go to the first).

How many reflections this speech gave rise to! And to begin with, in his exaggerated modesty (much applauded, so that he never has such success as when he declares he doesn't care about success), he is unwilling to consider that he has inscribed his name deeply in the history of the theater and that the French stage is not the same since his glorious efforts. But some in my part of the hall were concerned to hear him depict as a general abandonment a solitude for which he had voluntarily, patiently, and passionately worked. "Don't talk to the helmsman," he used to say. He had managed to call forth, more than anyone I have known, the most fervent devotion from many; no one was more surrounded by friends, more seconded, more beloved than he. The real desertion, the one from which he had most to suffer (but it was hard for him to speak of this), was that of the authors. He could hope, and I hoped with him, that the only thing lacking was the instrument (which he was providing) for a renascence of the theater to take place; new works, strong and young, called forth by the need he had of them, were of necessity going to pour in. . . . I thought so too. Nothing of the sort happened. And his immense effort remained without any direct relation to the epoch. He was struggling against the epoch, as any good artist must do. But dramatic art has this frightful disadvantage, that it must appeal to the public, count with and on the public. This is indeed what made me turn away from it, more and more convinced that truth is not on the side of the greatest number. Copeau, though claiming not to, was working for a select few. He wanted to lead to perfection, to style, to purity, an essentially impure art that gets along without all that. He frightens me when he declares that he was never closer to achieving his aim than in the Japanese *No* drama he was putting on, which an accident prevented him from presenting to the public, and of which I saw the last rehearsals. . . . A play without any relation to our traditions, our customs, our beliefs; in which, artificially, he achieved without much difficulty an arbitrary "stylization," the exactitude of which was absolutely unverifiable, totally factitious, made up of slowness, pauses, something indefinably strained toward the supernatural in the tone of voice, gestures, and expressions of the actors.

He frightens me even more when, as a conclusion to his lecture, he declared, in substance, that he was now fifty years old, still felt "at the height of his powers," game despite so many blighted hopes, ready to fight again. I should like so much that, ceasing to fight against the Chimera which has henceforth withdrawn into him, he should concern himself solely with completing that literary work of which he spoke at Pernand and which, at least, will survive. But neither is he willing to admit to himself to what extent his new religious convictions keep him from producing that work which refuses to go in the direction of his prayers; just as he refused to admit, to admit to himself, that between Catholicism and dramatic art there could be no alliance, save to the detriment of one or the other, and only through a distorting compromise.

It is indeed because Copeau's artistic ideal is visionary that he is a pathetic figure. I have always thought that there was something of Ibsen's Brand in his case. He too let himself be misled by an image of holiness, which mis-

leads only the noblest; but I do not know whether
Catholicism ought not to see in this one of the demon's
most perfidious snares, for that form of holiness can be
achieved only at the expense of others and much pride is
hidden in it.

18 January

I am leaving for Cuverville.

At the *N.R.F.* I encounter Malraux, who speaks to me
of my *Œdipe*.

"Yes," he says laughing, "Œdipus escapes the Sphinx,
but only to let himself be eventually gobbled up by his
daughter. . . . You ought to write an *Œdipus at Colonus*,
in which Œdipus, before dying, would repulse even An-
tigone."

And I imagine, as a sort of epilogue, a dialogue between Œdipus and Theseus. I think of a life of Theseus
(oh, I have been thinking of it for a long time!) in which
would take place (what I invent only today in the train
taking me to Cuverville) a decisive meeting of the two
heroes, each measuring himself against the other, and
throwing light upon, each in opposition to the other, their
two lives.[3]

25 January

Finished Sieburg's book.[4]

Even if the serious shortcomings that Sieburg reproaches
us with were real (and they are very close to being so,
but the fact that they are not *quite* so is enough to permit
me complete hope), the alternative with which he claims
we are faced would remain none the less inadmissible,
and nothing in this book proves to me that European
equilibrium cannot be re-established without France's
handing in her resignation. She owes it to herself to prove
that she is capable of evolving without necessarily repu-
diating her past. A renewal for which such a price was
paid would be tantamount to a bankruptcy. It is that
very past that must give birth to her future. But the

[3] This is precisely what Gide was to do in his *Thésée*, first published
in 1946 though the project goes back at least to 1911.
[4] Friedrich Sieburg's *Gott in Frankreich* (*Who Are These French?*)
appeared in French translation in 1930 as *Dieu est-il Français?* with
a preface by the publisher Bernard Grasset.

strength with which she clings to things is terrifying. It makes me think of Valéry's remark: "How many people are killed in accidents because of not wanting to let go their umbrella!"

France is no more obliged to adopt the pace of others than to impose her pace on other nations; but rather to change her pace herself and convince herself of the truth of the Gospel saying: "Neither do men put new wine into old bottles." That new wine may be French wine, even were it not to be recognized at first as French. Our country has many surprises in store for Sieburg (and for herself); she is rich in unsuspected resources. However inert its dough may often seem, it takes very little yeast to make it rise.

Three images are too many for the same thought, alas; but let us pursue the last one. The dough does not like the yeast. The yeast for her is the *foreign*. That yeast was often necessary (in literature of course) to bring out wonderful manifestations: Italian yeast for Ronsard, Spanish for Corneille, English for romanticism, German also; the works called forth in this way are no less French, and the blame heaped on me today for listening to the voice of the Russians is ill-founded. Despite the reproach, so often justified, of not taking the foreign into account, no literature perhaps more than the French has managed to be impregnated by it while still maintaining its own stamp and its peculiarities. It might even be said that, given the Frenchman's virtues (of clarity, restatement, tact, and ability to perfect), no other nation has greater need of the foreign; and that without a contribution from outside he would run the risk of fatally whittling down his substance if he did not, on the other hand, also possess inventive powers—which he most often succeeds in exploiting only much later, behind other countries.

Grasset in his reply to Sieburg is probably right in saying that Germany is in a stage of development that France has left far behind. But he is wrong in thinking that it is an advantage to be old. Germany has over us just that advantage, misunderstood among us, of youth.

France of late is beginning to show regard for youth. First sign of a rejuvenation.

. . .

I heartily scorn that kind of wisdom that is attained only through cooling off or lassitude.

My memory is no less good and it seems to me that it is but recently that *I know how to learn.*

And I have never suffered more from my insufficient education.

30 January

Received at last the issue of *Latinité* so long announced which contains an "impartial" inquiry into my "influence" in Europe.[5] There are still many critics who fancy that I have always been much concerned and preoccupied with my influence and that I wrote with the aim of bending and dominating the minds of my readers. I hoped to have given proof of the contrary, my sole desire having been until quite recently to write works of art, if not precisely impersonal, at least emancipated from myself, and which, if they exerted any action over the reader, could only help him to see clearly, to question himself, and force him to think, were it against me, to leave me.

But it is certain that, of late, my position is not the same. This is also because I see more clearly in myself and want much more definitely and vigorously what seems to me much more clearly preferable. In any case, and whatever it may be, the thing I am most bitterly reproached with is having worked for the emancipation of the mind. This seems unpardonable to the group that, on the contrary, aims only toward the most complete submission to authority, to rules, to tradition, etc. That group, which is very powerful, always uses the same weapons, which it always has at hand. The best reason it can find to prove that man *must* not change is that he *can* not change. For as soon as one glimpses the possibility of a progress, how can one fail to wish to obtain it? It is that glimpse of a possible progress that has so deeply *cultivated* my thoughts and modified my gait.

[5] The issue of *Latinité* for January 1931 contained a symposium on Gide conducted by V. de Laprade and J. Reynaud, with contributions from Germany (Emil Ludwig, Max Brod, Klaus Mann, Carl Stern-heim, Heinrich Mann, Arnold Zweig, etc.), Czechoslovakia, Italy (Lionello Fiumi, Alberto Consiglio, etc.), Rumania, England (Bernard Shaw and Francis Hackett), and France (Lucie Delarue-Mardrus, Rachilde, Jean Cassou, Drieu la Rochelle, Maurice Bedel, Francis de Miomandre, etc.).

The thing I notice above all in the hostile replies is that their authors are not judging me according to my books (which they admit not knowing) but according to the reputation that has been made me and which they are not concerned to verify as to exactitude. Even those of their side will gradually discover that I am not exactly like what they first thought me to be. Besides, those protests more than anything else have assured me of my reality, of my value; or rather, and more precisely, it is only in the light of them that I began to become aware of it. Originally I looked upon myself simply as an artist, and was concerned, in the manner of Flaubert, with hardly anything but the good quality of my work. Its profound significance, to tell the truth, escaped me. But is it not natural that that significance of the work, for any artist anxiously careful of his craftsmanship and *sincere*, should first elude its author? For his personality, whatever he may do, shows through in his work, and what takes on significance is not so much the work but himself.

31 January

Some people would be sufficiently tender-hearted, but they lack imagination to the point of not being able to imagine, even weakly, the sufferings of those who are not close to them. The far-away ceases to seem quite real to them and they read descriptions of the imprisonment and brutalities suffered by the "suspect" or "unorthodox" professors in Poland, etc., etc., in the same spirit as tales of horrors of past ages. It does not *touch* them. A clever novelist would be able to move them more. In that sympathy for imaginary misfortunes there is a certain flattering self-indulgence; the knowledge of real sufferings only embarrasses. One thinks: What do you expect me to do about it? And, in the certainty of one's inability to help, each one finds permission to sit back and do nothing.

As for feeling, through their very opinions, somewhat bound up with the oppressors and torturers, this never occurs to them. Obviously they feel and tell themselves that if they lived in the countries where such abominations take place, *they* would be on the right side. And isn't it because I tell myself that I should be *on the other side* that these stories move me to such a degree? Feeling on the side of those who are being oppressed *is a part of my optimism,* and I know that if I endured their sufferings with them, my optimism would not be stifled. It is not at the mercy of constraints. Profound optimism is always on the side of the tortured.

It is not at all that I feel more "human" today than at the time when no trace of such preoccupations could be found in my work. I simply took care to forbid them access to it, judging that they had nothing to do with art. I am no longer so sure of this, nor that anything can and must remain foreign to art; it runs the risk of becoming, it necessarily becomes, artifice if what is closest to the artist's heart is banished from it.

2 February

This morning wrote without too much difficulty this letter, of which I make a copy, for I can use it again:

DEAR MADEMOISELLE,

No, do not excuse yourself for the time you have taken by asking me to read your charming letter. But do not hope that I can find any to read your manuscripts with the attention that I feel sure they deserve. Nevertheless I should take that time, and quite willingly, if I thought that my advice on them could possibly be of any advantage to you; but I long ago ceased to believe in the virtue of any advice other than what one can give oneself.

This bit, however, which you will be able to extract from Mme de Sévigné's remark that I am inclined to quote to the too numerous young people, and particularly girls, who seek my opinion:

"When I listen only to myself, I do wonders."

Most sincerely, etc.

Worked considerably over the *Fandango de candil* by Granados[6] the last few days (since my return here), which I have the greatest difficulty merely getting into my head because of the incessant repetitions and half-repetitions—and which I am still far from playing in a way that satisfies me.

I am getting ahead with *Clarissa Harlowe.* I have reached page 220 of the second volume; but there are

[6] This dance, full of popular rhythm and color, is one of the piano pieces of the *Goyescas.*

five, of five hundred pages each. Rarely read a book with so much application.

3 February

Long and very interesting letter from Roger about my *Œdipe*. (Replied to him at length the same day.) He complains of the lack of breadth and development of my drama. But did not my intentional exclusion of all images, of every oratorical development, have necessarily to lead to this contraction? I do not know whether or not I am to regret it.

I reread his *Confidence africaine*[7] with the greatest satisfaction. Not a single lapse, not a single gap. Obviously one who can achieve such perfection in craftsmanship has every right to criticize and advise others; it is quite natural that he should ask of others what he demands of and obtains from himself, and especially when those others are his friends.

5 February

Yesterday reread aloud my *Œdipe* to Agnès Copeau and Em., who begged me to do so.

As a result, I have come to regret the letter I wrote to Roger the day before in reply to his criticisms. Through great fear of self-indulgence, I am most inclined to welcome criticisms; but decidedly Roger's did not seem to me well founded. Such as it is, I believe that my drama is what it had to be and what I wanted it to be.[8] It answers my requirements; satisfies me. A more ample ending would have thrown it off balance. Intentionally I suppressed all the amplifying overtones, which it is enough for me to awaken in the reader's mind.[9]

. . .

[7] *The African Confidence* (1931) is a short novel relating a curious case of incest in the words of the protagonist, by Roger Martin du Gard, referred to above as Roger.

[8] After writing "*ce que je voulais qu'il soit*" Gide adds in parentheses: "*qu'il soit, non qu'il fût,*" in order to indicate that his wish is fulfilled, and that he has intentionally avoided the traditional agreement of tenses.

[9] I believe, however, that in the third act I could have let myself go a bit more. Doubtless my reason intervenes too much. Nothing that is not intentional, motivated, necessary. What I used to call "God's share" reduced to nothing, through lack of confidence, lack of belief in inspiration, which has made me lack courage to write except when not dominated by emotion. One ought to be willing to write without knowing very well what one is saying, or especially what one is going to say. [A.]

And I receive a note from Roger, very saddening since it tells of an attack of phlebitis (only too clearly foreseen!), but which begins thus: "Forgive me my mean letter about *Œdipe*. Fate has already cruelly avenged you." So that I am, nevertheless, quite happy to have already told him of my gratitude for his frank criticisms.

"With talent you do what you will; when you have genius, you do what you can." I have forgotten whose is this wonderful remark (Ingres?).

The mother-in-law of Davidson (who is making a bust of me and at whose house I lunch today), a charming old lady of eighty-four, when—on the point of lighting a cigarette after the meal—I ask her if smoking bothers her, tells us that a similar question was put to her, before 1870, by Bismarck, in a train between Paris and Saint-Germain in which she happened to be alone with him. To which she replied at once:

"Sir, I do not know. No one has ever smoked in my presence."

Bismarck immediately had the train stopped so that he could change to another compartment.

8 March

Before leaving Paris, I had gone to rue de Villejust.[10] Saw Valéry; for the first time in months and years, *not tired*, not out of patience, in full possession of himself, fully *realized* so to speak, and filling his character to the very limits. In the course of the conversation he even said only once his customary "Furthermore I don't give a damn" (apropos of his article on women's suffrage which had just appeared in the *Revue de Paris*—a most remarkable article that I was not able to read until I got to Roquebrune).

I cannot help regretting, oh, quite selfishly, that Valéry has never made an effort to understand me better, and that the impression he has of me remains so substantially the same, the very one that Pierre Louÿs must have had at the time of our worst disagreements. To him, to them I represented the Protestant, the moralist, the puritan, the sacrificer of form to idea, the anti-artist, the

[10] For more than twenty years Valéry lived at 40 rue de Villejust, which has been rebaptized since his death as rue Paul Valéry.

enemy. I do not know how, despite that, there remained in Valéry's heart rather than in his mind so true a friendship for me. He has given me as many opportunities to assure myself of it as to assure myself also of his lack of understanding.

But from this I have merely suffered without ever harboring resentment for the fact that the clever construction of his mind had to exclude what constituted my justification and my life. Yet a more penetrating examination would, it seems to me, have readily shown him that our divergences are, after all, less *essential* than he may believe, than he insists on believing. Consequently, by very different paths to be sure, I constantly agree with him and subscribe to almost everything he writes, for which I most often feel nothing but an unlimited admiration.

18 March

Finished *Clarissa*.

For the third time (I believe it may even be the fourth) I gather up my strength to launch into Huxley's *Point Counter Point*, for I have been told that one must get beyond the beginning. But what can I think of a book of which I read attentively the first seventy pages without being able to find a single line somewhat firmly drawn, a single personal thought, emotion, or sensation, the slightest enticement for the heart or mind to invite me to go on?

Went as far as page 115 with great effort. Unreadable. Yet I have plenty of pluck for reading. I cannot even understand how there were people able to go on.[11]

19 March

The itch from which I have suffered for months (or, but with interruptions, for years) has recently become unbearable and, for the last few nights, has almost completely kept me from sleeping.

Besides, nothing appears on the outside; immediately under the skin, it is like a poison that wants to come out; an injection of extract of bedbugs. Can it get any more

[11] This passage is particularly piquant when one recalls that *Point Counter Point* was deeply influenced by, not to say modeled upon, Gide's *Faux-Monnayeurs*.

intense? It doesn't seem so. But it can enlarge, spread to the whole body. . . .

I think of Job looking for a piece of glass with which to scratch himself, and of Flaubert, whose correspondence, in the last part of his life, speaks of similar itchings. I tell myself that each of us has his sufferings and that it would be most unwise to long to change them; but I believe that a real pain would take less of my attention and would after all be more bearable. And, in the scale of sufferings, a real pain is something nobler, more august; the itch is a mean, unconfessable, ridiculous malady; one can pity someone who is suffering; someone who wants to scratch himself makes one laugh.

In the morning, after an almost sleepless night, I get up without any enthusiasm whatsoever, my brain beclouded as after (I suppose) smoking opium; lacking virtue, zeal, or appetite for work; longing to be at Cuverville, where I could put myself on a milk diet for a time; ready to drag miserably through the day.

20 March

As if, beyond pains or itches, there were nothing to bother a man! The last few nights I was intrigued by strange moans coming from the next room. Kept awake myself by the itching, I noticed that they did not cease all night long. They did not exactly bother me, thanks to the wads I put in my ears at night, but I should have liked to know what it was.

And yesterday evening, coming back from dinner and on the point of entering my room, I am stopped by my neighbor, who was waiting at his door. He is a little man, perhaps no older than I, but so worn out, so worn down that it seems as if death has almost nothing to take from him.

He wants to beg my pardon for the disturbance his groans may have caused me. He is suffering from asthma and emphysema and cannot keep from moaning. All this said in English in the most courteous way. I protest at once that he does not disturb me at all and that he can moan all he wants; pity him cordially and leave him with the wish that he may have a somewhat better night.

Doubtless, compared with his anguish, my itch is nothing at all. Let us live with our sufferings and not want to change them. These wise reflections allowed me to sleep a bit better.

Marseille, 31 March

Greatly enjoyed seeing Saint Exupéry again at Agay, where I had gone to spend two days with P. Back in France barely a month now, he has brought back from Argentina a new book and a fiancée. Read one, seen the other. Congratulated him heartily, but more for the book; I hope the fiancée is as satisfactory. . . .[12]

Tonio's stories are so strange and gripping that I should like to note them down at the moment of hearing them. He talks to us at length of his brother-pilot Guillaumet. Guillaumet was on the air-mail route from X. to Y. (?); there had been no news of him for six days. It was said that his plane had been caught in a storm while crossing the Andes; he must have fallen in the mountains, in a particularly inaccessible, unknown region, to which none of the inhabitants that the company had tried to send out searching for him had been willing to venture. . . .

Tonio de Saint Exupéry was dining in a big hotel in Buenos Aires when the news began to spread: Guillaumet was alive, had been found. The emotion was so great that everyone got up and embraced one another. Tonio saw him soon after and plans to write the story that Guillaumet told him of his amazing adventure.

The plane had come down in the snow at an altitude of nearly ten thousand feet. The storm was so violent that he had first to wait for forty-eight hours in the shelter he had dug under the plane. If he had not been alone, he would have lost his life, for a comrade would not have had his extraordinary resistance and Guillaumet would not have wanted to leave him. . . . Fortunately he had on him a small pocket compass that his chief had by chance given him a few days before. Neither rope nor piolet. No experience of mountain-climbing. No hope of getting out alive. And the thing that first made him set out was the desire to leave his body clearly visible, for it

[12] At this time Antoine de Saint Exupéry was known only for *Courrier sud* (*Southern Mail*). The book he had just brought back was certainly *Vol de nuit* (*Night Flight*), which appeared in 1931 with a preface by Gide. The story about Guillaumet now forms a part of *Terre des hommes* (*Wind, Sand and Stars*), which first came out in 1939.

occurred to him that his widow would have to wait four years before getting his insurance if there were any question of his being dead. But as long as he was walking, he might as well go toward salvation. And once on the way . . .

Nothing with which to warm himself. Nothing to eat. . . . But, above all, the great preoccupation of not going to sleep. To rest he chose rocks with such a slope that he could cling to them only when awake. Terrible temptation to let oneself go to sleep. The lure of the snow-fields; voluptuous torpor. . . . The third day, he slid to the bottom of a ravine, from which he gets out completely soaked. He has the constancy to go back, climbing a three-thousand-foot slope in order to dry himself in the first rays of the sun. And for four days, no food. He fears losing control of his thoughts and concentrates his entire will on the *choice* of those thoughts!

Courage in this case lies not in risking one's life, but on the contrary . . .

All this is what Tonio is to relate. I ask to go over his story, for I shall never forgive him for spoiling it. What our present literature most lacks is heroism.

My ear, or some even more subtle precision-balance or other, remains just as hard to please. One foot more or less to my sentence and it shocks me like a bad line of verse. I cannot endure being quoted wrongly (as so often), even if it were with the best intention in the world.

13 May

Lunched the day before yesterday at Sèvres, at the Bertaux', with J. Schlumberger, the Thomas Manns, and the Soupaults. I did not yet know Thomas Mann, who had been so kind to me on several occasions that I could not decently ignore his being in Paris. Meeting under excellent circumstances, which I am happy to owe to Bertaux. Very good lunch; most cordial atmosphere; natural and sprightly conversation. It was perfect.

Thomas Mann and especially his wife speak French perfectly. Moreover their pronunciation, when they express themselves in German, is so distinct that not a word escaped me.

I liked both of them enough to be eager to see them again. It seems to me that one can talk with him effortlessly of anything and everything.

Devout Spain[13] is burning her convents more ferociously than did ever the land of Voltaire. It can certainly be said that she richly deserves these excesses and that her ancient Inquisition prepared these long-range reprisals. And it would not even be necessary to go back so far. I doubt if that fury is a sign of real liberation, alas! There is something spasmodic about it that might well not last.

I should like to ask those who are shocked by such violences how a chick can get out of the egg without breaking the shell.

But above all I should like to live long enough to see Russia's plan succeed and the states of Europe obliged to accept what they insisted on ignoring. How could so novel a reorganization have been achieved without, first, a period of profound disorganization? Never have I bent over the future with a more passionate curiosity. My whole heart applauds that gigantic and yet entirely human undertaking.

Those who are most inclined to doubt of its success are precisely the *believers* who used to profess the greatest scorn for doubt as soon as it touched their religious convictions. They do not admit a faith so different in nature from their mystical faith. And faced with this miracle to be accomplished, a quite natural and practical miracle (so that it can be called a miracle only by misuse of the term), they play the skeptics; but, here too, the first condition of the plan's success is to believe obstinately that it will succeed. Far from defying intelligence, it calls for intelligence, which must triumph in this case.

Marseille, 4 June

Those pages from Mauriac's *Journal* in the June *N.R.F.* no longer find any echo in my heart. I no longer even understand *what is concerned here.* "Even in the state of grace," he writes, "my creatures are born of the murkiest part of me; they are formed of what subsists in me in spite of myself." What a confession! This amounts to say-

[13] Gide uses the expression "Satin Slipper Spain" because of Claudel's drama, *Le Soulier de satin* (1929), in which the heroine entrusts her satin slipper, as a symbol of her virtue, to a statue of the Virgin.

ing that if he were a perfect Christian, he would cease to have any material of which to make his novels. Is not this precisely what I told him? [14]

How anguished he is! And how I¹ like him thus! But what is the use of this anguish? May a time come for him when it will seem to him as vain and fanciful, as monstrous as it seems to me today.

But the mark is so deeply cut in him henceforth that he will think he is lost if he frees himself. The habit of living head-down forces one to see everything upside down. Any effort at righting the inverted image is imputed to pride. As if one could not be modest without bowing double! Or as if that natural modesty were not worth the modesty achieved through contortion!

And nothing is more sincere, most certainly, than these pages. Is not this just what makes them frightening?— that these torments, these struggles, these gratuitous, fanciful debates should become, for the believer, a real anguish; that authentically he should pity us for ceasing to know that anguish, for having escaped it, for being happy!

There was omitted from the periodical publication a page of that journal that Mauriac subsequently reinstated in the book, *Souffrances et bonheur du Chrétien*.[15] That page concerns a reading of my *Voyage au Congo* and bears witness to an affection that will surprise, even infuriate, many of Mauriac's readers. I am only too well aware what courage it takes today to speak of me in

---

[14] On 24 April 1928 Gide had written Mauriac a letter inspired by the latter's *Life of Jean Racine*: "You rejoice in the fact that God, before seizing hold of Racine again, left him time to write his plays, to write them *despite* his conversion. In short, what you seek is permission to write *Destins* [Mauriac's most recent novel at that moment]; permission to be a Christian without having to burn your books; and this is what makes you write them in such a way that, though a Christian, you will not have to disavow them. All this (this reassuring compromise that allows one to love God without losing sight of Mammon), all this gives us that anguished conscience which lends such charm to your face, such savor to your writings, and which must be so pleasing to those who, while abhorring sin, would be most unhappy if they had to cease being concerned with sin. You know moreover that this would be the end of literature, of yours in particular; and you are not sufficiently Christian to cease being a writer." It was this letter that caused Mauriac to write his essay *God and Mammon* (1929).

[15] *Misery and Joy of the Christian*, first published as a book in 1931.

certain environments without protesting in horror. Mauriac had already had this courage in the past.[16] How deeply those pages of his journal touch me and what an echo that affection finds in my heart is what I need to write down here, were it only for myself.

"And suddenly I am seized, not by Africa, but by this Gide so different from what the journalists have written of him, so human, so close to the earth. . . . His wonder before stones, plants, insects—nothing I admire more and *from which I feel farther removed.*" Nothing is better designed than the study of natural sciences to cure us of that anguish to which the pursuit of a metaphysical, inaccessible God necessarily leads. But those to whom that studious contemplation would be most advantageous turn away from it, and from the *reality* that their very anguish, and the belief in another reality, urge them to consider as merely a disappointing mirage (they arm and defend themselves against its attraction), an illusion. Yet there lies the only truth that man can achieve and embrace with some certainty, the patient study of which can bring about some progress for humanity. Those who strive to see with "the eyes of the soul" are those who have never really known how to observe.

(Charlie Du Bos, translating with Élisabeth Van Rysselberghe a passage from Keats's correspondence which concerned "snails' horns," was astonished and asked her on what part of the body snails had horns and confessed that he thought he had never seen snails.)

There are here two needs of the mind, so different that he who lacks one of them cannot understand the embarrassment this deficiency can cause to others.

But we do not adore the same God. And the only one

[16] Doubtless the most striking of those occasions was the preface Mauriac wrote for a reprinting of Gide's *La Tentative amoureuse* in 1922. It began: "Doubtless Claudel and Jammes, those good shepherd-dogs, scold and worry this lost sheep who carries his taste for conversion to the point of being converted every day to a different truth. Let us try, however, to understand in Gide a case of terrible sincerity: no trace in him of what Stendhal unjustly calls hypocrisy when he finds it in the men of the seventeenth century. It is true that the choice of a doctrine obliges us, at those moments when forces in us disown it, to continue doing it lip-service, until the return of grace. Gide is the man who would never be resigned to influencing, even for a moment, the automaton."

in which I can believe, diffuse in nature, I am willing to
grant them that he no longer deserves the name of God.
In order to be seen by us, he does not ask for faith, but
merely for attention. His mystery is all the greater for
being in no way supernatural.

Roquebrune, 12 June

The novel requires a certain slowness of progress that
allows the reader to live with the characters and become
accustomed to them. If they do things and make remarks
that, knowing them, we might just as well have been able
to invent for them, this does not matter; and we are even
amused to recognize them in such things and not to be
surprised. When I wanted to tell of them only what is
disconcerting, and leave to the reader the duty of filling
out their characters with everything that did not particularly distinguish them, I was probably not well advised.
It may seem that I did not know how to make them come
alive because I so readily gave them up as soon as their
outline was sufficiently sketched, and when portraying
them more fully and following them at greater length told
nothing more about them. This is because I have always
been bothered in the work of others by all that is not
essential and that the alert reader's imagination can supply
for itself. A concern for the lightest possible baggage has
always tormented me, and I do not like to let time make
that abstract of the essentials which I can just as well
achieve at once. Allow only the indispensable to subsist
was the rule I imposed on myself—nowhere more difficult
and dangerous to apply than for the novel. This amounts
to counting too much on that collaboration which the
reader will supply only when the writer has already been
able to secure it.

14 June

What they are to want has been chosen for them. And
that it is the best will not be questioned. No time, no
effort devoted to its pursuit, which they would consider
wasted time. It is precisely to this that the best part of us
is given, is devoted.

It is no longer a matter of restoring ruins, but of building anew on a ground that must first be tested. Everything must be questioned, doubted again; nothing must

be accepted but the authentic, from which all mysticism
is banished. I mean by mysticism: any blind belief.

16 June

Evolution of my thought? Without a first Christian formation (or deformation), there would perhaps have been
no evolution at all. What made it so slow and difficult
was the sentimental attachment to what I could not cast
off without regret. Even today I still have a sort of nostalgia for that mystical and ardent climate in which my
being was then inflamed. I have never again recaptured
the fervor of my adolescence, and the sensual ardor in
which I subsequently delighted is but its ridiculous imitation. At least so it appears to me, now that my senses are
aging. Oh, how easy it would be for me, even today, to
write emotional remarks on this subject that my reason
would disown tomorrow! Nothing is easier than to stir to
emotion when one does not hesitate to talk nonsense. It
is illusion that permits the lyricism of childhood. My
whole effort has been to achieve in myself a happiness
that could do without being illusory.

Then, to be sure, my youth had much to do with it;
the wild beating of a new heart; my love. . . . I could
nourish that religious fervor only with what soon appeared
to me as *inadmissible*.

Without that Christian formation, without those bonds,
without Em., who oriented my pious inclinations, I should
not have written *André Walter*, or *L'Immoraliste*, or *La
Porte étroite*, or *La Symphonie pastorale*, etc. . . . or
even, perhaps, *Les Caves du Vatican* and *Les Faux-
Monnayeurs* as a revolt and a protest. . . . But what else
I should have written in their place is utterly impossible
for me to imagine. Would the lack of a crisis have been
necessarily an impoverishment? It is quite useless to ask
myself this, and the question must go unanswered.

23 June

It is not in suffering, in adversity, that my optimism
finds a stumbling-block, but in the ugliness and malicious-
ness of men.

It is enough to discourage goodwill and make a laugh-
ing-stock of all self-immolation, all sacrifice.

I was not yet twenty years old when this shocking

truth had already occurred to me: that the very act of
sacrifice magnifies the one who sacrifices himself to the
point where his sacrifice is much more costly to humanity
than would have been the loss of those for whom he is
sacrificing himself. But in his abnegation lies the secret of
his grandeur. On the immolation of the best is built the
whole theater of antiquity; Nietzsche very well understood this.

Munich, 1 July

Frightful monotony of these *Cahiers* of Barrès (Volume
III).[17] A mind on the leash, always circling round its
kennel. He attached his collar himself; but Taine helped
him greatly in this.

The doctor whom Em. had come to consult in Paris
said to her at once:

"You must have had very delicate hands."

. . . She had the most exquisite hands that can be imagined. I loved them especially, not merely as a part of
her, but in themselves. She convinces herself and tries to
convince me that her hands lost their shape naturally; but
there is more to it: she deformed them by misusing them,
by making them undertake coarse duties for which they
were not made and which Em. assumed out of modesty,
abnegation, maceration, and for many virtuous reasons
that would have made me look with horror on the spirit
of sacrifice. And it was the same with her mind, gifted
with the most exquisite and rarest qualities, suited for
the most delicate preoccupations. Her natural humility
would not admit that she could be superior in anything
and thus she condemned herself to the most ordinary
occupations, in which nevertheless her superiority was
obvious. From witnessing, powerless, this progressive renunciation, which she even refused to recognize, I suffered
unspeakably. Had I complained of this, she would have
said that all these superiorities I saw her relinquishing
existed merely in my loving imagination. She really be-
lieved this and in this revealed herself to be superior to
those very superiorities which her virtue esteemed so
little.

[17] *My Notebooks* by Maurice Barrès appeared posthumously in eleven
volumes from 1929 to 1938, edited by his son, Philippe Barrès. Volume
III covers the period from May 1902 to November 1904.

17 July

There are certain days when, if I merely let myself go, I should roll directly under the Lord's Table. They think it is pride that withholds me. Not at all! It is intellectual integrity.

Paris, 19 July

Odd that such a row is kicked up about the printing errors in Proust's books, though he wrote rapidly— whereas in a text of mine, where every word is weighed, so little attention is paid to quoting me exactly. And since most often people quote only at second or third hand, it is that distorted quotation which, subsequently, is requoted by others. . . . I doubt if ever texts have been more often deformed and could suffer more from deformation than mine. This adds some bitterness to the pleasure brought me by Fernandez's book. He quotes according to Du Bos: "His thought carefully unwinds." I wrote: "his thought unwinds like silk" [18] (*Faux-Monnayeurs*, p. 390). Did Charles Du Bos already make the error?

Cuverville, 24 July

Read *The Bridge of San Luis Rey* by Thornton Wilder. It is literature, but of the best; and even with something more. Delightfully written, facing the past.

The Spanish revolution, the struggle of the Vatican against Fascism, the German financial crisis, and, above all, Russia's extraordinary effort . . . all this distracts me frightfully from literature. I have just devoured in two days Knickerbocker's book on the Five-Year Plan, which Marc Chadourne lent me.[19]

A half-hour to crawl down to the botton of those coal-mines without elevators; a half-hour to come up again. Five hours of work crouching in a stifling atmosphere. The peasant recruits desert; but the young formed by the new ethic enroll enthusiastically, eager to work for the progress of which they have been given a glimpse. It is a duty to be done, to which they submit joyfully. Ah, how well I understand their *happiness!*

[18] A misreading of *soigneusement* for *soyeusement*.
[19] H. R. Knickerbocker's *The Red Trade Menace: Progress of the Soviet Five-Year Plan*, was published in 1931.

27 July

In Paris again, but for only two days. Tomorrow, board meeting of the *N.R.F.* in the morning, and in the afternoon reading of Roger Martin du Gard.

I should like to cry aloud my affection for Russia; and that my cry should be heard, should have importance. I should like to live long enough to see the success of that tremendous effort; its realization, which I wish with all my soul and for which I should like to work. To see what can be produced by a state without religion,[20] a society without the family. Religion and the family are the two worst enemies of progress.

Cuverville, 28 July

The music of the sentence . . . today I attach less value to this than to its clarity, its exactitude, and that force of persuasion related to its profound animation.

These letters of Proust to Mme de Noailles discredit Proust's judgment (or sincerity) much more than they serve her fame as a poetess. Flattery cannot go further. But Proust knew Mme de N. well enough, knew her to be vain and sufficiently incapable of self-criticism to hope that the most exaggerated praise would seem to her the most deserved, the most sincere; he played with her as he played with everyone. And I see in these shameless flatteries less hypocrisy than an obsessive need of serving up to each individual what he would most like, without any care for truth, but simply for opportunism; and especially a desire to bring out and soften up the one on whom he blows hottest.

1 August

I scrupulously ruled out of my *Faux-Monnayeurs* everything that another might just as well have written, being satisfied with indications allowing one to imagine whatever I did not set out. I recognize that those neutral passages are the very ones that rest, reassure, and win over the reader; I alienated many of those whose laziness I should have flattered. But if I am told that I was incapable of doing what I did not want to do, I protest. What is easier than to write a novel like others! I am

---

[20] Without religion? Perhaps not. But a religion without mythology. [A.]

loath to do so, that's all, and no more than Valéry can I
resign myself to writing: "The Marquise went out at five
o'clock," or, and this is of a quite different nature, but
strikes me as even more compromising: "X. wondered at
length whether . . ."

3 *August*

The great danger is letting oneself be monopolized by
a fixed idea. Goethe managed to avoid it. Neither Tolstoy
nor Barrès did. At a certain age the field of vision frequently narrows. "Convictions" are bad; I hope to purge
myself of them in *Geneviève*.

I no longer hoped being able to work as well as I have
the last few days. I shall be able to judge the quality of
what I am writing only with a little perspective. Meanwhile I go ahead without rereading myself too much.

Very good piano-practice.

5 *August*

A man "in whom is no guile." I know no other which,
more than this word of the Gospel, has dominated my
life. It seems to me pretentious to say so. But, young as
I then was, yes, that is what I inscribed in my mind. It
seems to me today that "sincerity" and the effort to
achieve it *in oneself* are contained therein.

I have often noticed the care the cat takes not to
wound the field mouse with which he is playing (contrary
to the current opinion). He is less delicate with the
mouse that, more agile, might escape him. Still less delicate with the bird, when the latter is already capable of
flying away. But yesterday I surprised my cat in the
garden playing with a little wren, still unable to fly. With
what precautions his velvet paw pushed it, made it hop!
I was observing him from behind a window and could
intervene only rather late. The little bird did not have the
least scratch and did not seem otherwise upset. I put it
back into the bush from which it must have fallen, where
I saw it hop from branch to branch and where its parents,
soon after, were able to come and feed it.

On carelessly made or insufficient observations how
many fine theories are built up which do not bear examination!

September

To what a degree the same past can leave different marks—and especially admit of different interpretations.

Try all one's life never to do an insincere thing, not to write a single sentence that goes beyond one's thought in any way, and one can then hope to be called, at about sixty, a "play-actor" by an M.A.[21] This is a term he in no wise thinks of applying to all our masters in camouflage; he reserves it for me alone, accompanied by the epithet "magnificent," which excuses him for having none the less admired me, but explains why—after having seen through me—he now turns away. Most likely he took offense at the few words in my *Œdipe* where I make my Eteocles the author, like him, of a *Nouveau Mal du siècle*.[22] What pride! What pettiness! If he had plagiarized me less in the past, he would disavow me less vigorously today. I do not like that way, after having taken your fountain-pen, of moving away from you in order to avoid suspicion.

Sunday, 13 [September]

Reached Marseille at seven o'clock. Sailed at noon for Bastia. The odd and dull appearance of my traveling-companions makes me think I got on the wrong ship.

Splendid weather, but I learn that a dreadful mistral blew last night, that the sea was rough, that the ships entering Marseille were frightfully late. . . .

Most interesting conversation with a captain of the Foreign Legion. Very happy to learn his rank in the course of one of his tales: "At that time I was not yet a captain." (I have never been able to tell rank; and in a conversation with an officer am embarrassed to be reduced to calling him "sir.")

He relates, and very well too, the transfer to Sidi-bel-Abbès of a flag of the Legion bearing on one side of the rosette the initials L.É. (Légion Étrangère) and on the other L.N. (Louis-Napoléon), which had gone through

---

[21] Marcel Arland.

[22] *The New World-Weariness* was the title of an essay by Marcel Arland in 1924. Seven years later, as a way of mocking his overenthusiastic disciples, Gide attributed this title—together with that of *Our Unrest*, borrowed from Daniel-Rops—to the callow Eteocles of his drama.

both the Crimean and the Mexican Wars and been preserved until then at the Musée des Invalides.

Excellent crossing. But I am unable to surrender to joy
without repeating to myself: Still you! . . . Aren't you
ashamed? Make way for others. It is time. . . .

Calvi, Monday

Arrived at Ajaccio at about ten o'clock. Wild desire to
go back at once. Absurd longing, to want to begin the
past over again! The town seemed to be charming. Last
summer, I don't know why, I had been unable to see it. At
the period of the *Nourritures* I should have wept with joy
over it. The first rays of the sun were turning the houses
pink along the harbor. Large sea-birds were circling above
the ship. I needed a younger companion who would have
been stirred, he at least, by the discovery of what so much
stirred me once. I merely noted and with almost no rise
in temperature that it was quite worthy of stirring someone. Doubtless my exaltation was still greater than that
of the other passengers, but could that be enough for
me? I expect certain things of myself. . . . Yet I managed to keep myself almost joyful during the motor trip.
But at Calvi I do not find Paul V., or Véra, or little Jean.
They must have left already. . . . I dragged my boredom
out onto the quays of the harbor, barely able to smile at
the numerous children who recognized me. The wind is
rising. The return crossing will be bad. What have I come
to look for here? I hardly slept at all last night. I am
sleepy.

18 September

In a reply by Massis to a question asked by *Candide* I
read with amusement:

"Never, at the height of their fervor, did the wildest
Gidians among us speak of Gide with the enthusiasm and
ecstasy of these newcomers."

Decidedly you did not bury me very deep, my dear
Massis! And all those "Let's get out of here; he's beginning
to smell" of your declarations of my "bankruptcy" did not,
after all, do me all the harm you had hoped.

But you prefer to admit that you were wrong in your
prognostics about the postwar generation and to bury it

altogether in the same grave with me, rather than admit
that I was perhaps not so dead as you used to say.

19 September

That amazing difficulty, that near impossibility for the
vast majority of French people to imagine that others can
dress, eat, think, live, in short, otherwise than in France.
It is still the "How can one be a Persian?" [23]

(Siegfried speaks excellently of this and Curtius too,
who quotes him in a remarkable article in the *Neue
Rundschau* that he sends me: "*Abbau der Bildung.*" [24])

Native disposition, but encouraged by family upbringing and the teaching of the schools. Those who are already
French are taught to be French. Far from being released,
they are further imprisoned.

20 September

At Cuverville again after a week's absence. I return
sobered and cheered. Anxious above all for work.

Two interesting brochures are sent me from America:
André Gide and His Catholic Critics, and *Marcel Schwob
and André Gide* (*A Literary Affinity*).[25]

Strange that the first comparison—which was really inevitable—between Schwob's *Le Livre de Monelle*[26] and
my *Nourritures terrestres* should come from so far away.
It is true that the publication of *Monelle* attracted hardly
any more attention from critics and the public than did
the *Nourritures* three years later. At that time publishers
scarcely used publicity; and, moreover, the authors' pride
would not have consented to this.

On different planes, the exhortation of the two books
was the same, but it remained altogether intellectual with
Schwob. This is also why his little book was better received than mine in the beginning.

I do not think there was the slightest influence from
one to the other. It is simply that both of them testify to
a similar need. Of all my books there is none more spon-

[23] The summary of the French attitude to the Persian visitor in *Les
Lettres persanes* (*The Persian Letters*) by Montesquieu.

[24] "The Abolition of Culture."

[25] These are both articles by S. A. Rhodes; the first appeared in
Sewanee Review in October 1930 and the second in the *Romanic
Review* in February 1931.

[26] *The Book of Monelle* is a work of lyric exultation in the beauties
of nature and the joys of the senses, an appeal for self-fulfillment.

taneous, more sincere than my *Nourritures*. Besides, it is in great part made up of extracts from journals and note-books prior to *Monelle*.

Schwob bore me a grudge for this, I was told. My brutal book indecently crushed his delicate book. . . . He held it against me for sometime and I was deeply grieved, for his friendship was dear to me. Yet I yielded to too imperative a necessity for any considerations, even those of friendship, to withhold me from writing and publishing. I shall add that, however flagrant the resemblances were, that book was too intimately mine for them to be apparent to me at once, at least with enough force. In *Monelle* I was above all sensitive to all that separated it from life and found it, though exquisite, somewhat quaint. And the greater reality and more immediate contact with nature that my *Nourritures* offered were likewise what was to frighten the earliest readers off, what was to remain so long without assent, without echo. It was to those very elements by which my book differed most from Schwob's that, later on, it owed its importance.

Paris, 4 October

Dined with Copeau at the restaurant of the Vieux-Colombier. Maurras comes in shortly after us. Had not seen him for . . . probably thirty years. Copeau points him out to me. I should not have recognized him. Does he recognize me? I don't know. Besides, a pillar hides us from each other. . . . As we leave, Copeau tells me of his latest conversation with Maurras, several years ago. He imitates Maurras wonderfully:

"Léon Daudet is amazing: he likes Claudel!"

Whereupon Copeau, laughing:

"So do I."

"I prefer Racine."

"So do I."

Copeau has never seemed to me more lively, younger even; nor more affectionate. But the conversation wanders. Immediately after dinner he accompanies me to Roger's, where I had an appointment.

Long conversation about his play (*Un Taciturne*[27]) which has been under rehearsal at Jouvet's for a week.

---

[27] *A Man of Few Words* by Roger Martin du Gard concerns a case of unconscious homosexuality and its belated, shocked recognition.

Roger complains of not being able to find a young actor who is sufficiently attractive physically. X., who offers himself for the role, is intelligent and charming; but, says Roger: "No one in the audience will ever have a desire to kiss him on the mouth." The secret motive of the play, moreover, seems completely incomprehensible to Jouvet and to Renoir. Not the slightest tremor, not the slightest warmth. If sensuality does not enter in, the pistol-shot at the end has no justification. . . .

Roger is beginning to grasp that he was perhaps not right to assert that there is not a man, however little he may lean toward Sodom, who can remain insensitive to the appeal of a Ganymede. He must become convinced, however, that in this regard some remain utterly blind, totally indifferent to the *ignudi* of the Sistine Chapel and unable to see anything but aberration in the passage from Diderot's letter that the *N.R.F.* printed last year (quote it).[28] But even if the majority of the audience are capable of a certain partial comprehension, this would have to be prepared by a certain youthful warmth, a sensual charm, a possible appeal on the part of the young actor.[29] Jouvet wants there to be "no possible ambiguity"; he will avoid it so effectively that the secret desire of the "man of few words" will seem preposterous and his final deed an act of pure madness. All this might upset the play. And it will teach Roger that to succeed in the theater one must above all not try to get outside the conventions.

Cuverville, late October

Salvemini asks me to intervene in regard to Lauro de

[28] The passage, which Gide does not quote, is: "One would perhaps accuse oneself more easily of planning a major crime than of some slight obscure feeling that was vile and base. It would be perhaps less painful to write in one's account-book: *I have desired the throne at the expense of its present occupant's life*, than to write: *one day while I was at the bath with a large number of young men, I noticed one of surprising beauty and was not able to keep myself from approaching him.* This sort of examination would not be useless for oneself either." These lines occur in a letter to Sophie Volland dated 14 July 1762, which was published by André Babelon in the *Nouvelle Revue Française* for March 1929.

[29] I should speak in exactly the same way if it were a question of Hippolyte. The actor to whom this role is given must not be such as to make Phèdre inexcusable. [A.] The reference is, of course, to Racine's *Phèdre*.

Bosis.[30] He sends me all the documents he has managed
to gather together relating that hero's wonderful exploit.
I already knew most of them; they had been given me by
an intimate friend of Lauro de Bosis, particularly his letter
to the King of Italy, the one to the Italian people, and
the last will of the new Icarus. I cannot read these papers
without the greatest emotion; but what can I do? . . .

I must explain myself to Salvemini: despite my admiration for the young hero's deed, I lack something: belief in
liberty. It is most difficult for me to bring my own thought
to light. The notion of liberty, as it is taught us, seems to
me singularly false and pernicious. And if I approve the
Soviet constraint, I must likewise approve the Fascist
discipline. I am more and more inclined to believe that
the idea of liberty is but a snare. I should like to be sure
that I should think the same if I myself were not free, I
who cherish above all my own freedom of thought; but I
also believe, and more and more so, that man achieves
nothing worth while without constraint and that very rare
are those capable of finding that constraint in themselves.
I also believe that the authentic color of an individual
thought takes on its full value only when it stands out
against a background that is not itself multicolored. It is
the uniformity of the masses that allows a few rare individuals to rise, in contrast to it. The "Render unto Cæsar
the things which are Cæsar's, and unto God the things
that are God's" of the Gospel seems to me more than ever
a teaching full of wisdom. On God's side, freedom, that of
the mind; on Cæsar's side, submission, that of acts. The
single concern with the happiness of the greatest number,
on the one hand; on the other, the single concern with
truth.

But what I am writing of this here barely satisfies me.
This remains: constraint for constraint, Fascism's strikes
me as a return to the past, whereas that of the Soviets
seems a tremendous effort toward the future. That costly
experience interests humanity as a whole and may liberate

[30] The gifted young Italian poet and essayist, Lauro de Bosis (1901–
31), became an active anti-Fascist and, learning to fly for this purpose,
flew over Rome on 2 October 1931, scattering leaflets addressed to the
population and to the King. Chased by pursuit planes, he vanished at
sea on the return flight.

it from a frightful weight. The mere idea that it might be interrupted and forced to fail is insufferable to me, and that such a gigantic effort toward the never-yet-attempted might remain fruitless. The idols that they are overthrowing over yonder have long seemed to me the most oppressive among the false gods.

After the rehearsal of *Un Taciturne,* Martin du Gard's play, G. goes about repeating that he could never become interested in feelings he cannot experience himself.

Will he force me to think that homosexuals have more imagination than the . . . others? No, but they are more frequently called upon to exercise it.

30 October

The son of F., my tailor, provides me with a wonderful start for a theatrical character while I am trying on a suit:

"It needs to be full here," I tell him.

And he says at once:

"Yes, full . . . while being slightly . . ."

And he does not finish his sentence.

I imagine this quirk, much more deeply rooted and hence much more powerfully comic than a purely verbal quirk, and more revealing of character: each of his thoughts is accompanied by its shadow; he agrees with a reservation, but a reservation that remains vague and only half formulated. He says:

"Obviously . . . yet on the other hand . . ."

"Yes . . . but nevertheless . . ."

An actor who struck just that note, it seems to me, would be irresistible; like Simon with the "And all . . . And all . . ." of the old man in Chekhov's *Sea Gull.*

31 October

At Roger's play, rather lively protests were heard yesterday and the day before during the third act; first, at Thierry's exaggerated declarations to turn Joë away from the marriage, and again at the final revelation. One must expect to see these protests increase and become organized when people are no longer taken by surprise but know in advance toward what the play is heading. Many are those who deign to see in this only an indulgence toward the fashion of the day, the indiscreet playing-up of a "specialty" of the *Nouvelle Revue Française*. They are not willing to admit reality, since they are among those who claim doubtless that things do not begin to exist until they are talked about. They acted the same toward Russia; and toward so many other things. The system that consists in not crediting, not taking into account, whatever is displeasing or embarrassing is too simple; and sooner or later it turns back on those who practice it. In regard to the sexual question, I am filled with wonder when they shout, like Souday: "That's the limit!" when the subject is just beginning to be timidly treated. Such people indirectly provide justification for the hypocrisy and reassuring camouflage practiced by so many writers, and even the most famous, beginning with Proust. Truth, so long hidden from view, seems indiscreetly troublesome as soon as it begins to show itself. The few shy depictions that certain bold writers risk are still so timid, so reticent, that they shock without in any way satisfying truth; and since truth cannot be suppressed by not being proclaimed, it will of necessity eventually be revealed.

But what does the majority's lack of understanding matter here! The truthful writer is concerned with showing what is and not what people wish were so, even though he were to deplore that the world is as it is. "Such things happen," Roger Martin du Gard made Armand say in his play, "such things happen, even to the best people." For fear of protests, Jouvet successively dropped the "even to the best people," then the following day, "such things happen." Where will that get him? He has ceased to say it; but still "such things happen" just the same, and the indignation of conformists can do nothing about it.

The majority of the audience are willing to admit that the two women sleep together (though this moreover was not a part of Roger's intentions); but that Thierry should feel an attraction toward Joë, even unconsciously, and even though he resists it, this appears to them to be monstrous.

It is probably not exact that my thought has let itself be influenced by the need of my own self-defense. But rather my quest, before this problem that nature forced upon me and for which I had to find a solution.

An explanation is not necessarily an approbation; but most often people consider it useless to try to understand what they reprove.

1 *November*

I have just reread Bourdet's *La Prisonnière*, of which the first act at least offers such great analogies with Martin du Gard's play. The same quite indefinable mystery, the same switching onto wrong tracks as a result of a carefully contrived lack of understanding before an unsuspected, unsuspectable, and inadmissible proposition. How much more clever Bourdet seems to me here! That first act is extraordinarily well turned out. What ease! What grace! What sprightliness in the dialogue! . . . It is later on that Roger Martin du Gard gets ahead of him. However clever Bourdet's play may be, and perhaps because of its very cleverness, I am embarrassed by a sort of indirect flattery of the public's worst instincts. It seems here that the highest felicity can be achieved only in coitus. He pays no attention to this fact: that, even between people of "normal" tastes, perfect concomitance of the sexual spasm is extremely rare (among homosexuals likewise, moreover) and that the majority of couples cannot boast of having ever known it; basing the profound union of a couple on that alone is somewhat painfully paradoxical. I understand only too well the distress of Bourdet's hero when faced with the painful evidence of his inability to give his wife more joy, and his wife's inability to experience a sincere and complete joy with him. But that hero, whom he depicts at the outset as so noble, descends to the point of degradation when he bases his happiness on *that*. This secret drama is that of many couples and is what made Tolstoy say that of all tragedies the tragedy of the bedroom was by far the most frightful. There is nothing exceptional about it and there is no need to call upon homosexuality in this case; or else it would have to be granted that a very great number of men and women, apparently quite "normal," are unrecognized homosexuals . . . (besides, I am much inclined to believe this), ready to blow out their brains like Thierry rather than to recognize themselves as such. But is that really what people look for, and do they really look only for that—or even merely *especially* for that—in marriage? And is it not possible for marriage to become hell when it provides only that? I know certain respectable women, mothers of many children, who never did more than lend themselves grudgingly[31] to the sexual embrace, and would not have lent themselves at all if that embrace had not been the condition *sine qua non* of a maternity they desired. (Unconscious Lesbians perhaps.) And, on the other hand, certain worn-out husbands who have ceased to play the conjugal role except out of duty, and to make sure of their wife's fidelity, and to be left alone. . . . All this is not even hinted at in *La Prisonnière;* it would seem, according to Bourdet, that heterosexuality is enough to ensure happiness. The drama, after all, might be the same without his heroine's being "a captive"; I am not even sure that it might not have been better.

Paris, 12 November

Yesterday went to hear Giraudoux's *Judith.* Strange play. I was with Robert Levesque. The theater was only half full although it was only the tenth performance.

This morning I write to Giraudoux:

My dear G.,

I was struck last night at finding tickets for your *Judith* so easily. After having heard the play I am less surprised that the theater was not better filled; it is only at one's own expense that one forces the lazy public to think. Only the happy few[32] will be grateful to you for having dared a "drama of ideas." It required your amazing art to form a parallel for the abstract debate and to clothe it with a drama of passion. Yes, as I write this, I wonder if, in your mind, the drama of passion did not precede the drama of ideas and if the latter was not added onto it. For (the drama of ideas overflowing the other, and by far, in significance, scope, and weight) the pyramid seems to rest on its point. And this moreover is what allows it not to rest at all: it oscillates, vibrates, and trembles, without ever tottering. . . .

Making a problem of religious metaphysics turn upon a question of very special psychology . . . I accept this, but remain none the less embarrassed: if it is easy to admit that Judith should fall in love with Holophernes, on the

---

[31] This word appears in English.
[32] This expression appears in English.

other hand it is not easy to understand how she gets to the point of killing him. "Through love," she asserts. She has to tell us for us to know it. She proclaims it the more vehemently the harder it is for her to convince us. This remains subtle and does not strike the mind at once. As for me, I cannot but regret that the "miracle" is not based on an evidence that would render flagrant its falseness.

I do not send my letter. I should have to add that this play, though more important than *Siegfried* and *Amphitryon,* does not satisfy me as its predecessors did. Even the very serious debate involved seems intellectual play, a joust. The emotion of certain scenes hardly rises above the flickering and shimmering with which an over-precious style clothes them.

Have oneself treated—or kill oneself. No other possible solution to the problem raised by the case of Roger Martin du Gard's *Un Taciturne*—his cousin declares peremptorily in an article (moreover almost excellent) in *Les Nouvelles littéraires.*[33] As if all the "Thierrys" we know, and all those we do not know, had not each one found a personal solution. As if, in the play itself, Roger Martin du Gard had not taken care to make his Armand ("the only reasonable character in the play") exclaim: "You cannot make me believe that if Joë had reciprocated. . . ." Mme Théo remarked very judiciously that it is not only the discovery of his own love that pushes Thierry to suicide, but perhaps also, but perhaps above all, immediately recognizing it to be hopeless; and his jealousy. Thierry must have been dreadfully absorbed by his business not to become aware of his inclinations until so late. The characters of tragedy are always, more or less, idle people. It is hard to imagine a Hamlet harassed by the need to earn his living. The "to be or not to be" is a fruit of leisure.

Cuverville [*late December*]

Jammes, in search of a publisher, asks me to intervene in order to place a book that is "very gay in spots" which he has just finished writing "with considerable gusto and *currente calamo.*" He has created in it "a character by the name of Élie de Nacre."

[33] The cousin is Maurice Martin du Gard.

"He is," he tells me, "a fictionalized *you* who plays sidesplitting tricks on everyone." And he adds: "You will be the first to laugh."

He asks my authorization to call his book "L'Antigyde."

And since I reply at once that I consent (for it will not be said that I am keeping a child from romping), I receive a new letter which warns me: "Even if my mirror sometimes has a good time, you will forgive its *deforming whims* by reason of the sublime death that I help you to 'achieve' in Spain," etc., etc. To get to this: "I have not yet offered this book to any publisher. If you dangled it before Grasset's or Flammarion's eyes, and the request for it came from one of them through you, that would be pluperfect diplomatically."

I preciously preserve these two letters in order to convince myself that I did not invent them.[34]

[34] The letters have in fact been published in their entirety in the *Correspondance 1893–1938* between Jammes and Gide, edited by Robert Mallet (1948). *L'Antigyde* was brought out by Éditions du Mercure de France in 1932.

1932

M_{ost} often it happens that one attributes to others

11 January

only the feelings of which one is capable oneself . . . but this is the way one blunders. Among the refugees whom we aided at the Foyer Franco-Belge, there were very few who did not attribute the most interested motives to our charitable activity; in the eyes of all we were paid employees who, besides, took a little graft on the side, at their expense. What would have been the good of speaking of disinterestedness, of love of duty, of the need of doing service in our way and of reducing suffering? We should have been laughed at.

Knowing how to put oneself "in the place of others." X. puts himself there all right. . . . But it is always *himself* that he puts there.

Roquebrune, 12 January

Great and fine figure of my Uncle Charles, whom I went to see before leaving Paris. For some time he has been suffering from a cancer of the esophagus and is getting weaker day by day.

"Is it very painful?"

"It is not painful at all. But I am beginning to enter the descending curve." (He is entering his eighty-fifth year!)

Moreover he works as much and as well as ever.

His eyes have taken on a sweet look, a sort of amenity that I really believe I had never known him to have. I should like to be able to talk to him to tell him of my admiration, my affection. . . . But how hard it is to make oneself heard by him! And I am not alluding so much to his physical deafness as to that sort of instinctive refusal to listen, to believe, against which stumbles everything that is said to him, and which, even in his youth, discouraged those best disposed toward him. But suddenly he makes up his mind to talk a bit, and as I tell him that he ought to consent to be X-rayed:

"You wrote utterly inexact things about your grandfather. That he died without ever having consented to call in doctors is absolutely false. He saw many of them, on the contrary; masses of them; and even, at the end of his life, on the advice of Cousin Pascal, he fell into the hands of a mesmerizer who came and made passes over him."

Alas, everything I said of him is what had been told me by my aunt. But I hasten here to rectify this and shall try to retouch the portrait that I give of him in *Si le grain ne meurt* . . . (according to hearsay).

Not a word about what concerns him; but probably it weighs heavily on him. Is the portrait I sketched of him inexact? I do not believe so. Thibaudet sees in my portrait a "hatred" that was never in my heart. Quite the contrary. That portrait, however severe it may be, bears but very few reflections of the dreadful indictment my aunt forced me to hear, every time I saw her and almost to the very last moments of her life. The accusations she made—some of which, alas! were only too well founded, but which her passion exaggerated to the point of absurdity—became toward the end so painful for me, especially after Paul's death (for which she considered my uncle responsible), that I saw less and less of her. She failed dreadfully to recognize what constituted my uncle's extraordinary value and deigned to see nothing but insensitivity in his severity, in his disinterestedness nothing but hypocrisy, and nothing but twaddle in his theories. Those two creatures equally admirable in many ways, equally ill-adapted to conjugal happiness, equally un-understanding, as little as possible designed to get along together, remained all their life lamentably opposed to each other (with a sort of resigned, pathetic reconciliation two days before my aunt's death).

That couple, profoundly unhappy because of one another, remained utterly faithful to each other and allowed me to grasp the fact that the worst conjugal dramas are perhaps not those of jealousy.

16 January

I go back to see my uncle, who has declined considerably since my last visit. I find him quite weakened by fever. But his mind remains the same, as does his immalleability, if I may be permitted the expression. Looking for something pleasant to say to him, to shout to him rather, for he hears with more and more difficulty—and

while he is taking a bit of orangeade, all solid food being
forbidden him:

"They made it very well at Uzès."

"What did they make well?"

"Lemonade."

"Where?"

"At Uzès."

"Who told you so?"

"No one at all; I remember. . . ."

"Well, what do you know about it, then?"

"But I used to drink it myself."

"You have been back there, then?"

"No, I remember what I drank when I was a child."

"They didn't make lemonade."

"Yes they did; I remember it very well. It was a rice
lemonade."

"Why rice?"

"To take away the bitterness of the lemon; they used to
boil rice and pour the boiling water on cut-up lemons."

"But they did that only for intestinal upsets. You were
not ill at Uzès; why should they have made it for you?"

"Well, it is certain that I have drunk it and that I found
it very good."

My uncle eventually granted that, in fact, it wasn't bad.

And do not go and see in that resistance to others an
effect of age: I have always known him that way.

This bit of dialogue is an example of what almost all
conversations were with my uncle, and of the extreme
difficulty one had in making oneself understood by him.
I believe the fact that he had never been ill greatly increased that sort of impenetrability. Always equal and
consistent and faithful to himself, he could understand
others only through thought, and understand of others
only thoughts. Howbeit quite capable of emotion and of
the most sublime and keenest emotions, but of a general
nature; he remained as unconcerned as possible with the
individual and what differentiates. Not only did it fail to
interest him; I even believe he doubted that it could have
any importance, even exist outside the footless imagination
of writers. He lived among entities. Even love and friendship had to depersonalize themselves in order to find

access to his heart, which never beat so rapidly as for the
collective.

18 January

The sentences at which comprehension stops short and
even the most enlightened sympathy stumbles. . . . There
is perhaps none in which more perfidy has been seen than
the one from my dialogue with Félix-Paul Grève:

"I prefer making others act to acting myself."

If I explain it, I shall appear to be exculpating myself.
What is more natural, however, than to say to an adventurer whom one wants to hold at a distance: action
belongs to you, thought to me? The latter promotes the
former. As soon as I act I limit myself, etc. What else
could I say to him that would be immediately understood
by him? After all, I couldn't preach to him—and surely
he would not have listened to me. . . .

Moreover, did I not reproduce his triumphant reply?

No, that sentence did not "escape" me. One has only
to think of the person to whom I said it, of the person
I was in Grève's eyes, of the circumstances, etc. If it were
to do over, I could not say anything different; at most
perhaps I should explain a bit better? The astonishing
thing is that Grève, in answering me, merely recited the
teaching of my Nourritures. By taking over my role, he
pushed me to the right. On the whole, I took cover.

"If it may be that my teaching leads to crime, I prefer
that it should be you who commit the crime." This is
what my sentence meant. Grève was playing the role of
helot in my presence. Through self-esteem I tried to save
face; but I felt his advantage and that he got the better
of me. I was overcome by my "disciple" and was disavow-
ing my ethic if that was where it was to lead. The conflict
in feelings was too complex in this case for anyone to be
able to draw an argument from my sentence, it seems to
me. Seeing an affirmation, a profession of faith, the declaration of an ethic in that way of beating a retreat is risky,
to say the least. But the critic remains free to see in my
declaration an "involuntary confession."

21 January

Again insomnia. Nervous system overtense, at bay.
These last few nights impossible to find sleep until dawn

and when the whole house is awaking; and this despite
all precautions and what I take to try to sleep, which stul-
tifies me without making me lose consciousness a moment.
In the morning, however, I do not feel too tired and I
should work, if only bores would leave me alone. I am
going to try to arrange my life otherwise. This necessity
of going out for my meals (and there is no restaurant
near) wears me out. My mornings are completely devoured by correspondence, telephone calls, etc. I must
not make myself accessible until after noon and ask the
concierge not to bring up the morning mail. *Curiosity* is
my greatest enemy. It sometimes happens that I close my
door to everyone, and then run to the door at the first
ring. . . . Indispensable discipline. And stop telling myself, as I did recently in cowardly fashion, that henceforth
I shall write nothing worth while and that my work is
finished.

22 *January*

Article by Haraucourt (very kindly and quite unexpected, that Eugène Rouart sends me, taken from some
newspaper or other) on my *Œdipe*. He sees in my play,
above all, an opposition between free will and predestina-
tion. Many will do likewise and through my fault; for I
am well aware, and particularly became aware at the
rehearsals and through Pitoëff's interpretation, that I
indiscreetly emphasized that obvious conflict—which
tormented me greatly in my youth, but which long ago
ceased to disturb me and which, in my very play, seems
to me less important, less tragic, than the struggle (which
moreover is closely related to it) between individualism
and submission to religious authority. It is curious that
the first conflict just happens to appear with most force
in religious souls (particularly those of Christian background), for the ancients could likewise believe in predes-
tination, but without thinking they could, or should, elude
it. Perhaps if I had not raised that question at all—the
hero's struggle against Tiresias, of individuality against
religious ethics, it might have been even more tragic;
more apparent in any case. . . . But these problems are
closely and inextricably linked. No matter: whether or not
one is disturbed by determinism (either by accepting it or
by denying it), the drama remains the same and the op-

position between the perspicacious anti-mystic and the
believer, between the man blind through faith and the
one who tries to answer the enigma, between him who
submits himself to God and him who opposes Man to
God. The other cause "will soon be once and for all won,"
Haraucourt says quite rightly. It already is and consequently ceases to disturb us. If that were the only
thing "at issue" in my drama, it would not have had any
contemporary interest and would justify those who deign
to see in it only intellectual juggling. Moreover, I foresee
a time when *ethical* problems will interest only a few
timid souls.

25 January

These young people who send or bring you a manuscript
and ask advice of you do not know how much they put
you out. That is their excuse. It takes me hours to get to
know a book satisfactorily; when it is not so bad that I
can judge it from the first pages and drop it at once, when
I give myself to it, I do so wholly. And my work, once
interrupted, does not allow itself to be picked up immediately afterward. There is a prolonged back-wash in my
mind. . . . And also, afterward, I must write, or receive
the author and talk. I have there, on a shelf in my library,
fourteen begging manuscripts, which, if my eyes happen
to light on them, make me long to be dead.

Brussels, Saturday

Every degree between hatred and love, between the
hypo and the hyper, between any feeling whatever and
its contrary, as in physiology between the too much and
the not enough. We must add, in psychology, intermit-
tences and interferences, and always possibilities of doubt
as to the sincerity not only of the expression of one's feelings, but of the very feelings one experiences, or that one
thinks one is experiencing, or that one would like to experience or not to experience. All of which makes for
art, poetry, etc., but hardly makes for preciseness, certainty, science, etc.

Every degree between snobbery, the desire to frequent
people of high society, famous people, and the desire to
flee them on the other hand. My Uncle Charles often expressed that irresistible withdrawal before the famous. He
ceases to frequent a friend as soon as that friend achieves

fame. There enters into this the feeling that that friend, whom you used to help, can now get along without you. As for taking advantage of him, of his new situation, some pride or other turns you away from what might be helpful to you. All this mixed up, delicately blended, explains more or less that sort of reverse anti-snobbery (in which I greatly resemble my uncle) and the slowing down of some of my former relationships.

21 February

Answering a telephone call, I go to see Paul Valéry at about four o'clock and stay more than two hours talking with him. Those who have never known him cannot imagine the charming graciousness of his eyes, his smile, his voice, his kindliness, the abundant resources of his intelligence, the amusement of his sallies, the sharpness of his views—through so rapid an elocution, often so confused and mumbled that I frequently have to make him repeat many sentences.

A bad cold confines him to his room; he says he is worn out and looks it; his handsome face is lined with anxiety; harassed by the obligations of his fame, tormented by money questions, exasperated by the correspondence that cuts holes in his time (he shows me a letter from a general offering him a 250,000-franc diamond, "a real bargain"), much troubled by the general situation and convinced that the miserable work of political men is leading us to the abyss and all Europe with us. He reads me a declaration by Einstein, distinctly individualistic, to which he subscribes more willingly than to the Soviets. Impossible to build up a single front to stand against the ruinous claims of nationalists. He convinces me of this, and I leave that conversation greatly grieved, for I cannot doubt that he is right. The catastrophe strikes me as almost inevitable. I have come to wish most heartily for the upset of capitalism and everything that lurks in its shadow—abuses, injustices, lies, and monstrosities. And I cannot persuade myself that the Soviets must fatally and necessarily bring about the strangling of everything for which we live. A well-understood communism needs to favor worth-while individuals, to take advantage of all the individual's values, to get the best output from everyone. And well-understood individualism has no reason to be opposed to what would put everything in its place and bring out its value.

Cuverville, 25 February

I read with the greatest interest Stalin's new speech, which exactly answers my objections and fears . . . (speech of 23 June 1931); consequently I rally to it with all my heart.

So long as I glimpsed only miserable palliatives to a ruinous state of things, to lying credos, to cowardly intellectual compromises, I could still remain undecided, although all those things seemed to me more and more deplorable. And it appeared to me more and more clear against what my heart and mind rose up and wanted to fight; but I could not be satisfied with mere protest. . . . Now that I know not only *against* what but *for* what—I make up my mind. And I wonder at the fact that all those who used to reproach me with my "indecision" are all on the other side. They used to throw back at me that letter from Charles-Louis Philippe which I had myself quoted, that sentence which ended the letter: "Be a man: choose," as if they were unwilling to admit that one could make any other "choice" than theirs.

I know in their camp people of such great heart and such good will that, even convinced that they were wrong, it was indescribably painful for me to have to declare myself against them. But how can one fail to declare oneself, rather than see one's silence taken for acquiescence? Indifference, tolerance are now out of place, as soon as the enemy takes advantage of them and one sees prospering what one considers as decidedly bad.

26 February

That the ideas of Lenin and Stalin might overcome the resistance the European states are trying to bring against them is beginning to seem possible to those states; and this fills them with terror. But that it might be desirable for those ideas to win out is something they refuse to envisage. There is a great deal of stupidity, a great deal of ignorance, a great deal of stubbornness in their refusal; and also a certain lack of imagination that keeps them from believing that humanity can change, that a society can be built up on different foundations from those they have always known (even though they deplore them), that the future can be anything but a repetition and reproduction of the past.

"Everything begins over again," and "there is nothing new under the sun," they say. And Valentine: "If that famous plan were to succeed, it would take away all my pleasure in living"; as for me, this would happen on the contrary if the plan failed.

27 February

To cease advancing aimlessly and to head toward something . . . what an indescribable satisfaction! But was I not won over to the party even before it was formed and formulated its doctrines? And if my wishes too often remained vague, was not this in part because their realization seemed to me too distant? Emotionally, temperamentally, intellectually, I have always been a communist. But I was afraid of my own thought and, in my writings, strove more to hide than to express it. I listened too much to others and gave them more credence than I did myself, as much through sympathy as through lack of self-assurance, through incurable modesty, through fear of "being entirely of my own opinion." Events over yonder have taken this in hand and I am grateful to them for pushing me to it.

The fact that capitalist society sought support in Christianity is a monstrosity for which Christ is not responsible, but rather the clergy. The clergy has so effectively annexed Christ that it seems as if one could not get rid of the clergy today without casting out Christ at the same time.

Some people's faith remains so great that they distinctly see Christ weep over that desertion. How could that desertion fail to strike them as abominable?

Le Tertre, 5 March

I feel only too well my incompetence, and I feel it more and more while concerning myself with these political, economic, and financial questions that belong to a field in which I adventure timidly, urged on by an increasing curiosity. But what I feel more and more is the inextricable confusion of all these problems. Such questions are so complicated that the more one becomes involved in them the less one understands; at least this is true of me. Certain specialists in wartime would build up this or that prediction based on their calculations, this or that interpretation of the future—which seemed fatal, but to which events almost always gave the lie.[1] In such cases people talk (for the calculations were exact after all) of "the psychological factor," of "imponderables," which the technician was unable, or judged unnecessary, to take into account. But these are precisely my line, my field. I must not try to go beyond them.

Valmont, 30 March

Some time ago this notebook ceased to be what it ought to be: an intimate confidant.

The perspective of an even partial publication of my *Journal*, as an appendix to the volumes of my *Œuvres complètes*,[2] has distorted its meaning; and also fatigue or laziness, and the dislocation of my life, fear of losing what I ought to have put into books or articles which, through some lack of confidence or other, I despaired of writing satisfactorily. Even these lines I am writing without assurance. To be sure, I have already known periods of slackening enthusiasm, and I know that I got over them; but at that time I was young. Is there enough space left ahead of me, henceforth, to spring forth anew? For all the impetus acquired in the past does not seem to me of any help for what I now want to write. And this is above all the reason for my silence. I am in this sanatorium to rest, to take care of myself, to find out what I am still worth and whether or not I can still dare.

Cuverville, 21 April

I have got into the lazy habit of reading while walking, while eating, of not being able to go without reading. All the time I ought to give to meditation, to the imagination, to work, is absorbed by reading. My own thought yields to someone else's, or accompanies it, or fights it. I must

[1] I want to make an exception of my Uncle Charles Gide, whose predictions on the contrary always, or almost always, came true. [A.]

[2] The first extensive publication of the *Journals*, indeed, was made in the fifteen volumes of the *Complete Works*, but there it was divided according to notebooks rather than years and many names of individuals were omitted.

teach it the monologue again, or the kind of dialogue in which it does all the talking. How long it is since I have really worked!

"No," says É.G., "it cannot succeed" (*it* is the Five-Year-Plan) "because if it succeeded, we should be done for." ("We" is not France, but simply big banking interests.) He says this smiling charmingly and quite conscious of the weakness of the argument. I take real pleasure in seeing him again and am ever more sensitive to his qualities of mind and heart. They seem to me greater the less he tries to bring them out, as much through awkwardness as through modesty. Real virtues loathe the ostentatious; I am more and more convinced of this.

This too, this above all, withholds my pen: the thought, of which I keep reminding myself, that many things still dear to us will have neither value nor significance for those of whose coming I have a presentiment and whom my heart beckons. It is to them that I should like to speak, for them that I should like to write; but they will not listen to me. And besides they will do right, having no need, for their part, to hear what I, for my part, should need to tell them. My sympathy means nothing to them and little does it matter to them that I turn toward them. To grieve over this would be folly.

Cuverville, 6 June

I am making a great effort to get back to my book, to draw my *Geneviève* from lethargy. . . . Have I no further creative power in me? Or rather can I no longer become attached to my fiction? It no longer interests me; my mind is constantly leaving it. The novels of others do not hold me any more, and even of Mauriac's I have not been able to read more than fifty pages. . . .[3] How can one still write novels when our old world is crumbling around us, when something unknown is being formulated for which I am waiting, for which I am hoping, and which with all my attention I am observing as it slowly takes shape?

Darmstadt, June

No, I do not have to regret the more or less incongruous jokes that stud my *Œdipe,* but rather the program preface

---

[3] Probably *Le Nœud de vipères* (*Vipers' Tangle*), which first appeared in 1932.

in which I seem to attach special importance to them. I had written that preface specifically for the Antwerp public and at the express request of Pitoëff, who feared (and was right to fear) that that rather heavy audience would not dare laugh even though it felt like doing so. That preface, which I had forgotten, was reproduced, without my being aware of it, for the Parisian public, for which it was not at all suitable. The jokes in *Œdipe* displeased in general and even rebuffed some of the best disposed. This seemed to them merely a grinding out again of Meilhac or Hervé. I believe that it is to such "easy effects" in great part that my play owed its lack of success (despite the enthusiasm of some).

I have just witnessed the last performance of this same *Œdipe* at Darmstadt. The director, Hartung, had the very ingenious idea of supporting and motivating all the anachronisms of the play (which, consequently, ceased to appear forced) by a semi-ancient, semi-modern setting, mingling the column of a Greek temple with a projection on the backdrop of Notre-Dame de Paris. The actors themselves wore their tragic finery over an outrageously contemporary costume. The scenic illusion, consequently, was non-existent; but my desire not to try to achieve it became at once obvious, and when the chorus was heard to declare: "The action of this drama cannot get under way without . . ." etc., the audience was grateful to me for bringing them into collusion with me and understood that the interest of my play was elsewhere: in the clash of ideas, and that the drama took place on another plane from that of the ancient tragedy.

Cuverville, 11 June

I do not know what impression I may make on others; but on myself: utterly stupid. In conversation with X. or Y. my sole preoccupation is to appear to be following. (Oh, I am speaking of a conversation *in French!*) I remember those conversations which, as a child, I strove to understand, those conversations among "grown-ups." Nothing has changed. But I no longer have the excuse of youth. And if I have to hold up my end, I bring out nothing but squawks.

"Have pity on me and don't listen to me! I have nothing to say to you. And don't think that out of politeness

you have to pretend to give importance to what I say.
Everything I say and shall say to you is merely absurd.
Go on talking among yourselves then, just as if I were not
here. I should so much like not to be here. Why did you
invite me? I am sleepy!"

13 June

Indeed I do not insist that the tower in which I take
refuge should be an ivory tower! But I am no good if
I leave it. Glass tower; observatory in which I welcome
every ray, every wave; fragile tower in which I feel badly
sheltered; do not want to be; vulnerable on all sides; but
confident in spite of everything, and my eyes fixed on
the east. My desperate waiting, despite everything, takes
on the color of hope.

Christ's cross is a part of their armament. Offensive
weapon, or merely defensive? He who fights always claims
to be attacked. Sophistry of "legitimate defenses."

That enrolling of Christ is, of all the frauds, the most
shameful; of all hypocrisies, the most abominable perhaps.
"Not peace, but the sword," Christ himself said. That is
what they retain of his gospel of peace. They have so
effectively linked the idea of religion to the idea of country that it is in the name of God that they arm and
mobilize, and that no pacification seems possible except
by rejecting simultaneously both of them together, just as
the U.S.S.R. is doing at present.

The U.S.S.R. however does not intend to suppress the
various states; on the contrary, she supports and protects
them and, so doing, reveals her wisdom; but on the one
hand by mingling their interests, and on the other by
disaffecting them, as a chapel is disaffected, she suppresses
what might oppose them to one another. Only atheism can
pacify the world today.

That will toward atheism on the part of the Soviets,
however, is what most arouses against them certain really
devout minds. A world without God can only go toward
ruin, they think; only toward perdition a humanity without cults, without devotions, without prayers. . . . Why
do not these pious souls convince themselves that one
can never suppress any but false gods? The need of
adoring lives at the center of man's heart.

But religion, our religion, the only one, is a *revealed* religion, say those pious souls. Man can know the truth only through the revelation of which we are the guardians. Any felicity, any harmony achieved without the aid of God seems to them criminal; they refuse to consider it real; they deny it and with all their piety oppose it. They prefer humanity unhappy to seeing it happy without God, without their god.

In this new form they no longer recognize war—and that we are in the midst of it. If the cannons get to booming and the gases to spreading abroad, this will only be *as a confirmation.* War in the embryonic state, dissimulated war; but the starving of millions out of work is worth the machine-guns' harvest. The bourgeois feels safe; for how long? . . .

"Conversion to Communism has been fashionable in Germany for ten years," Curtius tells me.

"Here it is conversion to Catholicism. It is called simply 'conversion,' as if there could not be any other. But in heart as well as mind I have always been a communist; even while remaining a Christian; and this is why I had such trouble separating them from each other, and even more trouble opposing them to each other. I should never have reached this point all alone. It required people and events to educate me. Do not speak of 'conversion' in this case; I have not changed direction; I have always walked forward; I am continuing to do so; the great difference is that for a long time I saw nothing in front of me but space and the projection of my own fervor; at present I am going forward while orienting myself toward something; I know that somewhere my vague desires are being organized and that my dream is on the way to becoming reality."

Howbeit, utterly unfit for politics. Do not therefore ask me to belong to a Party.

Marseille

Much better impression of the sailing and fishing population of Cassis, where I go to join Roger Martin du Gard. In Marseille, indeed, it is not the masses, but the riffraff.

Of the power of the word. As soon as "sex-appeal" was

found, in the shelter of that word every pornography was admitted.

This makes me think of one of Abbé Mugnier's sallies, exquisite in my opinion, but requiring a certain finesse, I believe, to appreciate it. It takes place at some society dinner or other. The Abbé leans toward the elegant lady seated next him:

"Can you tell me, please, what we have just been served?"

"Why, Abbé, it is a roast of beef."

"Ah! God be praised; I feared it might be Chateaubriand." [4]

18 July

What one might have done is confused with what one should have done and by far prevails over what one has done. Let us call it, for greater simplicity: regrets. There is none that I have more trouble getting rid of than this one: circumstances and Em. contributing somewhat, that is to say: the climate and soil of Cuverville being slightly different, or Em. being less attached to that place and willing to settle elsewhere, I should have persevered in my attempts at gardening, which through many disappointments I did not pursue more than three years. And this would have kept me much more at Cuverville. It was only most reluctantly that I resigned myself to giving up, and only when I realized that with the earth and the sky against him no one could succeed. And let no one speak of inconstancy and restlessness. I should have persevered. What I most longed to do was to be able to study plants; with nothing or almost nothing for show, my garden would have been a sort of laboratory, would have recalled those botanical gardens in which each type of plant is enclosed. Horticultural hybridizations would not have concerned me so much as botanical species. I should have wanted to "force" certain ones, through care and selections; insist on getting from them all the perfection and beauty they hold in reserve. Every living matter is plastic.

And I hold that true philanthropy, likewise, ought to

___

[4] Chateaubriand is the common French name for a porterhouse steak; the Abbé is of course thinking of the writer.

be less concerned with saving "what was lost" than with
perfecting the human species, which also can and must
be improved. What it might be is the thing we should
become attached to; that is what we must help it to become, rather than bewailing its miserable withering, and
prolonging the existence of what is an insult to life. The
healthiest are already all contaminated by sympathy.

19 July

Tolstoy's withdrawal as an artist can be explained also
by the decline of his creative faculties. If he had still
borne in him some new *Anna Karenina,* one can believe
that he would have been less concerned with the Douk-
hobors and would not have spoken ill of art. But he felt
his literary career to be finished; his thought was no
longer swollen with poetic impulse. Already *Resurrection*
marked a notable decline. Who could regret that he did
not give us other works of decadence?

If social questions occupy my thought today, this is
partly because the creative demon is withdrawing from
it. Such questions do not take over the field until the
other has already surrendered it. Why try to overrate oneself? and refuse to recognize in me (what appears clear
to me in Tolstoy): an undeniable diminution? . . .

Did poetic force decrease in me with my Christian sentiments, as Em. tells me this morning? I do not believe so;
but rather with my perplexity. Each of my books up to
now has been the exploitation of an uncertainty.

23 July

They will strive to suppress everything of which they
do not at once see the use. Until their own leisure finally
achieved allows them to enjoy it in their turn, how could
they appreciate what it required so much "fecund laziness" and so much "scented leisure" to achieve? *Primum
vivere.* And I greatly fear, I confess, that the initial anxiety
for vegetables may first exile from our gardens all the
flowers. Consequently I admire nothing so much in the
U.S.S.R. as the organization of leisure, of education, of
culture. Probably the great need of cadres urged them to
it; but also the feeling that work, though it becomes a
necessity for every man, is nevertheless not the end of

man, and that every man must have his share of that leisure which, in our time, is still the privilege of but a few.

Cuverville, 29 July

Nothing to note. Dreadful confusion after reading the Trotskyite manifestoes that Pierre Naville lent me. But, however well founded certain criticisms may seem to me, it strikes me that nothing can be more prejudicial than divisions within the party.

7 August

I am leaving for Berlin without desires and without joy, already eager to come back, to be back.

Yesterday at Vogel's, Ehrenburg, to bring out the profound difference of the new generation in the U.S.S.R.:

"When those of my generation were recommended not to read a book, they rushed to that book and devoured it at once. Every prohibition of that sort was to them a recommendation. Quite on the contrary, as for the young people who are between twenty and twenty-five today, it is enough to tell them that a book is bad, for them not to try, not to be willing even, to open it. But the change in this case has taken place not only among the young readers, but also among those who advise them, who immediately preceded them, in those who tell the young: read this, do not read that. The young would not listen to them unless, having changed themselves, they deserved to be heeded by the young."

28 August

Back to Cuverville after a new sojourn in Berlin (the third this summer).

What has happened? The time came when, considering the little that was left me to live, I told myself: not a day to waste . . . and since then I have done nothing worth while.

Hold one's own at least. . . . But no, as soon as one ceases to be tensed toward progress, one falls back. . . .

September

Rather keep silent than complain. . . .

Berlin, 17 October

I give up the other notebook, of unlucky hue, in which I managed to write nothing but asininities and repetitions of what I brought out in October in the N.R.F.[5] (In psychology, the ass is a ruminant.) The last words I wrote in it: "rather silence than complaint," date from the month of . . . ?—Quite willingly I should have considered them as definitive "last words." I have not often wished to die (two or three times only) but rather to be already dead —for greater simplicity. I used to compare myself to Icarus, lost in the labyrinth from which so many mystics think they are able to free themselves only by a leap toward heaven. If my journal is not more full of wailing, this is because I take pleasure in writing only in a state of felicity. That resolution, already made in my youth, to let my work reflect nothing but joy (or rather an encouragement to living) may lead to believe, most deceptively, that I am accessible to nothing else. Just like the sundial that marks "only the happy hours." But my depression of late was due, as often, chiefly to fatigue. Harassed on all sides, I fled Paris to recover myself.

23 October

One cannot, however, succeed in making me believe in God by persuading me that it is healthier to believe in him! or more comfortable.

It is, on the contrary, precisely in the scorn of comfort that I become stronger and assert myself. And this is what makes me throw out from under my head Montaigne's "soft and smooth pillow." [6] It is perhaps also for the comfort it would take away from me that I wish for Communism; as it is also certainly for that reason that they fear it.

13 December

Solicited by the A.E.A.R.,[7] which wants to count me among its recruits, I reply: No, dear comrades. The only result of such an engagement would be immediately to keep me from ever writing anything again. I have declared as loud and clear as I could my sympathy (and the word is weak) for the U.S.S.R. and for all it represents in our eyes, in our hearts, despite all the imperfections

[5] In the October 1932 issue of the *Nouvelle Revue Française* appeared extracts from this journal covering the period 8 January 1932 through 14 June 1932 and entitled *"Pages de journal."*

[6] Montaigne spoke of his *"mol et doux oreiller"* of doubt.

[7] Doubtless L'Alliance Européenne des Amis de la Russie, which grouped sympathizers of the U.S.S.R.

that are still held up to us. I believe that my co-operation
(and in my case very precisely) can be of more real
advantage to your (to our) cause if I give it freely and
am known *not* to be enrolled. Writing henceforth according to the "principles" of a "charter" (I am using the
expressions of your circular), this would make whatever
I might write henceforth lose all real value; or, more
exactly, it would spell sterility for me. Do not see, in what
I am saying here, any desire for personal protection and
safety. Already I have proved more than once that I did
not fear to "compromise" myself when I judged it necessary. But those who read me today and upon whom I can
exercise (even without exactly wishing to) some influence
would not even listen to me any more as soon as they
could believe that I am thinking and writing under
orders.

29 December

Read with the keenest interest the beginning of Benda's
Discours à la nation européenne[8] in the proofs of the next
issue of the *N.R.F.*

I should not be surprised if Benda, a contemporary of
Proust and Valéry who like them is revealed late in life,
were to become one of our chief leaders. On rereading
those pages immediately afterward to Em., I regret that
the writing is sometimes a bit flabby.

René Schwob's book on me[9] could have as an epigraph
this sentence that I read this evening in Bossuet:
"It is impossible for him to teach well since he does not
teach in the Church." (*Œuvres oratoires,* Vol. III, p. 211,
ed. Lebarg.)

I told René Schwob that he reminded me of the doctors
of Monsieur de Pourceaugnac.[10] He cannot admit that
I am in a state of health and I owe it to him to be ill. He
takes for blackness everything that is not saturated with
certain rays.

That art and literature have nothing to do with social
questions and can only, if they venture into them, go

[8] *Speech to the European Nation.*
[9] *Le Vrai Drame d'André Gide* (*The Real Drama of André Gide*) by
René Schwob appeared in late 1932.
[10] The chief character in Molière's comedy of this name.

astray, I remain almost convinced. And this is partly why I have been silent since such questions have become uppermost in my mind.

We are just beginning to emerge from the mystical stage; but that the "fine arts" belong to it I am ready to believe and that they need that climate to prosper. I prefer not to write anything rather than to bend my art to utilitarian ends. To convince myself that they must be uppermost today is tantamount to condemning myself to silence.

1933

2 January

After *Le Grand Meaulnes*, read *Le Bal du Comte d'Orgel*, which I had never read either.[1]

Extraordinary assurance of this book; almost excessive. It has about it something of the wager and of acrobatics. The achievement is almost perfect (despite incomprehensible stylistic weaknesses for some fifteen pages toward the middle of the book). Far superior to all the other productions of Radiguet and to *Le Grand Meaulnes*, of which the interest becomes diluted; which spreads out over too great a number of pages and too long a space of time; somewhat uncertain in outline, with the most charming giving out at the end of the first hundred pages. The rest of the book chases after that first virginal emotion, trying in vain to recapture it. . . . I am well aware that this is the very subject of the book; but it is also its shortcoming, so that it was perhaps not possible to bring it off better.

An unrecapturable freshness. . . .

Such an *Œdipe*, and sublime, and in the grand style, and pure of line, and stripped of all dross, might probably have laid claim to some success, but it would no longer have offered any interest for me. In the jokes, trivialities, and incongruities of mine there is, as it were, a constant need of warning the public: you have Sophocles' play and I am not posing as a rival; I am leaving him the pathos; but here is what Sophocles could not have seen and understood, though it lay in his subject, and what I understand—not because I am more intelligent but because I belong to another epoch; and I propose to let you see the other side of the scenery, were it to be an obstacle to your emotion, for it is not your emotion that matters to me and that I am trying to evoke: it is to your intelligence that I am addressing myself. I intend, not to make you shudder or weep, but to make you reflect.

[1] *Big Meaulnes* (or *The Wanderer*, as it is known in English) was Alain-Fournier's only novel, for he was killed at the front in 1914. *The Count's Ball* was Raymond Radiguet's second novel, published after his death at the age of twenty.

4 January

Cardinal Dubois accepts an invitation to dinner at Rothschild's.

"Mouton-Rothschild" is served and a lackey half fills the Cardinal's glass, when the latter stops him and fills it up with water.

"What, Your Grace, are you baptizing my wine!"

"Don't be alarmed, Baron, I am cutting it."

Apparently apocryphal remark, but amusing all the same, especially if it implies the complete presence of mind of both interlocutors. Much less funny as soon as one imagines it to be invented; resulting quite naturally from the realization of two picturesque ways of describing the dilution of wine, and from the reflection that one of the two images can apply equally well to the Jewish practice and the other to the Christian practice. Put into the mouth of interlocutors, it takes on life and becomes amusing; you hear the voices, see the subtle smiles. . . . Throws light on the device for fabricating witty theatrical dialogue.

Montherlant is probably right when he says (and he says it magnificently) that youth rejects the idea of a peace that would offer no sustenance for its appetite for glory and its need of enthusiasm. But what Communism proposes to us today is a way of fighting war which demands of us more courage and permits of more heroism than war itself. In truth war would call for nothing but a blind submission.

That future war which we are forced to glimpse, abject in every way, will no longer have a place for heroism; so that that last allurement, that prestige it still holds for the noblest among our young men, will be taken from it.

New titles of nobility, new forms of holiness, of sacrifice, of heroism (and not at all as you say: new facilities), this is what we need. This is ignored only because of an absurd misunderstanding, a profound misappreciation of human nature and its mysterious appetites. It is you on the contrary who offer it stagnation in the inherited comfort that your effort is solely concerned with preserving.[2]

•   •   •

[2] Already in March 1910 I wrote: "Barrès! Barrès! Why do you not understand that what we need is not comfort (and I mean: intellectual comfort), it is *heroism*." [A.]

It seems to me very unjust to reproach the U.S.S.R. with being anxious only about material interests; but she is utterly right to take care of them *first*. And by ensuring education to all her people, by favoring and filling their leisure hours, she certainly shows that her aims do not stop there.

But in order to rebuild anew, one has to start from the ground itself.

Many are those who still confuse mysticism and spirituality and who believe that man can but crawl if religion does not support him; who believe that religion alone can keep man from crawling.

So it took two letters from correspondents (which it was unbecoming not to publish) to make *Les Libres Propos* decide to mention my *Pages de Journal*.[3] As it seems to me that the prolonged silence of that little review, and a most estimable one, is made up in great part of great admiration for my uncle (so that for them Gide is Charles Gide and there must not be any other Gide than he), and as my uncle had, even more than I, to suffer from an even more unjust silence, it is not of this silence itself that I shall complain. The thing against which I find it hard not to protest is the peremptory way they had, at the time of the publication of my *Voyage au Congo*, of establishing the fact that before bumping up against a few sorry exactions in French Equatorial Africa I had never managed to interest myself in men, solely absorbed as I was in the contemplation of myself. So that presumably it required that contact with the oppressed black race to tear me away from my "narcissism" and that there was less reason for being grateful to me for finally concerning myself with "social problems" than for holding it against me for not being earlier interested in them.

If I had kept a journal during my first trip to Algeria as I did daily in the Congo, most likely I should have spoken of the business of the Gafsa phosphates, which I was then able to follow closely, of the withdrawal of the White Fathers after the death of Cardinal Lavigerie, and especially of the arrival of barrels of absinthe to break down the natives, and of the expropriation of the Arabs

[3] *Extracts from the Journals*, published in 1932.

by the device of the Cazenave bank according to a monstrous method that I would probably have exposed. . . .

(And, on the other hand, if I had not kept that journal in French Equatorial Africa, I should most likely have brought back from my trip in the Congo only a few "landscapes" for a new *Amyntas*.) The feeling of my incompetence long kept me from speaking of what was not *my line*. It took the war to bring me to doubt of the value of "competencies," to convince myself that a specialist can be wrong like anyone else and that I had just as much right as anyone else, and even the duty, to speak.

Paris, 6 January

The truth is that I cannot resign myself to staying away from Em., nor dissociate my brain from my heart. . . . This is the secret of all my indecisions; my very reticences are the most passionate. But no, there is nothing to be done about it, nothing to be tried; "no man can serve two masters"—and "the man whose heart is divided is inconstant in all his ways. . . ."

Every time I see her again I recognize anew that I have never really loved anyone but her; and even, at times, it seems to me that I love her more than ever. And it is because it takes me away from her that every step forward is so painful to me. I can no longer think without cruelty. A "condition of anxiety" sufficient to explain many sleepless nights. . . .

Probably it is because I feel her suffer from it that each attack on Christ still hurts me so painfully. At times I come to wonder if it is not also because, without wanting to admit this to myself, without even knowing it or being exactly aware of it, I never completely ceased believing in him. Yes, believing in Him, in his immanent omnipresence, in that aggravation of his cross through our fault, etc. . . .

8 February

Too busy of late to keep this notebook up to date. Trip to Wiesbaden, where I find Stravinsky, with whom I am to work for Ida Rubinstein.[4] Complete accord.

[4] On *Perséphone*, an opera in three tableaux presented at the Théâtre de l'Opéra, Paris, by Mme Ida Rubinstein on 30 April 1934 and published the same year. The music was by Igor Stravinsky, the choreography by Kurt Jooss, and the staging by Ida Rubinstein and Jacques Copeau.

Even if there were but one inexact quotation in a whole
book, you can be certain that that is the one which will
be at a premium and will be reproduced everywhere. I
had warned Pierre-Quint, pointing out to him a tiresome
slip: he makes me say: "I am never what I think I am,"
whereas I had written quite differently and with much
more sense: "I am never *but* what I think I am."

"Do you want to bet," I added, "that that is the sentence among all others which the critics will remember?"
And this evening, in fact, I see that mistake reproduced in
an article by Thérive. It is the only quotation he makes;
it is wrong.

It seems to me that an alert, perspicacious critic could
have, should have, run down the mistake. One would have
to know me very little to accept as mine such a flat sentence. But all the rest of the article shows how little
Thérive knows me.

The sky above Europe and the entire world is so heavy
with storm; hearts are so full of hatred—that occasionally
one comes to think that nothing but a conflict of classes
could forestall today the mortal conflict of nations.

I am making a great effort to sober my thought with a
little wisdom, but what an error it is to believe that wisdom is always on the side of moderation! And those who
say: "rather war than revolution," how can they fail to
understand that the revolution would inevitably follow
the war, so that, by trying to avoid one, we should have
both?

14 March

Those who (René Schwob in particular) see my writings encumbered with the sexual obsession seem to me
as absurd as those who formerly claimed those writings to
be frigid. Sensuality remains, in their mind as in their
flesh, so closely linked to the object that awakens it that,
the object once changed, they fail to recognize it. Then,
warned by me, they saw that sensuality everywhere, after
having seen it nowhere. It influenced my will, they said,
distorted my thought, rotted my prose; each of my books
was impregnated with it. . . . How many stupidities they
wrote on this subject.

5 *April*

What would be Barrès's attitude in regard to Hitler? He would approve him, I believe. For, after all, Hitlerism is a successful Boulangism.[5] What made it prove abortive in France? Circumstances or men? Would the French people have let themselves be led into such excesses? Doubtless Hitlerism was favored by unemployment, poverty, and that constant irritation which France, alas, seems to have taken it upon herself to provide.

7 *April*

Since Germany seems bent upon getting rid of her brains, could not France offer to take in that "gray matter" that our neighbors seem to scorn?

Could not the French government, above and beyond politics, offer Einstein, forced into exile by Germany, a chair in the Collège de France, as was done in the past for Mickiewicz? A laboratory and the means of continuing his research. . . . In order to create a sort of foreign annex to this Collège, which would perpetuate an ancient tradition of receptivity of which France would have reason to be proud, it would probably not be hard to gather together the necessary funds. Shall we have enough sense to make this gesture before another country gets ahead of us? And this time what a fine reason we should have for being glad to be French!

I speak of this to Malraux, who promises to speak of it to Monzie.[6]

Roquebrune, 10 April

Quite rested already by the joy of being back here, despite the last two sleepless nights. A letter from Roger renews his request. I cannot succeed in getting up enough steam to dare writing. If only I could see Valéry. It would be up to him to do it. He at least would be listened to.

During the trip from Marseille to Menton I reread

[5] General Boulanger, named Minister of War by Clemenceau in 1886, later became a Royalist and threatened the Republic in 1888–9 as a popular dictator who might have seized power. Barrès was among his many admirers.

[6] Anatole de Monzie was then Minister of Education.

Vieille France[7] at one sitting. How could I have been so wrong at first? It is true that numerous changes have brought this book to perfection; now it is excellent. Great joy.

The moment is doubtless ill chosen for manifestations (declarations) of this type. And, even though I have an utterly different point of view from his, Fabre-Luce is right. Not that I believe at all that an agreement with Hitler is possible or desirable (there are too many implications and misunderstandings in it), but that, faced with Hitlerism, it is at present unwise to invite France's forces of resistance to relax. Voicing the claims of the extreme Left too soon, however legitimate they may be, amounts to inciting Hitler to come and crush them here, as he has just done in Germany.

I am not saying that the whole contribution of the past is of no use to me; but rather that that contribution might have been different. And I constantly recognize all I owe to those of my country, of my race, who brought me into being; what I owe likewise to that joint inheritance which takes no account either of races or of countries. But I tell myself, and keep repeating to myself, that the heritage of the past might have been different. I cannot imagine as any different the instruments of conquest over nature: the ax, the hoe, the sickle, or, later on, the rudder; but rather all those works of the intelligence according to which our judgment and taste have been formed. In the most complicated of machines I can admire the turning to account of laws that my intelligence can understand and subjugate to its own self-proposed ends, yet never modify. So that solely in their imperfection can those machines remain different.

The work of art infinitely varied.

And all the rest is fantasy. Future humanity will not consider it seemly to pay any attention to it, and Homer will be as if he had never sung. Child's play, all of it! We are entering a serious epoch.

· · ·

[7] First published in 1933, *Old France*, by Roger Martin du Gard, is a particularly unflattering portrait of a small town as seen by the postman on his daily rounds.

Et qui sait si les fleurs nouvelles que je rêve . . .[8]

But dreaming is now out of the question.

"It would be fine to grow old [9] if we advanced only toward improvement: it is a drunkard's gait, staggering, dizzy, amorphous."

I wonder if the last word, *informe,* does not signify in Montaigne's mind, rather "without beauty" than "without form"; better justified thus: *in-formosus,* the negation *in-* being more suitable to an epithet than to a substantive (I cannot find any other example where it is so linked). Littré gives no example of that acceptation. But the word in the example from Boileau that he quotes: "Tragedy, *informe* and coarse at its birth . . ." allows one to glimpse the passage that might have taken place from one meaning to the other. I am well aware that there is the Latin *informis,* from which the French comes directly; but it just happens that this word, when Virgil or Horace uses it, means rather "without beauty" than "without contour," and Montaigne, raised on those authors, remembers this.

11 April

This evening *L'Éclaireur de Nice* informs us that Einstein accepts the chair that Spain has just offered him at Madrid. The event is announced in large capitals; *L'Éclaireur* grasps its importance then.

I cannot admit that those qualified to make that offer in the name of France did not think of it. . . . What reasons did they have for not doing so? . . . I am seeking, and for myself too, excuses. . . .

---

[8] This is line 9 of Baudelaire's sonnet "L'Ennemi" ("The Enemy") in *Les Fleurs du mal.* After describing his youth as a darkling storm that ravaged the fruit in his garden, the poet states that he has now reached his intellectual autumn and must work to rebuild the flooded earth—

> And will the new flowers I see in dream
> Find in this soil washed bare and clean
> The strength to grow and the mystic food?
>
> O grief and pain! Time consumes our life,
> And, gnawing our heart with teeth like knife,
> The Enemy fattens on our lost blood!

[9] Montaigne wrote: "Il ferait bel estre vieil." [A.] This means: "It would be fine to be old."

As soon as the news of Einstein's exile appeared, I should have put forth the suggestion in *Marianne* or the *N.R.F.* Still better: instead of barking with the others at that public meeting, have that suggestion to the French government voted by acclamation by the large audience. How I blame myself for not having thought of this then!

Every good Frenchman should be inconsolable that France did not have the sense to make this fine gesture, which would have been so natural to her and in which we should all have recognized ourselves.

14 April

Is it a result of Malraux's intervention with Monzie? Yesterday's *Le Temps* announces Monzie's interpellation in the Chamber regarding the offering of a chair to Einstein. Bravo! But how can this be reconciled with Madrid's offer, which Einstein is already said to be accepting?

How can I recover that serenity of mind indispensable to work? I really believe I have lost it forever.

. . . That wretched creature in a doorway on the corner of the boulevard Saint-Germain and the boulevard Raspail. His coat pinned together with a safety-pin to hide the lack of shirt. A vacant stare. . . . I saw him again, two hours later, as I left the *Nouvelle Revue Française,* in the same place, in exactly the same pose, an image of utter despair. I tried to speak to him, but he seemed not to understand anything; he almost dropped the bill I slipped into his hand. Back at rue Vaneau, I could think of nothing else. . . .

That state of joy in which I intended to maintain myself, that joy has ceased to be anything but a very dim sputtering flame which I feel to be on the point of going out. I conceive a hatred, not so much for the rich who live in a condition of thoughtlessness, but rather for everything I am aware of possessing over and above. What brings me to the Communists is not theories, which I only half understand and am not concerned with, it is merely knowing that among them there are some for whom this state of things is *intolerable.* But there are such among Christians likewise. Why, how, do they happen to be the exception among Christians? It is, alas, only too easy to answer this question with another question: how can one consider intolerable what one believes to be willed by God?

25 *May*

I receive a visit from a young Communist of twenty-six, who looks only twenty; he is bringing me an article in which, if you take his word for it, he has forever shut up Benda; the latter, recognizing that he would have no reply to this, has presumably opposed the inclusion of this article in the *Nouvelle Revue Française*. The above-mentioned young man counts on me to go over his head. The interest of the party is involved in the acceptance of that article. It is not he (whose name I have forgotten) who is involved, but the cause, and I am betraying the party if I do not force Paulhan's hand. As I tell him that I have never wanted to make use of authority at the *N.R.F.*, that I have always left Paulhan complete freedom of choice, that, in short, I refuse to intervene, he declares while raising his voice that he is "stunned," profoundly disappointed, that after my declarations he had a right to expect me to support him and, since that's the way it is, he is ready to relate as loud as he can my falling away, my desertion. I tell him that this is blackmail; at once he exclaims: "To be sure; but legitimate blackmail. . . ." He talks louder and louder, gets excited, seizes me by the arm; eventually I put a chair between us. . . . "Is that really your last word?" he asks in his most threatening tone. And since I reply that I have nothing to add: "It's a pity! I am sorry for you, but you've asked for it. You will live to regret this."

This conversation amused me too much for me not to push it beyond reasonable limits, so that, toward the end, there were repetitions without making any headway. I especially enjoyed the confusion that X. insisted on maintaining between the fate of his article and the success of the cause; besides, he seemed rather sincerely convinced and, consequently, I rather liked him in spite of everything. (Several times he protested "that it was not a question of his article," to which I replied "that on the contrary it was a question solely of his article.")—Somewhat concentrated, the dialogue might be excellent. Young X. played rather well his role of zealot—after all, rather easy like all the roles of "stock" characters.

Cuverville, 6 June

I read in *Le Temps* of today:

"The European Anti-Fascist Congress met yesterday at
the Salle Pleyel with the participation of the foreign delegates. The representatives for France are: MM. Marcel
Cachin, Careille, Racamond, Cazaubon, Professor Prenant,
André Gide." I am eager to point out here that my acceptance of that congress was taken from me by surprise.
My categorical *refusal* having "come in too late," I received a letter of apology (to be found in the papers I
left in Paris), to which I in turn replied that, since the
error was committed, there would be still greater trouble
trying to correct it, for I should then seem to be *withdrawing* from a congress to which I merely did not want
to belong. I add that not one of the names of those men-
tioned in the letter (requesting my support) as future
members of the committee figures here.

I have received, since the Hitler crisis has been acute in
Germany, a dozen solicitations from different groups
whose objects, as it would seem from their declarations,
are the same, so that it is appropriate to wish them to get
together and not let their efforts be scattered. Having the
possibility of declaring myself when I want to and in the
way that seems suitable to me, I systematically refuse to
countersign any declaration whatever of which I have not
written the text. There is in this no desire whatever to
distinguish myself; and I very well understand how important it is, in any occasion of this sort, to group together,
to unite one's efforts; but I do not believe I have yet encountered a single proclamation of this type of which I
can completely approve and which did not distort my
thought on some point or other.

All interested opinions are suspect to me. I like to be
able to think freely and begin to fear being taken in as
soon as some advantage comes to me from the opinion I
profess. It is as if I were accepting a bribe.

By mood and temperament I am not at all revolutionary.
Furthermore, I personally have every reason to be pleased
with the state of things. But, you see, what bothers me is
just being in a position to be pleased with it; telling myself
that if you were not born on the right side, you would

perhaps not think the same; having to think: if you are a conservative, it is your advantages that you want to conserve and hand on.

Vittel, June

... In this sense one is quite right to speak of a "conversion." For just like the conversion to Catholicism, conversion to Communism implies an abdication of free inquiry, submission to a dogma, recognition of an orthodoxy. It happens that all orthodoxies are suspect to me.

The important thing, they say, is to *believe,* and all the rest shall be added unto them. After which they arrange for themselves and dress up for their purposes the teachings of the Gospel, and claim to reconcile themselves with God by recognizing that they sin, that they have sinned, that they are sinners. It is their way of being religious that makes religion hateful. It is in the name of Religion that they are fighting and this is why it is Religion that we are fighting.

But, I must admit it, what leads me to Communism is not Marx, it is the Gospel. It is the Gospel that formed me. It is the precepts of the Gospel, according to the bent they gave to my thought, to the conduct of my whole being, that inculcated in me doubt of my own value and respect of others, of their thought, of their value, and that fortified in me that disdain, that repugnance (which probably was already native) for all individual possession, for all monopolizing.

It would not be hard for me to set down the few words of Christ, to which I cannot even say that I am trying to make my conduct conform, so intimately have they become my flesh and blood; so that, if I abide by them, it is not at all as by external commands, but as by the very laws of my instinct, as by an inner necessity; so that I cannot elude them.

Vittel, 4 July

The mere idea of defending, of having to defend Christ against Communist comrades strikes me as profoundly absurd. It is against the Russian popes, the priests, etc. that I want to defend him, and to restore him to you. It is against religion that I am protesting, against the Church, dogmas, faith, etc.

But precisely because you, Communists, do not admit
the divinity of Christ, it is as a man that you must judge
him, and, consequently, you must note and admit that he
fully deserved being accused and condemned by the very
ones who are your worst enemies, by the powers against
which you rise up, by the representatives of wealth . . .
of Roman imperialism. And consequently Christ is one of
you.

14 August

It seems to me that the World Congress in preparation[10]
must pay quite special attention to honoring the young
people who refuse to take part in the game of war, English or American students, French school-teachers, "ob-
jectors" of all countries; to clearing them of that perfidious accusation of cowardice by which people try to discredit them and disqualify their conduct. It is important
to let them know, in reply to such calumnies, that we give
them our esteem, often even our admiration, knowing full
well that it requires more real courage to be opposed individually to a collective enthusiasm than to follow the
example, even if it were in order to face death; knowing
all the initiative that this personal courage involves, and
that it leads, not only to material sanctions, but also to
those, even more dreadful for some, of opinion.

It behooves this congress to propose this new form of
heroism to youth. Texts might help—such as this one
which I extract from the *"Notes"* (written under the inspiration of *Les Soirées de Saint-Pétersbourg*[11]) published
last December by the review *Esprit*. The author was
twenty-two when he wrote them, in April 1924; despite
this declaration he allowed himself to be incorporated into
the colonial infantry and was killed, the following year,
in the Rif War. Family reasons prevented giving his name,
says H. G., who hands on this posthumous message:

"Put everything at stake, risk one's life, give it on purpose for a Revolution, so that a step forward may be
taken—what is greater? But for these mad wars in which
men are sacrificed, not even to illusions, not even perhaps
expressly to the interests of a few . . . but to a sclerotic,
inhuman, soulless system that is turning in the same

[10] The World Youth Congress against Fascism and War.
[11] *The St. Petersburg Evenings* by Joseph de Maistre.

groove, that is taking a tail-spin, leading the world to some unimaginable slaughter, to some haggard and empty rage—for such wars, who will convince me of being a madman or a coward if I say: No?"

I do not hide from myself the fact that, faced with the Hitlerian threat, such declarations may seem to some particularly inopportune; on the contrary, I believe them more useful than ever at the moment when the nationalist fury of certain countries is becoming aggressive and may, through fear or emulation, lead neighboring countries into a parallel madness.

29 August

These last lines scarcely satisfy me, and I am quite aware of all that remains to be said. The question is rather: does all that the conservatives are protecting deserve to be saved?

It seems to me quite useless to reply: the best will always survive the shipwreck; for nothing seems less certain to me; and that confidence implies a mysticism that I resist elsewhere. I fear, very much on the contrary, that in this case the good may be swept away with the worst, and refuse to believe in a God who "will always recognize his own." In any adventure of this type one launches into the problematical and it is no good saying later on: "I did not intend just that"; for it is always just *that* that it was important to foresee.

It seems to me that there has not been brought out what, to say the very least, seems strange: that "mysticism" today is on the side of those who profess atheism and irreligion. It is as a religion that the Communist doctrine exalts and feeds the enthusiasm of the young of today. Their very action implies a belief; and if they transfer their ideal from heaven to earth, as I do with them, it is none the less in the name of an ideal that they struggle and, if need be, sacrifice themselves. And even, and this frightens me, that Communist religion involves, it too, a dogma, an orthodoxy, texts to which reference is made, an abdication of criticism. . . . This is too much. I very well understand the need of calling on authority and of rallying the masses to it. But here I give up; or at least, if I remain with them, it is because my very heart and reason advise me to do so and not because *"it is writ-ten . . ."* Whether the text invoked be by Marx or Lenin, I cannot abide by it unless my heart and my reason approve it. I did not escape from the authority of Aristotle or St. Paul to fall under theirs. Yet I recognize the necessity of a credo to bring together individual wills; but my adhesion to that credo has no value unless it is freely consented to. I add that, in the majority of cases, the so-called freedom of thought remains utterly illusory. And I understand very well that desire to unify thought which is today tempting Hitler, in imitation of Mussolini; but which can be achieved only at the price of what a frightful impoverishment of thought! The specific and individual value yields to some collective value or other, which ceases to have any intellectual value at all.

13 September

The case of Einstein, however, remains most peculiar; it is as a German that he refused to take up arms. If he consents to take arms today, he does so as an expatriate and to fight against his own country, the threat of which he is well qualified to judge sufficiently. We must listen to him, and also when he says that his feeling remains the same. In both of these declarations, although they seem to contradict each other, he has it in for the idea of Fatherland. (I mean the idea of Fatherland as the nationalists understand it: that form of idolatry.)

Cuverville, 27 October

I have loved Racine's lines above all other literary productions. I admire Shakespeare tremendously; but with Racine I feel an emotion that Shakespeare never gives me: that of perfection. Jean S., in a very interesting discussion, reproaches Racine's characters with not going on living once the curtain has fallen, whereas those of Shakespeare, he says very justly, appear for a moment before the footlights, but we feel that they do not end there and that we could find them again, beyond the stage. But I just happen to like that exact limitation, that nonprotruding from the frame, that sharpness of outline. Shakespeare, doubtless, is more human; but something quite different is involved here: the triumph of a sublime fitness, a delightful harmony in which everything enters in and contributes, which fully satisfies at one and the same time intelligence, heart, and senses. Man and nature, in his wind-swept plays, all poetry laughs, weeps, and vibrates in Shakespeare; Racine is at the summit of art.

5 December

"Besides, it's very simple," said that excellent lady at that excellent luncheon yesterday. . . . "Besides, it's very simple: if I didn't have servants I couldn't knit any more for the poor."

1934

Arrived the first. Came directly from Marseille. But changes at Rome and Naples, with stops of a few hours. It would be most ungracious not to recognize that Rome is splendid; more glorious, without a doubt, than yesterday; as exalting as possible. But at the same time it has lost much of that secret charm that used to fascinate me. Yesterday almost everything had to be discovered. The coals were burning under the ashes. Now everything spreads out and struts in broad daylight. What hides today, on the contrary, is poverty. Everything is clean, neat (i.e., cleaned up), sparkling. But nothing recalls Keats, or Stendhal, or Goethe.

Enforced visit (to get my ticket stamped) to the Mostra Fascista; great temporary exposition building, which would seem ridiculous, frightful, if it were not soon to be torn down, if it laid claim to permanence. Architectural journalism. In the inside, a number of rooms, very cleverly arranged, hardly exhibit anything but statistics, lists, photographs of "heroes," newspaper clippings relating the noble deeds of Fascism. An atmosphere utterly unbreathable for the work of art. But there can be no question of works here. This is the time of action; anyone who wants to can suppose that the rest will come along later.

On the other hand, Naples struck me as sordid, without charm; and the people swarming, more poverty-stricken, more ragged than ever. The alleyways all decked out with multicolored wash hung up to dry, as picturesque as ever; but I can no longer enjoy it.

I am occupying here (Villa Politi) a vast and very comfortable room; and the lure of the outside is not so great that I cannot work in it. It is a habit to be resumed; and also that of chatting with this notebook. I had let the preceding one be encumbered with social and political preoccupations that I want to banish for a time from my mind. Left in Paris that notebook, in which for weeks and months I have written nothing worth while. If only anxiety about the little time left me to live did not constantly come and stop, interrupt all impetus, I should still feel young enough, and, all together, healthier than at the time of "long projects and vast thoughts."

Yesterday I got back to *Geneviève*. Upon reading the second chapter to R. M. du G. in Marseille, ten days ago, it did not seem to me (as I feared) so bad but that I can and must continue it.

Rather irritated by the reading of *Manhattan Transfer* by Dos Passos, of which Yves Allégret had spoken so enthusiastically. Succession of images, probably exact, but so rapid that the retina cannot get enough of an impression. One retains nothing of it. And how many devices in the sense-notations! No echo; and it can lead only to despair. I find it hard to read to the end. None of these unsubstantial creatures interests me. Were they to disappear, the world would not be much impoverished. With none among them can I commit myself and become involved.

I have reread *Othello* for the sixth time, with an ever keener admiration. And it even seems to me that I was somewhat unjust in what I said of the lack of psychological novelty in Shakespeare's characters. Each of the characters, definitely in his place, lets one suspect sufficient mystery and shadowy background to feed infinite reflections. The drama is constructed between the imaginary verisimilitude and the invisible reality of sentiments. Wonderful subject, which is far from being exhausted by the action. And this is fitting.

11 February

The mystic: "You are turning your back to the light." "I do so to look at the rainbow."

I borrow this image from Goethe, whose second *Faust* I am rereading. Meanwhile I am saturating myself with Voltaire's *Contes*,[1] long and short, in the charming edition of Schiffrin,[2] and do not succeed, any more than I did before, in setting *Candide* far above all the others. I even

---

[1] The *Tales*, which include *Candide*, *Zadig*, *Micromégas*, etc.

[2] Jacques Schiffrin created the series of one-volume classics known as *Éditions de la Pléiade*, which for some time now have been published by Éditions Gallimard.

wonder if it is not to the slight naughty bits in it that *Candide* owes its remarkable fame. The satire in it often falls a bit short and in it Voltaire's laugh seems to me more a grin than elsewhere. He writes *Candide* to amuse himself; and while amusing himself he amuses. But one is aware also that he wants to prove something without one's being very well aware what, nor whom he is attacking. To show that man is innumerably unhappy on this earth, there is no need for so much wit. Religion teaches us this too; Voltaire knows this very well and at times it embarrasses him. If he were to return among us today, how upset he would be to have so little overcome many things that he either was attacking badly or else was wrong to attack; and to have played into the hands of so many fools! Goethe, if he came to life today, would find more satisfaction, or Montaigne.

Manosque, 30 March

The best thing would be to begin writing in this note-book again as naturally as if I had written in it the day before. Between old friends what is the good of excusing oneself for having gone so long without seeing one another?

That evening (I believe it would not be too hard to find the date again if only I first found my calendar), after an excellent conversation with Martin-Chauffier, at avenue Henri-Martin, I had dined at the tiny restaurant in the Place du Trocadéro where I used to go often a few years ago. I was returning home immediately afterward, somewhat melancholy and with no other plan than to go to bed at once. Place de l'Alma I was preparing to take the 19 bus when I am joined by Domi,[3] back from the Billancourt studio. He has not yet dined, but he intends to amuse himself a bit first. How joyfully I let myself be led toward the Byron in the Champs-Élysées! Both of us are enchanted by Eddie Cantor's *Roman Scandals*. And during the whole show I do not think too much of that little bite I gave to my tongue two days before, as I happen to do from time to time. (I cannot succeed in understanding how I go about it to bite myself like this; once

[3] André Gide's nephew, Dominique Drouin.

I bit so deeply that I went to the doctor, thinking he would have to sew up or finish cutting off the little piece of flesh I had half detached.) And that evening my tongue remained rather painful; I thought of it again, alone in the taxi taking me back to rue Vaneau after the show: all the same that little wound, however insignificant it may be, but repeated always in the same spot, might eventually give rise to a cancerous growth. . . . One must dare to look upon this coldly. It would begin with a sort of almost painless callus, about which I should not even dare consult the doctor; and when I should finally make up my mind, the doctor might well tell me: too late. Cancer of the tongue is well known; particularly hard to treat, particularly painful in a brief time, disagreeable for one's friends. If I were sure of it, what should I do?

No, no! I should not have to probe or question myself at length. Should I have the necessary guts?—Yes indeed. . . .

It has already occurred to me two or three times in life to envisage the possibility of suicide; but never, I believe, with so much force and clarity as that evening during the little time between the Champs-Élysées and the rue Vaneau in the taxi that dropped me at my door.

What does this gentleman want of me who is approaching me while I am paying the chauffeur?

"Monsieur Gide?"

I reply with a grunt, but he insists:

"You are Monsieur André Gide, aren't you?"

At this hour of the night in the now deserted street, what can he want of me?

"It is because," he says to me, the rumor of your suicide has been all over Paris this evening; I am a reporter on *Le Petit Journal* and, like many of my colleagues, I had come to get the details. . . ."

Thursday, 12 July

Savet played us some records of Mozart, Beethoven, and Bach. I really enjoyed only those of Bach (one of the Brandenburg Concertos, the third I believe). Beethoven struck me as heavy with rhetoric and redundancy.

Doubtless I was well advised to force myself for a long time to admire what was presented to me as admirable.

My natural penchant carried me toward Chateaubriand; I decided to prefer to him Stendhal, who taught me much more. There is no great advantage in letting oneself go too readily to one's tastes. Real education is the one that takes you into the unfamiliar. But an age comes when it is more important to assert oneself than to educate oneself. What strength he would then have who *pretended* nothing! It is time for me to dare to say everything that it is high time to dare to admit to myself.

14 July

That Russian lady thinks she has conquered me by telling me the tremendous pleasure she has got from my . . . *Symphonie inachevée!* [4] But the book of mine she prefers is my *Faux-Monnayeurs*, which she has reread so often that she almost knows it by heart. Yet from what she says of it, it appears that she is thinking of my *Caves du Vatican*. Thus fame very rarely offers an absolutely smooth bed for our vanity to lie down in.

22 July

Very interesting article by Crépet on the relations between Baudelaire and Mérimée. I did not know the latter's letter that Crépet quotes; in it Mérimée speaks of *Les Fleurs du mal* as of "a very ordinary book, in no wise dangerous, in which there are a few sparks of poetry such as one may find in a poor lad who is ignorant of life and who is fed up with it because a girl of easy virtue has deceived him." He adds that he "does not know the author but would be willing to bet he is a respectable simpleton." Crépet explains rather badly, in my opinion, the almost servilely obsequious attitude of Baudelaire in regard to Mérimée, just as in regard to Sainte-Beuve. I see in it rather that *incurable modesty* that I pointed out likewise in Dostoyevsky and that I understand only too well. Nothing more sincere, in one as in the other; whereby both were so secretly accessible to the Christian feeling despite all the resistance of their very legitimate pride. It was in the very excess of their modesty, since both were rich with that antagonism, that their pride sated itself; it never occurs to them that anything is *due them;* they beg. Each of them feels he is in dreadful need.

[4] Thinking of *The Pastoral Symphony,* she has called it *The Unfinished Symphony.*

23 *July*

These are the very doctrines of Barrès that are flourish-
ing in Germany today. I have been pointing out their
dangers for some time.[5] And it is no good saying that
Hitlerism exaggerates them to the point of absurdity or
that these doctrines, good for France, are bad for other
countries. They must necessarily lead to this as soon as
they cease to encounter a sufficient opposition, as soon as
they overcome that opposition. Barrès's followers of yesterday are ungracious not to recognize this, and have lost
all right to blame in this case what they wanted to see
happen in France. I do not even know whether or not I
was well advised to write that those doctrines could, in
their time, be useful to our country, so dangerous may
become the prejudice they inculcate. Did not Barrès likewise constitute himself the apologist of a certain expedient
justice that Hitler is preaching today? And was it not easy
to foresee that those fine theories, as soon as someone else
got hold of them, might turn against us?

Has Hitler ever promulgated anything more revolting
than what Barrès teaches his son, when speaking of his
governess: that Germans have no soul? This apparently
amounts to saying that one can kill them without scruples.
I do not want to give any importance to a paradox and
pretend not to understand what Barrès meant by that.
But, at the age he then was and however intelligent he
may have been, was little Philippe in a position to understand it? Did not such words run the risk of forcing that
young mind into revolt?—against his governess perhaps;
or against his father, which would have been much better.

24 *July*

Concern for "what people will think of it" has never
much stood in my way. Though it was often very painful
for me to sadden some for whom I had the keenest affection, I was always able to override this, judging that considerations of the heart must not sway the reason. But
here it is a question of not disappointing the hopes that
desperate creatures have laid in me. How could I fail to
take into account the sympathies that my declarations

[5] Notably in the now famous *Ermitage* review in 1897 of Barrès's
Déracinés (*The Uprooted*), later republished in *Pretexts*, and the essay
on *Nationalism and Literature* (1909).

have brought me? Yet to consider only the extremity of
my thoughts, to offer only their point, is a way of betraying those thoughts; I cannot. I hold that one always finds
a secret advantage in remaining utterly sincere were that
sincerity, in the beginning, to play into the hands of the
enemy.

In any profound confession there is more eloquence and
instruction than one might think at first. It is dishonest to
overrate oneself. Even of heroes and saints, it is useless,
it is dishonest, to reveal only the bust, to present an
affected image. Even the saints, even the boldest heroes
have known hours of weakness, of relapse, and of doubt.
The important thing is that they overcame them. The
sight of their very stumblings teaches us. There is some
encouragement for weaker men in seeing that those heroes
were, despite everything, only men, subject to the same
weaknesses as we; and, on the other hand, that in spite of
many weaknesses man can make himself a hero.

Finally, those objections, those reticences, which adversaries might bring up against me—is it not preferable
to show that I knew them by myself and that I have already replied to them? that my present conviction is not
the result of blindness? And does not that conviction come
out all the stronger because it has managed to overcome
everything that would weaken it? . . . But the point of
arrival is the only thing that matters to them, not the
slow and cautious development of the thought, which
nevertheless gives it, subsequently, its assurance.

25 July

It is good to have doubted everything afresh and to
stand on a thoroughly clean earth. But in order to start
out anew. Shall I be able to do so myself? Have I still
enough strength today? The young people who come to
me distinctly feel that I should like to delegate to them
all my powers. For a long time it can no longer be a
question of works of art. In order to listen to new, indistinct chords one must not be deafened by moans. There
is almost nothing left in me that does not sympathize.
Wherever I turn my eyes, I see nothing but distress
around me. Whoever remains contemplative today gives
evidence of an inhuman philosophy, or a monstrous blindness.

. . .

How cleverly my laziness puts forward all these fine sentiments! A flattering shelter that would be upset at once by a new burst of health.

It is not becoming to lay to virtue the weariness of old age. The table of successive renunciations would not lack eloquence, if one could get oneself to make such admissions without self-indulgence.

1 August

The young Czech Communist who comes to see me congratulates me on certain pages of *Prétextes* (*Nationalisme et littérature*, concerning Ricardo's theories[6]) which, he says, "are impregnated with a pure Marxist spirit."— So much the better! So be it! But, I beg of you, if I am a Marxist, let me be so without knowing it.

FOR A PREFACE

Companion of your solitude, young man who will read me later on, it is to you that I address myself. I should like you to derive from my writings strength, courage, and awareness; and scorn for false virtues. Do not sacrifice to idols.

2 August

I read in an article by Mauriac (*Le Temps* of 31 July), otherwise very good and well-intentioned: "Gide has written, I believe, that if he had been prevented from writing books, he would have killed himself." I never said that, and even less wrote it. Mauriac read it in a newspaper and repeats it in a newspaper, and that pretentiously absurd sentence will, thanks to the newspapers, be more read and commented upon than any of my books, as almost always happens with false quotations, which, like counterfeit coins, "drive out the good ones." New, excellent (and lamentable) example of the baneful present-day preponderance of the newspaper.

I note this out of great fear of having later on to assume paternity for that bombastic remark.

Ascona, 16 August

Wonderful hotel of the Monte Verità. Room so quiet

---

[6] The essay "Nationalism and Literature" first appeared in the *Nouvelle Revue Française* in 1909 and was reprinted in *Further Pretexts* in 1911.

that I immediately have a taste for work again. I share it
with Robert Levesque, who respects my desire for silence
and meditation. But this morning, entirely concerned with
bringing my correspondence up to date.

One is so wonderfully comfortable here that I shall not
allow myself to stay more than a few days; just time
enough to relax my nerves and to learn how to sleep again.
Ah, if only I had deserved this well-being by my work!
This is the way I want the places of rest and convalescence
in the south of the U.S.S.R. to be, this is perhaps the way
they are.

A little more light and air in my thoughts. But I dare
not yet yield to joy—which, nevertheless, would be so
natural to me here.

17 August

. . . and already my weakened senses carry a bit less
far desires that are a bit less nimble.

18 August

Am I still capable of completing a new work? I ought
not even to raise that question. But, around me and within
me, I feel so few permissions, I see so many obstacles rise
up! My self-confidence is so limited! The weight to be set
in motion seems to me in advance so heavy! My strength
so out of proportion to what I should like to undertake!
And, ahead of me, the time so short!

Yet I know from experience, and I go about repeating
to myself, that the triumph in art is achieved only through
a series of successive slight victories. Only the second-rate
is easy. I must struggle above all against this new enemy:
impatience.

Here everything bathes in a splendid azure, as at the
time of my *Nourritures*. If I did not constantly repeat to
myself (and why?) that I am old, I should barely feel
my age. Perhaps curiosity lures me somewhat less and
dawns seem to me less surprising. To the finest sunrises I
say: "Oh, let me sleep!" The world still has its charm,
but those rights over everything that I used to grant myself I am less inclined to recognize now that I know those
with whom I share them to be so few. Moreover this is not
a matter of age. I remain much more *moral* than I should
like.

13 September

Extremely (and I am almost on the point of saying: deplorably) open to sympathy, I let my mind be held in check, during the war, on a natural slope that would have taken it very far and was unable to put up any resistance (I reproach myself with it sufficiently today) to the rash enthusiasms of the friends who surrounded me at that time. At the Van Rysselberghes', in the constant company of Verhaeren, of Copeau, of Ghéon, of Schlumberger, of Vincent d'Indy, without exactly following their example, I did not have the force to protest. At least I considered it prudent to keep silent and gave all my time and almost all my thoughts to the work of the refugees with which I could busy myself without compromise. Invited to one of our dinners, my Uncle Charles Gide, who had in no way given up his freedom of thought, was amazed by the excess of our chauvinism (I say *our*, for I let myself be swept along); he could hardly risk a few reflections designed to moderate us, instantly jumped upon from all sides. "If he had gone on, I should have thrown my plate at his head," declared Ghéon immediately afterward. Must I regret not having been able, not having dared, at that time, to take a stand, to resist the influence? No, yielding to it myself allowed me to know it better and, consequently, allows me today to judge it—severely— and puts me better on my guard against it.

Cuverville, 19 September

Many newspapers have reproduced the declarations of M. Georges Bonnet on his return from the U.S.S.R. One sentence of his "travel impressions" allows me to understand better the confusion that usually arises concerning individualism. "The difficulty," says M. Bonnet, "has come from the peasants who have remained very *individualistic*. . . ." No doubt of it: Communism is against that kind of individualism and must fight it. But that bitter anti-interdependence of the peasants is but the caricature of real individualism, just as superstition is but the caricature of true religious feeling. One cannot be judged according to the other.

Obviously I suffer from the refusal of some. Yes, that obstination in refusal, the intentional lack of understanding, the hatred, is often extremely painful to me. But, on the whole, I *receive* much more than I had ever hoped. I readily convinced myself, when I was young, that I should not know any fame during my lifetime, that I should be discovered only later on, that my real readers were not yet born; on the other hand, I was absolutely certain of the value of my writings. I still have that self-confidence, that slight desire for immediate success; and the stir that some make about my name hardly does more than embarrass me. I have never longed for the success of an Anatole France, of a Barrès; the posthumous fame of Baudelaire, of Keats, of Nietzsche, of Leopardi is what I wanted, the only one that seemed to me really beautiful and worthy of envy. There is a misunderstanding in any popular acclaim (at least so long as the mass continues to be what it now is), something slightly adulterated with which I cannot be satisfied.

Obviously I suffer from the injustice of certain accusations. But were they deserved, I should suffer much more from them.

Cuverville, 1 October

I have forsaken this notebook, my mind occupied by that play (without a title yet) of which I have finished sketching out the first act.[7]

Read *La Fortune des Rougon;* reread *L'Assommoir.*[8]

I should like to write an article on Zola, in which to protest (but gently) against the present lack of appreciation of his value. I should like to bring out in it that my admiration for Zola is not recent and is in no wise inspired by my present "opinions" (simply those opinions allow me to gauge his importance better today); bring out that: barely out of school and in the midst of the Mallarmé circle, Pierre Louÿs used to recite to me, jumbled together with groups of lines from Hugo's *Le Satyre,* long passages from *La Faute de l'Abbé Mouret*[9] (among others) and inculcated in me his youthful admiration. For several years I have reread each summer several

---

[7] Probably *Robert ou l'Intérêt général* (Robert or the Common Weal), which was not published until 1944–5.

[8] *The Fortune of the Rougons* and *Assommoir* are both novels by Zola belonging to the series entitled *The Rougon-Macquarts.*

[9] *Abbé Mouret's Transgression* is another of the novels of *The Rougon-Macquarts.*

volumes of *Les Rougon-Macquart* in order to convince myself anew that Zola deserves to be placed very high— as an artist and without any concern for "tendency."

My predilection, immediately after *Germinal*, goes to *Pot-Bouille*.

Reread with the greatest advantage *Le Discours de la méthode*.[10]

[10] *Germinal* has the same title in English; both it and *Piping Hot* belong to the same series. *The Discourse on Method* is by Descartes.

1935

I feel today, seriously, painfully, that *inferiority*—of never having had to earn my bread, of never having had to work to keep body and soul together. But I have always had such a great love of work that that would probably not have diminished my happiness. Besides, that is not what I mean. But a time will come when this will be looked upon as a deficiency. There is something in it for which the richest imagination cannot provide a substitute, a certain kind of profound education that nothing, later on, can replace. A time is coming when the bourgeois will feel in a state of inferiority when compared with the mere workman. This time has already come for some.

Tangier to Fez, 23 March

If I did not constantly remind myself of my age, certainly I should scarcely be aware of it. And even repeating to myself, like a lesson one has trouble learning *by heart:* I am over sixty-five, I find it hard to convince myself and succeed only in persuading myself of this: that the space is narrow where my desires and my joy, my virtues and my will, can still hope to stretch out. They have never been more demanding.

Jef Last, who, beside me, is reading my *Nourritures terrestres,* makes me feel how wrong I was to write that I had favored "all the vices" in me. That is false; there is, in that declaration, a certain amount of defiance and bragging. For I cannot consent to call vice a penchant and tastes that were natural to me. From everything that procures an artificial intoxication, from everything that adulterates, depraves, and corrupts nature, I have always turned savagely away. And it is doubtless to this that I owe feeling younger today than I felt at twenty.

24 March

Jef Last is of the opinion that Ménalque's tale stands out as a blemish and mars my *Nourritures.* He is right. It is a bit that was added afterward; I wrote it, I recall, at Saint-Moritz, without interruption, to answer the request of Ducoté, who wanted to see me open the new series of *L'Ermitage,* of which he had just taken over the editorship.[1] It is there that this tale appeared, rather different in ethics from the already written pages of the *Nourritures,* which seemed to me too fragmentary for me to consent to release them at once. (Likewise *La Ronde de la grenade* appeared in the second number of *Le Centaure;* all the rest remained unpublished.[2])

Jef Last finds fault with Ménalque's ethics. He is right. I too disapprove of it and, even at that time, presenting it only with reservations, took care to ascribe it to someone else. This is true; but my partial disapproval remains almost imperceptible and the slight irony I thought I was putting into certain sentences ("the pictures that my knowledge of painting allowed me to acquire at a very low price") is not sufficiently marked. The figure of Ménalque is better drawn in *L'Immoraliste.* Here, in *Les Nourritures,* being confused with mine in certain regards, it might distort my intention and infringes on what remains most valuable in the work: the apology of destitution. I felt this so keenly that I tried to return to that intention in various assertions of Ménalque along the way: "my heart has remained poor," etc.—but which today strike me as comparable to those sophistries by which some rich people, who want to remain Christians, try to enlarge slightly the eye of the needle, whereby, without losing any of their wealth, to enter all the same "the kingdom of God."

28 March

. . . But the vast majority of men put up very well

---

[1] *L'Ermitage,* a monthly literary review, had existed since 1890, but it assumed new significance when Edouard Ducoté took its editorship in 1897 and secured contributors such as Claudel, Copeau, Gide, Gourmont, Jammes, etc. The *Récit de Ménalque,* later incorporated into Book IV of the *Nourritures terrestres,* appeared in the first issue under Ducoté.

[2] In *If It Die . . .* Gide tells that he wrote *The Round of the Pomegranate* "without any other pretension than a more supple obedience to the inner rhythm" at a time when he had the idea of, but had not written, *The Fruits of the Earth.* After its publication in the short-lived *Centaure,* edited by Pierre Louÿs, it too became part of Book IV.

with their poverty, do not suffer from it and are not even
aware of it. Whoever tried to shake them up and disgust
them with their sordid apathy would run the risk of playing the useless role of the agitated agitator of *Paludes*.[3]
By transferring the unrest of that book from the moral to
the social plane I believe I should only have limited it.
But it is easy to make that transfer in imagination. Fundamentally the unrest would remain the same. Fine function
to assume: that of *disseminator of unrest*.

With this so imperfect world, which could be so beautiful, shame on him who is satisfied! The *so be it*, as soon
as it favors a default, is impious.

> *Hossegor, 29 May*

Some are amazed (and, if they feel some affection for
me, are grieved) by the "confessions" they read in the
extracts from my *Journal* that were published in the
N.R.F. for May.[4] Thierry Maulnier, in *L'Action française*,
goes so far as to declare "without precedent" that recognition on the part of a writer of a dwindling of his creative faculties. It would seem, according to him, that the
vanity of writers is so great that they prefer to leave it to
critics and readers to notice this; and, in any case, if they
happen to become aware of it, they immediately take
great care to hide the horror of that realization. But to
me it just happens that that realization has nothing horrible about it; it seems to me quite natural to grow old
and I am no more ashamed of it than I should be of
disappearing. I believe that in the sincerity of an admission there is more eloquence and more to be learned than
in the cleverest pretenses of eloquence. My journal is full
of such admissions. Nothing seems to me more useless,
more absurd, than to overrate oneself; I like a portrait
if it is lifelike, not if it flatters me. Moreover I recognize
that I should perhaps not be so ready to make such admissions of weaknesses if I were quite sure that those weaknesses were to be definitive. But what somewhat reassures
me and makes me look upon them as not necessarily the

---

[3] The unnamed protagonist of Gide's *Marshlands* (1895) strives to
spread unrest and to stir his friends from their passive acceptance of a
humdrum life.

[4] Those extracts covered the dates 27 June 1932 through September
1932, ending with the notation: "Rather keep silent than complain. . . ."

result of age is that I have always known similar ones and often they were very prolonged. I believe that the simple admission I made at the time when I was suffering from them might bring some help to those who are too readily discouraged and have a tendency to think everything lost as soon as they have to put off until later on the realization of their hopes.

What a wonderful confirmation of my "proverb of hell" (it is with fine sentiments that bad literature is made) I find in Beaumarchais's *Les Deux Amis,* and even in his *Eugénie* (where there are nevertheless some charming scenes).[5]

It was not of medicine that Molière made fun, but of tradition. Let there be no mistake about it.

It is Lenin himself (and I am not putting these words into his mouth) who speaks of "the revolutionary democratic spirit . . . of early Christianity" before it had become a "state religion." If one believes Dujardin, who claims to have studied the "sacred texts" for ten years, many interpolations, in the Gospels as well as in the Epistles of St. Paul, were presumably slipped in to favor an expedient relaxing of principles.

Hossegor, 31 May

Wherever I go and whatever I do, it is always out of season. But I like it this way. Sole guest of a gloomy grand hotel (gloomy merely because it is empty) which will not begin to fill up before July. I shall be gone well before. I should like this country if only I could find someone to fall in love with; but I search the countryside in vain. . . .

At this Writers' Congress so many delegates from so many countries would still like to speak, ought to speak. But what can be done when faced with the eloquence of certain orators who go on at length? . . . to call for, it so happens, to insist upon, everyone's right to speak. The oratorical excess of a few reduces the others to silence. I am thinking in particular of that woman who represents Greece and who has been pointed out to me. I am told

[5] *The Two Friends* (1770) and *Eugénie* (1767) are both moralizing dramas written before the famous *Barber of Seville.*

that she is waiting her turn, waiting in vain. She made
the long trip, I am told, in fourth class—a painful trip,
painfully paid for by a group of workers, her comrades.
. . . It is most likely she that I see at a distance, on the
platform, in the second row, wearing a saffron-colored
peplum, seated alone. At once I approach her and, putting
into my voice all the sympathy I can:

"It is fortunate, comrade, that Greece is represented
here."

Then she, turning her beautiful face toward me and in
an undertone:

"I am India."

So that the unfortunate representative of Greece will
not even have the consolation of my remark.

. . . Judged from this angle, literature has ceased to
have any but a documentary interest.

"The only ones who should write," writes Poulaille, "are
those who have something to say." *Id est:* something to
relate. Those who have seen something.[6]

What an illusion! And how readily one feels, upon reading this or that reportage, for instance, that—however
important and passionately interesting it may be—outside
of what he has seen, the author has nothing to say to us.
The question begins precisely where Poulaille leaves off.

3 August

Cultivate the differences. . . . What misunderstanding
allows Guéhenno to reproach me with that? No need of
cultivating the rest, which will never be lost. But the
rare, the exceptional, the unique—what a loss it would be
for all if it happened to disappear! It goes without saying
that if the peculiarities are not genuine and are artificially
obtained, the game is off. One is not concerned with sham.
But man's figure deserves to be constantly enriched. Woe
to whoever attempts to reduce it! Or even merely to limit
its features. What has once taken place may repeat itself,
and any happy anomaly requires to be observed and
protected, at the risk of being reduced to the common

[6] The reference is doubtless to Henry Poulaille's *Nouvel Age littéraire* (*A New Literary Age*), a study of proletarian letters that came
out in 1930.

level of the whole. For it has everything against it, and, to begin with, opinion. Natural history, here again, can teach us, and the cautious work of experimenters. What care they lavish upon any vegetable or animal "sport," any rare variety, even though sometimes due to some accident of deficiency or disease (oh, Jean-Jacques! oh, Dostoyevsky!). Does one ever know in advance the advantage that may sometimes arise from it? What unexpected substitutions will result from a partial shortcoming?

Through anxiety, Guéhenno, to approve and espouse only the most general, most common sentiments of humanity, you impoverish it. I see that ideal figure of man with a thick common mass all haloed with individual possibilities. Is it necessary to repeat it again?—Any effort toward disindividualization in the interest of the mass is, in the last analysis, baneful to the mass itself.

What sensitive souls do not like is red. They have a horror of the shedding of blood, of shots. Let a few men find a sudden death in a fray, and they are shocked and what a row at once in the papers! They endure more easily the fact that thousands of starving people should perish, but little by little, without a sound and not too close to them. And, moreover, "the statistics are most likely exaggerated"; and *their* paper says nothing of it.

One sees come down from the mountain creatures without beauty or grace, as if hacked out of fir trees; most likely with a mentality of conifers. . . . Oh, how much more delicacy I felt in certain tribes of the Congo!

"*Reprendre du poil do la bête* (to take a hair of the animal): seek one's remedy in the very thing that caused the evil, begin over again." (Littré.)

That saying, which is overused today, is tending to get away from its original meaning. Those who use it probably think they are dealing with an image borrowed from riding and link it up with "getting back in the saddle," which probably seems to them more banal and, hence, less expressive. Yet it is the almost exact translation of the English expression: "take a hair of the dog that bit you" [7]

[7] In English in the text, followed by a literal French rendering.

—which has kept its original sense, even restricted until it is scarcely used, I believe, except for the drunkard who, on awaking, takes a drink of what made him drunk the day before.

It is good that the voice of the indigent, too long stifled, should manage to make itself heard. But I cannot consent to listen to nothing but that voice. Man does not cease to interest me when he ceases to be miserable; quite the contrary. That it is important to aid him in the beginning goes without saying, like the plant it is essential to water at first; but this is in order to get it to flower, and I am concerned with the blossom.

Nothing illustrates my thought better than this cynical and wonderfully ferocious remark of Valéry, so eloquent "in the domain of the absurd." It was a long time ago. We were young! We had mingled with the idlers who formed a circle around a troop of wretched mountebanks. It was, I recall, on the raised strip of pavement in the boulevard Saint-Germain, in front of the statue of Broca.[8] They were admiring a poor woman, thin and gaunt, in pink tights despite the cold. Her teammate had tied her, wrapped her up, skillfully from head to foot, with a rope that went around her I don't know how many times and from which, by a sort of wriggling, she was to manage to free herself. Sorry image of the fate of the masses; but no one thought of the symbol; the audience merely contemplated in stupid bliss the patient's efforts. She twisted, writhed, slowly freed one arm, then the other, and when at last the final cord fell from her, Valéry took me by the arm:

"Let's go now! *She has ceased suffering.*"

If one fails to understand the irony, the tragic beauty of this remark, it's a pity.

7 *August*

To all the outcasts, the bent under a yoke and the heavily loaded, the thirsting, the sore at heart, the aching —assurance of a compensatory afterlife! However fanciful it may be, would you dare rob them of that hope? Yes, if

---

[8] A statue of Paul Broca, professor of the medical faculty and senator (1824–80), until recently stood close to the Odéon métro station on the south side of the boulevard Saint-Germain between rue de Condé and rue Dupuytren.

it is to tell them: even "here below." Leave them eternal life, or give them revolution.

Or rather: rob them of eternal life, and you will have revolution.

I am not saying here anything that is not very banal; those of both camps are equally convinced of it, some to long for exactly what the others fear. But this is also what explains why Catholicism has so many ungodly partisans.

17 September

Finally finished the preface promised for a new edition of Henry Monnier, promised for a book of which I had had the idea.

Scarcely satisfied with these not very original pages, which caused me a lot of trouble and took considerable time.

Monnier is so little known today that I thought it timely not so much to comment upon him as to present him anew to readers. I was not able to place this sentence: "When he laughs, his laughter is mirthless. He laughs only when he is deriding."

There comes a time in life—and I believe that this time must come if one merely lives long enough—when the things one scorned in one's youth take their revenge, just as in the Greek tragedy Aphrodite or Dionysus takes revenge for Hippolytus' or Pentheus' disdain. Yes, today I am paying for my refusals of the past, of that long time when everything I knew to be transitory and belonging to politics and history seemed to me unworthy of real attention. The influence of Mallarmé urged me to this. I came under that influence without being aware of it, for it merely encouraged me in my natural tendency and I was not yet well aware, then, how important it is to beware of what flatters you and that the only real education comes from what goes counter to you.

Cuverville, 6 October

Not at all; my feelings or opinions in regard to *families* are not prompted by any resentment against mine. Here again I was favored; I have no reason to complain of *my* family; quite the contrary.

My arguments against families are, among others, the very ones that made Maurras write his little book on *Les*

Monod.[9] The family spirit is opposed to the individual as
well as to the state; because of the inheritance, the interests it arouses are almost always sordid; or more exactly,
it makes *interest* win out everywhere. It gives encouragement to a sort of favoritism and mutual aid, without care
for the real value of people. It props each one up and
drives him definitely along a path to which heredity
already directed him, and from which he can most often
get away only by a very painful effort of recovery, by a
revolt that may compromise his intellectual equilibrium
in the other direction.

But "where can one be better off than in the heart of
the family?"

To be sure! Shame on those who seek comfort ahead
of everything in life.

Maurice Lime came to see me the day before yesterday;
his work at the factory leaves him free only Saturday
afternoon or Sunday. I was happy to be able to tell him
all the good I thought of his book,[10] read very attentively
this summer. He is still a very young chap, rugged, with
an open laughing face and eyes that look straight at one.
At once I feel utterly at ease with him, and am grateful to
him for not treating me as a bourgeois, but as a comrade.
Already with Jef Last I felt that sort of sudden and violent
liking that leaps over artificial barriers and only derives
more force from the hateful social differences. In relations
among "bourgeois" there is a bit of connivance (I was
about to say: complicity), a bit of that abject feeling of
those who "have cared for the pigs together";[11] one has
the same habits and wears the same shoes. Whereas here
communion is established at once on the deepest and most
sincere basis.

[9] Beginning in 1897, Charles Maurras consistently attacked the
Monod family as a symbol of "foreign" and Protestant infiltration into
French intellectual life. His chapters entitled *"Les Monod peints par
eux-mêmes"* ("The Monods Depicted by Themselves") began appearing in 1899 in *Action française* with the subtitle: *"Histoire naturelle et
politique d'une famille de protestants étrangers dans la France con-
temporaine"* ("Natural and Political History of a Family of Foreign
Protestants in Contemporary France").

[10] *Pays conquis (Conquered Territory)*, first published in 1935.

[11] This expression, most common in the negative or interrogative,
implies the great familiarity of those who have worked together.

28 October

La Bruyère's remark about "coming too late" when "everything has been said," which is so often and too indulgently quoted [12]—makes people forget the very important paragraph 107 of *Les Jugements:*

"If the world is only to last a hundred million years, it is still in all its freshness, and has but just begun . . . what new things will spring up in arts, in sciences, in nature, and, I venture to say, even in history, which are as yet unknown to us! What discoveries will be made! What various revolutions will happen in states and empires! What ignorance must be ours, and how slight is an experience of not above six or seven thousand years!" [13]

Why is this passage never quoted? I was stopped short by it, yesterday evening.

THE REFUGEE

He rings just as I was about to go out. I have an appointment with the dentist; am already late. No one to open the door and tell him: "Monsieur is not in." I come lacing up my shoes. The refugee begins an endless story to explain to me that his case ought to interest me particularly. He takes out of a leather briefcase an album containing many signatures of celebrities, urges me to add mine; this is odious to me. When he hears me sniffle, he thinks he is showing kindness by exclaiming: "Have you a cold?" He would like to move me to pity; but I haven't the time to be stirred. "Come back another day; you see that today I cannot . . ." "I had already come yesterday." Now that he has me, he wants to take advantage; this is awkward of him; he only succeeds in irritating me; he feels this and wastes a little more time excusing himself. All the hope he had put in my advice, my help, my aid, is deflated. His voice trembles, he tries to find words. . . .

And all day long I carry about my remorse for that

---

[12] "After about seven thousand years, during which there have been men who have thought we come too late to say anything that has not been said already. The finest and most beautiful ideas on morals and manners have been swept away before our times, and nothing is left for us to gleam after the ancients and the ablest among the moderns." (Translation by Henri van Laun of *The Characters of Jean de La Bruyère.*)

[13] From the same translation.

insufficient help, for my abruptness, for my impatience. If I had only taken down the poor fellow's name and address, as I generally do. But no, no way of making up. . . .

Intolerable *moral feeling* of deficiency, of indigence (I am the indigent one in this case).

30 October

The lines of Baudelaire, exquisite among all:

> *Mainte fleur épanche à regret*
> *Son parfum doux comme un secret*
> *Dans les solitudes profondes,*[14]

which I still prefer to those of Gray which they translate so miraculously:

> *Full many a flower is born to blush unseen*
> *And waste its sweetness on the desert air*

—these lines betray a sly anthropocentrism that is charmingly naïve: it seems, according to Gray or Baudelaire, that the flower's scent and the softness of its colors have no other aim than to caress the eye or nostrils of man. Small matter if the "deepest of solitudes" in which the flower blooms is peopled by a thousand similar flowers, to whose approval it would be natural for the flower to be more sensitive than to the eying and sniffing of men—if it can be said that it is sensitive to anything. But that is just where the mystery lies: why and how does all this become, when it passes through man's senses, harmony?

He who signs R. K. in *Le Temps* of the 1st of December confuses everything in order to reduce to absurdity my remark: "The caterpillar that really wants to know itself would never become a butterfly" (to which Brunschvicg most pertinently writes me that the caterpillar does not really know itself unless it succeeds in knowing in itself even its possible metamorphosis)—I invite him to meditate on this: that the expression "I know myself"

---

[14] Many a flower regretfully
    Pours forth its perfume so secretly
    Sweet in the deepest of solitudes.

These lines are from the poem "Le Guignon" ("Bad Luck") in *Les Fleurs du mal*.

is never used except in a restrictive sense ("I know my-self: I do not . . ."), and that in a broadening sense, on the contrary, "I no longer recognized myself," which is always followed by the assertion of something or other of which one would not have thought oneself capable.

And this allows me to believe that my paradoxical sally none the less contains, despite what R. K. may say of it, a large share of truth.

No, it would be false to say that my opinions, my thoughts, have not changed, and it would be dishonest of me to claim it. But the great, the very important change is this: I had thought, until quite recently, that it was important first to change man, men, each man; and that this was where one had to begin. This is why I used to write that the ethical question was more important to me than the social question.

Today I let myself be convinced that man himself can-not change unless social conditions first urge him and help him to do so—so that attention must first be paid to them.

But attention must be paid to both.

It is also, it is in great part, the stupidity and dishonesty of the attacks against the U.S.S.R. that today make us defend her with a certain obstinacy. They, the fault-finders, will begin to approve her just when we shall cease to do so; for they will approve her compromises and concessions, which will make the others say: "You see!" but by which she will wander from the end she originally pursued. May our eyes, while continuing to focus on that end, not be led, thereby, to turn away from the U.S.S.R.

1936

When "it's not going right," I walk up and down in my room, then, somewhat through impatience, I seize almost at random a book from my shelf (not one of those books lying on my table which I am "in the course" of reading, but one of those old constant companions, which are always there, to which everything brings me back) and open it really at random. This "random chance" would make me believe in the devil or in providence, for I fall at once, almost every time, on the page, on the sentence, on the words I just happen to need to start off again. Thus it is that yesterday Browning offered me a short poem I had never yet read: "The Lost Leader," which it seemed he had written particularly for me and just for the present moment. (This is not the first time that Browning bucks me up and counsels me.) I understood that it was about Wordsworth (don't try to be smart: a note in the book told you explicitly)—who, after having been enthusiastic about the French Revolution, turned about and took sides with the defenders of "order." Not every line in the poem, the note says very fairly, can be exactly applied, moreover, to Wordsworth—who served Browning only as a pretext, his falling away only as a starting-point, for a poem; one more opportunity for Browning to depersonalize himself in order to put himself momentarily into someone else. This someone else is not Wordsworth in this case, but whoever becomes indignant over his falling away. Despite his perpetual alibis, through them, it is nevertheless Browning speaking to us here; and, particularly here, it is his voice that I recognize:

> *Shakespeare was of us, Milton was for us,*
> > *Burns, Shelley, were with us,—they watch from their graves!*
> *He alone breaks from the van and the freemen,*
> > *He alone sinks to the rear and the slaves!*
>
> *We shall march prospering,—not thro' his presence;*
> > *Songs may inspirit us,—not from his lyre;*

Deeds will be done,—while he boasts his quiescence,
  Still bidding crouch whom the rest bade aspire:
Blot out his name, then, record one lost soul more,
  One task more declined, one more footpath untrod,
One more triumph for devils and sorrow for angels,
  One wrong more to man, one more insult to God! [1]

I stop, for of the quivering emotion of this poem I feel that very little subsists in my translation. And I spoke of it only for this reason:

What an amazing anthology one could make (in which would figure for instance the page of La Bruyère I copied out recently) grouping and bringing out of all the great writings of the past the revolutionary element. It seems that school work consists in taming the classics; they appear tempered, sobered, softened, inoffensive; familiarity has dulled their sharpest weapons. They cannot be *properly* read without giving them back some of their edge.

                                                      At sea, 12 February

Flee! Inhabit for a time some abstract, hollow, and unfurnished region or other, in which to abstain from living, from judging, yet without betraying or deserting any cause.

We were to leave Marseille yesterday at four o'clock; but, because of the strikes, the loading had not been completed before night. It was during dinner that the *Canada* imperceptibly got under way.

Marcel de Coppet, now Governor-General of French West Africa, with whom I am traveling, got me a very comfortable cabin. I feel very reduced, very well-behaved. Yesterday I was still running a temperature of 100.4 degrees, and all these last few days doubted if I could leave. No curiosity; almost none; rather acquitting a sort of duty, or obligation, toward myself: the hope that, once there, I shall be grateful to myself for having gone. Yet, right up to the last moment, I hoped for the little calamity that would keep me from going and would allow me to think: "What a narrow escape!"

Remained stretched out all morning, soaking in emptiness, incapable of thinking, even of reading. At about

[1] Gide has quoted but these dozen lines of the poem in his own translation.

eleven o'clock we enter a foggy region in which the ship advances slowly, timidly, and blowing its foghorn.

At moments one even doubts whether we are still advancing; then a sort of barely perceptible pulsation gives evidence of the ship's effort.

14 February

I finish *Journée* by Claire Sainte-Soline, which, in its good parts, is in no way inferior to Marguerite Audoux. Certain dialogues with the old aunt, while the latter is seeking a justification, are excellent. Much less successful the imaginary monologues following the crime.

Read with the keenest interest almost the whole July issue of *Esprit*.

19 February

If all goes well (and the weather is radiant), we shall reach Dakar in three hours. It is eight now. I still have to shave, change, close my bags, and finish *Much Ado about Nothing*. Gave up noting day by day; I should have had to be more astonished. During the whole crossing, saw nothing alive in the sea but a paltry flying fish. A flock of sea gulls was still flying yesterday after the sun had set, and again this morning they escort us before dawn.

I have read *Billy Budd*.[2] Finished *Faust*. Considerable poetry of Goethe, in the Insel-Verlag edition that Ernst Robert Curtius gave me at Bonn in 1930. Read Colette's latest book[3] with very keen interest. There is in it much more than a literary gift: a sort of very peculiarly feminine genius and a great intelligence. What choice, what order, what happy proportions in an account apparently so unbridled! What utter tact, what courteous discretion in confidence (in the portraits of Polaire, of Jean Lorrain, of Willy above all, of "Monsieur Willy"); not a touch that fails to hit its mark and to mark itself in one's memory, sketched as at random, as if while playing, but with a subtle, accomplished art. I constantly skirted, brushed against that society that Colette depicts and that I recognize here, artificial, sophisticated, hideous, and against

---

[2] By Melville. [A.]

[3] *Mes Apprentissages*. [A.] In *My Years of Apprenticeship*, Colette tells of her marriage to Monsieur Willy and her beginning to write for his signature the now famous *Claudine* series. Some of the best episodes concern the music-hall singer Polaire, whom Willy dressed and promenaded as a "twin" of Colette.

which, most fortunately, an unconscious residue of puri-
tanism put me on guard. It does not seem to me that
Colette, despite all her superiority, was not somewhat
contaminated by it.

Saint-Louis, 8 March

Last night I had a strange dream. I had not gone to
sleep until very late in that improvised room of the Aleg
outpost, both doors of which, to get a draft, remained
open onto the vast night, giving access, together with
breaths of warm air, to a multitude of bats that wait until
morning to cling to the beams of the ceiling and go to
sleep in turn.

My dream had transported me into a large drawing-
room full of people. I was smoking a big cigar and considered this quite natural though I have not lighted a
cigar more than three times in my whole life. A lady,
whom I knew very well in my dream and yet did not
recognize, approached me to say that the odor of the cigar
bothered her. I then went to a window and, opening it,
threw my cigar out. Beneath the window lay a broad
terrace with a balustrade and, in a row along the balustrade, a few armchairs. It happened that my cigar, carelessly thrown, had fallen on one of them, and someone
pointed out to me that it was going to burn the chair.
Then, without stirring, by an effort of the will, I made
the cigar rise up and return to me like a boomerang. It
floated for some time in the air, as if hesitating, and then
bumped, with the end I had first had in my mouth and
which was still a bit damp, not exactly between my
lips, which I was opening to receive it, but against this
spot on my left cheek—just where there plopped a dropping from a bat sleeping above my head; this awakened
me. It was dawn.

Cuverville, 16 May

The annoying habit I have recently assumed of publishing numerous pages from this journal in the *N.R.F.*
(somewhat from impatience and because I was not writing
anything else) has gradually detached me from it as from
an indiscreet friend to whom nothing can be trusted without his repeating it at once. How much more abundant
my confidence would have been if it could have remained
posthumous! And even while writing this, I imagine it

already printed and calculate the reader's disapproval. At times I get to the point of thinking that the absence of echo of my writings, for a long time, allowed them everything that constituted their value. It was important to assure my words a survival that would allow them to reach future readers. I am extraordinarily embarrassed by this immediate repercussion (approbation as much as blame) which will henceforth greet everything that falls from my pen. Ah, the happy time when I was not listened to! And how well one speaks so long as one speaks in the desert! To be sure, it was certainly to be heard that I spoke, but not right away. The odes of Keats, the *Fleurs du mal,* still remain as if enveloped in that silence of their contemporaries, in which their eloquence is amplified for us.

17 May

I consequently tore up all the work done at Saint-Louis, as I had torn up the result of my work at Syracuse. I was obliged to bow to the facts: that third chapter of *Geneviève* was worth nothing. It was worse than bad: undistinguished. Useless to try to redo it; were I to spend months more on it, I should not make it any better. It is better to cut it out, leave the book unfinished, and not wear out on it my remaining fervor. The second chapter, moreover, ends in such a way as to offer a sort of possible conclusion—æsthetically at least—although precisely opposed to what I had planned. I should have liked to make Geneviève catch hold of herself after her mother's death, say to herself: "The way I take hardly matters, but only where I am heading." This was to be the beginning of the third chapter, and I strove in vain to slip this sentence into the very end of the second; it would have ruined everything. I preferred to give up.[4]

And now I take up again *L'Intérêt général,* which I had given up hope of completing successfully. I like certain scenes: the ones I wrote with the least effort and uninterruptedly. But what efforts, later on, to make the transitions! If, according to Marx, I took the working time as a measure of value, that play would certainly be my masterpiece. But this is playing with words. I just happen to be

[4] In its final state, published in 1939, *Geneviève* has but two chapters and does not contain this sentence.

reading (with great interest and advantage) the little
book by Schaeffle, *The Quintessence of Socialism* (1874),
that Marcel Drouin lent me.

✿   ✿   ✿

Paris, 3 September[5]

. . . A tremendous, a dreadful confusion. Dined with
Schiffrin, who is trying to cling to me and to find some aid
in my conversation. He speaks to me of his "disappointment" in the U.S.S.R. and of Guilloux's;[6] relates the long
conversation they had on the way back. I argue: the word
"disappointment" seems to me inexact; but I do not know
just what to suggest in its place.

We try out on Marc's phonograph some of the records
that were given me by the U.S.S.R.; but, as I very much
feared, the only one I really desired (the wonderful
chorus of Caucasian women heard in Moscow, then at
Tiflis) is not there. Probably charged with "formalism."

Marc spreads a bit more gloom over us by his story of
the exclusion (from the union) of that carpenter who
consented to help some comrades for a moment outside
the regular hours of work.

Come home very tired after having dined with Schiffrin
at the Corsican restaurant near Lipp's, I resume a little
equilibrium and serenity only by reading, before going to
sleep (i.e., before trying to), long successions of wonderful lines in *Dieu* and *La Fin de Satan*.[7]

5 September

Seen Malraux again. Clara M. receives me alone at
first. Then the three of us go to dine together (and very
well!) Place des Victoires, at a restaurant where he had
already taken me. And for two hours I am in awe before
his dazzling and staggering flow of words. (Oh! I am not
giving any pejorative meaning to this expression—which,
originally at least, did not have any. I add, however, that
it is natural that it should have taken on one—that the
auditors and victims should have given it one, out of
revenge.) As with Valéry, André Malraux's great strength

[5] Back from the trip to the U.S.S.R. [A.]
[6] On his voyage André Gide was accompanied by Jef Last, Jacques
Schiffrin, Eugène Dabit, who died at Sebastopol on the return journey,
Pierre Herbart, and Louis Guilloux.
[7] *God* and *The End of Satan* are both by Victor Hugo.

lies in caring very little whether he winds, or tires, or "drops by the wayside" whoever is listening and who has hardly any other anxiety (when I am the one listening) but to seem to be following, rather than to follow really. This is why any conversation with those two friends remains, for me at least, somewhat mortifying, and I come away rather crushed than exalted.

Shopping at the Bon Marché, where I lunched while reading the report of the Moscow trial (which the *Journal de Moscou* of 25 August gives in detail)—with an indescribable discomfort. What to think of those sixteen men under indictment accusing themselves, and each one in almost the same terms, and singing the praise of a regime and a man for the suppression of which they risked their lives?

Read at the Gallimard bookshop Pierre Naville's preface to a study by his brother Claude on me.[8] Obviously intelligent preface. But what can I think of the criticism he makes of all of my work (until my "conversion") of not letting itself be influenced by the great social events taking place at the time when I wrote that work? Type: Archimedes at Syracuse. If the great literary works of the time of Louis XIII and Louis XIV showed a reflection of the Fronde, if we heard in them an echo of the Royal Tithe, perhaps Pierre Naville would have more consideration for them; but they would have lost that superior serenity which has made them last. As for me, I hold, quite on the contrary, that when social preoccupations began to clutter my head and heart, I wrote nothing more that matters. It is not fair to say that I remained insensitive to such questions; but my position in regard to them was the only one that an artist must reasonably take and which he must strive to maintain. As for Christ's "judge not," I understand it as an artist *too*.

7 September

We are plunging into a tunnel of anguish, the end of which cannot yet be seen. Last night, before going to sleep, I read a few chapters of *L'Esprit des lois*.[9] I like

[8] *André Gide et le communisme* appeared in June 1936.
[9] Montesquieu's *Spirit of Laws*.

that style of Montesquieu's, which holds the reader's attention and forces him to read slowly.

This morning I finish an article on Dabit and dictate it
to Mme Aurousseau. I had received a visit from Louis
Gérin, to whom I "preached." He took it very well, moreover. Having gone out very late, I lunched at Lipp's,
then went to pick up Clara Malraux and take her to
Père-Lachaise. I had told Dabit's parents that I would not
be present at the burial; but I feared my absence might
be badly interpreted, that it might be taken for disdain.
. . . I did well to go. There are a great many there;
people of the lower classes especially, and, among the
literary people, nothing but friends whose grief was genuine. Very keen emotion. The father obliged me to walk
beside him, with the immediate family. The speeches by
Vaillant-Couturier and Aragon presented Dabit as an
active and convinced partisan. Aragon in particular insisted
on Dabit's complete moral satisfaction in the U.S.S.R.
. . . Alas! [10]

Returned to the N.R.F. with Gaston and Raymond Gallimard, Schiffrin, and Clara Malraux; the Paulhans had
returned separately. I go back to rue Vaneau after a long
conversation in Paulhan's office.

I am writing this out of duty. My heart is like a sponge
of melancholy, and I know not where to turn.

17 September

I had a strange dream, from which I awakened just as
it was turning into a nightmare; and this is what allows
me to recall it.

I was in a bedroom in which Paul Valéry, in bed, was
dictating as Milton used to dictate. It was clear that he
was very ill, too ill to write himself. In a corner of the
room someone, who might well have been Claude Valéry,
was taking the dictation; or at least he was supposed to
be writing; but when I looked at him, he was busy non-

[10] In his *Retouches (Afterthoughts on the U.S.S.R.)* André Gide
records that Dabit "told me more than once that he was relying on
me to speak out" and quotes an article by Pierre Herbart and a letter
by Jef Last, both of whom shared Dabit's room during the last weeks
of his life, to the same effect. Last adds: "I dare to state that the
book Gide has written was the very thing Dabit expected and demanded of him."

chalantly sharpening his pencil, while Valéry continued to utter sentences the importance of which came partly from the fact that they would perhaps be his last. And I felt fall upon me, like a command, the urgent obligation to make up for the secretary's default. I took out my fountain-pen and on a sheet of notebook paper that suddenly happened to be in my hand began to write. But there begins the nightmare. Valéry's pronunciation was more indistinct than ever; there were many words that I heard, or understood, badly; and that I did not dare ask him to repeat, in view of his great weakness.

I had already covered a half-page as best I could; and if I had awakened ealier, I should have remembered other sentences; each one in turn seemed to me of great importance, sublime. I recall only the last one, which, having awakened, as I say, I felt the need of noting at once. Here it is: "Just an AH ago, we were literary clocks." I had interrupted him, not understanding very well; and, not daring to ask him what that meant, I found it more expedient to ask him how AH should be written. He replied at once, with some impatience:

"It doesn't matter: A or AH" . . . and I then understand that he was expressing a period of time. That meant: the time required to say: *a* (or *ah!*). As for the rest, I wrote it on trust, wondering whether he had said: *pendule,* or *pendu,* or *perdu.*[11] It was, in any case, admirable.

Nice, 2 October

Have ceased to keep this notebook up to date, all the time I was at Cuverville, entirely absorbed by writing my reflections on the *U.S.S.R.*[12] Written directly and rapidly, there is much to be criticized in them. Necessity for a preface to warn the reader at the outset.

These last two evenings spent with Roger Martin du Gard. Each new encounter consolidates and deepens our friendship. I like the fact that he has adopted to such a degree Pierre Herbart and Marc, both of whom get along with him marvelously. Since he questioned us yesterday about the new laws in the U.S.S.R. regarding homosexual-

[11] The meaning would of course be very different, since *pendule* means clock, *pendu* means hanged man, and *perdu* means lost man.
[12] His *Retour de l'U.R.S.S.* (*Return from the U.S.S.R.*), which came out in French in 1936.

ity, the conversation is prolonged on this subject. We discuss the merits of that law. Does it really protect the family as it claims to do? I maintain that a libertine and debauched heterosexual can bring more trouble into a family than would a pederast. Herbart judiciously points out that the periods in which pederasty has been accepted seem in no wise to have been marked by a fall in the birth-rate.

I maintain that the man who looks upon woman exclusively as an instrument of pleasure and sees in her only a possible mistress is hardly eager to get her with child; and as I risk this (which is perhaps not so paradoxical as it may seem at first): that the married homosexual profits by having his wife occupied by pregnancy . . . Roger, with a huge laugh, exclaims that: "there is certainly not one in a thousand who ever thinks of that."

(The odd thing—but this reflection comes to me only subsequently—is that not for a moment did we envisage the question of lesbianism, which, however, might turn a woman away from maternity far more than would the homosexuality of a husband.) But if I note here, very incompletely, the gist of our conversation, which remained after all not very serious and merely skimmed a very grave subject, it is because of this reflection of this morning: Roger, for any psychological question whatsoever (and even, or especially, when functioning as a novelist), intentionally eliminates the exception, and even the minority. Whence a certain banalization of his characters. He is constantly asking himself: what takes place, in this given case, most generally? The "one in a thousand" does not claim his attention; or else it is to reduce this case to some great general law (in which, to be sure, he is right). But it is in order to discover that general law that the exception, quite on the contrary, concerns me, that it calls forth my most vigilant attention and that I consider it so instructive.

It is the taking into consideration of the exception (as I have already said) that leads to the most important discoveries: that of radium and radioactivity, for instance —or already that of the weight of air, when people deigned to notice that nature did not always "abhor a vacuum."

. . .

Volume XII of my *Œuvres complètes* has finally just appeared. From thirteen to fifteen volumes in all were foreseen. There will most likely be sixteen or seventeen. And still more if I continue to live and write. The subscribers will be, according to their mood, delighted or annoyed. The latter would have a right to protest, it seems to me, for they will find themselves committed to more than they were told to foresee. The last time I saw Malraux we discussed the problem at length and sought a solution likely to satisfy all and sundry.[13]

Meanwhile the fear of cluttering that publication, which claims to be complete, with writings of a very different nature and in a way extra-literary, often withholds my pen. If they deserve to be gathered together in turn (and the subscribers have a right to ask for them), they will have to form a sort of appendix to my strictly literary work; which the subscribers would have a right to refuse —a supplementary volume which, on the other hand, could be sold separately. This would set me at ease once more and give my pen its freedom again.[14]

[13] It was eventually decided to limit the edition to the fifteen volumes to which subscribers had committed themselves, with the possibility of later volumes, similar in format, to be sold separately. With Volume XV, moreover, substantially all of Gide's work published prior to 1932 (the date at which the publication of the *Complete Works* began) had been included—with the notable exception of *The School for Wives* and *Robert*, held over to be grouped with *Geneviève* of later date.

[14] This desire was realized when Gide allowed Mme Yvonne Davet to gather together his extra-literary writings under the ironic title of *Littérature engagée* (*Literature of Commitment*), issued in 1950.

1937

What has got into me this morning? This sudden desire *Paris, 7 May*
to write anything whatever in this notebook. . . . Simply
the night was a bit better. The preceding nights, atrocious.
I should like to slip away among the Negroes; find a
place where I could smile in freedom. The season is too
advanced, I fear, for Morocco or Dakar. I deemed it reasonable not to give myself leave until after having finished
my book. (Everything most absurd that I have done in
life has always been done in the name of "reason.") And
then I dared not get too far away from Cuverville. I took
Retouches[1] to the *N.R.F.* last Tuesday. The week has
only three work-days because of the Feast of the Ascen-
sion. Now I shall have to await the proofs. . . .

Yesterday evening I knocked about wildly from Clichy
to Pigalle, then from Pigalle to Clichy, not making up my
mind to dine before nine o'clock; then starting out again
in pursuit of adventure, of pleasure, of surprise, and
finding nothing but dullness, banality, and ugliness. Took
the métro to get home; done in; but I was counting on
fatigue to assure me a passable night; and, altogether, I
succeeded.

I had taken along *Écuador*, which, after the exquisite
quality of *La Nuit remue*, disappointed me.[2] Michaux
was still groping there; now he writes with assurance;
every word carries. But I did well to continue: from
p. 127 onward it is much better (the voyage in a native
canoe). Here and there, excellent.

What else did I want to say? Everything, now, seems
to me a repetition. . . . And that preface to Thomas
Mann's *Letter* that I promised to write![3] . . . Ah! I

[1] *Retouches à mon Retour de l'U.R.S.S.* (*Afterthoughts on the
U.S.S.R.*), which came out in 1937.

[2] Both *Ecuador* and *Night Stirs* are by the poet Henri Michaux.

[3] Thomas Mann's letter in reply to the Dean of the Faculty of
Philosophy of the University of Bonn, which had withdrawn his honorary degree, was published in French in 1937 with other essays under
the title, *Avertissement à l'Europe* (*Warning to Europe*), prefaced by
Gide; and in English (also 1937) as *An Exchange of Letters.*

should like to shout "Pax" and step out of the game. My
work-table (if I may use the expression) is not more encumbered than my brain. I should have held to my ethical
system; it was good; but receptivity was a part of it;
and now everything is upset to such a point, overturned
and mixed up, that I haven't the heart for the task of
putting everything back in place, and that, and that too.
We are entering a new era, that of confusion.

Went to meet Élisabeth Herbart at the Gare Saint-
Lazare (back from London). Nothing is more odious to
me. With my infirmity of not recognizing anyone, I drift
about, bump into anyone whatever with both heart and
head, haggard, bewildered. And naturally I missed her.
Returned home exasperated, ill.

Ecuador suddenly becomes delectable from the native
canoe on. "Although I speak more often of misfortune, I
also have a lot of little enjoyments."

Cuverville, 13 May

Faithless, I have not been able to oblige myself to keep
this notebook up to date. And yet I was counting on it to
get me *out of my indifference*.

I have given my book to the printer; I have already
received the proofs. I ought to feel liberated. I keep
repeating this to myself; but all those preoccupations of
yesterday still inhabit me and I take no interest in anything else. I cannot manage to disengage my mind. As
soon as I am not absorbed by some precise occupation, I
feel vague, wandering idly. I should like to forget everything; live for a long time among naked Negroes, people
whose language I didn't know and who didn't know who
I am; and fornicate savagely, silently, at night, with anyone whatever, on the sand. . . .

I see nothing but distress, disorder, and madness everywhere; but justice mocked, but the right betrayed, but
falsehood. And I wonder what life could still bring me
that matters. What does all this mean? What is it all
going to lead to, and the rest? Into what an absurd mess
humanity is sinking! How and where to escape?

But how beautiful the last rays were this evening, gild-
ing the beech grove! . . . Alas, for the first time I am

not associating myself with the spring! And now, those
pathetic songs of birds, in the night. . . .

14 May

I did well to write those lines, yesterday. It purged me.
This evening I feel quite reconciled with the universe
and with myself.

27 June

To feel oneself an exceptional being; I sobbed with
fright when I first made that discovery, but I had to resign
myself to it, and already I had sufficiently accepted the
exceptional not to be very much surprised when I had to
become aware of it likewise in sexual matters. No, my
surprise came rather, later on, from discovering that, in
this domain at least, the exceptional (I mean: what was
presented to me as such) was, after all, rather frequent.

The feeling of the exceptional I experienced, still quite
young, upon noting that often I did not react as others
did; as the common run of others. And try as one might
later on to humiliate oneself, to depreciate oneself, to want
to be vulgar, to refuse oneself to every distinction, to try
to melt into the mass and like it, one remains none the
less a creature apart. That feeling of differentiation the
child may feel while still very young and by turns with
sorrow, even with anguish, and very rarely with joy.

28 June

I see less well and my eyes become tired more quickly.
I hear likewise less well. I tell myself that it is probably
not bad that there should withdraw from us progressively
an earth one would have too much trouble leaving—that
one would have too much trouble leaving all at once. The
wonderful thing would be, at the same time, to get progressively nearer to . . . something else.

30 June

Nothing more useless than that thirst for education
which still torments me. If I could break with that habit
of thinking that my time is wasted as soon as I remain
unoccupied! That unrelieved recourse to the thought of
others, partly through fear of being left alone with mine,
is a form of laziness. I even come to congratulate myself
on the weakness of my eyes, which will soon refuse too
constant readings.

9 August

The need Pascal [4] has of making man despair and of
undermining his joys with the sole purpose of precipitating
his conversion, that systematic depreciation of the gratuitous, of art ("what a vanity is painting . . ."), of everything that distracts man from the necessity of death—
strikes me as much more fruitless than pleasure itself.
How much wiser seems to me Hebbel's witticism: "What
is the best thing the rat can do when caught in a trap?—
Eat the bacon."

Just as fruitless seem to me Mauriac's considerations
regarding Lawrence and what a Lady Chatterley may well
become in old age.[5] If I have any remorse today, it is indeed for not having taken better advantage of my youth.
When pleasure invited me, I used to refuse my body to
harmony; it was only much later, only too late, that I
understood what a reliable guide is desire. I used to local-
ize God in a certain suprasensual region, inaccessible or
almost, toward which I tended with an Alpinist's ambition,
and grace was not vouchsafed me.

Goethe was a great help to me, and botany. It is odd
that Catholicism, so ready to point out pride as soon as
man wanders from the teachings of the Church, does not
deign to see that same pride in resistance and refrac-
toriness to natural laws. And why not dare say, as Catholicism did for Descartes: "I cannot forgive Pascal." That he
should wail is all right; his wailings are very beautiful;
but that he should want to force us to wail; that he should
go so far as to write: "I can approve only those who,
wailing, seek," is not this enough to make one exclaim
that one approves only those who find; who find with
shouts of joy?

24 August

When one has formed a false idea of someone and that
person subsequently acts and speaks and writes in such a

[4] Whose *Pensées* Robert Levesque is reading, beside me, in the new
edition of the N.R.F. [A.]

[5] In an article entitled *"Eros,"* first published in *Le Figaro* and later
reprinted in the first volume of his *Journal*, François Mauriac asks: "In
twenty or thirty years, what will Lady Chatterley do with her game-
warden? Will they continue the same gesture until death? When
satiety comes, aged, ignoble, they will seek to feed elsewhere that lust
too skillfully exercised not to go on dominating during decrepitude. I
think of that dreadful book: *The Old Age of Lady Chatterley*."

way as to contradict that original false impression one
had formed of him, one is much more likely to accuse
him of hypocrisy than to recognize that one was mistaken
about him.

3 *September*

The great secret of Stendhal, his great shrewdness, consisted in writing *at once*. His thought charged with emotion
remains as lively, as fresh in color as the newly developed
butterfly that the collector has surprised as it was coming
out of the cocoon. Whence that element of alertness and
spontaneity, of incongruity, of suddenness and nakedness,
that always delights us anew in his style. It would seem
that his thought does not take time to put on its shoes
before beginning to run. This ought to serve as a good
example; or rather: I ought to follow his good example
more often. One is lost when one hesitates. The work of
translating, for this, does a disservice. Dealing with someone else's thought, it is important to warm it, to clothe
it, and one goes seeking the best words, the best turn of
expression; one becomes convinced that there are twenty
ways of saying anything whatever and that one of them
is preferable to all the others. One gets into that bad
habit of dissociating form from content, the emotion and
the expression of the emotion from the thought, which
ought to remain inseparable.

For instance, I should like to say just now that: "If
others wrote less, I should have more enjoyment in writing." . . . Well, I've said it! Why should I look for anything better than this sentence? It is the first one that
came to mind; it expresses my thought perfectly. But my
mind goes over it again and again, examines, criticizes it,
and tries to perform upon it that little operation of weath-
ering, of destruction, that it is better to leave to time,
which will take care of it. And in saying this I myself fall
into that fault with which I am reproaching others.

What more would I like to express? That this super-
abundance of written matter, of printed matter, stifles me
and that in Paris, where it all piles up, overflowing the
insufficient bookshelves onto tables, chairs, the floor even
and everywhere, my thought can no longer get in motion,
nor breathe. I am like Pompeii under the rain of ashes;
and do not want, by writing myself, to add to it. When

I happen at times to open one of these new books, it almost always seems to me that modicum of truth and novelty it brings would improve by being said more briefly —or might not be said at all. So that, when the desire to write seizes me, I hesitate and wonder: is it really worth saying? Have not others said it before me? Have I not already said it myself? And I keep silent.

25 October

All these young people from whom I receive letters begging encouragement or counsel do not imagine (that is their excuse) the time it takes to answer them. They imagine even less that the book they are keeping you from writing would answer them, and many others at the same time. But each of them would like an individual reply to questions that are not individual at all.

Cuverville, 30 October

What keeps me from writing now is not lassitude, it is disgust.

15 December

"The imagination imitates. It is the critical spirit that creates," said Wilde (in *Intentions*); of all Wilde's aphorisms there is none that seems more paradoxical at first and less worthy of being taken into consideration. By defending it, one runs the risk of passing for a sophist oneself. What was my astonishment, my joy, to find, most unexpectedly, this same profound and fecund truth when thumbing at random through Diderot's *Œuvres complètes* —and set forth by him almost in the same terms: "Imagination creates nothing; it *imitates*." [6] I took pleasure in quoting this sentence opposite Wilde's paradox in an article on "the forsaking of the subject in the plastic arts." This morning, opening the first number of the sumptuous review *Verve*, in which that article appears, my eyes fall at once on the sentence: "Imagination creates nothing; it *invents*." A zealous proofreader, too zealous, thought he was doing right to correct a text that was obviously faulty in his eyes.

[6] *Salon de 1767* (Assézat edition, Vol. XI, p. 131). [A.]

DETACHED PAGES

I

(Recovered Pages)

Of all the "great authors" (I can employ this term without smiling), those who have taught me the least, doubtless, are the French. And how could it be otherwise? I have them in my blood, in my brain; even before reading them, I was made of them. They are of the same stuff as I. I can learn to reason with Descartes; if I reason differently, it will seem to me that I am indulging in nonsense. But certain peoples do not reason at all, which nevertheless live. Reasonable and reasoning I am irremediably, willy-nilly; whatever I do, my mind assimilates nothing that has not first passed the toll-house of my reason. But what I want to get by, oh! without fraud, are foreign matters that my own country does not produce spontaneously.

✳

La Bruyère's "everything has been said" long benumbed France. Even today the great majority of Frenchmen believe that nothing remains but to repeat and that "the whole of man" is to *repeat* better and better, something, to be sure, of which the French acquit themselves more readily than any other people in the world and from which they draw great pride. And the worst is that La Bruyère's remark follows the direction of our race and flatters a natural disposition to the point of not allowing one to distinguish what is the native share and of making one wonder whether the Frenchman could have done much better with a different permission, listening to another counsel. No matter! I cannot keep from believing that the best education is not the one that favors one's penchants and that a somewhat vigorous nature, such as ours, finds advantage in opposition, in constraint.

Since leaving childhood behind, I have been bumping into this judgment of La Bruyère's and have never ceased rising up against it. But my protest is fed today by other much graver considerations which I want to try to set forth, though suspecting the slight welcome they can hope for in France. French through and through, I am yet speaking as a Frenchman unable to admit the discredit that France so often seems eager to deserve.

That man has made himself what he is, what pride! That a God made man, what devotion! But what matter? The important thing is that man was achieved (were it even by God) only slowly, progressively. This is what is repugnant to all religion and particularly to the Catholic religion. I read just yesterday this impertinent assertion that "a certain degree of knowledge was attained at the earliest time when man began to think" and, as an immediate corollary, obviously, that that degree "cannot be surpassed." The most terrifying thing is that this assertion is presented as "dwelling in the consciousness of every Frenchman"; the most saddening thing is that there are indeed very few Frenchmen who do not accept it. And Gourmont himself, elsewhere so perspicacious and so resolutely atheistic, maintains this disconcerting thesis: that no less genius was required to invent thread or the needle than to discover the laws of gravitation or the transmission of waves. And this, if I am willing to admit it, merely carries the problem back beyond the time when needle and thread, when man himself, were not yet invented. But Gourmont starts from this in order to try to establish a so-called law of intellectual *constancy* which would forbid man's ever having been less intelligent (I was about to write: less a *man*) than he is today; not seeing that such a claim remains irreconcilable with the doctrines of evolution that he professes; for after all, if man has always been what he now is, one is forced to admit that he issued complete from the hand of a Creator.

✳

I had rather early put myself on guard against the notions that I owed to habits inculcated by my parents, to my Protestant formation, to my country even; not at all that I had a prejudice that they were bad, but at least I intended not to readmit them until after having proved their excellence myself, after having made them appear before me, compared to others, weighing them in my critical scales and assuring myself that they rang true.

I did not become aware until much later, and even only very recently, that many of those notions—I mean of those that I had admitted after examining them—were the product, often indirect, of my social condition, of the favors of fate (which had caused me to be born in a well-off, comfortable situation, sheltered from material worries), of the society in which I had lived, to which my parents belonged, and, to state it more simply: of my *class*. This word, just a short while ago, meant very little to me. I knew men to be more or less well-to-do and, my inclination taking me toward the least favored, I had scarcely had any but poor friends—that is to say, obliged to earn their living, and often very painfully. None the less, problems of a social nature hardly interested me, and my mind deigned to take a fancy to and concern itself only with the problems that seemed to me common to all men. And doubtless I had first to recognize how bad was a form of society that guarantees the happiness of a few privileged people at the expense of the majority's poverty in order to become aware that many of those notions I had admitted and considered acceptable, over which my mind labored, had taken shape thanks to that inequality and belonged themselves to a system that seemed to me worthy to be condemned. I did not condemn those notions at the same time, for to some of them I owed my art and what constituted in my eyes my *raison d'être;* but at least they seemed to me suspect and I began to look at them askance, and especially those that flattered my class, those in which the bourgeois class could find support, comfort, and justification.

My most severe scrutiny was directed toward any notion from which I might have some advantage. I had a sort of cantankerous predilection in doing so; yes, a reverse predilection. But even this critical work, as I must recognize, remained bourgeois, and I am well aware that, less favored, I should not have been able to undertake it. This is indeed partly, I thought, why those of the working class so easily accept others' ideas; why so often (some say: always) incitement to revolution comes from the bourgeois class, even though addressed to the masses and unable to prosper without them.

There is doubtless in Rousseau's theories less paradox and madness than people enjoy saying. The unfortunate thing is that they were theories and that sometimes passion prompted them. I cannot believe that man, as he claims, is "naturally good." The taste, the need, the very sense of truth are not to be found either in children or in primitive peoples. That utopia in the past dangerously distorts any project, any prefiguration of the future. But how can one fail to admit, and precisely because they fashion man and educate him, that civilization is responsible for many a downfall, society for many a wasting away? Man is to be made, to become, and that *good man* (not "naturally good," but a product, but a work of culture and art)—the great grievance against society is for having done so little, labored so ineffectively to achieve him.

What I especially do not like in Rousseau is his esteem for ignorance. The misuse man has made of the discoveries of science is not enough to incriminate science, but man himself who misuses it.

It goes without saying; and if the fire burns us, we shall not put it out merely for that reason.

What I blame Rousseau for is speaking of "laws of nature" when it is a matter of human affairs. Natural laws cannot be modified; there is nothing that man institutes, there is nothing human, that cannot be modified—beginning (or rather: ending) with man himself.

No, it is not exactly a fashion, for fashion comes from the outside, though responding to unconscious inner demands. But I believe that the war left all minds in a semiemotional disposition particularly vulnerable to that sort of contagion. Griefs, unwontedly grave reflections, particularly all those about the brevity and basic insecurity of life, certain despairs apparently insurmountable without supernatural aid, a great need for affection, the disuse, in the ordinary humdrum, of all the heroisms that war had brought to white heat, a need for abnegation, of proving one's nobility to oneself, of serving the public welfare, and of sacrificing to higher interests embarrassing peculiarities, of enlisting—yes, all this enters in, and many other things besides. It is a state of mind or of soul that the war created. A certain friend of mine amuses himself (and I find fault with him for it) by considering our new converts as "gassed men." And what I find fault with is being amused by it; but I believe he is right to consider all these conversions as by-products of the war (including my *Numquid et tu . . . ?*). For there is not one of these converts whose mind did not contain some fissure (which a somewhat subtle and searching psychological examination always allows one to discover) through which the mystical gas could penetrate. Add to this the fact that, in this new state, each *neo* finds his advantage; and if one is quite surprised to encounter in each of them all his most shocking original shortcomings, one learns that they ceased to be shortcomings since he began offering them to the Lord; so that each of them never felt more himself, the proud man more proud since he is proud in the name of that Truth he henceforth possesses, the wrathful man since his wrath is holy, and the simpleton since he has recognized the pitfalls of intelligence and given up to his superiors the care of having thought for him. So it is for each of them. There are excellent ones among them; they were excellent in the past; they have the modesty to believe that they owe that excellence to their conversion. Those exquisite souls find their place here without admitting to themselves that, under any banner, they would have been exquisite; but I cannot judge their religion according to them; simply: that religion suits them and probably better than any other. What warns me, amazes me, is that the tree can also bear such frightful fruit. For, there is no gainsaying it, it is that tree that bears them, and in order for that tree to be able to bear such fruit, there must be something bad in its sap; and was it not You Yourself, O Lord, who taught me to judge the tree by its fruits?

II

(Summer 1937)

In the little unfinished book of Lenin, *The State and the Revolution,* which is so important and of such weight, there is a sentence that holds my attention. "Until now," he says, repeating an idea dear to Marx and Engels moreover, "there has not been a revolution that, in the long run, has not led to a strengthening of the administrative mechanism." I am quoting from memory and would not swear that these are exactly his words; but I believe I am not betraying his thought. In any case it is the very idea that his whole book develops. And in this consideration he finds encouragement to undermine more thoroughly the complex apparatus of the state. For if preceding revolutions led simply to a strengthening of the very thing they were trying to destroy, this is because those revolutions were incomplete, he thinks; they did not go far enough. That writing dates from 1917. If it is unfinished, this is because Lenin considers it more important to act than to write. He performed the complete revolution. In order to achieve it, and completely, all sacrifices were admitted. At last the revolution wins out, has won out. This was twenty years ago. And now what is the status of the U.S.S.R.? Dreadful bureaucracy, administrative mechanism has never been stronger. Never mind the "until now": that little sentence remains true and Lenin could still repeat what he wrote in 1917.

In Marx's writings I stifle. There is something lacking, some ozone or other that is essential to keep my mind breathing. Yet I have read four volumes of *Das Kapital,* patiently, assiduously, studiously; plus, from end to end, the volume of extracts very well chosen by Paul Nizan.[7]

---

[7] In 1934 had appeared a volume of selections from Marx entitled *Morceaux choisis,* with an introduction by Henri Lefebvre and Natan Guterman; the extracts representing Marx as a philosopher had been chosen by Paul Nizan and those representing him as an economist by J. Duret.

Of Engels, the *Anti-Dühring*.[8] Plus a number of writings inspired by and on the subject of Marxism. I have read all this with more constancy and care than I brought to any other study; and more effort too; with no other desire than to let myself be convinced, to yield even, and to learn. And each time I came away aching all over, my intelligence bruised as by instruments of torture. I went about repeating to myself: you must, knowing full well that I was not looking for pleasures, that having nothing to do with Marxism. But today I think that what especially bothers me here is the very theory, with everything, if not exactly irrational, at least artificial (I was about to say artful), fallacious, and inhuman it contains.

I think that a great part of Marx's prestige comes from the fact that he is difficult of access, so that Marxism involves an initiation and is generally known only through mediators. It is the Mass in Latin. When ones does not understand, one bows down. Throughout all of Marx's writings (with perhaps the sole exception of the *Communist Manifesto*—and even there . . .), his thought remains scattered, diffuse, in a nebulous state; never does it coalesce or achieve density. Aside from the two famous slogans: "Proletarians, unite," and "It is not a question of understanding the world, but of changing it" (wonderful formula), one cannot manage, from page to page and chapter to chapter, to find a sentence that stands out and isolates itself from a confused magma. And the happy reception of Marxism comes likewise from the fact that not letting itself be gripped by any such projection, its enormous mass escapes seizure, and attack, too nebulous to crumble and weather. Blows simply sink in and never seem to carry.

*

I care very little whether or not my writings conform to Marxism. That "fear of the Index" that I used to express in the past, the absurd fear of being found in error by the pure Communists, bothered me greatly and at length, to such a degree that I no longer dared write. What I am saying will seem very childish. But I don't

[8] *Herrn Eugen Dührings Umwälzung der Wissenchaft* (*Herr Eugen Dühring's Revolution in Science* (*Anti-Dühring*), by Friedrich Engels.

care. I am not interested in showing myself off to advantage, and I believe that I am most inclined to set forth my weaknesses. But now I am free of that sterilizing fear. And that fear has taught me a great deal; yes, much more than Marxism itself. The discipline I imposed on myself for three years has not been without advantage; but today I find greater advantage in liberating myself from it than in continuing to adhere to it. That plunge into Marxism allowed me to see the essential thing it lacked.

Did it require the failure of the U.S.S.R. to lead me to think thus? It is but the illustration of my blighted hope. And one first tries to tell oneself: it failed through infidelity. Then one again hears ring out the sinister words: "There has not been a revolution that has not. . . ."

Oh, how right you were to see in my coming to Communism a matter of sentiment! But how wrong you were not to understand that I was right! According to you, the only communism that matters is the one that is reached through theory. You speak as theoreticians. To be sure, theory is useful. But without warmth of heart and without love it bruises the very ones it claims to save. Let us beware of those who want to apply Communism coldly, of those who want, at whatever cost, to plow straight furrows on a curving field, of those who prefer to each man the idea they have formed of humanity.

*

It is noteworthy that certain pure theoreticians of Marxism expect, hope, demand of society, of the social state, what they in no wise begin by achieving in themselves. For the Christian, the revolution takes place within himself. I should like to be able to say: within himself first; but most often that revolution is enough for him; while the outer revolution is enough for the others. These two efforts, these two results, I should like to be complementary and believe that, often, they are rather artificially opposed.

A constant need of reconciliation torments me; it is a failing of my mind; it is perhaps a good quality of my heart. I should like to marry Heaven and Hell, *à la* Blake;[9] reduce oppositions and most often refuse to see anything but misunderstandings in the most ruinous and fatal antagonisms. "Individualism and Communism . . . how can you claim to reconcile those adversaries, even in yourself?" my friend Martin du Gard said to me laughingly. "They are water and fire." From their marriage is born steam.

What a sorry need of hatred I feel everywhere today! A need of opposing all things that ought to understand one another, complete one another, fecundate one another, join together! . . .

[9] André Gide translated Blake's *Marriage of Heaven and Hell* in 1922.

1938

Preparing an anthology of Montaigne, I am rereading *6 January*
wonderful passages in the *Essais* analogous to those in
my *Journals* published in the latest issue of the *N.R.F.*,
which made some express amazement and regret that
at sixty-seven I should already be speaking of getting
old.[1] These passages in the *Essais* were written when
Montaigne was thirty-nine.

Kaola[2]

Pleasant house in which we are camping. Everything in
it is as clean as can be, doubtless; for how can one keep
being invaded by black beetles—or cockroaches.[3] I always confuse them, like porpoises with dolphins.

Night of anguish. Went to bed early, very sleepy; but
stiflings. Stomach churning; never again take that frightful
soft and sticky meat which is called "fish" in this country.

At midnight I decide to have recourse to dial. Badly
closed tubes, which open and scatter the lozenges in my
valise. In the bathroom, where I go to get some distilled
water (but a mistake was made: the bottle contains
syrup), I surprise cockroaches in the act of copulating.
I thought they were wingless; but some (probably the
males), without taking flight, unfold enormous trembling
wings. When I am ready to go back to bed, I notice rising
above the top of the wardrobe opposite my bed the erect
head of a python, which soon becomes but an iron rod.

Got up at dawn. The main road, which passes our
veranda, becomes active: a whole nation is going to
market. Very "road to India."

[1] Gide's *Pages de Journal* (*Extracts from the Journals*) published in
the *Nouvelle Revue Française* for December 1937 covered the period
6 June—30 October 1937. *The Living Thoughts of Montaigne*
presented by André Gide was published in 1939 by Longmans, Green
& Co. in New York.

[2] Altogether concerned with the report that I was to furnish the
Committee of Inquiry which had sent me to French West Africa, I
took, during this trip, but very few personal notes. The rest has no
literary interest and does not belong here. [A.]

[3] The French has three words here: *blattes, cancrelats,* and *cafards,*
all of which mean "black beetles" or "cockroaches."

Bafoulabé

The astounding thing is not that Pabo Sissoko should be a fetishist (like every member of the three tribes of Bafoulabé)—the astounding thing is that he has not ceased to be, and a convinced fetishist, despite reading Descartes, Spinoza, Plato, etc. He talks of Frazer, Lévy-Bruhl, and refutes them. He speaks with authority and vehemence and considers that I was quite wrong to add notes in the account of my *Voyage au Congo*. My original observations were exact, he says: the rectifications according to Lévy-Bruhl are not. He negates the "prelogical" state, a pure invention of theoreticians, he says.

His great master is Fustel de Coulanges; it is toward *La Cité antique* that he turns; there it is that he finds his chief support.[4]

He knows that he himself (like all those in his family) is *also* a panther. But no connection with the criminal human panthers.

Kita, 1 and 2 February

Convince oneself once and for all that the moral value of people does not depend on their political color.

He who makes great demands upon himself is naturally inclined to make great demands on others.

X. replies alternately: "Useless to build roads; there are no products," and: "Useless to produce; there are no roads to transport the products."

11 February

Left Kankan at 5.40 a.m., our special train scheduled twenty minutes ahead of the regular train.

Reached Mamou at 5.30 p.m. I am paid military honors. The people of the administration in dress uniform, with all medals flying; in my colored shirt and khaki trousers, lamentably untidy, I remind myself of *The Government Inspector*.[5] Strive to make up for the undress of my costume by an excessive dignity in bearing.

On the road from Mamou to Dalaba, at night, we pass in the opposite direction a rather large animal that the chauffeur asserts to be a panther; for a moment it stops,

---

[4] *The Ancient City* by Fustel de Coulanges was first published in 1864; it shows the strength of religious institutions in ancient societies.
[5] Gogol's famous play.

dazzled by our headlights. Many rather big birds, with easy sweeping flight, rise up before the car, one after another; goatsuckers, I believe.

Likewise encounter with a serpent, about a yard long, on the side of the road. We are walking while the chauffeur is repairing a blowout. The serpent remains motionless; from a distance we throw stones at it. Close to, it is merely a strip of cloth.

Delaba, 18 February

I find here, probably left by mistake, a rather recent issue of *La Revue de Paris*, in which I read the wonderful pages of Valéry that are to be appended to Noulet's book.[6] Valéry has never written anything perhaps that delights me more. (I often have this impression with him.)

✿   ✿   ✿

Paris, 12 March

That contemptible comedy that we all play more or less and to which I should like to lend myself less than so many others, so that my writings find in this very refusal their chief value.

The anxiety we have for the figure we cut, for our personage, is constantly cropping out. We are showing off and are often more concerned with making a display than with living. Whoever feels observed observes himself. Yet there are some tormented by the constant anxiety of presenting a more authentic image of themselves, in closer conformity with their inner reality. There are others who make a great effort and would like to be taken at their face value, but their face value does not represent what they really are. Hypocrites? . . . Not altogether.

I had accompanied Élisabeth to the Gare de Lyon. Her train left at eight o'clock. The morning was radiant; I could not make up my mind to go back home. I went near by to pick up Robert Levesque, whom I had not seen since my return from French West Africa; invited him to go with me to the Jardin des Plantes, where I

---

[6] Valéry's fascinating *Fragments des mémoires d'un poème* ("Fragments of the Memoirs of a Poem") eventually appeared as an appendix to *Paul Valéry* by E. Noulet in 1938. This essay is a brief spiritual autobiography explaining how he abandoned, and then returned to, poetry.

wanted to see my chameleon again. Not managing to feed him, I had turned him over to the Vivarium, where he is stuffed with cockroaches for lack of flies, rather rare in this season. "Timothy," the only one of his species, cuts a very elegant figure beside two enormous chameleons from Madagascar, the color of cinders. He immediately decked himself in grass-green, spotted with black; this is his dress costume.

I feel again that extraordinary serenity which Butler said he experienced in the contemplation of big pachyderms; which I enjoy indistinctly in this place where all human activity is devoted to the study of animals and plants. Probably the way of communing with God that most satisfies me is that of the naturalists. (I do not know that of the astronomers.) It seems to me that the divinity they approach is the least subject to caution.

Chatted almost an hour with Auguste Chevalier, with great profit and pleasure.

As soon as I return to that atmosphere of the natural sciences, I tell myself again: I missed my vocation; it is a naturalist that I should have liked to be, should have been.

It is easy for a pederast to appear chaste in the eyes of a heterosexual. On the other hand, the truly chaste man is readily suspected by the homosexual of being himself merely a homosexual trying not to be and resisting himself, or ignorant of himself. Such suspicions, it must be added, are rather often founded.

Chastity more rarely follows fear, or a resolution, or a vow, than it is the mere effect of lack of appetite and, sometimes even, of distaste.

─────────────────────────── 7

Paris, 21 August
Finding myself quite alone and with almost no work to do, I decide to begin this notebook, which, for several months, I have been carrying with me from one halting-

⁷ This double ruled line, which appears without commentary in the French edition, marks the death of Mme André Gide which occurred on 17 April 1938.

place to another with the desire to write in it anything but this; but since Em. left me I have lost the taste for life and, consequently, ceased to keep a journal that could have reflected nothing but disorder, distress, and despair.

Last night my eyes fell, almost by chance, on a line of Baudelaire that it seemed to me I did not yet know. This line corresponded so curiously to my present state that it seemed to me Baudelaire had written it particularly for me and for this precise moment in my life. And yet this line owes a little of its extraordinary incantatory power to this: that it generalizes and urges us to consider as a banal law, applicable indifferently to all, what we were perhaps flattering ourselves we were alone in knowing.

> *When our heart has once its harvest reaped,*
> *Living is painful. 'Tis a secret known to all.*[8]

Moreover, this is just what the words "secret known to all" say. Baudelaire is skillful in entrusting to a few words that at first *look like nothing at all* his most profoundly painful truths.

> *I tip my urns one by one*
> *For one more drop from each.*[9]

That is Victor Hugo, but the sound of the voice is the same; the two images meet to depict a like distress, which is mine and that of any person who feels the ground, on which his confident foot trod, now yielding.

Since she has ceased to exist, I have merely pretended to live, without taking any further interest in anything or in myself, without appetite, without taste, or curiosity, or desire, and in a disenchanted universe; with no further hope than to leave it.

All the work of my mind, these recent months, was a

---

[8] The lines:

> Quand notre cœur a fait une fois sa vendange,
> Vivre est un mal. C'est un secret de tous connu

are from "Semper Eadem" in *Les Fleurs du mal.*

[9] The lines:

> Je penche tour à tour mes urnes pour avoir
> De chacune une goutte encore

are from the poem "Paroles sur la dune" ("Words on the Dune") in *Les Contemplations.*

work of negation. And not only did I put my value in the past, but that past value seemed to me imaginary and not worth the least effort to recapture it. I was, I still am, like someone sinking into a stinking morass, looking all around him for anything whatever that is fixed and solid of which to catch hold, but dragging with him and pulling into that muddy inferno everything he clutches. What is the good of speaking of that? Unless, perhaps, so that someone else, desperate like me, will feel less alone in his distress when he reads me; I should like to hold out a helping hand to him.

Shall I get out of this quagmire? I have already gone through periods of opprobrium when the apostle's cry sprang to my heart: "Lord, save us: we perish!" And I even know how to utter this cry in Greek. For it did not seem to me that any salvation was possible without some supernatural intervention. And yet I got out of it. But I was younger. What does life still hold in store for me?

I cling to this notebook, as I have often done: as a system. A system that used to work. The effort attempted in this way seems to me comparable to that of Baron Munchausen tearing himself from the morass by pulling himself by the hair. (I must already have had recourse to this image.[10]) The wonderful thing is that he manages to do so.

23 August

I have again been interrupted. It was Maurice Saillet who, as we had agreed by telephone, came to pick me up at seven o'clock. I had gone after him, around noon, at Adrienne Monnier's, for she has entrusted her shop to him and lent him her apartment.[11] Saillet deserves that kindness. I found him beaming. He has an almost too handsome face and an extraordinary distinction of manner, which does not fit with his hoarse, almost grating voice, which makes one think of the worst "doubled" films. I remain chatting with him very pleasantly for almost an hour; then he accompanies me to the door of the *Mercure de France,* where I greatly enjoy seeing Léautaud again.

[10] No earlier use of the image can be found.
[11] Mlle Monnier's excellent bookshop on the rue de l'Odéon was called La Maison des Amis des Livres. It was first opened in 1917 and was long a center of cultural life.

I believe that after a short time I should manage to be quite natural with him. But I am still too anxious to agree with everything he says in order to put him more at ease and to get from him those vast bursts of very sonorous laughter, which, as he hinted, do not spring from a very gay heart. Launched into the subject of the presumptuousness of the young of today, he is inexhaustible and relates amusingly and with self-satisfaction some very spicy anecdotes.

We agree that "in our time"—that is, when we were young—we should never have had the "nerve" to disturb our elders in order to make them read our awkward literary attempts and to beg of them advice, which, moreover, we were not at all inclined to follow. Léautaud is sinking into a sort of most delightful *subjective absolute*. He is particularly intractable in matters of language, refusing to admit sins against grammar. A girl came, last year, to his office (he tells the story), eager to consult the old collections of the *Mercure*. They are arranged on shelves. And when she saw them: "I didn't realize," she exclaimed, "that they took so much space!" Whereupon Léautaud: "Mademoiselle, we are accustomed to receive here only people who speak French." [12] And he goes on with an enormous laugh and in his fine, sonorous voice.

"But can you imagine that hussy who doesn't *realize!* . . . For several months I accepted being a 'reader.' It was Duhamel who had begged me to be. But I couldn't put up with it very long. Reading mediocre manuscripts —I don't know of any more maddening task! Besides, it went rather fast. At the first mistake in French—well, for instance, when I encountered an *aimer de . . . j'aimais de regarder . . . elle aimait de se promener . . .* in the wastebasket!" [13]

However great may be his admiration for Valéry (we are speaking in particular of his so remarkable and quite recent essay on the notion of *liberty*[14]), encountering an

---

[12] The verb *réaliser* strictly means "to make real," though it is coming more and more to have the sense of "to be aware."

[13] The verb *aimer* should strictly be followed by the infinitive directly, but the *de* is becoming more frequent in speech.

[14] "Fluctuations on Liberty" (1938) was included in the 1945 edition of *Regards sur le monde actuel* and hence in the American edition (*Reflections on the World Today*).

aimer de makes him stop reading. I wonder if perhaps he has not, in my writings too, stumbled on that expression, which I do not find so detestable and of which one could find some examples even in our best writers.

25 *August*

At Cuverville since yesterday evening. I am rereading, hoping to take advantage of the impetus, some of the pages written these last few days; but they strike me as so woolly that I wonder if I am to continue. Jean Hytier's book on me,[15] which I discover at the Gallimard bookshop (for, out of discretion doubtless, he did not send it to me and I was ignorant of its existence), had somewhat instilled new life in me. I think that nothing better has been written on my work and I like the fact that, following the recommendation of a sentence from my *Journal* that he uses as an epigraph, he takes, to judge that work, an æsthetic point of view. Yes, that book comforted me . . . would have comforted me: for what remains to me today of what constituted my value?

26th *in the evening*

What does not seem to me quite fair, on the other hand, is holding my grief responsible for my languid condition; it is my grief that led me to it; it is not especially that which keeps me in it. And I am probably not in very good faith when I convince myself of it. I find in it a too easy excuse for my cowardice, a cover for my laziness. I was expecting that grief, I foresaw it for a long time, and yet I imagined my old age, in spite of grief, only as smiling. If I cannot succeed in attaining serenity again, my philosophy is bankrupt. To be sure, I have lost that "witness of my life" who committed me not to live "negligently" as Pliny said to Montaigne, and I do not share Em.'s belief in an afterlife which would lead me to feel her eyes upon me beyond death; but, just as I did not allow her love, during her life, to influence my thought in her direction, I must not, now that she is no longer, let weigh upon my thought, more than her love itself, the memory of that love. The last act of the comedy is no less good because I must play it alone. I must not sidestep it.

[15] *André Gide*, published in Algiers in 1938 and reissued in Paris in 1945.

5 *September*

A succession of splendid days; a pure, radiant sky; as soon as it rises, the sun spreads an opulent felicity over the fields even though the harvests have been gathered; it seems that everything that breathes ought to feel happy. And, faced with this display of beauty, my heart remains indifferent, almost hostile. Since she has no longer been here, invitations to happiness are an intrusion upon me. What serenity in the azure! What divine indifference to the infinite misery of man!

Free at last and with no tie left, like a kite with the string suddenly cut, I toppled over, diving soul-first toward the ground, where I crashed.

Braffy, 13 September

Listened to Hitler's Nuremberg speech on the radio. The call to arms permits a facile eloquence, and it is easier to lead men to combat and to stir up their passions than to temper them and urge them to the patient labors of peace. The flattery springs from this: that the affirmation of strength contains a permission of stupidity.

If I have written nothing further in this notebook for several days, it is partly because I have got back to work. Schiffrin came, and during the fortnight he spent with us, I went over with him the proofs of my *Journal*. With Marcel [16] I spent from two to four hours each day going over in detail my translation of *Antony and Cleopatra*. The considerable improvements we made in it have made me feel my first version to be very defective; but I believe it almost excellent now. At a distance of ten years it would perhaps appear to me full of imperfections; not of errors; that does not seem to me possible, for we not only examined at great length all the doubtful passages in the text but also read patiently and meditated over the numerous explanatory annotations of the commentators in the excellent edition by R. H. Case that gathers them together. Nothing was better designed than this work to renew my enjoyment in living. Marcel likewise, who obviously took very great pleasure in it. Our understanding was complete, as in the early years. The proof pages became covered with changes, and numerous passages had so much written between the lines as to become almost

[16] Marcel Drouin.

incomprehensible for the printer. Schiffrin would then transcribe them with tireless care and patience. The work was finished the eve of my departure for Braffy.

22 September

Yesterday evening I finished rereading the first two hundred proof pages of my *Journal* for the Pléiade edition.[17] Now I can turn altogether to the preface for Shakespeare:[18] It bores me and I shall say nothing worth while in it; yes, nothing worth the trouble of saying. Chores! chores! but they are better than the idleness that I do not yet know how to turn to contemplation.

Finished also *Les Jeunes Filles en fleurs* (which I notice that I had never read completely) with an uncertain mixture of admiration and irritation.[19] Though a few sentences (and, in spots, very numerous ones) are insufferably badly written, Proust always says precisely what he wants to say. And it is because he succeeds so well in doing so that he delights in it. So much subtlety is, at times, utterly useless; he merely yields to a finicky need of analysis. But often that analysis leads him to extraordinary discoveries. Then I read him with rapture. I even like the fact that the point of his scalpel attacks everything that offers itself to his mind, to his memory; to everything and to anything whatever. If there is waste here, it's just too bad! What matters is not so much the result of the analysis as the method. Often one follows attentively, not so much the matter on which he is operating, as the minute work of the instrument and the slow patience of his operation. But it constantly appears to me that if the true work of art cannot do without that preliminary operation, it really begins only with that accomplished. The work of art presupposes it, to be sure, but rises up only after that original operation has ended. The architecture in Proust is very beautiful; but it often happens, since he removes none of the scaffolding, that the

[17] That edition first appeared in the summer of 1939.

[18] Gide was to write the foreword for the edition of Shakespeare's *Complete Plays* (translated by various hands) to be published in the Pléiade collection.

[19] *A l'ombre des jeunes filles en fleurs* (*Within a Budding Grove* in the Scott Moncrieff translation), which first appeared in 1918 and won the Goncourt Prize, is the second part of Marcel Proust's great work, *Remembrance of Things Past*.

latter assumes more importance than the monument itself, in which one's glance, constantly distracted by the detail, does not succeed in grasping the whole. Proust knew this, and this is what made him, in his letters and in his conversation, insist so much on the general composition of his work: he was well aware that it would not be obvious.

7 October

I always have to make an effort to get back to this notebook after I have forsaken it for some time. Since the 22nd of September we have lived through days of anguish[20] and "people" might be surprised not to find any echo of them here. But whoever concluded from my silence that I was indifferent to "public affairs" would be greatly mistaken. Merely the reflections I felt able to make hardly seemed to me in their place in this notebook; and if I ceased to write anything in it during all that time, this is because they filled my whole mind. Even though the events of history seem to me to escape at one and the same time both the will and the foresight of men, it seemed to me that reason (if not justice and right) was winning a victory over force; but I am not so convinced of this that I was not considerably shaken in my optimism by the admirable letter Jef Last wrote me. He is willing to see in the Munich conversations nothing but a shameful defeat, which can only result in a new strengthening of Hitler and new claims; for us, nothing but new withdrawals and with dishonor. Would Germany have yielded to a firmer attitude, or at least to a less tardy firmness? Would a war have ensured the triumph of justice? or merely that of brute force?

8 October

Anniversary, today, of my marriage.[21] A day that I made a great point of spending with her, occasionally rushing back from a great distance. During these recent days of anguish I got to the point of ceasing to be sad that she is no longer here; she could not have endured all this. . . .

I am becoming gradually accustomed to the idea of

[20] The Munich crisis.
[21] André Gide and Madeleine Rondeaux were married on 8 October 1895.

having to live without her; but, without her, I am no longer interested in my life.

25 October

Yesterday at the Valérys'; exquisite and charming luncheon. I feel much more at ease with Paul since I have learned to limit the havoc wrought by his conversation. His extraordinary intelligence gives him, more than anyone else, a right to scorn. I know, better than in the past, how to get around his crushing superiority. Or, more exactly, I pay less attention to some of his annihilating statements and the fact that he recognizes no value in what is not quoted on his market. Moreover, there are many of his scornings that I share; but if I had to limit my approbations to his, I should feel too impoverished.

I accompany him to the radio council and sit beside him, around the green table. The name of the *Iliad* having been pronounced, Paul leans toward me and in a low voice:

"Do you know anything more boring than the *Iliad*?"

Dominating a sudden protest, I find it more . . . friendly to reply:

"Yes, the *Chanson de Roland*," which makes him agree at once.

Valéry's system involves a sort of austerity (and this is what makes him so admirable in my eyes) and renunciation of which I do not feel at all capable.

I cannot involve the whole world in my grief. Everything goes on *as if nothing had happened*—and I too, as if nothing in my life had been changed. This is partly because everything she represented for me subsists untouched by her death. She was a direction of my heart; and already during her lifetime her voice, at times, seemed to me to come from a great distance.

4 December

For lack of a productive work, which the broken-up life of Paris does not permit, I am wearing out my impatience by going over the proofs of my *Journal* for the Pléiade collection.

In spots I should like to add notes. Thus I read under date of 22 August 1930: "That self-indulgence to which

love invites us, drawing from us not the best but what is
most likely to please the other; you do not so much raise
him as he debases you. . . ."

I maintain that reflection which, in the great majority
of cases, alas, seems to me fair. But I protest that I was
not thinking of myself when writing it; it was but the best
of me that I could offer to Em., and if at times I felt
quite hampered by my love, that illusion came from the
fact that the least good occupied a great deal of place
in me.

23 December

No, no . . . it is with her that I had begun the game.
Since she has withdrawn from it, I am no longer capable;
I have lost interest in the great game of life and long
to withdraw in turn.

In that October issue of the *N.R.F.*, in the midst of
one of the most successful portraits by Suarès, I bump into
this stupefying sentence: "Gabriele d'Annunzio is the
greatest writer of Italy for at least the last three hundred
years." And what of Leopardi? My astonishment was
communicated to Suarès; and in the January issue, of
which I have just received the last proofs, he makes up
for it as best he can; as he had made up, in the past,
for Dostoyevsky. He was "holding him in reserve," it
seems. And this time: "What do you say of Leopardi?" "I
am not saying anything about him: I am keeping him."
For Suarès never admits that he has made a mistake; that
is utterly incompatible with his ideas of "greatness," of
his greatness.

Rather than confess that he had forgotten Leopardi,
or that he didn't know him, he prefers to explain that,
for him, Leopardi remains outside of Italian literature
since it never knew how to take death or suffering seriously
. . . so that, in order to save his stake, he now sacrifices
Dante to his vanity.

What bothers me in Suarès is not at all the error in
judgment, the failure to appreciate or the forgetting, to
which we are all subject, involving on his part return,
rectification, and retraction—as it happened for him in
regard to Goethe, to Nietzsche, to Dostoyevsky, to Leopardi, and as it will soon happen, I hope, in regard to

Chopin. What bothers me is the need of hiding that initial stumble and, by advantageously camouflaging the past, passing off the clever recovery of a supple mind for a congenital infallibility. What pettiness I see in that constant regard for his figure, in those affectations, that manner of dressing, that fear of being caught in undress, in a natural state! . . . What is the use? In the past I somewhat frequented Suarès. He has a charming nature and I have never found him greater than when he was least preoccupied to seem so.

But he will take what I am saying as an insult, as a black and sly perfidy. It is not so much that he is susceptible, touchy; but he strives for an isolation that helps him to think himself incomparable. Being great does not suffice him; he likes himself only when superior.

And yet how well he spoke of Stendhal, in Milan, on the steps of the Scala, dapper and trim, but always shedding some of his trimness, and all the more charming as a result!

25 December

I enjoy all the more chatting with Roger Martin du Gard as I enjoy less and less chatting with others. Each new conversation with him is added to the vast ensemble of a conversation begun long ago, interrupted, resumed, and, after all, always the same, just as my perpetual mute dialogue with Em. was always the same. And, just as with Em., Roger and I are constantly of the same opinion. Conversation does not oppose us; it teaches, warns, and enlightens us. It is, for me at least, extraordinarily enriching and profitable, and (perhaps I should say: above all) I enjoy it.

1939

7 January

Do you think of making the most of (but have you merely noticed?) the repeated weak beats of the third, at the height of the accompaniment of the Nocturne in D flat (op. 27)? Have you noticed that they fall contra-tempo in exactly the same way as the double beats of the dominant in the slow part (in major), so extraordinarily *nocturnal* likewise, and so ecstatically beautiful, of the Scherzo in B minor?[1] Make it be like that drop of crystal which the tree-frog (or the toad perhaps) drops into the heart of the purest summer nights. Did Chopin think of it himself? . . . In any case, Paderewski did when he played the piece. On that crystalline note, at once detached from all the rest and melting into it, the whole landscape was suspended.

And, in both pieces similarly, as if lifted by ecstasy, it rises eventually (in the Nocturne a half-key and in the Scherzo a whole key), to fall back soon after, swooning with an excess of joy.

I had got to the point of playing that Nocturne very well; one of those that are most susceptible to misinter-pretation. Anyway, it is not one of those I prefer. . . . When I think of the farewell I said to music,

My heart almost bursts[2]

and it does not seem to me that death can take anything from me, now, that has meant more to me.

Marseille, 26 January

Before leaving Paris, I was able to finish going over the proofs of my *Journal*. Upon rereading it, it seems to me that the systematic suppression (at least until my loss) of all the passages relative to Em. have, so to speak, *blinded* it. The few allusions to the secret drama of my

---

[1] Both works are by Chopin.

[2] The line *A peu que le cueur ne me fend*, which Gide quotes here, appears early in François Villon's *Testament*, where the poet is lament-ing his lost youth.

life become incomprehensible through the absence of what would throw light on them; incomprehensible or inadmissible, the image of this mutilated me that I give there, which presents, in the ardent place of the heart, but a hole.

Obsessed by the thought of Spain's atrocious agony.

For a long time I have not traveled alone. I needed a younger companion, a pacer; I used to espouse his joy. Will this solitude that I am imposing on myself today urge me toward work? or rather toward despair? . . . I no longer have that intrepid curiosity which used to launch me into adventure, nor that desire and need of scaling or of rounding mountains and capes to see what is hidden on the other side. I have seen the sinister reverse of too many things. . . .

I am taking with me but few books:

Joseph in Egypt by Thomas Mann;

Dichtung und Wahrheit;

Les Chroniqueurs du moyen âge in the Pléiade collection;

Les Pages choisies of Claude Bernard;

a La Fontaine, and

The Birth of Philosophy by Nietzsche[3] in the recently published translation by Geneviève Bianquis—which I was reading yesterday in the train and have just finished in Marseille. I copy from it: "The greatest loss to touch humanity is the miscarriage of superior types." In a manner of speaking, for the saddest thing, it so happens, is that humanity is not *touched* by it.

Probably I shall go and meet Robert Levesque in Greece during the Easter vacation. Nothing recalls me to Paris before May. Here I am free, as I have never been; frightfully free, shall I still be able to "try to live"? . . .[4]

[3] The titles of Mann's novel and Nietzsche's work are given in French, whereas Goethe's *Truth and Poetry* is in German. *The Medieval Chroniclers* in the Pléiade edition was edited by Albert Pauphilet and, like the *Selections* from Claude Bernard, had recently appeared.

[4] The last words are from a line in the final stanza of Paul Valéry's "Le Cimetière marin" ("The Cemetery by the Sea"), a poem opposing contemplation and action:

> Le vent se lève! . . . il faut tenter de vivre!
>
> (The wind is rising! . . . one must try to live!)

10 September

Yes, all that might well disappear, that cultural effort which seemed to us wonderful (and I am not speaking merely of the French effort). At the rate at which we are going, there will soon not be many to feel the need of it, to understand it; not many left to notice that it is no longer understood.

One strives and strains one's ingenuity to shelter those treasures from destruction; no shelter is safe. A bomb can do away with a museum. There is no acropolis that the flood of barbarianism cannot reach, no ark that it cannot eventually sink.

One clings to wreckage.

11 September

My body is not so worn out that life with it has ceased to be bearable. But as for giving a reason, an aim to one's life . . . Everything is suspended in uncertainty.

War is here. In order to escape its obsession, I am going over and learning long passages of *Phèdre* and of *Athalie*. I am reading *The Atheist's Tragedy* of Cyril Tourneur and Eichendorff's *Taugenichts*.[5] But the oil lamp throws a poor light; I must close the book and my mind returns to its anguish, to its interrogation: Is this the twilight or the dawn?

19 September

I doubt if I have ever enjoyed more propitious conditions. But my mind is open only to anguish. I do not even try to escape the preoccupations besieging us. In this dreadful struggle now beginning, everything for which we live is at stake, and the sacrifice of those dearest to us may not be able to save those values. One would like to put them in safekeeping, like the stained-glass windows of the churches; but those very precautions isolate and detach them from life; they are beginning to become like objects in museums, which will perhaps survive the catastrophe, to be found later on with amazement.

I have forsaken Racine, these last few days, for La Fontaine and learned by heart again some ten of the

---

[5] *The Atheist's Tragedy* first appeared in 1611. *Aus dem Leben eines Taugenichts* (*The Happy-Go-Lucky*, or *Leaves from the Life of a Good-for-Nothing*) by the German romantic poet Joseph von Eichendorff dates from 1826.

fables. La Fontaine's perfection is more subtle but no less exigent than Racine's; it fills less space with an apparently more negligent art; but one has only to give it sufficient attention: the touch is so discreet that it might go unnoticed. Nothing is farther from the romantic insistence. It goes on at once, and if you have not understood, that's just too bad. It is impossible to imagine a more discreet, apparently less intentional art. To such a degree that one wonders if one is not sometimes adding to it, if La Fontaine is really conscious himself, in certain lines or expressions, of all the emotion they contain; one is also aware of an element of cunning and that one must enter into the spirit of the game at the risk of not altogether understanding him; for he takes nothing seriously. Oh, how far we are from the war with him!

Everything in his behavior seemed to say: since he has ceased to love me, nothing matters to me. But I still loved him and, indeed, I had never loved him so much; but it was no longer possible for me to prove it to him. That was by far the worst of it.

30 October

No, decidedly, I shall not speak on the radio. I shall not contribute to pumping oxygen into the public. The newspapers already contain enough patriotic yappings. The more French I feel, the more loath I am to let my mind be warped. If it regimented itself, it would lose all value.

I doubt that it is very fair to write, as Lucien Jacques did in 1914 or 1915, about certain particularly ridiculous utterances: "Is it so hard to keep silent?" and am aware how painful silence is when one's heart is overflowing; but I do not want to have to blush tomorrow for what I should write today. Yet if I keep silent, this is not because of pride; I am almost inclined to say that it is because of modesty and even more of uncertainty. I may be, and I often am, in agreement with the majority; but the approval of the majority cannot become in my eyes a proof of truth. My thought does not have to follow the fashion, and if I do not think it more valuable from the mere fact that it is different and isolated and separate, at least it is when it differs that it seems to me most useful to express it. Not that I take pleasure in that difference, having otherwise great trouble in doing without agreement, and not that the thoughts seem to me less important when widely shared; but it is less important then to express them.

It is by insisting upon the value of the particular, it is by its force of individualization, that France can best and must oppose the forced unification of Hitlerism. To-day, however, it is essential to meet one united front with another, and, consequently, to enter the ranks and be a part of the unit. Temporarily, it is said. . . . Let us hope so. Moreover, isolated voices can no longer make themselves heard today. My unseasonable thoughts, until better times, I will store up in this notebook.

Are my thoughts, then, so very different—and so often so today—from those of others? Perhaps not. But in that case why should I express in an undertone what others excel in shouting? As soon as I do not differ, I keep silent. It is partly because I am definitely aware only of my differences, whereas I am no longer sure of anything as soon as I am in agreement.

1940

1 January

Of all these streets, tell us why
You chose the darkest of all?
And why you always try
To stay in the shade of the wall? [1]

7 *February*

One must expect that after the war, and even though victors, we shall plunge into such a mess that nothing but a determined dictatorship will be able to get us out of it. One can see the soundest minds gradually progressing in that direction (if I am to judge from myself, as the fellow says), and many insignificant facts, one little decision after another, which taken singly seem absolutely wise and altogether unavoidable, are progressively accustoming us to that idea.

. . . So that one could guess their opinions merely by knowing to what they are insensitive. It is easy to remain a conservative when one is well taken care of oneself and but little touched by the misfortune of others.

Their mind moves in a dry world, boiled down like a problem. At first I tried to believe that they were urged to Communism by a tormenting love for our brothers; I was not able to mislead myself for long. Then I tried to believe that those dry, insensitive, abstract creatures were bad Communists, that they were doing a disservice to a noble cause, and I refused to judge the cause according to them. But no, I was mistaken altogether, from top to bottom. The real Communists, as I was told, as it was proved to me, were they. They were following the line exactly; and it was I who was wrong by introducing the heart, with which they had no concern, and grounds of judgment they claimed to do without. And first of all when I claimed

---

[1] *Dis ce qui, de toutes ces rues,*
T'aura fait choisir la plus sombre?
Pourquoi toujours tu t'évertues
A rester du côté de l'ombre?

to preserve through Communism my individuality, my individualism. There could and must be no question but of equality, of justice. The rest (and it was that remainder that especially mattered to me) belonged to Christianity. And slowly I came to the conviction that when I thought myself a Communist, I was a Christian, if it may be that one can be a Christian without "believing," if Catholicism as well as Protestantism did not put above everything else and as a condition *sine qua non:* Faith. So that, with either one side or the other, I could not and would not come to terms. It's a pity: were it not for that damned question of belief which unfailingly makes my reason bristle, I should get along well enough with the latter, at least as to the virtues they advocate, but which very often they convince themselves that Faith allows them to do without.

Anything I buy at the expense of others I cannot enjoy.

In increasing that of others lies my greatest joy.

15 February

I should have been quite capable of being "converted" at the last moment—I mean at the hour of death, in order not to cause her too much suffering.

And this is what made me long rather to die at a distance, in some accident or other, of a sudden death, far from my family, as Montaigne likewise wished to do, without any witnesses ready to attach to those last moments an importance that I refused to grant them. Yes, without any other witnesses but chance and anonymous ones.

18 May

Admirable night. Everything swoons and seems to be enraptured in the light of an almost full moon. The roses and acacias mingle their scents. The undergrowth sparkles with fireflies. I think of all those for whom this so beautiful night is the last and I should like to be able to pray for them. But I have ceased even to understand very well what the words "pray for someone" mean; or rather, I know that they can no longer mean anything for me. They are words that I have carefully emptied of all meaning. But my heart is filled with love.

· · ·

Through a sense of decency I am concerned in this notebook only with what has nothing to do with the war; and this is why I go for so many days without writing anything in it. Those are the days on which I have not been able to rid myself of the anguish, not been able to think of anything but *that*.

21 May

How hard I find it to tell myself that there are things I am no longer of an age to do and that I should do better not to try!

Or at least I tell this to myself all right, but without convincing myself. So that, after all, I do those things none the less; but afterward I am almost done in.

I am writing this seated on the edge of a road above Vence, on my way back frome a dangerous climb, tiring because there was no path, through undergrowth that became thicker and thicker as I approach the summit, which is constantly withdrawing and which, eventually, I give up reaching.

Great effort without any reward other than the satisfaction of my vanity (for the landscape from the top was much less beautiful than I had a right to expect from my trouble) and the joy I take in new plants: a small spurge forming a cluster close to the ground, which I believe I had never seen before; a geranium with very broad purplish-red flowers; a little member of the lily family similar to asphodels. . . . A bit lower down, the poppy-red cistus dotted the moor, and occasionally, rising from among the rocks, robust valerians. Not a butterfly.

O incurably frivolous people of France! You are going to pay dearly today for your lack of application, your heedlessness, your smug reclining among so many charming virtues!

25 May

That systematic disindividualization toward which Hitlerism strove prepared Germany wonderfully for war. And that is especially the point, it seems to me, on which Hitlerism is opposed to Christianity, that incomparable school of individualization, in which each is more precious than all. Negate individual value so that each one, fused into the mass and adding to the number, is indefinitely replaceable; so that, if Friedrich or Wolfgang gets killed, Hermann or Ludwig will do just as well, and that there is no occasion to be greatly grieved at the loss of this or that one.

Letters from young men at the front, letters from Belgian refugees; enough to fill one's heart with tears and horror. May tomorrow not bring still worse.

A telegram from Marc,[2] which at first I do not very well understand, urgently advises me, in the name of an imaginary Dr. Dubois who has been consulted, to begin at once my treatment in the Pyrenees. This is obviously because he judges that there is peril in remaining—or, if not peril, immediate danger; and this after talking with the Ministry of the Interior. Who knows even if D. did not especially beg him or commission him to warn me?

But I haven't the heart to go and leave behind me the Bussys and all those at Cabris. The danger is no greater for me than for them. The Bussys, to whom I transmit the telegram, tell me they have made up their mind to stay, whatever happens—unless, of course, a general command is given to evacuate Vence; most improbable . . . !

30 May

The social question! . . . If I had encountered that great trap at the beginning of my career, I should never have written anything worth while.

Vichy, 8 June

The roads are cluttered by wandering families fleeing at random and without knowing where. Children have got lost, whom the wretched parents are seeking. Last night, through the open window of my room giving onto the end of the park, I thrice heard a heart-rending cry: "Pierre! Pierre!" and almost went down to find the poor demented man who was uttering that call, desperately, in the night. And for a long time I could not go to sleep, ceaselessly imagining that distress. . . .

This morning I speak of it to Naville. He too heard the cry all right; but, he tells me, it was the night watchman,

[2] Marc Allégret.

who shouts: *"Lumière! Lumière!"* [3] when he sees a lighted
window, like mine.

14 June

That "important announcement" that Reynaud is holding in store for us, Naville thinks that . . .

Yes, that is it. And one ceases to understand where
that "soul" or that "genius" of France may still be that
they are claiming to save in spite of everything. Its very
support is going to be taken away from it. From now
on (and this was clear even the day before yesterday),
the struggle is useless; our soldiers are getting killed in
vain. We are at the mercy of Germany, which will
strangle us as best she can. Despite everything, we shall
shout very loud: "Honor is saved!" resembling that lackey
in Marivaux who says: "I don't like people to show dis-
respect for me" while receiving a kick in the rear.

Doubtless there is no shame in being conquered when
the enemy forces are so far superior, and I cannot feel
any; but it is with an indescribable sorrow that I hear
these phrases that exhibit all the shortcomings that have
brought us to our ruin: vague and stupid idealism, ignorance of reality, improvidence, heedlessness, and absurd
belief in the value of token remarks that have ceased to
have credit save in the imagination of simpletons.

How can one deny that Hitler played the game in
masterful fashion, not letting himself be bound by any
scruple, by any rule of a game that, after all, has none;
taking advantage of all our weaknesses, which he had
long and skillfully favored. In the tragic light of events
there suddenly appeared the deep decay of France, which
Hitler knew only too well. Everywhere incoherence, lack
of discipline, invoking of fanciful rights, repudiation of
all duties.

What will the well-intentioned young men who yesterday were concerned with remaking France do with the
miserable ruins that will remain? I am thinking of War-
saw, of Prague. . . . Will it be the same with Paris?
Will the Germans let the best of our energies breathe and
recover themselves? They will not limit their attention
solely to our material ruin. Today we cannot yet envisage
the frightful consequences of the defeat.

[3] "Lights! Lights!"

We should not have won the other war. That false victory deceived us. We were not able to endure it. The relaxing that followed it brought us to our ruin. (On this subject Nietzsche spoke words of wisdom. *Thoughts out of Season.*) Yes, we were ruined by victory. But shall we let ourselves be taught by defeat? The evil goes so deep that one cannot say whether or not it is curable.

Pétain's speech is simply admirable: "Since the victory, the spirit of enjoyment has won out over the spirit of sacrifice. People claimed more than they served. They wanted to save effort; today they are meeting misfortune." It cannot be better expressed, and these words console us for all the *flatus vocis* of the radio.

23 June

The armistice was signed yesterday evening. And now what is going to happen?

24 June

Yesterday evening we heard with amazement Pétain's new speech on the radio. Can it be? Did Pétain himself deliver it? Freely? One suspects some infamous deceit. How can one speak of France as "intact" after handing over to the enemy more than half of the country? How to make these words fit those noble words he pronounced three days ago? How can one fail to approve Churchill? Not subscribe most heartily to General de Gaulle's declaration? Is it not enough for France to be conquered? Must she also be dishonored? This breaking of her word, this denunciation of the pact binding her to England, is indeed the cruelest of defeats, and this triumph of Germany the most complete, by getting France, as she hands herself over, to debase herself.

And so many ruinous illusions! We see the cost of it today. We shall have to pay for all the absurdities of the intangible Versailles Treaty, the humiliations of those who were then the defeated, the useless vexations, which used to enrage me in 1919 but against which it was useless to protest; the shameful abuse of victory. Now it is their turn to abuse.

What a lack of psychology we revealed then, when infatuated with our triumph! As if the wisest thing would

not have been to hold out one's hand to the defeated,
help him get up instead of striving to crush him even
more, absurdly and without being aware that this merely
fed his rancor and stiffened his will. But how can you
persuade anyone, when it is a matter of politics, that
generosity is not always and exclusively reserved for
dupes? Probably it would have been fantastic to count
on "gratitude," but the best way of preventing Hitler was
not to provide him a justification.

Moreover, great historic events are invested with a
character of such inevitable fatality that the great man
who directs things seems to me much more created *by*
events than *for* them. My sentence is not very clear;
but neither is my thought. I mean that in the formation
of any great statesman one must consider as tremendous
the role of *circumstances*. Nothing differs more from
poetic genius. And yet the perfect blossoming of a masterpiece corresponds, likewise, to some participation of the
seasonable,[4] to the preliminary mood of the public, to
its unconscious anticipation.

6 July

I am advancing more and more easily in the *Gespräch-
ungen mit Goethe*[5] and am making undeniable progress
in the understanding of German. This is partly because
I never let a word go by until I understand it completely. Had I shown the same zeal for learning in my
childhood, where would I not be today! But it always
seems to me that I am merely beginning really to know
how to learn, to take advantage. What joy I find in
diligence!—and a semiforgetfulness of the present anguish.

Goethe recovers in the *Second Faust* all his greatness,
which he somewhat lost in the common run of the *Conversations*. At times one hears him utter almost embarrass-
ingly heavy sentatious remarks. The only thing that
saves them is the tone of smiling guilelessness present
throughout.

7 July

And we shall still continue to accuse Germany of "being
short on psychology"! . . .

---

[4] This word appears in English in the French text.
[5] Eckermann's *Conversations with Goethe*.

The thing seems to me to have been prepared with consummate cleverness: France and England are like two puppets in the hands of Hitler, who now amuses himself, after having conquered France, by aligning against her her ally of yesterday. I can see nothing but an invitation to England to hurl herself, through great fear, on our fleet, in that clause of the armistice which did not ask (at least at first) that it be handed over, but left it "intact," bound simply by a mutual promise (which allowed Pétain to say that at least our "honor" was untouched).

Was it not obvious that England should come to fear that that entire fleet might eventually be turned against her, and that Germany, if only the luck began to turn, would not hesitate to throw that decisive weight into the scale? It was better not to run that dangerous risk.

I doubt that this sudden turn surprised Hitler much. He was counting on it, I would swear; perfidious, cynical if you wish, but here again he acted with a sort of genius. And what I wonder at the most is perhaps the variety of his resources. Since the beginning of the war (and, indeed, since long before) everything has taken place exactly as he had foreseen it, wanted it; even with no delay; on the appointed day, for which he can wait, letting the engines that he has wound up and that must not explode beforehand act stealthily. No historic game is known or can be imagined that is more skillfully engineered, that involves so little chance. . . . Soon the very people he is crushing will be obliged, while cursing him, to admire him. He does not seem to have been mistaken in any of his reckonings; he correctly evaluated the power of resistance of each country, the value of individuals, their reactions, the advantage that could be drawn from this, with everything involved. Oh, how our shocked bewilderment, our honorable indignation in face of the English attack at Mers-el-Kebir must have amused him, and the sudden souring of our relations with England! [6] To have got the French aviation, already half decommissioned, to return to the field and, as a reprisal, to

[6] On 4 July 1940, after the French Admiral Gensoul had refused the British terms offered by Vice-Admiral Somerville, the English fleet bombarded French units off Mers-el-Kebir, near Oran.

bombard the English ships is wonderful! And, further-more, we shall have to be grateful to Germany and Italy for canceling their prohibition at once in order to allow us to strike out likewise against what becomes "the common enemy" and thus to give us—indeed!—full permission to help the Axis. We have been prettily maneuvered, without even being aware of it, by Hitler, the sole master of the circus ring, whose sly and hidden smartness surpasses that of the great captains.

One awaits with breathless curiosity the next chapter of this great drama he had so minutely and patiently elaborated.

I should like to be told which of his insults that made us call him a monster, which of his contempts has not been found, and proved in practice, to be motivated. His great cynical strength consisted in not deigning to take account of any token values, but only of realities; of acting according to the prompting of an unhampered mind. He has never taken any but others in with fine words. One may well hate him, but he most decidely has to be taken into account.

13 July

It requires considerable imagination, and of the rarest type: imagination within the reasoning faculty, to visualize the remote consequences of a defeat and the way in which each may suffer from it. Solidarity among all the citizens of a nation is not very firmly established, at least in France, and but little *felt;* it remains an abstract thing; and, moreover, for many has very little existence in reality. It would have been appropriate, not exactly to create it, but to inculcate this feeling among the masses and the school-children. To tell the truth, it is through the privations it involves, and only thereby, or almost, that the great majority will feel the defeat. Less sugar in one's coffee, and less coffee in one's cup—that is what they will feel. But since they will be told that it is the same in Germany, these privations will seem to them due not so much to the defeat as simply to the war; and they will not be altogether wrong.

The whole education of children ought to tend to raise their minds above material interests. But try to talk to the farmer of France's "intellectual patrimony," of which

he will be very little inclined to recognize himself as
an heir. Is there one among them who would not willingly accept Descartes's or Watteau's being a German,
or never having existed, if that could make him sell his
wheat for a few cents more? I fear that we shall be
obliged to witness a retrogression, an obliteration of noble
values, or at least their volatilization into the realm of
mysticism; and this will be at one and the same time
the most serious and the most imperceptible of the items
on the "bill."

My heart is quite restored and reinvigorated by Mozart's wonderful Concerto in D Major admirably played
by Wanda Landowska, of which I have just heard the
recording over the radio. Strength and kindness, grace,
wit, and tenderness—none of these is absent from that
work (which I recognize note by note) any more than
from the perfect playing of the artist; one of my regrets
will be not having heard her more often.

16 July

From Vichy, where he had to return, Arnold Naville,
that most faithful friend, sends me an article from Le
Temps of 9 July on "The Youth of France." (I am
generally a very regular reader of Le Temps, but cannot get it here.) That article, which makes him angry,
takes me to task and denounces, among others and specifically, my influence over youth as a public danger,
probably on the basis of the titles it quotes of two
of my books, Le Traité du Narcisse and L'Immoraliste.[7]
It is "against that considerable, but baneful, influence that
there must be a reaction today," it says, for I have
presumably "founded a lamentable school, forming a
vain and deliquescent generation." But did not people
take pleasure in pointing out that the men of that generation had fought rather valiantly in 1914? Yes, to be sure,
it would say, but only those, it so happens, who managed
to escape my fatal domination. What a strange idea that
anonymous author of the article has of the kind of influence my works exerted! If only he could know the
letters I receive from the young. Protest, as Naville would

---

[7] The Treatise of the Narcissus and The Immoralist were first published, respectively, in 1891 and 1902.

like me to do? As both judge and accused, I cannot. Besides, what is the use? In addition, that old accusation of *"corrumpere juventutem"* is more likely than praises to assure fame; this is generally known anyway, and how ill founded it usually is. But in this sorry period it might get my writings banned. It is not up to me, it is up to youth itself to defend me; up to those who have read me to prove that I have not perverted them. Doubtless the education of youth is today the most important task. The article in question implies that people are inclined, as in the past, to take youth, and themselves, in with empty phrases. The tendency toward grandiloquence is a shortcoming that I fear we shall not get rid of so soon. It is especially important to teach to children (and for this purpose to possess it first oneself) what bears the beautiful name of *clairvoyance*. This is also what we most lacked before and during the war and what we most lack today, if I can judge from this article. To develop the critical sense in the child ought to be the first and most constant effort of the teacher. There is nothing better against "nazism."

17 July

Read much German of late. I am learning lists of words, patiently copied into a little notebook that I carry on my walks. It is probably a little ridiculous at my age to still try to learn, and all this effort is quite useless; but the moment I am not stretching toward something, I become mortally bored and cease to enjoy life. And yet I tell myself that it is the state of pure and simple contemplation that it would be appropriate to achieve and in which it would be good to go to sleep. My mind is not yet sufficiently at peace for that; still too curious, too greedy.

19 July

The incompetence of our military leaders comes partly from the fact that, outside of war and so long as it is not taking place, their knowledge remains theoretical and ceases to correspond to the technical progress that the adversary takes great care to let them overlook. They cannot practically keep in training. What skill would one have a right to expect of a carpenter, even though he knew his plane thoroughly, if he had never been allowed to use it previously on some boards and thus to acquire experience of his trade? Those across the way had been able to keep their hand in. Hitler had educated them in a series of easy victories. They came upon us already tried in combat.

In addition, what about the superiority of their arms, of their number, of their discipline, of their impetus, of their confidence in their leaders, of their unanimous faith in the Führer? What did we have to set up against them but disorder, incompetence, negligence, internal divisions, decay? But what is the good of going back over all that? In the present state of France she was no longer in a position to hope for victory. I am almost inclined to say that she did not deserve it. So that it soon appeared that she had hurled herself into the adventure, or rather that she had let herself be dragged into it, with dangerous improvidence. So that one can think today that it would have been much better for her had she been conquered in 1918 rather than to win that deceptive victory which put the finishing touches on her blindness and put her to sleep in decadence.

25 July

I made a point of writing in this notebook yesterday; but these few days' interruption and my moves have broken the thread. It required the stagnation and idleness of Ginoles to permit an attempt at focusing my thought. Again I feel nothing in me but confusion and disorder.

Read and reread much Goethe of late: some poems, the beautiful introduction to *Farbenlehre*, and, urged on by Eckermann's admiration, the *Novelle*, which really is unbelievably silly (*blissful*).[8] Goethe could not have written it at present. It is doubtless impossible to speak of progress in the realm of art, but he would have seen that nothing but the specific individuality of the notations can sustain the interest of such a tale, in which everything is invented, constructed "at will"; and to prove what? That kindness achieves more than violence? . . .

---

[8] The *Novelle* was translated by Thomas Carlyle as *Goethe's Novel* and by others as *A Tale*; the *Farbenlehre* is known in English as *Goethe's Theory of Colors*.

That the wildest forces of nature, when tamed, can be of use? . . . That poetry and music overcome the most savage instincts? . . . That the trusting simplicity of a child wins out when brutality fails? . . . Obviously; but what wins out here is artifice. A work of art cannot be achieved by the mere application of good rules; and moreover those that Goethe has applied in this brief tale are most debatable. Likewise, Goethe would blush today at many of his reflections on painting, which Eckermann has handed down to us. The arts have evolved in a manner that he could not foresee, and certain great painters have appeared all of whose work rises up against his theories. It is amusing to note that in many other fields likewise the most advantageous path has been cut in a direction in which he foresaw nothing but a dead end. And, furthermore, this which is very serious: his whole intelligence, however spontaneously inquisitive it was, did not keep him from thinking that he had to direct his curiosity away from what he judged human intelligence to be incapable of ever achieving (Lord! how complicated my sentence is!—but no more so than my thought) and in regard to which inquiry seemed to him useless: astronomy or prehistory, and any problem concerning origins, initial formations. . . . Some of the lofty problems he refused to envisage, through fear and dislike of disappointment, are the very ones in which the mind, subsequently, has risked its boldest excursions and with the most amazing advantage.

Will it be said that France had ceased to be the great nation whose role she continued to play? Just the same, I see no other nation on earth that can assume that role today in her place, and it is essential to convince her, to convince oneself, of this.

If tomorrow, as it is to be feared, freedom of thought, or at least of the expression of that thought, is refused us, I shall try to convince myself that art, that thought itself, will lose less thereby than in excessive freedom.

We are entering a period in which liberalism is going to become the most suspect and least practicable of virtues.

28 July

Indulgence. Indulgences. . . . That sort of puritan rigor by which the Protestants, those spoilsports, often made themselves so hateful, those scruples of conscience, that uncompromising integrity, that unshakable punctuality, these are the things we have most lacked. Softness, surrender, relaxation in grace and ease, so many charming qualities that were to lead us, blindfolded, to defeat.

And, most often, mere ignoble absence of constraint, listlessness.

Les Ronds de cuir, which I have just tried to reread, has plunged me into a fit of indescribable blues.[9] "It's Daumier," I am told. Not at all! Daumier was satire; Daumier stigmatized what Courteline seems to put up with. He delights in abjection, sides with the trickster, the malingerer. What can one expect from such second-rate humanity, the portrait of which is only too exact, alas! Kindly, indulgent portrait in which so many Frenchmen recognize themselves; or at least one recognizes so many Frenchmen!

Sorry reign of indulgence, of indulgences. . . .

Ah yes, I laugh with Courteline, at times irresistibly; but the laughter over, nothing remains but despair.

12 August

The *N.R.F.*

"The only ones in whom they recognized real ability were their friends," it used to be said. Would it not have been fairer to say: "The only ones they recognized as friends were those who had real ability"? The group that was formed here, contrary to all the surrounding groups, deigned to take into account only the quality of writings and not their color. Nothing was harder to get accepted, even by some of our contributors.

As for me, I maintain that there is no country in Europe that has more to lose from a unification of opinion, of thought, and that is more impatient of it, than France. Yet that is what we tend toward today.

---

[9] Georges Courteline's novel in tableau form, *The Stick-in-the-Mud Pen-Pushers* (or, as we might say today, *The Chair-Borne Infantry*), depicts French bureaucrats. Though first published in 1893 and a favorite with the French, it has never been translated into English.

26 August

How at one and the same time can the days seem to me so tragically short and I be unable to fill them? Is not that perhaps the chief evidence that I am aging? If only I could harness myself to some long task! . . . I have tried to get back to the preface for the *Anthologie;*[10] but I have such trouble formulating the least thought that it seems to me I have forgotten how to write. Everything I experience at present is too remote from words; I am marking time in the moving sands of the inexpressible.

28 August

I am rereading Kafka's *The Trial* with an even greater admiration, if that is possible, than when I discovered that amazing book.

However skillful Groethuysen's preface may be, it does not wholly satisfy me; it tells us far too little about Kafka himself. His book eludes all rational explanation; the realism of his descriptions is constantly encroaching upon the imaginary, and I could not say what I admire the more: the "naturalistic" notation of a fantastic universe, but which the detailed exactitude of the depiction makes real in our eyes, or the unerring audacity of the lurches into the strange. There is much to be learned from it.

The anguish this book gives off is, at moments, almost unbearable, for how can one fail to repeat to oneself constantly: that hunted creature is I.

31 August

I did not know these *Études critiques* of Gobineau, which I find in Loup's library.[11] I read in the first of these studies:

"Whatever may be said against our century" (written in 1844), "the best literature can boast of such names as Béranger, Lamennais, George Sand, Hugo, Lamartine; with such lights an epoch might go astray, but it could

[10] Doubtless his *Anthology of French Poetry*, which was not published until 1949.

[11] *Critical Studies* (1844–8), not published until 1927, is a collection of Gobineau's neglected journalistic criticism of Balzac, Musset, Gautier, Heine, Jules Janin, and Sainte-Beuve. Loup is Mme Mayrisch.

not be justly said that it has lost its feeling in matters of art."

Such a judgment, on the contrary, simply shows to what a degree that "feeling" was lost; for Gobineau is merely repeating here the opinions of his epoch. He is not revealing his own taste here: the first three names he cites may well surprise us today, but they then enjoyed, and particularly the first one, universal approval. Goethe frequently speaks of Béranger in dithyrambic terms,[12] which lead us to wonder if we are not unjust and if nothing really remains of a work that then seemed so worthy of admiration. I have recently skimmed through again the collection of Béranger's *Chansons*[13] without finding a thing in them that does not seem to me vulgar, flat, and tedious. Does this amount to saying that our epoch has better taste? Or merely a different taste? I often stop to wonder if, among the writers we praise and the artists we prefer, there are not some from whom the following generation will turn away. On the other hand, the men of the future will be amazed that we failed to recognize at once as important some to whom we have failed to give what will be thought their due, which will be subsequently showered upon them, as was done for Baudelaire and Rimbaud.

In Renan's time the tendency was to consider the most serious literature as the most lasting; and this was very stupid. But are we any wiser today in our preferences, and will they not likewise amaze the men of the future?

5 September

To come to terms with one's enemy of yesterday is not cowardice; it is wisdom, and accepting the inevitable. "*Untersuchen was ist, und nicht was behagt,*"[14] Goethe says excellently. Whoever balks at fate is caught in the trap. What is the use of bruising oneself against the bars of one's cage? In order to suffer less from the narrowness of the jail, there is nothing like remaining squarely in the middle.

I feel limitless possibilities of acceptance in me; they

[12] See quotation from Lamartine. [A.]

[13] Various collections of Béranger's *Songs*, expressing perfectly the spirit of the average man, appeared from 1815 to 1833.

[14] "To investigate what is and not what pleases."

in no wise commit my innermost self. The much greater
risk for the mind is letting itself be dominated by hatred.
As for restricting my comfort and pleasures, I am quite
ready. To tell the truth, my aging body cares little. It
would probably not be the same if I were twenty, and I
consider that the young are more to be pitied today than
the old. In order not to have to distort one's thought,
it will perhaps be necessary to keep silent; those who
will have to suffer most from this are those who have
not yet spoken.

9 September

I have been braver in my writings than in my life,
respecting many things that were probably not so respectable and giving much too much importance to the
opinion of others. Oh, what a good Mentor I should
now be for the man I was in my youth! How effectively I
should be able to drive myself to extremities! If I had
listened to my own advice (I mean: the man I once
was, listening to the one I am today), I should have
gone around the world four times . . . and I should
never have married. As I write these words, I shudder
as at an act of impiety. This is because I have remained
nevertheless very much in love with what most held me
in check and that I cannot affirm that that very check
did not get the best out of me.

I believe that it is harder still to be just toward oneself than toward others.

27 September

In Dubious Battle by John Steinbeck. Impeccable translation of a most remarkable book. If I were less tired,
I should enjoy praising it. But I could do so only at too
great length. It is the best (psychological) portrayal
that I know of Communism, and perfectly lighted. If
it leaves the capitalist and bourgeois counterpart in the
shadow, at least it very cleverly gives one a glimpse of
this in the dialogues, and that is enough. The main
character is the crowd; but from that amorphous and
vague mass there stand out various individuals in whom
the variegated aspects of the problem are set forth without the discussion's ever cluttering and interrupting the
action. And likewise there stand out against the vast
general movement, in harmony or opposition with the

great wave of common interests, the passions or individual interests of the leaders or minor characters; and all this presented so fairly that one cannot take sides for or against the flood of demands any more than the author has done. The legitimacy of those demands, like the outcome of the struggle itself, remains "dubious." Especially dubious the legitimacy of using treacherous means to bring about the triumph of even the most legitimate cause. But Steinbeck reveals admirably (yet without *demonstrating* anything) how those who are refused all other means of fighting are led and forced to treachery, injustice, deliberate cruelty; and how the noblest and most generous characters are distorted thereby. Whence the great distress inherent throughout this beautiful and painful book.

When a certain stage of history is reached, everything appears in the guise of a problem. And man's responsibility increases as that of the gods decreases.

It devolves upon man alone, in the final reckoning, to solve all these problems which he alone has presumably raised.

12 October

Art inhabits temperate regions. And doubtless the greatest harm this war is doing to culture is to create a profusion of extreme passions which, by a sort of inflation, brings about a devaluation of all moderate sentiments. The dying anguish of Roland or the distress of a Lear stripped of power moves us by its exceptional quality but loses its special eloquence when reproduced simultaneously in several thousand copies. Isolated, it is a summit of suffering; in a collection, it becomes a plateau. I sympathize with the individual; in the multitude I become bewildered. The exquisite becomes banal, common. The artist does not know which way to turn, intellectually or emotionally. Solicited on all sides and unable to answer all appeals, he gives up, at a loss. He has no recourse but to seek refuge in himself or to find refuge in God. This is why war provides religion with easy conquests.

14 October

Certainly I am making progress in German. And yet it does not seem to me that I am reading *Lotte in*

Weimar today much more easily than I did *Der Zauber-berg* a few years ago.[15]

Oh, why did I not put forth such an effort in my early youth! But at that time it seemed to me much more important to taste life directly, to push away the screen of books and everything education interposed that might hamper the sincerity and innocence of my vision. Was I wrong? I cannot get myself to believe so. And even if I thought so, what could I do about it? Nothing more useless than regrets.

There are always certain regards in which the most intelligent of women, in her reasoning, remains below the least intelligent of men. A sort of conventional agreement takes place, involving considerable regard for the sex "to which we owe our mother," for many a lame argument that we should not accept if it came from a man. I am well aware that, nevertheless, their counsel may be excellent, but on condition that we constantly rectify it and expurgate from it that element of passion and emotivity which almost always, in a woman, sentimentalizes thought.

To love the truth is to refuse to let oneself be saddened by it.

23 November

I finish rereading *Werther* not without irritation. I had forgotten that he took so long to die. It is drawn out and one would eventually like to take him by the shoulders and push him. On four or five occasions what one hoped to be his last sigh is followed by another even more ultimate. . . . Frayed departures exasperate me.

Then, to rest my mind and reward me (for I read German only with effort and difficulty), I turn from German to English. Each time I plunge again into English literature I do so with delight. What diversity! What abundance! It is the literature whose disappearance would most impoverish humanity.

The sole art that suits me is that which, rising from unrest, tends toward serenity.

[15] *Der Zauberberg* (*The Magic Mountain*) appeared in German in 1924, and *Lotte in Weimar* (*The Beloved Returns*) in 1939. Both novels are by Thomas Mann.

25 November

Looking for the moments of life that one would most enjoy reliving, I begin to wonder if they are not those of pure physical pleasure; I mean of purely sensual pleasure, in which no element of sentiment or thought was involved. But I do not say that those are the moments I should be most willing to relive, for however great may be the nervous agitation they cause us, our inmost self is not greatly enriched by them.

But what is the use of writing down these risky ratiocinations instead of enjoying simply and immensely the divine spectacle unfolding before my eyes. The last, still warm rays of a sun about to disappear behind the last shoulder of the mountains are flooding the rolling landscape at my feet, giving the village houses, there on the left, a caressing farewell kiss and bathing with a golden tranquillity the bench where I have sat down to write. From each valley bluish columns of smoke arise and spread out broadly as a shroud would spread over the world on the point of going to sleep. . . .

December

I find it hard not to be convinced that we should be much better off if we had had the sense to recognize loyally our debts toward America. The great effort our country would have had to impose on itself in order to acquit them, the rule of discipline, the discomfort, would have been salutary to her, while preserving her sentiment of national honor, which, alas, she learned to value too cheaply as a result of the violence done it on that occasion. I think that our French leaders underestimated the French people at that time, when it was not difficult to convince them that their dignity, that the right to hold up their heads and hearts, were worth the few vexatious restrictions they would have had to accept, which, perhaps, by the recovery that one could legitimately expect from them would have spared us today's trials, much harsher and more mortifying.

19 December

All human acts involve more chance than decision.

Jean S. points out to me that if I claim God to be the product of man, I ought likewise to admit this for the

Holy Virgin, and indeed a product that it is much easier to achieve much more readily.

A novelist's imagination or anything that ordinarily constitutes a creator is not generally attributed to me. On the other hand, the critical mind is granted me; according to them, that is my strong point; it is esteemed and many of my judgments of still unclassified works were premonitory, it is recalled. . . . None the less, if, on the subject of this or that new book, I happen not to share the opinion of Peter or Paul, I am the one who rereads the book and wonders whether I am right, not Peter or Paul.

1941

My torment is even deeper; it comes likewise from the fact that I cannot decide with assurance that right is on this side and wrong on the other. It is not with impunity that, throughout a whole lifetime, my mind has made a practice of understanding *the other person*. I succeed in this so well today that the "point of view" it is most difficult to keep uppermost is my own.

In this vacillating state of mine what decides, too easily, is sympathy.

Oh, I should like to be left alone, to be forgotten! Free to think in my own way without its costing anyone anything and to express without constraint or fear of censure the oscillation of my thought. It would develop in a dialogue as at the time of my *Enfant prodigue* and would simultaneously put forth branches in opposite directions. This is the only way that I might more or less satisfy myself.[1]

[1] "Neither victors nor vanquished!" I do not much like that slogan. It implies on both sides a pretense so flattering for our self-esteem that I am suspicious. A "collaboration" such as is proposed to us today could not be "loyal" when it is thus based on a lie. It is doubtless fine and noble and reassuring after a boxing match to see the opponents shake hands, but there is no question of denying that one has beaten the other. We are defeated. As soon as we showed any inclination to doubt this, our opponent would be able to remind us of the fact; let there be no doubt about it. And if he helps us to get to our feet today, this is only to allow us an effort from which he plans to reap the profit. He supposes quite rightly that our labor and the production we can supply will be better (or, to speak more clearly, that our output will be greater) if we are not reduced to slavery and if we keep the illusion of working freely and for ourselves."

"Is it therefore your opinion that we should refuse to play this game?"

"Perhaps be a party to it at first, and, if possible, without too much bitterness, but also without illusions, in order to avoid, subsequently, too bitter a disappointment. Shall I tell you just what I think? I believe it is good for France to bend for a time under the yoke of an enforced discipline. Just as she was not capable, in the depths of moral laxity and decay into which she had fallen, of winning a real victory over an enemy much better equipped than she, a united, resolute, tenacious, and pugnacious enemy skillfully led by a man with his mind made up to override all the scruples that weaken us, all the considera-

I doubt if I would use that freedom of expression which is denied us today especially for the purpose of protesting against despotism. Yes, I wonder if this constraint does not hamper me even more in the other direction, for it takes away any value from everything I might think just now or say that might seem to be in agreement with *them*. Any advantage one may derive from it taints thought with self-interest.

Consequently, forgetting (or forcing myself to forget)

---

tions that stand in our way; just so I do not believe France capable today of rising to her feet again all alone and solely by her own efforts. I say 'today' but as early as 1914 I wrote: 'We have everything to learn from Germany; she has everything to take from us.' I abide by that formula."

"Do you not feel something mortifying, insulting, and intolerable in what you are saying?"

"The most elementary wisdom consists in taking things, people, and events as they are and not as one would like, or would have liked, them to be. A wisdom we have often lacked, for we have a great tendency to take words for things that exist and we are satisfied with a bit of eloquence. One has to play with the cards one has."

"We hold excellent trumps."

"But they are scattered and we don't know how to use them properly. This is what keeps me from being too upset if the conqueror, with his fine method, assumes responsibility for our hand, temporarily."

"Those trumps will not endure giving up their freedom of self-determination."

"Too much liberty led to our downfall."

"And then you are leaving out the fact that the conqueror will not tolerate our revealing ourselves, in any domain whatever, as superior to him. He will manage in such a way as to subjugate our virtues and talents and to discredit those that will not submit; our virtues and talents, our men of virtue and talent."

"That may be, but what can we do about it? Besides, it occurs to me as we are talking that the only virtues and talents I really value are uncooperative.

"The uncooperative will be brought to heel. Yes, I recall that remark of yours that you quote. But I also recall another remark I have read in your *Journal*. It too comes from the period of the other war. 'I sometimes think,' you wrote, 'I think with horror' (and, to be sure, it was justified!) 'that the victory we are longing for is that of the past over the future.' Well, you must be satisfied: this time the forces of the future have triumphed."

"And, indeed, nothing saddens me more than seeing France at present expecting her salvation to come only from an attachment to everything about her that is oldest and most worn out. Their fine 'National Revolution' gives me a pain in the neck. If our country is to be reborn (and I firmly believe that it will be), it will be in spite of that and against that. I expect our salvation to come from what is getting ready in the shadows and cannot emerge into the light of day until tomorrow." [A.]

that constraint for a time, if I let the voice of hell speak out, I hear it whisper in my brain:

"But after all, why and against what are you protesting? Have you not said yourself: 'The family and religion are the two greatest enemies of progress'? Were you not wont to look upon humanity as it still is— prostrate and sprawling—as abject? Were you not wont to scorn heartily the paltry interests that keep man from rising above himself? Did you not even write, at the time when your mind was bold: 'I do not love man; I love what devours him'? [2] A paradox doubtless, but not altogether. You meant, if I understood you correctly, that nothing great or beautiful is achieved but by sacrifice, and that the loftiest representatives of this miserable humanity are those in whom the sacrifice is voluntary. Have you not constantly denounced as the worst obstacle the cult of false gods? Are you not to be grateful to me for paying no attention to what you were accustomed to call so properly 'fiduciary values'—that is, the ones that have no other reality than what we grant them? Did you not discover, when you used to indulge in gardening, that the only way of preserving, protecting, safeguarding the exquisite and the best was to suppress the less good? You are well aware that this cannot be done without apparent cruelty, but that such cruelty is prudence. . . ."

Immediately the other voice speaks up, heard perhaps less by my brain than my heart: "Why are you speaking of the *best*? The work undertaken by him who aims to be the great gardener of Europe is not so much superhuman as inhuman. Probably, if he were to complete it, there would remain on earth neither a voice to moan nor an ear willing to hear it; and no one left to know or to wonder whether what his force is suppressing is not of infinitely greater value than his force itself and what it claims to bring us. Your dream is great, Hitler; but for it to succeed costs too dear. And if it fails (for it is too superhuman to suceed), what will remain on earth, after all, but death and devastation? Until the present moment this is the most obvious result of your under-

[2] Spoken by Prometheus, the hero of *Le Prométhée mal enchaîné* (1899).

taking, and everything suggests that it will be the only one."

11 February

A racy style that is almost excessively so. . . . Oh, how I like Colette's way of writing! What unerring boldness in the choice of words! What a nice feeling for the nuance! And all without seeming to pay attention—the exquisite result of a painstaking elaboration.

"I sat down rather glum before a piece of work undertaken without appetite and forsaken without decision." This "forsaken without decision" is a marvel of the intentional, discreet to the point of going unnoticed by the average reader, most likely, which delights me.

After *Bella-Vista*, which is quite recent, I take up *La Maison de Claudine*,[3] which I did not yet know. I enjoy reading in it: "Neither my brothers' enthusiasm nor my parents' disapproving amazement got me to take an interest in *The Three Musketeers*." Yes, I am glad not to be the only one who failed to lose his heart to Dumas père when my companion in boredom is Colette. Quite recently again, during the three weeks when I was kept in bed by an attack of nephritis, Mme Théo brought me *Monte-Cristo* at my request, but it soon fell from my hands without awakening the slightest curiosity for the complicated tribulations of its puppets.

To declare that one looks upon oneself as the most perfect representative of classicism at the present time— what could be more immodest! I did so, Massis, only after having written that I held modesty to be the first virtue of the classics, and thus I snatched away with one hand the gift I was making with the other. But it pleases you to recall from my sally only the presumptuousness without deigning to see that the affected presumptuousness was itself but a joke. I even added, as I recall, for greater humorous effect: "The best representative of classicism, with Gonzague Truc and Julien Benda," [4] in order to be quite sure of not being taken

---

[3] *Bella-Vista* appeared in 1937 and *Claudine's House* in 1922.

[4] The passage is found in the *Billets à Angèle* (*Notes for Angèle*) in the *N.R.F.* of 1921, reprinted in *Incidences*.

seriously. But Massis never uses anything from a writing
but what can serve his thesis. He is one of the most dishonest minds I know, for whom everything is fuel when
he wants to burn someone else.

23 February

Another "Proverb of Hell," [5] a fine one, that I invent for
Jean Schlumberger, who tells me he no longer attaches
any importance to, or at least no longer feels bound by,
the remarks on Thucydides that he wrote in 1913, which,
after copying them in this notebook, I reread to him the
other day. He has developed; his point of view of today
seems to him superior to the one he shared with Thucydides . . . in short:

> *The promise of the caterpillar*
> *Binds not the butterfly.*

I am reading, in another connection, a most amazing
book by Joubin on the *Métamorphoses des animaux
marins.*[6] It contains many subjects for dramas. But I imagine the dialogue between two intimate friends (or
husband and wife), one of whom had passed from one
condition to another—through progress, he would say—
whereas for the other it would seem treason not to remain faithful to his original rule of conduct.

6 March

My soul has remained young to such a degree that I
constantly feel as if the septuagenarian I indubitably am
is a role I am playing; and the infirmities and failings
that remind me of my age come along like a prompter
to call it to my mind when I might be inclined to forget it. Then, like the good actor I want to be, I slip
back into character and pride myself on playing the
part well.

But it would be much more natural for me to surrender to the coming spring; I am merely aware that I
no longer have the proper costume for that.

On Malraux's recommendation I am reading (after
several tales by Chekhov translated into English) *The
Devil,* by Tolstoy, without managing to see what he finds

[5] A recollection of the "Proverbs of Hell" in William Blake's *Marriage of Heaven and Hell,* which Gide translated.
[6] *The Metamorphoses of Aquatic Animals* by Louis Joubin (1926).

particularly wonderful in it. But I note this revelatory
sentence that might be quoted as occasion arises:

"The idea of baring his secret to his uncle, whom he
did not esteem, the thought that he was about to reveal
himself to his uncle in the ugliest light and humiliate
himself before his uncle, was pleasing to him" (p. 364).

Nice, 12 April

. . . At that time my speech was akin to song, my gait
to dance. A rhythm carried my thought along, ordered
my existence. I was young.

La Croix, 15 April [7]

Yesterday evening, going to the shore alone, I saw the
beach covered near the water-line by the washed-up
remains of an odd little animal I had never seen before.
Its flat body looks like an oval disk varying from three
to five inches long, quite translucent in the center, but
with edges that darken to a most intense purplish blue.
Above the oval rises like a comb a sort of transversal
sail, colorless and almost transparent, to catch the wind.
And I saw that the near-by waves were covered with
hundreds or thousands of these frail skiffs, which the
breeze was slowly bringing in to run aground on the
beach. Observing the nearest ones, I saw that the inner
surface of each disk was covered with delicate tentacles
like those of starfish. I wondered if they were not one
stage of a zoophyte, but believe rather that it was an
adult animal, the name and description of which I shall
try to find in the Brehm at Les Audides.[8] I was filled
with wonder and more deeply moved than I could have
been by the most beautiful landscape.

17 April

That Péguy is a great figure, and particularly noble
and representative, goes without saying; I consider admirable his very life and many a page of his *Jeanne d'Arc*,
as well as numerous others scattered throughout his
Cahiers.[9] But those lines from *Ève* which are quoted
everywhere today and over which everyone goes into

[7] The date "1ᵉʳ avril" in the Paris edition marks a hasty correction
of a misprint in the page-proof.

[8] Gide is referring to the *Illustrated Life of Animals* by the German naturalist Alfred Edmund Brehm.

[9] Most of Péguy's writings appeared in his own periodical *Cahiers de
la quinzaine*.

raptures belong among the worst I have read and the
worst that were ever dashed off in any language.

Honor, integrity, good faith—merely to pride oneself
on them amounts to relinquishing them somewhat.

10 May

If the English succeed in driving the Germans out of
France, a party will form in our country to balk at that
deliverance, to discover that the recent domination had
something to be said for it, since it at least imposed
order, and to prefer it to the disorder of freedom. A
freedom for which we are not yet ready and which we
do not deserve. Freedom is beautiful only because it
permits the exercise of virtues that it is first essential to
acquire. How much time will be left me to suffer from
this period of turbulence? Shall I live long enough to
see the dawn breaking beyond the confusion and not to
die in despair?

16 May

"Why do you French always have (and nothing but)
half-tones, nuances, and reticence in matters of color?" I
was not aware of this and hardly understood Rosenberg
when he said: "In Russia we like fresh and bold colors,
daring tones, gay oppositions. In France everything seems
monotone and dull, whether clothing, draperies, or stage
sets and those of life itself. Nothing but whispers, refined subtleties, discreet allusions; in contrast to them,
with our violent tastes we seem to ourselves good-
humored savages."

Shortly after that conversation there came to Paris the
Russian Ballet bringing its well-known dash and new life.

6 June

"Unselfconsciousness"; yes, this is indeed the proper
word, and Montherlant uses it wonderfully. He excels in
passing off as a virtue (and what is more, as a rare
virtue) and "freedom of mind" what, I fear, is but an
egotistic lack of interest in public affairs. He indulgently
quotes a remark by Gourmont and it can be felt that
the war "does not bother" him either. Many people are
well enough off not to have to suffer much from the
restrictions, and they look upon the present situation as
better than merely tolerable. They would be hypocritical
not to admit this simply and to assume a contrite ap-

pearance, for the poverty of others touches them but little and sympathy does not bother them; but there is nothing to boast about in that. The remarks of the "rat who has withdrawn from society," whether he is an artist or a philosopher, always smack somewhat of his cheese.

14 June

I like being a "victim" of the Legion. I do not like the fact that it should be for so small a reason.[10]

I was kept from speaking not so much by the threatening letter of M. de Tissot as by the insignificance of my lecture. Brave that threat in order to say so little! Not worth it. . . .

At first I congratulated myself on the hundred and eighty (soon after there were two hundred and forty) members of the Legion who handed in their insignia *"de suite"* by way of protest.

But of that little adventure nothing remains, as far as "public opinion" goes, but this: that they prevented me from speaking and that I was silent "recognizing that I was wrong and giving in to their reasons," as the papers said. Any article that might have clarified the matter would have been stopped by censorship.

12 June

The shortest night of the year.

The last four days have been more beautiful than one can say; more beautiful than I could endure. A sort of call to happiness in which all nature conspired in a miraculous swoon, reaching a summit of love and joy in which the human being has nothing further to wish for but death. On such a night one would like to kiss the flowers, caress the tree trunks, embrace any young and ardent body whatever, or prowl in search of it till dawn. Going off to bed alone, as I have nevertheless to decide to do, seems impious.

1 July

Of all Molière's plays, it is decidedly *Le Malade imaginaire* that I prefer. It is the one that strikes me as the most novel, the boldest, the most beautiful—and by

[10] On 21 May 1941 Gide was to give a lecture in Nice on the poet Henri Michaux, but this was made impossible by the newly formed SOL or fascist-inspired Legion in the service of the Vichy government. The lecture was published in July by Gallimard under the title *Découvrons Henri Michaux* (*Let Us Discover Henri Michaux*).

far. If that play were a painting, how people would wax
enthusiastic over its *substance*. When Molière writes in
verse, he succeeds by dint of expedients; he knows many
a little device to satisfy the requirements of measure and
rhyme. But, despite his great dexterity, the alexandrine
rather distorts his tone of voice. That tone is utterly
natural in *Le Malade* (and in *Le Bourgeois Gentilhomme*). I know no more beautiful prose. It does not
obey any definite law, but each sentence is such that not
a single word could be changed without spoiling it. It
constantly achieves a wonderful plenitude, muscular like
Puget's athletes or Michelangelo's slaves and as if swelling, without bombast, with a sort of lyricism made up
of life, good humor, and health. I never tire of rereading it and shall not cease praising it.

2 July

I reread, immediately after, *Le Bourgeois Gentilhomme*.
However fine and wise certain scenes may be, an intentional drawing-out of the dialogues allows me, by comparison, to admire even more the tight texture of *Le
Malade imaginaire*, so solid, so thick, so sturdy. And
what solemnity, what a *"schaudern"* each scene receives
from the secret contact with death. It is with death that
everything sports; it is made a sport of; it is made to
enter the dance; it is invited thrice, whether by little
Louison or by Argan himself with his wife and later
with his daughter; death is felt prowling about; it is
seen reconnoitering; it is braved and flouted; even to the
death of Molière himself, which comes at the end to
round out atrociously this tragic farce. And all that, in
the bourgeois key, achieves a grandeur that the theater
has never surpassed.

4 July

I propose this reform in which I see no disadvantage.
Without completely suppressing dictation, which can first
accustom children to relate writing to sound, *proofreading*
might occasionally be substituted for it with a view to
teaching them spelling. The teacher's task would be
vastly simplified and the child would take great interest
in this. It would not be difficult to draw up the text of
a galley involving a certain number of mistakes that the
teacher would know. A copy would be given to each

pupil. There would be—let us say twelve misprints to correct. Grading would be easy and the emulation more definite, the most deserving pupil being the one who had corrected all twelve. This method would have the further advantage of teaching the pupils the technique of proof-reading, which might later on be a help to some of them; but, above all, it would put them on their guard against the authority of the printed word, which too often inspires awe.

9 July

That letter from Malaquais, dated 18 June, still lies on my table. If I knew where to write him, I should have done so long ago. I can hear him accuse me, accuse Pierre: we are forsaking him, we are tired of him; besides, he had foreseen this long ago; and his bitterness does not stop with us, but overflows onto the whole human race. . . . He finds all sorts of reasons for our silence except the real one: that he neglected to give his address.

14 July

. . . I was obliged to recognize my error and that it was Christian virtues I hoped to find in Communism.

17 July

In reading Valéry one acquires that wisdom which consists in feeling a bit more stupid than before.

19 July

I no longer write an affirmative sentence without being tempted to add: "perhaps."

X. talks of himself with great modesty, but constantly.

I also read in Montesquieu.

"Wonderful maxim; not to talk of things any more after they are done."

Excellent remark to quote to those who ask me for explanations of my books.

20 July

A new issue of *Poésie 41* brings me some surprising poems by Aragon.[11] This is the best I have read in

[11] Four poems entitled *"Les Nuits"* ("Nights") appeared first in the fourth issue of *Poésie 41* (May–June 1941), a small and excellent poetry review published by Pierre Seghers at Villeneuve-lès-Avignon in the Gard. These poems, entitled individually "May Night," "Dunkerque Night," "Night of Exile," and "Night in the Deep South," were reprinted in *Les Yeux d'Elsa (Elsa's Eyes)* the following year.

poetry for some time and the most authentically new. I feel the need of writing this here, for I had not at all enjoyed his most recent books and feared he might henceforth be almost lost to us.

26 July

I come away delighted from Catherine's dancing class, which I have just attended.[12] No doubt but that daily training of this type gives the body that undergoes it slimness, grace, and decision. Spiritualization of desire. But it is desire none the less. Desire for something or other. And if the body is ugly, nothing can be done about it.

Were I a ballet-master, I should go and recruit on the beach some of those little Italians (perhaps French boys) with tanned bodies whom I was watching yesterday on the beach and whose elegant and rhythmical way of swimming I was admiring. Trained in dancing, they would seem so provocative that, out of regard for public morals, no one would dare to "produce" them.

29 July

The last part of life. . . . Rather listless last act; recalls of the past; repetitions. One would like some unexpected rebound and one doesn't know what to think up.

9 August

I had never before seen lizard's eggs. Six were brought me. Rather like the snake's eggs I used to dig up as a child in the old sawdust by the Val Richer sawmill. Big enough so that I thought they must be those very large green lizards which used to amaze me, and which, I am told, are rather common in this region. They were ready to hatch and from one of them that we broke open there emerged a small fully formed lizard, but still having its unresorbed nutritive sac on its side. It wiggled for a few minutes. We buried the other five in a pot full of dirt, and examining the pot four days later, we noticed that nothing remained of three of them but empty shells. The little ones, having hatched, had got away. I hastened the hatching of one of the two remaining eggs, cutting the soft shell with a razor blade. The little lizard came out slowly then, having gauged the weather, trotted off with astonishing agility, with as complete assurance in

[12] Catherine is André Gide's daughter.

his movements as an adult and as if in no wise surprised by the sudden discovery of the outer world.

22 August

Long succession of days during which the soul is willing to live in distraction and makes no further effort to get closer to God.

23 August

I ought to confess honestly that I have ceased to know just what that image hides. In this case it is less a matter of a situation than of a spiritual state. One cannot get closer to what is everywhere. It is much rather a question of a transparency of the soul that allows us to feel Him. The majority of men do not know that *state of communion;* but it brings the soul, the entire being, such a delightful felicity that the soul is inconsolable after once having known it and then allowed it to slip away.

This is partly what makes me, without believing in any definite God, really enjoy only the company of pious souls.

Quietism? No; but constantly in a state of effort and stretched toward something indefinable and adorable, toward a higher condition in which the individual is lost and absorbed—to which I see no other name to give but the very name of God.

10 September

I am reading with lively interest Bunin's book on Tolstoy. He explains him wonderfully and at the same time explains to me why I feel so ill at ease in contact with Tolstoy. What a monster! Constantly bucking, revolting against his nature, forcing one to doubt his sincerity at all times, being in turn everything and everybody and never more personal than when he ceases to be himself; arrogant in renunciation, constantly arrogant, even to the point of not being reconciled to dying simply like everyone else. But what anguish in that final struggle, that of a Titan against God, against fate! I admire him perhaps; but I can feel in harmony and in agreement only with the humble, the modest. For me, Tolstoy remains an *impossibility.* Cinelli compared him with St. Francis; what an absurdity! Tolstoy contrasts with St. Francis with his whole being and entire complexity, his ostentation, and even his effort toward a spectacular desti-

tution; forever putting on a show for himself, for him
simplicity is but a further complication. Protean, his most
complicated "creations" are never more than a simplification of himself; he who is capable of becoming so many
persons becomes forever incapable of real sincerity.

I am rereading Genesis for Catherine's intention; and
this afternoon, Ecclesiastes and the Song of Songs. To be
sure, the last two works contain useless repetitions (harmonious in the Song of Songs) and dull parts; but also,
and above all, pages of such beauty, of such solemn
grandeur, that I know nothing in any literature that is
superior or even comparable to them. If these books of
the Bible were architectural monuments, one would willingly make a several days' trip to see them, like the ruins
of Baalbek or the temple of Selinus. But they are within
reach; and numerous are those who can enjoy only what
has cost them dear. Besides, attention is turned away by
the reputation of this book for aiming at edification, and
by the boredom one consequently expects from it. It is
left to priests and ministers; good for converts! A profane
person has no concern with being catechized. Is it not
"the word of God"? Is it not necessary to "believe" it in
order to be interested in it? Some are convinced that the
interest I take in it is but a survival of my Protestant
formation. Every good Protestant, as is known, "is born
with a Bible in his hands." The Catholic hardly reads
it at all; no, not even directly the Gospel; the catechism is
enough for him, and the prayer-book with "the Gospel
for the day."

11 September

To what a degree I miss a piano, my piano! . . . On
certain days that need, that longing for music, becomes a
sort of almost physical pain. The other day, alone at
Germaine Taillefer's while waiting for her, I reread the
delightful Sonata in B-flat major, a marvel of grace and
emotion; then the slow Étude of Chopin in E-flat minor.
I noted that it would take me probably but a half-hour
to learn it by heart again. To be able to get back to the
piano . . . I should enjoy moments of complete happiness.
What prevents me from doing so? The physical conditions
in which I am living, but, above all, the obsessing fear

of bothering the neighbors, a fear that in my case increases with age, becoming almost pathological. As if the neighbors worried about *us*!

15 September

It is more than difficult for me to believe that the life of the soul can be prolonged beyond the death of the body. But even if I could manage to do so (moreover, I do not go to any great effort in this direction), it is utterly impossible for me to imagine that very hypothetical afterlife otherwise than as the continuation of a trajectory, and this would suffice to free me from worry, if by chance I had any.

One cannot imagine a more beautiful view than the one I enjoy, at any hour of the day, from the window of my room in the Grand Hotel. The town of Grasse opposite me dominated by the cathedral, whose tower breaks the line of the distant mountains, the harmonious disorder of the houses forming a series of terraces on the slope down to the deep ravine separating me from the town. While I am writing these lines the sun is finishing its course and, before disappearing behind the heights of Cabris, is pouring an ineffable golden light over the walls, the roofs, the whole town. A veil of rain has come to hide the mountainous background of the picture so that the cathedral tower, bathed in the last rays, now stands out against a bare sky, so it seems; on the left, another, smaller tower. The dinner hour struck some time ago and yet I cannot leave this sight.

Begin my life over again?   I should try at least to put a bit more adventure into it.

30 September

I understand, because I share it, the tendency of the aged toward avarice and shall not forgive myself the costly comfort of the very good Hôtel Adriatic, where I nevertheless decided to stay, unless I succeed in working while here. In my youth, urged on by a not very exacting demon, I used to work under any circumstances whatever, anywhere whatever. Today that demon voices certain demands. In order to stay at my writing-table I must like the room. But I have seen too many poverty-stricken people of late not to be constantly aware that the amount of comfort I allow myself would be luxury to them, not to wonder constantly if the work this comfort will allow me justifies such an outlay.

17 October

For whoever complains that the sudden turn of national feeling is not based on the central opinion of the country:

Of necessity a turn is always taken on the wing-tip. Not on the wing-tips but specifically on *one* wing. Though a revolution may call itself "national," it always marks the victory of a single party.

31 October

I finish Pearl Buck's *The Mother*. It is a fine book, which I blame myself for having read in translation. Probably what I am about to say of it would be even more noticeable in the original: it is a Chinese book, but equally, and even more, a Protestant book. I mean by this that the author is visibly brought up on the Bible, whence that sort of austerity, of nudity in the narration; whence that grandeur, that nobility without ostentation, that lofty resignation; the very tone of the narration, often, is Biblical.

And I plunge immediately afterward into *The Good Earth*.

1942

I open a new notebook to begin this new year, leaving the other but half filled. Wrote nothing further in it since tying myself down to those regular articles for the *Figaro*, lacking time and furthermore having no heart to write anything in it.

I have aged frightfully of late. It is as if I were getting away from myself. Oh, without any melancholy! It seems to me that I shall take leave of myself without regrets.

Catherine might have bound me to life; but she is interested only in herself—and that does not interest me.

I have again become interested in work and enjoy a semblance of happiness at my writing-table. My thought takes shape easily, so long as it is not profound; and in my articles I merely touch the surface of thoughts. I remain without opinion in the face of events, wondering at times whether I shall be able to find a place and a *raison d'être* in the new universe that is confusedly taking shape. This I believe: that it can have no relation to this farce of a "national revolution," which I cannot take seriously. The real heartbeats of France are hidden and cannot let themselves be heard. For the moment everything is but temporary outward show, boasting, and deceit. The soil is still too far from firm for anything to be built on it. Everything depends on . . .

It is almost midnight. I am sleepy. Let us put off till tomorrow the continuation of these ratiocinations.

I finish *Sartoris*.[1] Have begun to reread *Egmont* in a volume of Goethe lent by Theodor Wolf, whom I went to see this afternoon.

2 January

In what I wrote of Catherine I intended but very little censure. I am not displeased that that child should develop uncommonly and in a way that is rather baffling for those who are following her. She resembles me much too much not to force me to think that I was like what she

---

[1] By William Faulkner.

is today and that I should have acted likewise without that great love which, almost at the outset of life, raised me so far above myself. But up to now she has shown no love or persistent attention but for herself, and if I add that her voice is getting beautiful and that, on certain days, she can be full of charm and grace, this is enough, in her eyes, to make her accept all the rest. Despite her egotism, she has always shown an interest in others, and in a way of which I am particularly appreciative: as a novelist, so to speak, and I think now: as an actress.

I had rejoiced immoderately over those lessons I was preparing to give her in Nice, but I soon had to come down a peg. All her time is taken up with other lessons (dancing, singing, elocution), which merely direct her attention to herself. She never gets away from herself from morning to night, and even the little reading she does on the outside interests her only in so far as she can bring it into some relation with herself. I had been delighted to see her become enthusiastic about some sonnets or other by Heredia; she said she wanted to know others. I took pleasure in giving her *Les Trophées* in a very decently bound copy I had found at Grasse. But her desire disappeared at once and I don't believe she ever even opened the volume. I experienced such disappointments with Marc; it was enough for something to come from me for the curiosity he had evinced to die immediately. It is as if first one and then the other had to defend himself against me. It is better thus, I try to convince myself.

1 February

Many ways of saying a thing; most often the best form is the one that comes to mind at once. It is that spontaneous style that delights us in Stendhal. It always seems that one is taking his thought by surprise as it jumps out of bed before dressing. But there are other ways of writing well. I do not like thought to bedeck itself, but rather to concentrate and stiffen itself; the manner of Montesquieu and of Tacitus. Following Dorothy Bussy's example, I launch into the *Life of Agricola*. Each sentence is full, heavy, taut. I tarry to weigh every word; they fill my heart and mouth. At the outset I am seized. What authority! How much I prefer that sort of wild austerity to grace! I took the book with me; I read it while walking and, without exhausting its bitter essence, ruminate one of those vigorous maxims in which the will stiffens:

"Memoriam quoque ipsam cum voce perdidissemus, si tam in nostra potestate esset oblivisci quam tacere."

"Subit quippe etiam ipsius inertiæ dulcedo, et invisa primo desidia postremo amatur." [2]

22 February

The moment when one begins to detach oneself somewhat, when one ceases to cling so firmly to the branch. Soon one will be ready to pick. Is it so hard to die as people think? Doubtless one has only to let oneself go; the mistake lies in hanging on too much to life.

Those who protest most against Rousseau's influence and point out how pernicious it is are the very ones who are most shocked that he should have turned over his offspring to a foundling home. On the contrary, they ought to congratulate him on this, judging that Rousseau never did anything wiser; if indeed his influence was pernicious . . . if indeed he ever had any children.

10 April

There was a time when, painfully tormented and plagued by desire, I used to pray for the time when the flesh, subjugated, would let me give myself completely to . . . But give oneself to what? To art? To "pure" thought? To God? What ignorance! What madness! This was tantamount to believing that the flame will shine brighter from the lamp that has run out of oil. Abstract, my very thought goes out; even today it is the carnal in me that feeds it, and now I pray: may I remain carnal and full of desire unto death!

I have always thought that we raise children badly in France, and perhaps this is the chief thing of which I accuse families.

Public garden looted. No guard. The children trample the lawns, break the branches of trees, strip flowering bushes of their buds. And not a parent to put a stop to this absurd havoc, which they don't even much enjoy.

[2] "We should have lost memory as well as voice, had it been as easy to forget as to keep silence."

"Besides, the charm of indolence steals over us, and the idleness which at first we loathed we afterwards love." (Translated by Alfred John Church and William Jackson Brodribb.)

It is merely a matter of destroying and of keeping from anyone what ought to belong to all. Is this a question of the French temperament? Or merely, as I should prefer, of upbringing? Nation unworthy of the liberty they claim; makes one constantly and everywhere long for policemen, keepers of the peace and of order, fences, and "keep off" signs.

From the moment when I realized and convinced myself that *man is responsible for God* . . .

And the wonderful thing is that by believing he was saving humanity Christ did actually save it.

Likewise it may be said that prayer creates God.

It is good to let the child think that God sees him, for he must act as if within the sight of God and make of that his *conscience*.

The considerable number of things I have not said because they seemed to me too obvious, too much of the type that "goes without saying" and not worth saying. . . . And yet when one finally lets oneself go, or forces oneself, to write them, one is amazed to see how many people are still surprised by them and ready to declare that one has never written anything more remarkable.

As I open my *Journal*, my eyes fall on this passage in which I already said (23 August 1926): "The most important things to say are those which often I did not think necessary to say—because they seemed to me too obvious."

It is independently of our will that ideas take shape in us and develop. There exists for them a sort of "struggle for life," [3] of survival of the fittest, and some of them die of exhaustion. The sturdiest are those that feed, not on abstraction, but on life; they are also the ones that are hardest to formulate.

The history of an idea would be interesting to write. It may also be that an idea dies. Yes, it would be a fine subject: the birth, life, and death of an idea. If only I could count on enough time to write it. . . .

11 April

Where had I got the idea that it was all over, that

[3] In English in the original.

spring had ceased to interest me and would never seize hold of me again? For days now, since the weather has become fine again and the air is warm, I feel that I have the soul of a migratory bird and think only of setting out. I book a berth on the ship leaving Marseille for Tunis on 2 May. Ah, why am I not already there! Everything will have begun already. Again I am going to miss the Overture.

I note in the review *Foreign Affairs* (issue of January 1942), which my new friend Keeler Faus of the U.S. Embassy lends me, as a footnote to a long article "Russia and Germany," signed X.:

"General Karl Adolf Maximilian Hoffmann was one of the greatest German General Staff officers in the last war. . . . His mother was descended from the Du Buisson family. Like him, and like the great Moltke, nearly all the great German army leaders of the past hundred years, with the characteristic exception of Ludendorff, have had some Huguenot ancestry." [4]

Has a list ever been drawn up of the exiled families, of the gifts that France made to foreign countries through the Revocation of the Edict of Nantes?

5 a.m., 5 May [sic—*4 May ?*]

The *Chanzy* left Marseille yesterday at about 11 a.m.

10 o'clock [*4 May ?*]

Had coffee at about nine. I had kept a piece of Cantal cheese from last night's dinner. All the bread one can eat, or almost. The rather heavy swell had reduced the number of diners; the able-bodied enjoyed what was intended for the absent ones. Already at lunch a much more abundant fare than for a long time now on land. Animal delight in at last being able to eat one's fill. I very much need to build myself up. The last days in Marseille did me in. So many hours chasing from office to office to get the necessary visas, identification marks and stamps; had I been alone, I believe I should have given up. But Ballard, the ever obliging, accompanied me everywhere, kept an eye on me, palliated my lapses, omissions, or distractions. At the last moment, after our farewells, he came back to remind me that I had forgotten to check my trunk: I have to hurry back to the pier and chase from one fantastic

[4] Quoted in English in the original.

place to another. All very Kafka. I keep thinking of *The Trial.* Feeling of not yet "having put everything in order." If one had to go through so many formalities to die. . . . Material for a wonderful tale. "You can't go away *like that.*" . . . But at least then one has no right to take anything along. That would be one of the finest chapters of the book: detachment. Roger Martin du Gard is amazed that death, the idea of death, causes me so little worry. Were it not for apprehension of the final pangs (perhaps, after all, less dreadful than they seem from a distance), I really believe I am rather soberly resigned. I have had my fill on this earth. A certain happy equilibrium is worked out and one reaches the end of the banquet without much wanting it to go on longer. Others are waiting for one's place; it is their turn. . . .

I reproach myself for not having sent an interzone card to Jeannie Valéry from Marseille to tell her at once my delight in seeing Paul again, more gallant, more real, more charming than ever.[5] And never have my friendship and admiration for that incomparable personality seemed to me keener and more unqualified. I experience nothing but joy in noting his incontrovertible superiority and his widespread influence, which are tempered by the most charming graciousness. I hold myself to be but very little in comparison with him, but have learned not to suffer from this. He no longer stands in my way; I have accomplished my work on a different plane from his—which I understand too well and admire too much not to admit that that work of mine has no place in his system and no value in his eyes. He is right, and my friendship even approves him for not "considering" me. His marvelous intelligence, though with nothing inhuman about it, owes it to itself to be strict and exclusive. In comparison with which I seem to myself to be wallowing in approximation. The most wonderful thing is that his mind, without abandoning any of its severity, has managed to preserve all its poetic value, managed to contribute to poetic creation that very severity which might have been thought hostile to art and which, on the contrary, makes of Valéry's art such a consummate marvel. I admire the unflinching direction

[5] Correspondence between the so-called "free zone" and the "occupied zone" of France was then limited to postcards.

and victorious persistence of his effort. No one in our
time has more effectively or more consistently aided intellectual progress; no one could more legitimately write:

> *I know where I am going*
> *And want to lead you there,*[6]

nor was capable of leading so far.

9 a.m., 5 May

Slight swell. On awakening, Africa is in sight, very
close. Then it withdraws and the coastline recedes.

Another great delight in Marseille was the meeting
with Jean-Louis Barrault. Marc, who was awaiting me
when the train from Nice got in, had taken me to dinner
with him and Madeleine Renaud the first evening in a
cheap little restaurant near the station, where Barrault
ate his meal in a hurry before going to the radio station
where he was to read some scenes from *Le Soulier de
satin*.[7] Wonderful face instinct with enthusiasm, passion,
genius. In his company Madeleine Renaud, with charming
modesty, remains in the background. Neither in him nor
in her am I aware of any of the actor's usual unbearable
shortcomings. Talented enough to remain simple.

I saw both of them again the day before leaving,
lunching with them at their invitation in a very good
restaurant on the square where the wide avenue du
Prado begins. Barrault urges me insistently to finish my
translation of *Hamlet* for him; and I have such confidence in his advice that I should like to get to work
at once.[8] I am much pleased to learn that he and Sartre
are close friends. In their company, through a keen
personal affection, I feel my hopes rejuvenated.

It is good to be able to direct one's admiration toward
the future. It would be a source of despair if one had to

[6] The lines:

> *Je sais où je vais,*
> *Je t'y veux conduire,*

are from Valéry's poem, *L'Insinuant*. Gide, quoting from memory,
gives them as:

> *Je sais où je vais*
> *Laisse-toi conduire.*

[7] Claudel's play, *The Satin Slipper*, which Barrault later staged at the
Comédie-Française.

[8] André Gide's translation of the first act of *Hamlet* had appeared in
the Franco-American review *Échanges* in December 1929.

be satisfied with this renaissance commissioned by order that is offered us today, this mediocrity so willingly accepted.

15 May

The wonderful toccata by Bach played by the Philadelphia orchestra, though written for the organ; but I prefer it on the piano, where the different parts stand out better. It does not seem to me that Bach's music has much to gain from the coloration the orchestra gives it, however well it may be applied (as it is here), which tends to remove (or to hide) that almost mathematical necessity toward which the music tends. This amounts to humanizing it excessively. The music triumphs over that attempt, to be sure; and it may be said that if Bach had known at his time the resources of the modern orchestra, he would have taken advantage of them, as he did of the surprising sonorities of certain instruments in the Brandenburg Concertos for instance. But he did not do so, and there is a certain element of treason in bringing out and emphasizing the latent harmonic or melodic possibilities (as Gounod did for the first Prelude of the *Well-Tempered Clavichord*). After this emotional humanization I should like to hear again, in all the abstraction of a blueprint, that celestial edifice which, it seems, can be brought closer to man only by taking it farther from God.

Sidi-bou-Saïd

As soon as I had realized that God was not yet but was becoming and that his becoming depended on each one of us, a moral sense was restored in me. No impiety or presumption in this thought, for I was convinced at one and the same time that God was achieved only by man and through man, but that if man led to God, creation, in order to lead to man, started from God; so that the divine had its place at both ends, at the start and at the point of arrival, and that the start had been solely in order to arrive at God. This bivalvular thought reassured me and I was unwilling to dissociate one from the other: God creating man in order to be created by him; God the end of man; chaos raised up by God to the level of man and then man raising himself up to the level of God. To accept but one of them: what fear, what obligation! To accept but the other: what self-satisfaction! It ceased to be a matter of obeying God, but rather of instilling life into him, of falling in love with him, of demanding him of oneself through love and of achieving him through virtue.

8 June

Science, to be sure, progresses only by everywhere substituting the *how* for the *why*. But however remote it may be, there is always a point at which the two interrogations meet and fuse. To achieve man . . . billions of centuries would not have sufficed if chance alone had contributed. However anti-finalist one may or can be, one encounters here something unacceptable, unthinkable; and the mind is forced to admit a propensity, an inclination encouraging the groping, vague, and unconscious progress of matter toward life and consciousness; then, through man, toward God.

9 June

But how slow God is in becoming! . . .

La Marsa, 12 June

The time is approaching, and I feel it quite close, when I shall have to say: I must give up.

The absurdity of all that is maddening. It is enough to make one believe that civilization, our Western civilization, will never recover from it. . . . The fact that that collaboration with Germany, so desirable and so much desired by us at a time when the majority, when public opinion, considered it impious (I mean in 1918), should now be proposed to us, imposed on us by the very ones who once considered it unthinkable; that it should become for us a sign of defeat, a mark of submission, abdication, and abjuration . . . torments one's conscience, or mine at least.

I do not believe in *Liberty* (we are dying of its idolatrous cult) and am ready to accept many a constraint; but I cannot bow before certain iniquitous decisions, give even a tacit consent to certain abominations.

1 July

"Just when and from what moment onward will you

deign to admit that an adversary who constantly and in all domains reveals so flagrant a superiority deserves to win out?"

"But then this is the end of freedom of thought. . . ."

"Will *you* be able to carry your liberalism to the point of allowing me to think this freely?"

"To think what?"

"That the path pointed out to us as the most desirable by good Father X., for instance (whom I love and venerate), aiming to restore in us a feeling for the sacred and to obtain from us an intellectual submission, without inquiry or verification, to truths recognized in advance and beyond discussion—that that path is as dangerous for the mind as the path of Hitlerism, to which it is opposed, and perhaps even more dangerous, and I shall shortly tell you why. It is in the name of those accepted and indisputable truths that the Church once condemned Galileo and that tomorrow . . . Does the whole effort of a Descartes, of a Montaigne even, have to be repeated? People had ceased to realize just how and why that effort had been so important, so emancipatory. Despotism can be opposed only by another despotism, to be sure, and it is an easy matter for Father X. to maintain that it is better to submit to God than to a man; but, for my part, I can see on both sides nothing but an abdication of the reason. In order to escape a very obvious danger, we hurl ourselves toward another, more subtle and not yet obvious, but which tomorrow will only be the more dreadful. And thus it is that the seemingly most solidly established civilizations collapse, in a way that soon ceases to be comprehensible. As for ours, a few years earlier we should not have thought it possible; and even today very rare are those who recognize in this so-called recovery and pseudo-revival of France, in this return to the past, in this 'withdrawal to one's minima,' as Barrès used to say, the most tragic result of our defeat, the true disaster: almost unintentional and half-unconscious relinquishment, by the best, of the possessions acquired most slowly and with the greatest difficulty, the hardest to appreciate and the rarest of all. . . .

"I admire martyrs. I admire all those who are able to

suffer and die, whatever may be the religion for which they do so. But even if you were to convince me, dear Father X., that nothing can resist Hitlerism but Faith, I should still see less spiritual danger in accepting despotism than in that form of resistance, considering any subordination of the mind more harmful to the interests of the mind than a yielding to force, since force at least in no way commits or compromises the mind."

"Yet if it is in the name of Faith, through Faith, that we succeed in driving the enemy out of France . . ."

"I should indeed applaud the remedy by which we had overcome a great malady. But subsequently how much time and vigilance and effort should we need in order, as Sainte-Beuve said, to 'cure us of the remedy' "?

6 July

Reread with the keenest interest the two *Henry IV's* and *Henry V* of Shakespeare (read at Saint-Louis in Senegal, but I did not remember them sufficiently); *The Way of the Lancer* by Boleslavki (excellently translated, it seems to me); I have on my table the *Mémoires* of Rœderer[9] and a typescript of Simenon's *Pedigree,* plus a huge novel in manuscript by Amrouche's sister. I should like, however, not to leave Shakespeare before having read also the fifteen acts of *Henry VI* and *Richard II,* with which I should have begun.

12 July

The most fragile part of me, and the one that has aged most, is my voice, that voice which even about ten years ago was still strong, supple, modulated—that is, capable of moving from the grave to the sharp as I wished—a voice over which I had complete mastery and could play as an actor does, which I had, moreover, greatly exercised through frequent readings to a small, family audience and the habit I had adopted of reciting poetry while walking. Above all, it was tuned just right. Now my ear alone is in tune; consequently I have ceased to sing save in thought.

[9] This short title could refer either to the *Louis XII and François I, or Memoirs for Use in Writing a New History of Their Reigns,* or to the actual recollections of the same author: *Concerning Bonaparte: Journal of Count P. L. Rœderer.*

16 *July*

I ought never to travel without a Montaigne. If I had
the *Essais* at hand, I should look up the remark he makes
about La Boétie: "I have lived more negligently" (since
he left me). Jean Lambert, in his article on Schlumberger (*Fontaine,* number 21), attributes it to St. Augus-
tine: "I had lost the witness of my life," he presumably
said in *The Confessions,* "and I feared that I might not
live so well." It may be that this remark is there, but is
it not the precise translation of these words that I read
in the letters of Pliny the Younger (Letter XII, to
Calestrius Tiro): "*Amisi vitæ meæ testem. . . . Vereor
ne negligentius vivam*"? That sentence, which charms us
and makes us reflect, was perhaps but a commonplace
in antiquity, one of those banal remarks that were used
for each bereavement? [10]

Sidi-bou-Saïd, 1 September

Finished the translation of *Hamlet* yesterday. As much
as twenty years ago I had translated the first act (La
Tortue brought out a very fine edition of it), which all
alone caused me more trouble than the five acts of
Antony and Cleopatra. I thought I had forever forsaken
such exhausting labor. I returned to it at the request of
Jean-Louis Barrault with an adolescent's zeal and an
old man's patient equanimity. For almost three months
I have devoted from six to eight hours a day to it and
taken relaxation from it only to put into shape for the
Figaro my "Advice in regard to *Phèdre*" (then in regard
to *Iphigénie*). I should certainly not have persevered if
my version had not seemed to me greatly superior to all
the earlier ones, and especially much more adapted to
the stage and to delivery by actors. I had within reach,
not so much to help as to encourage me, the translations
by F.-V. Hugo, Schwob, Pourtalès, and Copeau. This
last one alone seems to show some regard for French;
all of them sacrifice rhythm, lyrical power, cadence, and
beauty to mere exactitude. I believe that, in this regard,
the translations of the last century were preferable.

[10] Pliny says of the death of an old friend, Corellius Rufus: "I have
indeed lost the witness, guide, and teacher of my life. To sum up I
shall say what I said to my companion Calvisius when my grief was
fresh: 'I am afraid I shall live more carelessly now.' " (*Letters*, I, 12.)

The great advantage of this work: I could tackle it at any time, always ready for this type of effort, which I was inclined to prolong for three or four hours at a time. Mme Théo urges me vigorously, and with the best arguments in the world, to give henceforth my best attention to my *Journal*. She is doubtless right, but the quality of this journal comes precisely from the fact that I write in it only in answer to some call and urged on by a sort of inner necessity. For some time now I have felt no need to open it again and have lost sight of myself. I become aware again how hard it is to reinterest oneself in something one has abandoned. All my thoughts are elusive; for some time I have been living and feeling only through sympathy; at least my affective faculties are as keen as in the best period of my youth.

Solitude is bearable only with God.

September

Still at Sidi-bou-Saïd. Thanks to the charming hosts who are lodging me, I find rest, comfort, calm, and salvation here. From the terrace of the villa I watch the plain as it swoons. Exhausting heat, which I am ashamed to endure so badly. And, for the first time in my life, probably, I am making the acquaintance of what is called nostalgia. I think of the mysterious forest interior at La Roque in which the child I was could not venture without trembling, of the edges of the pond thick with flowering plants, of the evening mists over the little stream. I think of the beech grove at Cuverville, of the great autumn winds carrying away the russet leaves, of the rooks' call, of the evening meditation beside the fire in the calm house on its way to sleep. . . . Everything I owe to Em. comes to mind and I have been thinking constantly of her for several days with regret and remorse for having so often and so greatly been in arrears with her. How often I must have seemed to her harsh and insensitive! How ill I corresponded to what she had a right to expect of me! . . . For a smile from her today, I believe I should forsake life and this world in which I could not overtake her. . . .

16 September

"When he used a word," John Dover Wilson says of Shakespeare in his excellent introduction to *Hamlet,* "all possible meanings of it were commonly present to his mind, so that it was like a musical chord which might be resolved in whatever fashion or direction he pleased." [11] This is what constitutes the force of his poetic incantation and this is what the translator must make a point of preserving. He must constantly fear, by being too precise, to limit the flight of the imagination.

The human soul (and why fear using this word to designate that complex of emotions, tendencies, susceptibilities joined together by a bond that is perhaps merely physiological) has shadowy, changing, intangible contours, constantly modified and subject to modification according to circumstances, climates, seasons, and all influences, so that the tensest and most vigilant will has great trouble maintaining in it a semblance of cohesion. In itself already sufficiently rebellious to description and analysis without that confusion which language contributes by using the same word, "love," to designate two tendencies of such different nature that they are opposed. Around this word and by reason of its misuse there has grown up a sort of false mystery, which would be rendered ridiculous if language turned to another word to signify love as charity rather than the one used for love as concupiscence; for desire and for the gift. But such lexical poverty is itself revelatory; it reveals that slipping from one to the other is always possible. But no matter; many a problem in this domain seems psychological and is artificially created by an improper use of words. It would not be useless to study the vocabulary of other languages, which perhaps do not suffer, in this regard, from the same poverty as does French.

29 September

Finished reading *Die Jungfrau.*[12] The end is even more absurd than all the rest. Schiller's only excuse is the ignorance still prevailing in his time as to the very docu-

---

[11] The quotation is given in English in the original.
[12] Schiller's drama *Die Jungfrau von Orleans* deals with Joan of Arc.

ments of the great trial. For fear of doing him an injustice and underestimating him, I want to reread *Don Carlos*, which is incomparably better, if my recollection of it is exact. But how great Goethe seems beside Schiller! How heavy with meaning the least of his works! Each is born of a need, an inner prompting. Schiller's *Die Jungfrau* is unmeaningful and nothing in it seems motivated save by a childish desire for scenic effect. (I also want to read Kleist's *Penthesilea*.)

1 October

Beside which Shaw's *Saint Joan* (which I am rereading with very great satisfaction) seems a marvel of intelligence, of appositeness, and of ingenuity.

9 October

Let myself be kept for dinner last night by Jean Amrouche after a fine game of chess. His friend Jules Roy, the very likable aviator, come in from Sétif, invited us as his guests. After the meal we went to the Halfahouine, which was especially lively on the next to last evening of Ramadan. This morning got up at five thirty because of Suzy's leaving. When I came in last night I had found a short letter from her, since she didn't expect to see me again—such a nice letter that I immediately made up my mind to kiss Suzy good-by. After having got up, unable to go to sleep again and not feeling like doing so, I went out. Radiant morning. I had taken with me the first volume of the *Histoire du peuple d'Israël*, which I had begun reading, but did not open it. Tried in vain to call to mind the whole of Baudelaire's *Crépuscule du matin*.[13] Contemplated at length a group of poverty-stricken children, half covered with sordid rags, obviously homeless. They were lying under a portico, one across another, trying to sleep, but tormented by flies and probably devoured by vermin, occasionally scratching themselves furiously under their tatters. Tunis is full of a poverty that is beyond help. Homeless children seemingly even much more lamentable than the *"besprizornis"* of Sebastopol, who at least seem lively and gay, probably now become valiant soldiers of the Red army. Insouciance of that hopeless youth,

[13] "Morning Twilight" is one of the poems of *The Flowers of Evil*. *The History of the People of Israel* is by Renan.

stuff of which the "social question" is made. Dream of a society that would not allow of any outcasts.

There are those who would like to ameliorate men and there are those who hold that that cannot be done without first ameliorating the conditions of their life. But it soon appears that one cannot be divorced from the other, and you don't know where to begin. Some days humanity strikes me as so miserable that the happiness of a few seems impious.

10 October

As for collaboration with Germany, nothing would have been more desirable, and for each of the two countries, each one having exactly what the other most lacked. But today events have made it so that the "Gaullist" elements greatly predominate in France, in number and even more in quality. This involves, in my case at least, no discredit for the marshal; on the contrary; he seems to me to be playing as best he can a difficult game, and the future will perhaps prove that even at the moment of the armistice he got out of it with the least prejudice to France (if indeed an event ever *proves* anything). I gladly subscribe to these remarks from the letter I received yesterday from Roger M. du G.: "I confess to being very susceptible to the style and accent of his speeches. It is said that they are written for him; now B., now G., now another are cited. . . . Nonsense! Each of his messages has an authentic ring that belongs indeed to the same man and that generally goes rather straight to my heart. His very mistakes are not lacking in either straightforwardness or natural nobility.[14] It will require perspective to throw light on the secrets of the *Pétain enigma,* and one of my great regrets is that I shall die without knowing . . ." Knowing what? Whether Pétain was not, at heart, the most "Gaullist" of us all; but it was important above all not to let this be seen.

13 October

One catches cold with a temperature of seventy-seven after days and nights spent in a Turkish bath. I know I shall not escape. . . .

[14] Need I add today (1949) that this opinion, which I then shared with my friend, we could neither of us keep for long? [A.]

The slow accumulation of very small, modest efforts. I recall the wonderful cry of the man in Dante's Hell (I was not yet twenty when I heard it for the first time, and what a lesson I drew from it for a long time thereafter!):

> *Were I but carrying so light a load*
> *That in a hundred years I gained an inch,*
> *Already had I set out on the road.*[15]

Real old age would be giving up hope of progress. I am not made for contemplative stagnation and enjoy only effort.

I am reading the *Penthesilea* very slowly, letting nothing pass without understanding and feeling it completely, with indescribable rapture. Kleist makes wonderful use of German syntax, and this makes it possible to appreciate its resources, its subtle license, its suppleness. The fine tangle of the sentence, in which he frolics, remains almost impossible in French, where the function of uninflected words is most often indicated only by their position. Enough to form two very different nations.

19 October

And this morning, in order to understand if possible the working of her mind, I ask Chacha to explain her remark of last night, but with all the respect I owe to her advanced age. It seems clear to me that a confusion has got fixed in her mind: the short time the water took to boil leading to the rest, endowing the water with a sort of attribute of speed. None of this reasoned out at all, of course; in an uncivilized way.

At this time when everything is rationed, she wastes gas in an odd way, putting the water on to boil for no reason at all, then saying, when she puts it back on the fire: "Oh, it will boil fast; it's already been heating for a half-hour!"

The Siamese cat, fed almost exclusively on fish in peacetime, now is quite willing to eat bread. Chacha tells me so this morning: "He eats anything now!" Then,

[15] *Inferno*, XXX, 82–4. [A.]

as if saying: "What a disaster!" she adds: "Ah, he certainly can be said to choose the right time!"

Twenty times a day, about anything or anyone: "What a poison!" And about the events of the war: "Ah, all that's very complicated!" I should have said at the outset that she comes from Martinique.

19 October

Corydon remains in my opinion the most important of my books; but it is also the one with which I find the most fault. The least well done is the one it was most important to do well. I was probably ill advised to treat ironically such serious questions, which are generally handled as a subject of reprobation or of joking. If I went back to them, people would not fail to think I am obsessed by them. People prefer to envelop them in silence as if they played but a negligible role in society and as if the number of individuals tormented by such questions were negligible in society. And yet when I began to write my book, I thought that number to be much smaller than it eventually appeared to be and than it is in reality; smaller, however, in France than in many other countries I came to know later, for probably in no other country (with the exception of Spain) do the cult of Woman, the religion of Love, and a certain tradition of amorous intercourse so much dominate manners or so servilely influence the way of life. I am obviously not speaking here of the cult of woman in its profoundly respectable aspect, nor of noble love, but of debasing love that sacrifices the best in man to skirts and the alcove. The very ones who shrug their shoulders when faced with such questions are those who proclaim that Love is the most important thing in life and consider it natural that a man should subordinate his career to it. They are naturally thinking of love as desire and of sensual pleasure; and in their eyes desire is king. But, in their opinion, that desire loses all value and does not deserve to be taken into consideration the moment it ceases to be in harmony with, and similar to, theirs. They are very sure of themselves, having Opinion on their side.

Yet I believe I said in that book just about everything I had to say on this most important subject that had not been said before me; but I reproach myself with not having said it as I should have. None the less, certain attentive minds will manage to discover it there later on.

12 November

Occupation of the French "free zone" by Germany and of North Africa by the U.S.A. . . . Events deprive me of any desire to say anything. Always tempted to think that it has no importance *basically* and does not interest me, even were I to lose my head thereby.

28 November

Yesterday very pleasant lunch at the Ragus', whom I always enjoy seeing, with the young Boutelleau couple, Jean Tournier, and Mme Sparrow.

The events of Toulon are being commented upon and, as almost always, they allow of very different interpretations.[16] Dr. Ragu, in better form than ever, judges them very severely. To him that heroic scuttling of our fleet seems comparable to the suicide of a disloyal employee cornered by recognition of his crime, escaping punishment and taking refuge in death: an absurd act resulting from an original notorious blunder. I suspect that this interpretation must likewise be Roger Martin du Gard's. This action on the part of the officers of the French Navy explains their attitude at Mers-el-Kebir: an order was given them, doubtless, to sink their ships rather than to let them be of use either to the English or to the Germans. But this amounted to setting one's point of honor above the very interests of the country and I can easily see why reason protests against this. Despite everything, this shows a preference for oneself over the cause, and this leaves the conscience ill at ease. One wonders, without being able to approve. In the dreadful dilemma they had got into, the only choice they had was between suicide and slavery. No loophole possible, no means of escaping. As soon as our fleet failed to decide at once in favor of keeping up the fight, it became useless or dishonored. Accepting the conditions of the armistice was tantamount to a delayed scuttling. Alongside the English, that fleet might have rendered very great services; now

[16] The French fleet in the harbor of Toulon was scuttled on 27 November 1942.

it serves merely as an example of the evils of obedience when personal conscience ceases to acquiesce in the commands received.

11 December

Finished *Le Rouge et le noir* in the night during a rather heavy bombardment. As for the reflections I noted yesterday, Stendhal himself brings his hero to make them in the last chapters of the book, and this sets off strikingly everything that precedes. One comes again on some very beautiful pages after long, boring passages that, it seems, were written rather perfunctorily. The reader, with Julien, "was tired of heroism" as he says, having become fully conscious of the vanity of that incentive which operates only in relation to "the idea of a public and *of others*" (Chapter xxxix). This at last re-establishes a scale of values. It was high time!

But in the first part there are easily a dozen marvelous chapters distinguished by incomparable novelty, briskness, and boldness such as would make a deep impression on the mind of a sensitive young reader just awakening to life.

In every street of Tunis many Italian or German soldiers; the former flabby, haggard, and wearing soiled uniforms, devoid of dignity and quick to show insolence; the Germans well equipped, clean, disciplined, appearing simultaneously smiling and resolute, probably ordered to show themselves pleasant and considerate toward the civilian population, to make their domination desirable, and going about it just right. Everywhere considerable munitions and armaments. . . . I fear we may be in for a long siege.

The official communiqués on both sides are most contradictory, each one announcing nothing but victories, retreats on the part of the enemy, and encircling of enemy forces. The mind stifles in this atmosphere of organized falsehood.

26 December

NOTICES in three languages (French, Arabic, and Italian) are abundantly posted on the walls of the city. They make known to the Jews that before the end of the year they will have to pay the sum of TWENTY MILLIONS as an aid to the victims of the Anglo-American bombings, for which *they are responsible,* "international Jewry" having, as it has long been well known, "wanted and prepared for the war." (The Jewish victims are naturally excluded from the number of people to be aided.) This is signed by "General Von Arnim, Commander of the Axis forces in Tunisia."

31 December

Last day of this year of disgrace, on which I want to close this notebook. May the following one reflect less somber days!

Doubtless I no longer cling much to life, but I have this fixed idea; *to last.* To make myself and my dependencies last a little while longer: linen, clothing, shoes, hope, confidence, smile, graciousness; make them last until the farewell. In view of this I am becoming economical, parsimonious of everything in order that none of this should give out ahead of time, through great fear that this war may be drawn out, through great desire and great hope to see the end of it.

1943

No electricity. We dine as early as six o'clock, for the gas is likewise cut off while we are sitting down at the table in the light of a single candle. Bombs again fell on Tunis at noon and at five o'clock; the results of the explosions are terrifying. Jean Tournier has been busy with a team of youths the last few mornings extracting corpses and wounded from under the ruins of a block of houses in the Arab town that had been demolished by three bombs early in the week. They counted between three and four hundred victims. It was impossible to help in time those who were calling for help from the cellars where they were walled off. And clusters of corpses, already rotting, continue to be brought out from under heaps of masonry, beams, and rubble.

And this is probably but the prelude to more violent bombings, which keep one from feeling safe anywhere. Hope of escaping narrows from day to day.

Invited by the Ragus, I lunched this first day of the new year at the civilian hospital together with the Boutelleaus. The latter arrive very late: a bomb has just fallen on the house of Mme Sparrow, the eminent Polish doctor who is lodging them. A telephone message (the hospital's exchange is still working) warns the Ragus that Mme Sparrow cannot come. Taken by surprise in her bed, where a severe headache had detained her, she had to rush out in pajamas. The bomb buried itself in the ground without exploding, cutting through the cellar of the building. They are thinking of exploding it, and a police cordon is keeping people at a distance from the block of evacuated houses. The evening before, I had entrusted to Gérard Boutelleau the two notebooks of my journal (the entire year 1942), which Hope Boutelleau had very kindly offered to type for me. Besides, fearing a house-search, I was anxious to put them in a safe place. Gérard B. had the greatest difficulty getting through the cordon of German police and getting hold of the manuscripts. This is what made him so late. It is hoped that the artificially provoked explosion will not do too much harm to Mme Sparrow's apartment. They left us immediately after the meal to make sure of this.

After their leaving we examine at length the plan of fleeing to Nabeul. It is essential to make sure that we are not rushing toward a greater danger: many country houses and farms have been sacked by Arabs and their inhabitants massacred. It is a sort of organized Jacquerie[1] protected by the German army, which is eager to make a good impression on the native population, drunk with its demands. Rather a bomb than butchery.

6 January

Bombs fell last night on the avenue Roustan barely sixty yards from the house of which we are occupying the fourth floor. The explosion blew in a French door of the room in which I was sleeping and broke a large and heavy mirror in the living-room. By an extraordinary stroke of bad luck we had not made sure the windows were unlocked because of yesterday's wind. A rather large bomb-fragment cut through the wooden shutter and knocked out the lower pane of one of the living-room windows.

9 January

Roosevelt's speech holds out the bright productive prospects of American factories, which, he declares, are now producing all alone more submarines than the factories of Germany, Italy, and Japan combined. Likewise for tanks, cannon, machine guns, and all other war supplies. Fine! He also speaks of the draft that is increasing the American army from two to seven million men (I think). But he doesn't speak, and can't speak, of the military value of those men. It is harder to achieve than machines; long training and practice are lacking. And the flaunting of that numerical and material superiority, if it is not accompanied by a moral superiority, far from reassuring me, worries me. What is the good of giving all those figures? Stalin cleverly hid his, so that the power of the Russian army took the world and Germany by surprise.

[1] The peasant uprising of 1358 as a result of the English invasion of France during the captivity of King Jean II.

11 January

All she expected of me and I was unable to give her
—indeed, that was due her . . . there are days when I
constantly think of it. Ah, if the soul, as you were eager
to persuade me, is immortal and if yours still has its
eyes fixed on me, may it realize that I feel eternally in-
debted to you. . . . But no, in my case, since I cannot
believe in an afterlife, this is not the form my regret
takes; I merely think of all the attentions I should have
had for her, and I await, and shall await, the smile with
which she would have rewarded me. In what a state of
blindness I have lived!

28 January

I read with amusement in Johnson's *Rasselas* (1759):
"I have been long of opinion, that, instead of the tardy
conveyance of ships and chariots, man might use the
swifter migration of wings; that the fields of air are open
to knowledge, and that only ignorance and idleness need
crawl upon the ground"; and a little further: "If men
were all virtuous I should with great alacrity teach them
all to fly. But what would be the security of the good, if
the bad could at pleasure invade them from the sky?" [2]

29 January

When, upon leaving my next to the last year of school,
I began to go out and to frequent a few salons, I readily
realized that the thing most needed in them is an ear,
each person being more attentive to what he says himself than to what others say. Nothing flatters people more
than the interest one takes, or seems to take, in their
conversation. I paid little attention to mine as a conse-
quence, attributing value only to the written word, and
prided myself on becoming a perfect listener. ("You listen
with your eyes," Wilde told me.) Thus it is that I was
well considered though remaining silent. But now, with
age, I am the one who is listened to; but I express myself so badly that I disappoint as soon as I open my
mouth. Everything that is dear to me and matters to me
remains far this side of my lips, out of reach as it were,
and I utter nothing but banalities and nonsense. I am
worth something only when faced with blank paper.

I take less and less interest in conversation, in what

[2] In the original, the quotations are given in English.

is called "an exchange of ideas," except with a few rare intimate friends. Most often I strive merely to flatter in order to please, tormented by the desire to be liked. What a weakness! And how I admire those who, like Victor, pay no attention whatever to that! Fortunately it is not the same in my writings, where I override and am very little concerned with "what will be thought of it." At least this is the way I did in the time when one could still write and publish freely. If I had handled my pen as I have my tongue, my writings would be valueless, though they would doubtless have enjoyed a greater, and especially an earlier success.

30 January

Ah, how harsh this separation from my loved ones seems to me certain days! How long this wait is! Can I even hope to see them all again? If it may be that, after this perilous passage through the war, I myself am still alive . . . What care I take to save myself for them until that day! It is this, almost as much as curiosity, that still makes me cling to life. Am I going to last long enough to see the following chapter? And how, in what condition, shall I find those I have so long lost from sight? How will they have stood the test? It is doubtless going on for many months more. And I think the worst is still ahead of us; in comparison to it, what we have already endured is nothing.

4 February

Boswell is indubitably superior to Eckermann. A pity that Johnson remains so inferior to Goethe. His wisdom is wonderfully representative of that of his time, but never rises above it. He has very racy sallies and retorts, but one listens to him without real profit, constantly aware of the limitations of his genius. Constricted, moreover, by the credo to which he constantly renews his allegiance; but one wonders whether without that curb he would have been able to venture very far. He remains a man of letters throughout everything, and one is grateful to him for this. His style is rich, full of images, consistent, rhythmical, and, as it were, succulent; in comparison Swift's seems fleshless. None the less, if Johnson seemed to dominate his time, he did so, I think, especially by his mass. He overwhelmed.

6 February

My dreams are often *auditory* as much as they are *visual;* but it also occurs to me to dream that I am *reading* sentences; they take shape in my mind as if without my knowing it, it seems, since I have the impression of discovering them; they take me by surprise. What an odd comedy one thus puts on for oneself, supplying the subject of the surprise and the amazement likewise. I recall having already noted some examples of this: one is simultaneously the accomplice and the dupe. I also wonder at the extent to which the remarks heard in dream correspond to the characters who make them, characters that are often much more lifelike in what they say and their tone of voice than in their external appearance, which is often vague and uncertain. Often, indeed, it is solely by the remarks they make that I recognize them. At first I don't know who the companion is walking beside me; and suddenly, on hearing him speak, I think: why, it's Marcel![3] And taking a better look at him, I tell myself: how he has changed! On seeing him, I should never have recognized him; but on hearing him, I know without a shadow of a doubt that it is *he.*

Where could I have been walking with Marcel? It was on the seashore among rocks lashed with spray. "When one is facing the sea," said Marcel, "it is impossible to think of anything." "That is what allowed Hugo to write poetry," I retorted.

10 February

Sorry need of insulting and vilifying one's opponent, a need equally common to both sides, which causes me to listen so painfully at times to the radio broadcasts, those from London and America as well as those from Berlin and Paris-Vichy. What! Do you really think that all the intelligence, nobility of heart, and good faith are solely on your side? Is there nothing but base interests and stupidity among your opponents? Or perhaps you will tell me that it is good to convince the masses of this, for otherwise they would have less heart in the conflict? It is essential to persuade the soldier that those he is being urged to massacre are bandits who do not

[3] Marcel Drouin.

deserve to live; before killing other good, decent fellows
like himself, his gun would fall from his hands. It is a
matter of activating hatred, and one blows on passions
to make them glow brightly. It takes brutes to fight
brutes; consequently they are turned into brutes.

Recognizing the good points and virtues of the enemy
has always been my weakness, and it might make me
pass for a traitor among the partisans of either camp.
This is indeed partly why I should keep silent today
even if I were given license to speak. Today there is
room only for falsehood, and it alone is listened to. And
everything I am saying about it is absurd. . . .

11 February

. . . for it is not a question of the few decent people I
might find in the opposite camp or country, but rather
of the principles and ethic animating them, which are
weighing on my head and chest, which keep me from
breathing, from thinking, from loving, which suppress
me. It is against that, not against them, that I am protesting and struggling.

13 February

There is and always will be in France (except under
the urgent threat of a common danger) division and
parties; in other words, dialogue. Thanks to that, the
fine equilibrium of our culture: equilibrium in diversity.
Always a Montaigne opposite a Pascal; and, in our time,
opposite a Claudel, a Valéry. At times one of the two
voices wins out in strength and magnificence. But woe
to the times when the other is reduced to silence! The
free mind has the superiority of not wanting to be alone
in having the right to speak.

I feel that I spring from French culture and am bound
to it with all my heart and mind. I cannot get away from
that culture without losing sight of myself and ceasing to
feel myself. But I believe that the idea of the mother
country, which is so greatly abused in wartime (when
it becomes indispensable for leading men to fight and
uniting them under a single flag), is hard to anchor
solidly in the heart of the vast majority of the untutored,
unless by a deceitful simplification. Mystical interests
elude them or are almost indifferent to them. It is essential to group individual interests in a cluster around an

entity, which is France. This can be done around a tree trunk only by removing its branches.

17 February

Numerical superiority, superiority in equipment, and in overwhelming proportions; the Anglo-Americans have this and boast of it. They have proclaimed it over and over and seem to rely on it. Their inactivity is going to leave the Russians all the honors of victory and Stalin is beginning to put forward the idea that he has conquered all alone. The communiqués from London now insist on the difficulties of the contest (in Tunisia) put off from day to day, which, they say, will of necessity be very costly. Will this be to exaggerate tomorrow the merits of a victory or to attenuate the shame of a defeat? Whom will they persuade that the contest was easier on the Russian front?

I cannot share the optimism of some who think the Germans will withdraw from Tunis without fighting, that resistance will be made in front of or behind that city, which is said to be undefendable, and that Bizerte rather than Tunis will be the center of the heavy fighting that is foreseen. I expect much worse ordeals, in comparison with which those of yesterday will seem but "a poor rehearsal." It is not even certain that we shall come out alive from the hell I foresee, and the days of semi-happiness that we are still living are perhaps the last.

I picked up Keats's *Odes* again. A half-hour was enough to learn them completely by heart again (at least the *Ode to a Nightingale* and the *Ode to Autumn*). I believe that likewise if I applied myself to piano practice again, I should have hardly any trouble relearning almost all of Chopin's études, the few preludes and fugues of Bach that I used to know by heart, etc.; but I cannot make up my mind to sacrifice the time it would take for my fingers to recover a semblance of dexterity. Besides, the feeling that I am being listened to has become unbearable to me. If I could practice without being heard by anyone and on a good piano, I think I should nevertheless get back to it; and very soon I should be giving many hours to it. . . . The intensity of my practice in the past came from this: disapproval of the virtuosos who play in such a way as to show themselves off at the expense of the composer they are interpreting. Now, I can no longer

claim at all, at present, to surpass them. From my practice today I should derive but too unsatisfactory a pleasure; it is better to preserve intact my regret for that lost
paradise.

18 February

I finished Boswell yesterday evening. Those thirteen
hundred pages can be read almost without a single moment of fatigue or boredom. To what a degree Johnson's robust intelligence is paralyzed or held in check
by his religious convictions and his perpetual fear of
going beyond them, Boswell implicitly admits himself,
though sharing his convictions, and that through them
"he had perhaps, at an early period, narrowed his mind
somewhat too much, both as to religion and politics."
And it is not one of the least interests of this book that
it allows us to follow the intentional narrowing of that
fine free thought. "He was prone to superstition, but
not to credulity," Boswell appropriately says. This is
the regard in which his book is most instructive, despite
him: we see, by example, how a vigorous mind can remain entangled in dogma.

Same scorn as in Goethe, same lack of curiosity, for
problems concerning origins. No more than Goethe does
Johnson suspect the lesson that can be drawn from the
study of primitive peoples. "One set of savages is like
another," Johnson declares[4] (15 June 1784), and he immediately directs his attention elsewhere. The egg that
ethnologists will later hatch had not yet been laid; any
curiosity in that regard seemed useless and unprofitable.

25 February

Before twenty, many a man thinks he is clever indeed
to discover that man acts only through interests. And
naturally he thinks only of the lowest, vilest interests.
For if he were willing to admit that the most immaterial
chimeras as well as the most sublime imaginations or
conceptions can sometimes *interest* man to the point of
taking precedence over vulgar interests, we should not
be far from agreeing. But this does not get us very far
toward recognizing that the man who, out of a feeling
of duty or to preserve an ideal, gives his life does so
because he takes pleasure in his very devotion to duty

[4] In the original, all quotations from Boswell are given in English.

and finds satisfaction in his sacrifice. For, after all, in
order to stir a man something is required: desire or
pleasure or need. This alone matters: what, for you, precedes all the rest? As for the motives of self-esteem, La
Rochefoucauld exposed them in such a way that there is
no need of going back over them, but perhaps you have
not read him. The Church herself is ready to admit that
"the will always works toward what it likes most," as
Pascal writes (*Provinciales,* Letter XVIII), and "One
forsakes pleasures only for greater ones" (Letter to Mlle
de Roannez).

3 March

Yesterday, shortly before noon, a more intense bomb-
ing than any of last month. I was at the civilian hospital
when it began. Dr. Ragu took me out on the terrace over-
looking the whole city just in time to see many columns
of smoke rise. Far as we were from the explosions, we
heard the whistle of the falling bombs. An icy wind was
blowing, which made me go in rather soon and I thus
saw arrive soon after cars and wagons loaded with
wounded. The Arabs were immediately sent to the Sadiki
hospital, the Italians to the Italian hospital; the French
alone were kept and sent to wards where, as Ragu told
me later, a frightful confusion reigned. I regret not having
accompanied him on his rounds. In front of the hospital
gate was grouped a crowd of poor people, with whom
I mingled for a time vainly seeking some face to look
upon with pleasure. Nothing but congenitally diseased,
deformed, poverty-stricken outcasts, ugly enough to discourage pity. A great anguish of grief weighed upon
that sorry humanity. They were waiting to be allowed
to approach the victims, and this could not be done until
after the latter had received first aid. I saw some on
stretchers as they left the ambulance, disfigured by
hideous wounds, with only half a face left; others deathly
pale and eyes closed, perhaps already dead. . . .

Lunch at the hospital, then returned to town immediately after. Learned on returning to avenue Roustan that
all the window-panes in my room had been blown out.
About thirty yards from the R.s' house a bomb destroyed
the buildings of the registry office.

No more electricity; no more gas; no more water.

7 March

The *Journal* notebook (January to May 1942) that I had entrusted to Hope Boutelleau for typing fell into the hands of the Italian police at the time of the house search at Sidi-bou-Saïd; the Italian police handed it over at once to the German authorities, who, I am told, were concerned by certain passages, and particularly the one ending with these words: ". . . It is useless to claim that, had we not declared war, Germany would have respected France, whom she knew, better than we did ourselves, to be weakened and incapable of resisting her for long." Alas, I had not waited for this war to think what seemed to me evident and what even Germany with the best will in the world could not have prevented. Was it not inevitable that a young nation, conscious of its strength and trembling at the recollection of an unjust defeat, injured in its pride by the most blundering of treaties, deprived by it of a possibility of colonial expansion as an outlet for a prolific population crowded within its frontiers, that such a nation should soon strive, as soon as she was back on her feet, to overflow onto ill-defended neighboring lands, insufficiently populated by an aging nation, numbed with comfort, listless and languid? . . . Yes, long before the war France stank of defeat. She was already falling to pieces to such a degree that perhaps the only thing that could save her was, is perhaps, this very disaster in which to retemper her energies. Is it fanciful to hope that she will issue from this nightmare strengthened? I believe she is at present pulling herself together.

13 March

The din of the explosions tears me from sleep at about nine. And while I am dressing in haste, new detonations much nearer make me rush to the window. In the direction of the harbor I see vast white clouds rising, which filled the sky for more than an hour. A very bright white glow continued for a long time to light up the horizon powerfully, the result no doubt of some tremendous fire. Amphoux, who had joined me in the living-room, judges that it is much closer to us than the harbor. I see another bomb fall on the left, in the direction of the Majestic, certainly less than a hundred yards from our house. And almost immediately afterward people run in the avenue Roustan, under our windows, carrying stretchers and hastening toward the scene. The wave of terror has passed; there is nothing to do but go back to bed, since I am beyond the age of being able to help the victims. But in expectation of a new wave that may perhaps strike us, remaining on the alert, I do not dare yield to sleep. No one can feel safe from such a blind aim; and why should I be spared? One feels the blast from near-by explosions pass over one like the flapping of a shroud.

16 March

The very pleasant young German officer, a student of art history and friend of Ernst-Robert Curtius, whom I went to see yesterday at the Rose de Sable, told me that in Rome, where he began his military service and was stationed more than a year, the books of the Pléiade collection[5] are so sought after that the few booksellers who still have some ask up to two thousand francs (in our money) for them (quoted up to four and five thousand francs in New York, Keeler Faus wrote me at the beginning of the war). It was that collection, created and edited so intelligently by Schiffrin, that Jean Schlumberger and I had such trouble getting accepted. We had to insist and to struggle for almost two years before reaching an understanding. "I don't see what you consider so remarkable in it," X. persisted in saying. Initiative in admiration is an extremely rare thing; here, too, nothing but followers are found. I recall a conversation with the chief bookseller (I might as well say the only one) of Dakar, during my first stay in French West Africa, who said to me of the Pléiade books: "No, sir, our clientele doesn't like those books; they have no chance of success. No, the colonists don't want them." Then, taking out a hideous large illustrated edition of some then popular author: "Here, this is what they like." If I saw him again today, probably he would assert that he

[5] A series of French classics, well printed on thin paper and leather-bound, which is now published by Librairie Gallimard. A single volume contains all of Montaigne; another, all of Rimbaud; Balzac's *Comédie humaine* appears in several volumes. In the summer of 1939 Gide's *Journal 1889–1939* came out in this series in a volume of over 1,300 pages.

never said such a thing, or even that he was one of the
first booksellers to sell and to recommend to his clients
the Pléiade collection; but I am sure that my memory
is not wrong on this point.

The charming F. V. Arnold is the first, and only, German to whom I have spoken in Tunisia. I hesitated to
meet him, then decided that my reticence was absurd.
We did not speak of the war. He told me simply, in the
beginning of our conversation, how embarrassed he felt
by his uniform. He enjoys declaring his great admiration
for Thomas Mann's *Lotte in Weimar*,[6] then takes out of
the breast pocket of his military tunic a tiny edition of
Goethe's *Divan*, no larger than a cigarette-lighter, which,
he says, helps him over many difficult periods. He also
speaks enthusiastically of Jünger. The war can never make
me look upon such representatives of Germany as enemies; but he knows and feels himself to be an exception
and expects to be crushed in a world in which he will be
unable to find a *raison d'être*.

                                                    19 March
. . . All the slight infirmities of great age, which make
such a miserable creature of an old man. Glandular res-
torations, I suppose, succeed on a much smaller scale.
With changes in temperature, for instance, the organism
now reacts only too weakly. I have to have recourse to
a whole series of drawers and vests, which I take off
and put back on twenty times a day. If occasionally I
try to escape that bondage and convince myself that it
is becoming a mania, I am sure to suffer: I catch cold
and am down for some time with a cold. Just now I
am wearing, one over the other, three pairs of drawers,
and at times, in order to remain motionless for some
time in this frigid room, have to pull on my pajama
trousers over my trousers or wrap the lower part of my
body in a blanket. My mind almost never succeeds in
forgetting my body, and this is more harmful to work
than one can say. Besides, the unbearable itchings constantly keep my mind from soaring. At night those itchings become worse; it seems as if they stand guard to

[6] Published in 1939, this novel was translated the next year as *The
Beloved Returns*.

keep sleep from approaching me; and I don't know what
position to take for sleeping: first one part of me, then
another, gets numb. Since I have got much thinner, an
insufficient cushion of flesh fails to keep me from being
indiscreetly aware of my skeleton. One has to go on
living, however, constantly reminding oneself that it all
might be much worse. . . .

27 March

It is that constant, somewhat Quixotic need, almost an
idée fixe, of correcting, of reforming, not only myself but
others that often made me so unbearable, first to Pierre
Louÿs, then to so many others, but that would make me,
I think, so good a citizen of a real republic. How could
it have failed to make Victor take a dislike to me,
accustomed as he is by his parents to have everything
his own way, never reprimanded by them, but adulated,
turning his desires into laws and never encountering anything but indulgence for his shortcomings? How could
he have discerned, through my continual thrusts, the
interest I took in him, for which, besides, he cared nothing? For him I was simply the spoilsport. A Protestant,
of course! . . . In that quarrel with Victor I had all the
wrongs on my side; almost all.

If there returns to France a period of well-being, soon
enough for me still to take advantage of it, I promise to
treat myself more generously. I have always been very
"close" about myself, and this has often made me look
like a miser; I was really a miser only when I alone was
concerned. I was eager to prove to myself that I could
be satisfied with little. But now that I have proved that
and know where I stand, I think I shall cease holding
my appetite, or even my greed, in check. I managed to
be an ascetic; I remain a sensualist. There are certain
elegances less suitable to the young than to old men and
I should like not to leave too unprepossessing an image
of myself. Just now I am making everything last, linen,
shoes, suits; I have to! But it seems to me that nothing
will be too good for me afterward. . . . I am writing
this without believing in it too much. For probably such
a general poverty awaits us after the war that it will

encourage me, I suppose, to even more parsimony than in the past.

Moreover, I have no great hope of surviving this period of horror.

10 April

Documentary value of literature: this alone matters to them. They would judge painting more soundly and, even without any special competence in the matter, would at least know that exactitude or, in a portrait, resemblance plays but a small part in the value of a picture. But reporting is far from having purged literature as much as photography managed to free painting of certain adventitious values. People suspect that qualities of technique alone confer on a canvas chances of survival and that what the painter represents, what is called the "subject," matters relatively little. But in a book everything is more mingled, confused, and the "subject" matters much more. Yet the interpretation of the subject, the resemblance with the thing represented, its profound resemblance, and the personal mark of the writer who sets it forth and sets himself forth, his style—all this enters into play, constitutes the value of the work and keeps it from falling into oblivion in a short time. To create a lasting work is my ambition. As for the rest: success, honors, acclamations, I make less of them than of the slightest particle of true glory: bringing comfort and joy to the young men of tomorrow. Oh, not limit life to oneself, but help to render it more beautiful and more worthy of being lived! I do not believe in any other after-life than in the memory of men; just as I believe in no other God than the one that is formed in their minds and hearts, so that each of us can and must contribute to his reign.

Oh heavens, yes, I am well aware in what sense I could say with Valéry that "events do not interest me." None of the things I cherish spiritually is dependent on this war, to be sure; but the future of France, our future, is at stake. Everything that still concerns our thought may disappear, sink into the past, cease to have for the men of tomorrow anything but an archaic meaning. Other problems, unsuspected yesterday, may trouble those to come, who will not even understand what constituted our reason for existing. . . . (I am writing this without really thinking it.)

But at last events are ceasing to crush us. The deeds of Leclerc's division are rehabilitating the French army. The British Eighth Army produces an air of heroism that makes one's heart beat faster. On our radio set, now repaired, I anxiously listen to the news, hear it again in German, in English, in Italian, on the alert for a bit of information not given in the other language, and as if my attention could hasten the future.

19 April

Art—called upon to disappear from the earth; progressively; completely. It was the concern of a choice few; something impenetrable for the "common run of mortals." For them, vulgar joys. But today the chosen few themselves are battering down their privileges, unwilling to admit that anything should be *reserved* for them. By a somewhat silly magnanimity, the best of today desire: *the best for all.*

I can imagine a time coming when aristocratic art will give way to a *common* well-being; when what is individual will cease to have a justification and will be ashamed of itself. Already we have been able to see the Russians reviling whatever manifests an individual feeling, no longer admitting anything but what can be understood by anyone whatever; and this may become anything whatever. Humanity is awakening from its mythological numbness and ventures forth into reality. All these children's baubles will be relegated among the obsolete; those to come will not even understand any longer how for centuries people could have been amused by them.

. . . *Withdrawing himself into some obscure retirement and patiently expecting the return of peace and security.*

(Gibbon, Chapter xvi.)

20 April

I finish *Richard II.* Odd play in which no further curiosity as to events maintains one's interest after the second act; nothing further but poetic ground swells. Most amazing sketch of the King's flabby character. Those two great families of Shakespearean characters: the men of action and the irresolute men, whom he opposes to one another in many of his dramas. And often the irresolute man is the center of the play, of which the very subject becomes his deterioration and retrocession before the other, better equipped than he for life. The first often gifted with the most exquisite qualities; the other stronger because less scrupulous. Whence, so often, the sacrifice of the best.

Did Freud know and cite the Duke of York's slip when saying to the Queen, after having just learned of the death of the Duchess of Gloucester:

Come, sister—cousin I would say—pray, pardon me.
(Act II, Scene ii.)

As soon as I have read it, I reread *Richard II* almost entirely. One of the least perfect, the least constructed of Shakespeare's dramas, but one of the strangest, one of the heaviest with poetry.

What to do with such a line:

Rouse up thy youthful blood, be valiant and live,

which I cannot succeed in scanning satisfactorily.

Days as if stolen from life. . . . It is now already eight spent in this retreat, rather gloomy despite the extreme kindness of my hosts and companions in captivity. They have been cloistered for almost six months, not even daring to show their faces at the window or especially to appear on the balcony in full view of the neighboring terraces, even less to risk themselves in the streets, where one is exposed to mass round-ups. That my own person is sought by the German authorities is not thoroughly proved. Arrested as a suspect? Suspected of what? No, but perhaps a lawful prize as a witness likely to talk and whom they prefer not leaving to the English. This is what was suddenly told me, and that I should do better to "hide out," as so many others were doing, without further delay. Even though I find it hard to convince myself that, if it came to that, my person or my voice could be of any importance, it was better not to run the risk of a forced voyage and sojourn in Germany or Italy.

Numerous hostages, undesirables or suspects, have been sent back to France of late; but many of the planes transporting them have been brought down on the way and no convoy is seen off without anxiety.

28 April

The finest subjects for drama are suggested to us by natural history and particularly by entomology. My *Saül* [7] was inspired by the odd discovery I had made of the chrysalis of a hawk-moth; it preserved its perfect form with the minute indication of the butterfly that was to issue from it; yet I noted at once that it was not capable of any of those slight quivering movements under the influence of tickling which reveal the latent life of ordinary chrysalises (at least the ones belonging to these butterflies). At the first pressure of my fingers the fragile envelope broke, which preserved but the form of the original animal; under this very thin and fragile sheathing many little cocoons had usurped all the space; they belonged to a sort of sphex, doubtless. . . . And I did not understand how the original animal, now devoured, had been able to find strength enough to achieve this deceptive pupation. Nothing revealed on the outside its total disappearance and the victory of the parasites. Thus, I thought, my Saül would say: "I am utterly suppressed."

And I learn this morning that the caterpillars of the *Lycænidæ*, after an initial period of vegetarian feeding, are carried off into an anthill by the ants, who enjoy the bit of honey secreted by their dorsal papillæ just as they do the milk of the aphis. But, deprived of vegetable food, those caterpillars change their diet and soon devour the entire nest of ant-eggs. Too bad for the ants! Thus it is and only thus and only in the anthill that the development of those caterpillars can reach completion.

Amazing "subject" of a drama! Not of a La Fontaine fable, but of a drama, and here is the first act: the caterpillar, a future butterfly, gets itself invited to the ants' house; all this, naturally, in the world of men and transposed to our scale.

[7] Gide's drama on Saul and David was first published in 1903.

8 May

While I was writing these lines yesterday, the Allies were already entering the city. This is what everyone said yesterday evening. This morning, awakened at dawn by a dull, constant, indeterminate sound, which seemed like the roar of a river. I dressed in haste and soon I saw the first Allied tanks approaching, cheered by the people from the near-by houses. You can hardly believe that what you have been so long waiting for has taken place, that *they* are here; you don't yet dare believe it. What! Without any further resistance, battles, or fighting? . . . It is over: *they are here!* The amazement increases even more when we learn from the first of these liberators to be questioned that these tanks and these soldiers belong to the Eighth Army, the very one that we thought was held in check in front of Zaghouan, that glorious army which came from the Egyptian frontier after having swept Libya, Tripolitania, conquered the Mareth Line and the Wadi Acarit Line, and whose progress we had followed from day to day in southern Tunisia. How are they the first to get here? Which way did they come? There is something miraculous about it. One imagined the liberation and entry into Tunis in many ways, but not like this. In haste I close my bag, my suitcase, and get ready to return to the avenue Roustan. No more reason to hide. All the hunted people of yesterday come out of the darkness today. People embrace one another, laughing and weeping with joy. This quarter near the nursery, which was said to be peopled almost exclusively with Italians, displays French flags at almost every window. Quickly, before leaving my retreat, I shave the four weeks' beard and go down with the companions of my captivity into the street, where they have not dared appear for exactly six months. We enter the wildly rejoicing city.

19 May

Reread *The Tempest;* amazed to recognize everything in it so well. Strange drama, which leaves one more unsatisfied than any other by Shakespeare, probably because no other awakens such lofty demands. Nothing unexpected in these symbol-characters: each of them, in

order to represent the better, becomes superlative. Once
the situation is established, the action unfolds without
trouble, without digression or hitch. Everything is a
matter of course in this exemplary display at the door
of the theater, where everyone, full of his role, adheres
to it and maintains it, as correct as in a tintype. Only
the relationship between Ariel and Prospero remains dis-
turbing and devoid of rigidity:

> *"Do you love me, master? No?"*
> *"Dearly, my delicate Ariel."*

It is charming, but it remains a bit brief,

22 May

No school edition, at least in those I have been able
to see (and I should be curious to consult on this subject the big edition of La Fontaine I left in Paris, wondering if perhaps it is not more explicit[8]) alludes to the
most amazing faculty frogs have of swelling up their
gullet like a goiter, like pigeons in the mating season,
and of projecting on one side of the mouth, as I have
seen done by camels in heat, a sort of huge blister, or
growth, a vibrant and yapping apparatus that is indeed
one of the strangest things one can imagine.[9] The article
"Frog" in the big Larousse dictionary makes no allusion
to it either. And yet it is that odd characteristic which
explains and motivates the fable of *The Frog Trying to
Be as Big as an Ox*. No doubt but what La Fontaine was
able to contemplate one day, as I did myself at La
Roque, this extraordinary spectacle: on a broad lily pad
floating on the surface of a pond, two frogs illustrating
and miming that fable in exemplary fashion. One of them
a mere spectator, and the other swelling up to the burst-
ing-point, his way of courting and manifesting his desire,
with oblique glances at the other one:

> *Look carefully, sister!*
> *Tell me, is this enough? Have I not achieved it?*

[8] No mention of that peculiarity in that edition either (June 1945).
[A.]

[9] "In the male, two *vocal bladders* can issue from a crevice that ex-
tends back to the shoulder; such pouches are sometimes as large as a
hazelnut." Brehm (June 1945). [A.]

In the ignorance of this fact, that fable may seem arbitrary and somewhat absurd. This is its justification, which ought to be pointed out to children to show them that here again La Fontaine proves to be an observer and remains close to nature, probably much more than any other writer of his time.

I am not at all among those who rather disdain those first fables of La Fontaine. The subsequent ones, more amply developed, have quite different qualities; but the initial ones have a density, a weight, a substance *à la* Breughel that delights me; and particularly that gem *The Wolf and the Lamb*. Not a word too many; not a line, not one of the remarks in the dialogue, that is not revelatory. It is a perfect object. But the taste for perfection is being lost, and I foresee a time when it will even cause people to smile indulgently as one smiles at children's games, when the *"quod decet,"* harmonious ponderation, the nuance, and art, in short, will yield to qualities of impact and to practical considerations, when the fact alone will matter. "Somber pleasure of a melancholy heart." [10] it will be all up with you! Here begins the virile age, the era of reality.

23 May

Always frightful mental confusion on the eve of departure. You take leave of friends, and they all want to see you once more. This morning the Amrouches, the Florys, Pistor, and a captain of the Leclerc division who wanted to be introduced to me, young Guy Cattan, were crowded into my room while Bourdil, Amrouche's brother-in-law, was hastily finishing my portrait. I try to find the pleasantest thing to say to each one of them. Meanwhile, while still posing for Bourdil, I start with Amrouche a game of chess, which he wins without difficulty, for I have lost my presence of mind. Besides, I have been playing much less well for some time now and my attention soon wanders. And I don't know yet whether it is really the day after tomorrow, Tuesday, that I am leaving; nor at what time; nor what I have a right to take with

---

[10] *"Jusqu'au sombre plaisir d'un cœur mélancolique"* is a line from the next to the last poem in La Fontaine's *Amours de Psyché et de Cupidon* (*The Loves of Psyche and Cupid*), Book II.

me in the plane; nor how nor when the rest of my luggage will catch up with me. How much simpler with death; the sudden command to leave *everything*.

On checking up, I find that I do not leave until Thursday. Horrors! I shall have to repeat all the farewells.

Algiers, 26 June

I dined, then, yesterday evening with General de Gaulle. Hytier, who accompanied me, had come to pick me up in a car at about eight. The auto took us to El Biar, directly to the villa whose terrace overlooks the city and the bay. We moved into the dining-room almost at once and took our places, Hytier and I, on the two sides of the general. On my right sat the son (or the nephew) of General Mangin; I did not catch the names of the other guests, two of whom were in civilian clothes, all of the general's entourage. We were eight in all.[11]

De Gaulle's welcome had been very cordial and very simple, almost deferential toward me, as if the honor and pleasure of the meeting had been his. People had told me of his "charm"; they had not exaggerated at all. Yet one did not feel in him, as one did excessively in Lyautey, that desire or anxiety to please which led him to what his friends laughingly used to call "the dance of allurement." The general remained very dignified and even somewhat reserved, it seemed to me, as if distant. His great simplicity, the tone of his voice, his attentive but not inquisitorial eyes, filled with a sort of amenity, were such as to put me at ease. And I should have been completely so if I did not always feel in the company of a man of action how remote the world I inhabit is from the world in which he operates.

I had just read with very keen interest, and why not say with admiration, many pages by him that were excellent, even capable of making one like the army, presenting it not as it is, alas, but as it ought to be.

[11] Jean Hytier recalls that the two civilian guests were Gaston Palewski (1901–   ), who was named director of de Gaulle's private cabinet in July 1943, and René Pleven (1901–   ), then Commissaire aux Colonies after having organized the colonial resistance in Africa; he has been several times Minister since 1944 and in July 1950 became Premier.

Reminding him of the remark he quotes to the effect that Jellicoe had all the qualities of Nelson save that of knowing how *not* to obey, I asked him how and when, in his opinion, an officer could and should take it upon himself to disregard a command. He replied most appropriately that this could only be at the time of great events and when the feeling of duty entered into opposition with a command received. Some of the guests then entered the conversation to compare military obedience to the obedience required by the Church. One could have continued much further than we did. The conversation soon dropped and I did not feel strong enough or in the proper mood to start it anew.

After the meal the general suggested to me that we take a little walk on the terrace. This amounted to offering me the opportunity of a private conversation, and I took advantage of it to speak to him at some length of Maurois. In the general's writings a sentence had somewhat surprised and hurt me, I told him, the one in which he states that he met Maurois only once and hopes never to see him again. I tried to explain Maurois's attitude, which, I said (and this was going rather far on my part), would have been very different if he had been better informed. I added: his eyes will soon open when he talks with the friends who are at present expecting him here. Maurois is wrong because he has been deceived. He thinks it is his duty to remain faithful to the marshal, and he is all the more inclined to think so because that duty pains him and, in acting thus, he is setting all his former friends against him.

The general's features had stiffened somewhat and I am not sure that my rather vehement defense did not irritate him. (Less sure, and this is worse, that my arguments were all valid, it seemed to me after having seen Maurois again.)

We spoke next of the advisability of creating a new review to group together the intellectual and moral forces of free France or those fighting to free her. But this was not carried very far either. He then told me how much he suffered from the lack of men.

"Those who ought to surround you," I told him, "are,

alas, under the wooden crosses of the other war." One has to play out the game with the hand one has. The trumps are not numerous.

We joined the rest of the company again and all went back into the drawing-room. The rambling conversation began to languish and I think everyone was grateful to me for breaking up the gathering soon. I thought sadly of what that interview might have been if Valéry had been in my place with his competence, his clairvoyance, and his extraordinary *presence of mind.*

I had spoken to the general, during our brief private conversation, of the resistance in Paris and particularly of that session of the Academy in which Valéry opposed addressing congratulations to the marshal as some academicians proposed. The general was thoroughly informed about it all.

He is certainly called upon to play an important role and he seems "up to it." No bombast in him, no conceit, but a sort of profound conviction that inspires confidence. I shall not find it hard to hang my hopes on him.

Fez, November

What would have happened *if* . . . Everyone is free to fashion imaginary events in his own way and according to his own opinions; whence facile convictions. This is what puts me on guard against History and urges me to prefer greatly "natural history," in which we have a constant check on facts and can always refer back to them; in which the "if" becomes an instrument of experiment, allowing new observations. Who, for instance, would dare to maintain that the butterfly is the same creature as the caterpillar if the fact of the metamorphosis had taken place but once? . . .

Anti-Barrès: I note in *The White Devil* by Webster (first scene):

We see that trees bear not such pleasant fruit
There where they grew first, as where they are new set.

In *Hamlet,* from one end to the other of the drama, nothing bolder, nothing more skillful, than that sort of shift which takes place from scene to scene by which each decisive action on the part of Hamlet is preceded by a sort of try-out of that action, as if it had some trouble fitting into *reality*. Already at the very beginning of the drama, in the dialogue with the ghost; then in any one of Hamlet's ways of behaving, toward his mother, with the King, with Ophelia . . . first he outlines the action, awkwardly. And we find this everywhere, in the double apostrophe of greeting to the players, so disconcerting, yet less so than the pantomime preceding the performance of *The Murder of Gonzaga*. Before the successful realization, there is always a failure.

1944

Every day I take myself by the shoulders and force myself to go for a walk, sometimes rather long. Unfortunately the outskirts of Fez are scarcely inviting and discourage curiosity: the country is all open and does not even offer the surprise and amusement of new plants. Everywhere the same little marigolds, which began to flower in about mid-January; clumps of scilla, of which nothing is left now but clusters of leaves. I still walk along at a good pace, but get tired quickly.

The example of Cardan, whose autobiography I am now reading in a German translation, urges me to speak more of my health. The condition of my liver and kidneys has greatly improved by itself and, altogether, I should be very well were it not for this tendency toward a cold and an almost constant hoarseness. The most unsatisfactory thing is sleep. Every evening I go to bed in apprehension of the few hours of anguish, often really painful, that I shall have to live through before being able to go to sleep. And again I am tormented by itchings, often unbearable, the whole length of my legs or between my toes. As for my mind, I feel it to be as active as in my best days, and my memory, which I am diligently exercising, has never been so good, at least for the poetry I am asking it to retain; for I believe that for the little details of life it is weakening; this is partly because I grant them less and less importance.

On my walks I always take along a book; but it often happens that I return without having opened it, having preferred to let my mind wander aimlessly or to recite, all along the way, the most recently learned of La Fontaine's *Fables* (of which unfortunately I find only the second volume here): *La Mort et le mourant, La Fille, Les Souhaits, Les Deux Amis, Le Paysan du Danube, Le Rat qui s'est retiré du monde, Le Rat et l'huître,* the long *Discours à Mme de La Sablière,* which opens Book

X, and the fable of *Les Deux Rats,* which follows it.[1]

In the garden of the Villa Brown the lavender iris have been in flower for the last twelve days; recently, a few rare jonquil-narcissus; in the wild state, oxalis, fumitory, arisarum, hawkweed; this is all, I believe.

Reading is invading the hours that were filled, even last week, by the polishing and typing of the extracts from my *Journal* that I am giving to *L'Arche,* which are to appear immediately afterward in a volume published by Charlot.[2] I am reading especially German and English, but have just devoured one after another eight books by Simenon at the rate of one a day (this was the second reading for *Long Cours, Les Inconnus dans la maison,* and *Le Pendu de Saint-Pholien).*[3]

6 February

After several almost sleepless nights I make up my mind to use the new soporific that Denoël had sent me from Rabat, hypalène,[4] which, besides, did not begin to act until very late, after a long period of very painful anguish. Deprived of sleep, I am not good for anything. The gears of my brain get choked up; the springs of my will relax. But upon issuing from the fountain of youth that sleep is for me, I am not too much aware of my age and can believe myself to be still hale. The outer world recovers its savor for me and I take a new interest in life.

During the hours of sleeplessness I go over this or that series of verses, beginning for instance: *"Iris, je vous*

[1] "Death and the Moribund," "The Girl," "The Wishes," "The Two Friends," "The Peasant from the Danube," "The Rat Who Withdrew from Society," "The Rat and the Oyster," "The Discourse Addressed to Mme de La Sablière," and "The Two Rats, the Fox, and the Egg" figure in Books VII–XI of *The Fables.*

[2] The monthly literary review *L'Arche* was founded in Algiers in late 1943 under the patronage of André Gide, with an editorial board consisting of Maurice Blanchot, Albert Camus, and Jacques Lassaigne; Jean Amrouche was editor-in-chief. The first issue appeared in December 1943 and was at once compared to the former *Nouvelle Revue Française.* In 1945 *L'Arche* was transferred to Paris, where it continued to appear until the summer of 1947. The Algerian, later also Parisian, publishing house Charlot published the review.

[3] *Ocean Voyage, Strangers in the House,* and *The Hanged Man of Saint-Pholien* are all novels.

[4] *Hypalène,* a product of Laboratoires S.I.T.S.A., is a combination of barbituric acid with other ingredients, but with no narcotic agents.

louerais," [5] and am not satisfied until I reach the end. That fear that my memory may fail me urges me to keep it in training without respite. A sort of avarice is involved in this, which differs only in its objective from the need that the old feel to hoard; after all, just as ridiculous, just as useless. Feeling everything slip away, one clings to trifles. But almost as much as the miser's false treasures, it remains external to oneself and is not integrated. . . .

If I had not abandoned the piano, *The Well-Tempered Clavichord* would be better than La Fontaine's *Fables;* closer to serenity.

Denoël appears to be greatly affected by the appendix to *Attendu que* . . . ;[6] and I am affected in turn, not by that appendix with the too conspicuous title: *Dieu, fils de l'homme,* but by the sorrow it causes him. And yet I cannot regret either having written those pages or even having divulged them. What I have expressed in them is close to my heart, and in regard to the religious question I can be neither "indifferent" nor merely skeptical. It is as a "believer" that I speak and that I set up my reason against their faith. Abandoning my reason, I should doubtless easily recover certain emotional accents that would touch Denoël as much as those of my *Numquid et tu* . . . ? I know how to achieve them; I have the recipe for that false profundity. Every cry of distress finds an echo in pious souls; every recognized need for supernatural help. Every cry such as: "O Lord, save us or we perish!" What separates us from such souls is the claim, which they consider impious, of doing without divine aid. Denoël foresees in it a drying-up of lyricism. To him that sort of smugness of the soul seems antipoetic. And doubtless in the "shadows of Faith" lyricism readily spreads its

[5] "Iris, I should praise you," is the opening line of La Fontaine's "Discourse to Mme de La Sablière," at the head of Book X of his *Fables;* it contains more than 170 lines.

[6] *Considering that* . . . , published in Algiers by Charlot in 1943, contained much of the material issued the same year as *Interviews imaginaires (Imaginary Interviews)* in Paris, Yverdon, and New York editions plus two dialogues entitled *"Dieu, fils de l'homme"* ("God, Son of Man"). Those dialogues were subsequently included in the New York edition of *Pages de Journal, 1939–1942* (Pantheon Books, 1944). They express Gide's mature and personal religious credo.

wings. . . . But the lyric state is not far from seeming to me a childish state, which the adult soul somewhat scorns. I could still lend myself to that game (and I should even be perhaps caught in it); but this could not be without some pretense and some sort of dishonesty.

7 February

An order has reached me to return to Algiers at once. The telegram comes from the Ministry of the Interior: a precise and urgent summons constituting an official mission, with which I must comply. I had not taken quite seriously an earlier telegram from Amrouche, calling me equally urgently: I thought that, considerably worried about my fate and exaggerating the danger of the uprising, he, as a friend, wanted to provide me a way out, leaving me free to take advantage of it if need be. On receiving the second telegram, I went to see General Suffren, and this morning I am informed by telephone that arrangements have been made for me to return to Algiers tomorrow evening by the plane which will come to get me at Meknes. So be it.

On the way to Gao, 3 April

Maison Blanche. Waited in vain for the happy accident that would have kept me from leaving. Raynaud and Morize accompanied me to the airfield, whence we take off at 7.30. Very cloudy sky.

I must have dropped off for scarcely a half-hour, and already we are flying over an utterly different country: sand-colored, covered with strange signs, with a sort of mysterious writing, inhumanly and incomprehensibly beautiful; elementary; nothing living or even merely vegetable mars it.

9.30

Blue-white sky. It is beginning to be sumptuously hot. Half-hour stop at El Golea. Conversation with two very likable mail and radio directors of that place. One of them comes from the Congo. Beautiful harmony of the palm trees on the pure sand; it gives me a sensual pleasure to encounter this again.

Gao

I cannot succeed in despising the joys of the flesh (and, besides, scarcely try to). A mishap to the plane that was to take us back (a providential mishap, I shall say) allowed me to enjoy one of the keenest the evening before last; all my memories of Gao radiate around it.

Had I carried quinine with me and taken some at once, I should doubtless have held up better; but I was unable to find any until the third day; that is to say that the kind Mme Pinson was good enough to give me some.

[*Algiers, 21 May*]

Today, 21 May, I finished *Thésée*.[7] There still remain large parts to rewrite, and particularly the beginning, for which I had not yet managed to find the proper tone. But now the entire canvas is covered. For the past month I have daily and almost constantly worked on it, in a state of joyful ardor that I had not known for a long time and thought I should never know again. It seemed to me that I had returned to the time of *Les Caves* or of my *Prométhée*. Furthermore, exalted by events and the recovery of France. The friends surrounding me here have been perfect. I owe them much and without them should never have been able to bring my work to a happy conclusion. I should like to dedicate my *Thésée* to each of them in particular (besides, they are not numerous), as a sign of my gratitude.[8]

I also owe much to the beautiful books of Charles Picard; to those of Glotz, so sensitively intelligent (to mention only the moderns).[9]

". . . Among the Greeks, as among the Hebrews, wherever the foreign element mingled most intimately with the native element, in Attica as in the tribe of Judah, there was formed the cream of the nation." (Glotz: *Greek History*, p. 286.) Most interesting remark and of wide application.

Nothing amuses me so much as work, not even the noble game of chess, in which I get beaten every day by Jean

[7] *Theseus* was not published until 1946, first in New York (Pantheon Books) and then in Paris.

[8] Indeed, when the work appeared, it was dedicated severally to Anne Heurgon, to Jacques Heurgon, and to Jean Amrouche.

[9] Charles Picard (1883–   ), known as an authority on pre-Hellenic religions, has written extensively on Crete, as has Gustave Glotz (1862–1935), professor of Greek history at the University of Paris and author of *The Ægean Civilization*.

Amrouche. Delighted to learn that Minos was already addicted to it, if we are to believe the archæologists.

"In those days of old, Minos was at ease and the gods were cramped." (Glotz, p. 560.)

"Sometimes they [the Romans] would make a peace treaty with a prince under favorable conditions; and when he had fulfilled them, they would add others such that he was forced to begin the war again." (Montesquieu: *Grandeur et décadence,* Chapter vi.)

The young people who come to me in the hope of hearing me utter a few memorable maxims are quite disappointed. Aphorisms are not my forte. I say nothing but banalities, nothing but platitudes to them; but, above all, I question them; and that is just what they prefer: talking about themselves. I listen to them and they go away delighted.

6 June

ALLIED LANDING IN NORMANDY.

Tipasa, 12 June

I am finishing, in great gulps, *Sense and Sensibility;* less enthralling doubtless than *Pride and Prejudice* or than *Emma* (as far as I can remember), but with an admirably deft draftsmanship and perfectly filling its frame. Comparable to certain portraits by Ingres, or rather by Chassériau. The sky is rather low, rather empty; but what delicacy in the depiction of sentiments! If no major demon inhabits Jane Austen, on the other hand a never failing understanding of others. The element of satire is excellent and most delicately shaded. Everything takes place in dialogues, which are as good as they can be. Certain chapters reveal a perfect art.

Finished, the same day, Malraux's *La Lutte avec l'ange,*[10] in which I recognize what he read to me at Cap Martin, in other words almost everything. I had hoped that he would bring his narrative to a more nearly perfect state. There is still much to criticize in it and, however gripping it may be, it is still very far from what

[10] Malraux's unfinished novel, *The Struggle with the Angel,* bearing the sub-title of *The Altenburg Walnut-trees,* first appeared in Switzerland in 1943.

it might have, and ought to have, been. Often, too often, he does not use the words that are called for, and many a sentence remains so imperfect, so ambiguous, that one would like to rewrite it or else say to him what as a child, he relates, he would have liked to say, hidden behind a desk in the Academy, to the "Great Writers": "Come now! Begin that over again, now." I could cite many a sentence whose syntax is indefensible (among others, the one with which the father's notes begin; I stumble on it just as much on a fourth reading as on the first; and the description of the first men carrying the gassed men out of the contaminated zone). The excessive use of abstract terms is often prejudicial to the narration of action. One must not try simultaneously to make the reader visualize and make him understand.

I plunge into *Twelfth Night*, forsaking *The Longest Journey*, in which I cannot manage to get sufficiently interested. Last month I patiently read *Howards End*, of which I retain almost nothing but a great esteem for Forster.

Without being too impolite, I should like to take leave of myself. I have decidedly seen enough of myself. I no longer even know whether or not I should still like to begin my life over again; or else, I should do so with a little more daring in affirmation. I have sought much too much to please others, greatly sinned through modesty.

25 June

For the last few days I have been applying myself to Latin again, with much more pleasure and much less difficulty than I should have thought, and reviving my first raptures by going over again rapidly the second book of the *Æneid*. It seems to me that I understand everything much better than I did then. And I now hold the key to Latin verses: it is enough to place the accents properly, without too much concern for the longs and shorts; then everything comes naturally. It is simple. Why was this not taught me at school instead of trying to teach me when a syllable is strong or weak, which comes out quite naturally when the verse is properly scanned? But it is first essential to get rid of that absurd habit, which was still prevalent then, of pronouncing Latin words "in the French manner"

—that is, by always putting the accent on the last syllable, which distorted everything.

I give about three hours a day to Virgil. While walking, I continue reading *Humphrey Clinker;* and in the intervals, Rabelais's *Quart Livre.*[11]

10 October

I am awaiting with apprehension my call to Paris, where many of those I should have taken the most pleasure in seeing again will not be, I fear; where I shall encounter nameless and numberless difficulties, troubles, and fatigues that I don't know whether I shall be strong enough to bear, any more than the inevitable cold. I am not risking any project and filling frightfully empty days as best I can with the assiduous study of Latin and with reading.

---

[11] *The Expedition of Humphrey Clinker* (1771) is by Tobias Smollett; Rabelais's *Fourth Book* continues the adventures of Pantagruel.

1945

The U.S.S.R. . . . I should astonish many people by telling them that there is probably no country in the world where I should more like to return (aside from "wild" countries, virgin forest, etc.).

Some think that I have a bad recollection of the trip I made there (in 1936, I believe) and that the two pamphlets I subsequently published are the result of a disappointment; this is absurd. I wrote them in the same way and in the same spirit as I pointed out, on my return from the Congo, the colonial abuses that had sickened me down there. And those who became angry over my criticisms of the U.S.S.R. were the very ones who had most applauded when the same criticisms were directed against the by-products of "capitalism." There they admired my perspicacity, my need to disregard camouflage, my courage in denouncing. In Russia, they suddenly said, I had been incapable of understanding anything, of seeing anything. And if some admitted the justice of my observations, at least they considered them untimely. At most a few imperfections were admitted among comrades, but the time had not yet come to speak of them. One had to realize the over-all success and close one's eyes to the temporary, inevitable deficiencies. . . .

Outside of those "deficiencies" I liked everything there. Nowhere yet more beautiful landscapes, nor, to inhabit them, a people with whom I felt more readily in a state of sympathy, in a state of communion (though I did not speak their language; but it seemed that that mattered little, so easily was that sympathy established through looks and gestures).

I am speaking of the people, of the "masses"; for what made me suffer there was seeing the social classes taking shape again despite the vast and bloody effort of the revolution, convention winning out over freedom of thought, and falsehood over reality.

Doubtless Stalin was very clever to give all his atten-

tion, first and above all, to the Red army; events have
justified him flagrantly; and it matters little now that
he did this by relaxing in other regards. For was it not
love of the land and of individual property, often a
religious feeling also, that, much more than clinging to
Marxist theories, made the Russian forces so valiant and
victorious? Stalin grasped this and showed that he had
grasped it when he opened the churches again. . . . But
I think that the justice of some of my accusations will be
readily recognized; in particular the one about the oppression of thought. What I said of this remains true, and that
oppression is beginning to be exercised, in imitation of
the U.S.S.R., in France. Any thought that does not conform becomes suspect and is at once denounced. Terror
reigns, or at least tries to reign. All truth has become
expedient; that is to say that the expedient falsehood is at
a premium and wins out wherever it can. Solely "right-
thinking" people will have a right to express their thought.
As for the others, let them keep silent, or else. . . . Doubtless one can overcome Nazism only through an anti-Nazi
totalitarianism; but tomorrow it will be essential to struggle
against this new conformism.

1946

January

That turn of mind (that vicious turn of mind) that people used to blame in me was what saved France. An attitude of insubordination, of revolt; or even initially and simply an attitude of inquiry. . . . So that, as if by chance, my former accusers suddenly and all together turned up on the wrong side: Béraud, Massis, Mauclair, Maurice Martin du Gard . . . without a single exception so far as I know—and it could not have been otherwise.

Academy? . . . Yes, perhaps, accept becoming a member if without solicitations, grovelings, visits, etc. And immediately afterward, for my first deed as an Immortal, a preface to *Corydon* declaring that I consider that book as the most important and most "serviceable" [1] (we have no word, and I don't even know if this English word expresses exactly what I mean: of greater usefulness, of greater service for the progress of humanity) of my writings. I believe this and it would not be difficult to prove it.

The most useful . . . I do not say the most successful. Its very form hardly satisfies me today, nor that way of avoiding scandal and attacking the problem through a feigned proxy. It is partly because at that time I was not sufficiently sure of myself: I knew I was right, but I did not know to what a degree. . . .

Aswân, 21 January

The Ponte Santa Trinità (in Florence) destroyed . . . a marvel of harmonious equilibrium, of slimness and of bold grace, which moved me as much as the most imposing architectural feats of Egypt. I like what exalts man and not what bows him low and humiliates him.

Were I to open my shutters in the morning on

[1] In English in the text.

. . . the flowery shores
Watered by the Seine . . .[2]

it would be a delightful surprise. These black boulders of granite breaking the course of the Nile are beautiful; but I do not admire them any the more for having, originally, been more amazed by them. I shall not try to put order into my thoughts. What's the use?

Nothing bothers me so much as the fame of a landscape (for the work of art it is not the same at all: admiration gives it stuff and density; its surface is nourished by successive interpretations; here I am bothered only when fashion enters into it—as it did recently for Emily Brontë and today for Kafka; but when this or that Greek or Latin writer is involved, what a joy to share the emotion of Goethe or Montaigne!). Before these black rocks of Aswân too many imbeciles have swooned. . . .

The letter from Mme X. that the hotel porter gives me this morning exasperates me, for it says: "We must have certain sensations in common, those that you must have irresistibly felt here when faced with the black rocks on these pink mornings." No, madame, faced with these black rocks, I felt nothing at all. I am a gentleman; and the emotions I might have had politely made way for yours.

Wadi Halfa

Often I am gnawed by a feeling (which sometimes gets to the point of anguish) that I have something more important to do (than what I am doing and am concerned with at present). If I had to die in an hour, should I be ready?

Assiduous, daily rereading of the last books of the *Æneid*. From three to four hours every day. These last books seem to me today to be in no wise inferior to the first.[3] Or at least, if perhaps less perfect in form and more scattered in interest (more confused, especially in Book

---

[2] The opening of the famous *Vers allégoriques à ses enfants* (*Allegoric Lines to her Children*) by Mme Deshoulières (1638?–94) reads:

> Dans ces prés fleuris
> Qu'arrose la Seine
> Cherchez qui vous mène,
> Mes chers brebis:

[3] Exaggeration. [A.]

XII), constantly revived by charming inventions, in which pity is mingled with horror, tenderness with heroism, the sentiment of glory and human dignity with fright.

24 February

At Nag Hamadi, where I find the same charming welcome from Dr. and Mme Girardot, of whom I had such a pleasant memory. Unexpected meeting with Jean-Paul Trystram, whom I take a keen and deep pleasure in seeing again. He is going to Afghanistan to take up a post as professor at Kabul; he accompanies us in a jaunt through the sugarcane fields and to the dam.

Yesterday evening I receive this letter from an unknown named Bernard Enginger; it is so significant that I want to set it down here:

For five years I have been wanting to write you. At that time I discovered your *Nourritures terrestres;* I was seventeen. I could not tell you how it upset me. I have never been the same since. I want to tell you of my respect and my admiration. Hundreds of letters like this one must have reached you. That is not the only thing I wanted to write you.

I struggled against you for five years. Your Ménalque knows enough to say: "Leave me." That is too easy. I struggled against that spiritual tyranny you exercised over me. I loved you, and certain passages from your books helped me to live in the concentration camps. In you I found the strength to tear myself away from a middle-class, material comfort. With you I sought "not so much possession as love." I cleared everything away to be new for the new law. I liberated myself. That is not enough. "Free for what?" That is the dreadful question. At last I detached myself from you, but I have not found any new masters, and I remain quivering. The terrifying absurdity of the Sartres and the Camuses has solved nothing and merely opens horizons of suicide.

I still live with everything you taught me. But I am thirsty. All young people are thirsty with me. You can do something. And yet I know that one is alone, always.

I do not expect from you a convenient solution for my little problem. That would be too easy, a collective solution. Each one must find his way, which is not the same as his neighbor's. But a glimmer from you might indicate the direction to take. . . . If there is a direction.

Oh, *Maître* . . . If you only knew the confusion of all our youth. . . . I do not want to waste your time. I have not said everything I wanted to say. There would be too much to say.

This is an appeal I am throwing out to you. Forgive my awkwardness: I know that you do not like sympathy.[4]

None the less, I want to tell you of my tremendous admiration and the hope I put in you.

Believe me, *Maître,* faithfully and respectfully yours,

BERNARD ENGINGER

Hotel de Paris, Cairo
(until 27 February)
on the point of leaving for
Pondichéry

At Suez he will take the same ship as Trystram, who is going to Afghanistan by way of India. I entrust to him a first hasty letter, which scarcely satisfies me. Then, after deliberation, write this, without much hope of still being able to reach B. E. at Cairo—and that is why I make a copy:

DEAR BERNARD ENGINGER,

Rushed by Trystram's departure, I wrote you too hastily yesterday evening. This is what I should rather have said to you:

Why seek "new masters"? Catholicism or Communism demands, or at least advocates, submission of the mind. Worn out by yesterday's struggle, young men (and many of their elders) seek and think they have found, in that very submission, rest, assurance, and intellectual comfort. Indeed, they even seek in it a reason for living and convince themselves (let themselves be convinced) that they will be more useful and will achieve their full value when enrolled. Thus it is that, without being really aware of it, or becoming aware of it only too late, through abnegation or laziness, they are going to contribute to the defeat, to the retreat, to the rout of the spirit; to the establishment

[4] Obvious allusion to a sentence in my *Nourritures:* "Not sympathy, but love." [A.]

of some form or other of "totalitarianism" which will be hardly any better than the Nazism they were fighting.

The world will be saved, if it can be, only by the *unsubmissive*. Without them it would be all up with our civilization, our culture, what we loved, and what gave to our presence on earth a secret justification. Those unsubmissive ones are the "salt of the earth" and responsible for God. For I am convinced that God is not yet and that we must achieve him. Could there be a nobler, more admirable role, and more worthy of our efforts?

PS.—Yes, I am well aware that I wrote in my *Nourritures:* "Not sympathy, but love." But I too, and before anyone else, following my own advice, "left my book" and went beyond. Even in regard to oneself it is essential not to come to a stop.

[Paris,] 22 November

My seventy-seventh birthday; I get up a little before six o'clock with the sudden resolution to begin to keep this journal again, interrupted since . . .

If that resolution does not hold beyond a few days, I shall tear out this page; for it is useless to leave a trace of such an uncertain commitment; without importance; Yvonne Davet, without suspecting it, has done a great deal, by the cult she has made of me, to disgust me with myself. I can understand Schwob covering the mirrors in his apartment; my image, that reflection of me that I constantly encounter, thanks to her, is becoming unbearable to me; I bump into it; I bruise myself on it.

25 November

I have always had for Léautaud an almost keen affection; consequently I am hurt by a certain remark of his, quoted by Rouveyre from a letter addressed to him in which Léautaud speaks of my "hypocrisy," my "duplicity," and my "little deceits." . . . Very curious to know on the basis of what anecdotes that opinion could have been formed. As a result of what ill-natured gossip? . . .

Perhaps Léautaud, reading the wholly affectionate praise I make of him in the pages sent recently as a contribution to the revival of the *Mercure de France*,[5] will think that

[5] Those pages, entitled *"Le Mercure de France,"* appeared in No. 1000 of the *Mercure*, which bore the date 1 July 1940–1 December 1946; they are reprinted in *Feuillets d'automne (Autumn Leaves).*

I wrote them as a sort of reply to his accusations, so that that very praise will appear, in Léautaud's eyes, as one more "little deceit." What an odd process of *deformation* can take place, unconsciously or almost, in the minds of the most perspicacious and best-informed! Thus it is that any portrait of another comes to resemble the painter as much as the model or more. . . .

2 December

Finally let myself be taken to *King Lear* last night. No effort to get there. Enid MacLeod comes to pick me up in an Embassy car, which is to bring me home likewise. Élisabeth, though having already seen the play the day before yesterday, accompanies me. Everything is arranged in the best possible way. But as soon as I am in the box (exactly facing the stage) or very soon after the curtain goes up, a mortal boredom begins to numb me, a rather special sort of boredom that I hardly ever feel save in the theater. There are pauses, suspenses, slow moments, preparations of effects, that are unbearable. Like a child at the Châtelet, I wait for the set to be changed.

As for Olivier, he is without contest a great actor. The fact that he can, with the same success, impersonate one after the other the dashing young officer of Shaw's *Arms and the Man* and old Lear is amazing. And the whole company surrounding him is definitely above average, completely homogeneous; excellent ensemble. But shall I dare write here what I think of *King Lear*? Yesterday's production strengthens my opinion: I am almost on the point of considering that play execrable, of all Shakespeare's great tragedies the least good, and by far. I constantly thought: how Hugo must have liked it! All his enormous faults are evident in it: constant antitheses, devices, arbitrary motives; barely, from time to time, some glimmer of a sincere human emotion. I cannot even very well grasp what is considered as the difficulty of interpretation of the first scene: difficulty of getting the public to accept the King's naïve stupidity; for all the rest is in keeping: the entire play from one end to the other is absurd. Only through pity does one become interested in the tribulations of that old dotard, a victim of his fatuousness, his senile smugness, and his stupidity. He moves us only at the rare moments of pity that he himself shows for Edgar and for his sweet fool. Parallelism of the action in the Gloucester family and in his: the bad daughters and the wicked son; the good Edgar and the kind Cordelia. The white hair in the tempest; the brutality unleashed against weak innocence . . . nothing that is not intentional, arbitrary, forced; and the crudest means are employed to seize us by the guts. It has ceased to be human and become *enormous;* Hugo himself never imagined anything more gigantically artificial, more false. The last act ends with a gloomy hecatomb in which good and evil are mingled in death. Olivier's company handles it as a sort of final apotheosis *à la* Mantegna: living tableau, skillful grouping; everything is there, even to the architecture of arcades framing in the admirably ordered ensemble. Art triumphs. One has only to applaud.

The enthusiastic audience acclaims Olivier and his company.

Strange part played in that drama by papers and missives, presented, stolen, falsified; up to seven times, if I counted aright.

1947

Buchet's book that Y. D. had sent me when I was in Egypt has just come back to her today.[1] Had I already read it? A note to his essay on Valéry, which I remembered, makes me think so; but up to that note (p. 133; that is to say, close to the end of the volume) everything seemed to me unfamiliar. Rather absurd criticism; for, after all, taking into account only my *Journal*, it is easy for him to prove that I am merely an erratic individual, incapable of producing any work; easy, but not quite fair. He argues as if I had been the author only of that *Journal*; and this allows him to talk of a "perpetual frustration" and of my vain and constant effort to hide this. At most he mentions *Paludes*; of the other books not a word.

I was very much behindhand with contemporary drama, if not with the drama of Marcel Achard, yet I did not yet know either his *Colinette* or *Une Balle perdue*, which I have just read with a certain rapture, partial with *Colinette* and almost constant with *Une Balle perdue*.[2] (Neither *Malborough* which is inexistent, nor *Voulez-vous jouer avec moâ?* which is rather disappointing.) As for Salacrou's drama, unbelievably uneven, I informed myself attentively of six plays. Excellent scenes in *Un Homme comme les autres* and the first two acts of *La Femme libre*. *L'Inconnue d'Arras*, alas, does not justify its claims; this is a pity.[3] At present I am absorbed by Stève Passeur. Too early to speak of him. . . .

---

[1] *Écrivains intelligents du XXᵉ siècle* (*Intelligent Writers of the Twentieth Century*) by Edmond Buchet appeared in 1945. Its three parts are entitled: "Marcel Proust or the Power of the Abnormal," "André Gide According to His *Journal* or Intelligence against Life," and "Paul Valéry and the Limits of Intelligence."

[2] *Colinette* (1942), *A Wasted Bullet* (1928), *Malborough Goes to War* (1924), and *Will You Play with Me?* (1923) are all comedies combining a comic gift of nonsense with a peculiar poetry.

[3] *A Man Like Anyone Else* (1936), *A Free Woman* (1934), and *The Strange Woman of Arras* (1935) are all comedies by Armand Salacrou. The last named, employing an expressionistic technique, was overpraised by its producer, Lugné-Poe, and by some of the critics.

I consider Sartre's *La Putain respectueuse* as a sort of masterpiece. I did not at all like his last two long and boring novels; but *La Putain* . . . since the excellent stories of *Le Mur* he had written nothing stronger or more perfect.[4]

Neuchâtel, November

A Swedish interviewer asked me if I did not regret having written any particular one of my books (I do not know whether he was thinking of *Le Retour de l'U.R.S.S.* or of *Corydon*). I replied that not only did I not disown any of my writings, but that I should certainly have bade farewell to the Nobel Prize if, in order to obtain it, I had had to disown anything.[5]

(Letter that was not sent, but it is worth setting down, since errors are hard to kill.)

SIR:

Allow me to protest against the article *"L'Italia di Gide"* that appeared in your paper[6] with the signature of Massimo Rendina. He intensifies the suspicion I have always had in regard to interviewers. I cannot point out all the errors contained in his article and particularly in what he makes me say: for I did not know Carducci, or Pascoli, or Benedetto Croce. It was not in Paris but in Florence that I frequented d'Annunzio. I do not recognize any of the remarks he attributes to me regarding the latter, or regarding the existentialists and Sartre.

AUTUMN LEAVES

Neuchâtel

I shall be able to say: "So be it" to whatever happens to me, were it even ceasing to exist, disappearing after having been. But just now I am and do not know exactly what that means. I should like to try to understand.

. . .

[4] The play *The Respectful Prostitute* was first presented in Paris in 1946; the stories of *The Wall* came out in 1939. The novels are *The Age of Reason* (1945) and *The Reprieve* (1945), the first two parts of *Roads to Freedom*.

[5] André Gide was in Neuchâtel in November 1947 when informed that he had been awarded the Nobel Prize for Literature.

[6] *Il Giornale dell' Emilia-Bologna*, 14 December 1947. [A.]

Please, leave me alone. I need a little silence around me in order to achieve peace within me.

What a nuisance you are! . . . I need to collect my thoughts.

"Free thought. . . ." X. explained to me that true freedom of thought had to be sought among *believers,* not among such as me.

"For, after all, your mind is fettered by logic."

I granted that it required a special freedom of thought to believe in miracles and all the rest, and that I could clearly see that his mind did not object to admitting what seemed to me (and to him) contrary to reason. That is the very essence of Faith. Where you can no longer observe or prove, you must *believe*.

"And if you refuse to believe," he concluded, "stop telling me and claiming that you love freedom."

Basically I was well aware that I was not a "free thinker."

Faith moves mountains; yes, mountains of absurdities.[7] To Faith I do not oppose doubt, but affirmation: what could not be is not.

Hence I shall refuse to consider finality in nature. According to the best advice, I shall everywhere substitute, systematically, the *how* for the *why*. For instance, I know (or at least I have been told) that that substance the silkworm discharges while making his cocoon would poison him if he kept it in him. He purges himself of it. To save himself he empties himself. None the less the cocoon, which he is obliged to form under threat of death and which he would be unable either to imagine or to fashion otherwise, protects the metamorphosis of the caterpillar; and the caterpillar cannot become a butterfly unless emptied of that silky poison. . . . But I am indeed forced at the same time to admire the way in which the *how* joins the *why* in this case, fusing with it so intimately and with such a tight interweave that I cannot distinguish one from the other.

And likewise for the mollusk and its shell. Likewise constantly and everywhere in nature the solution is inseparable

[7] See the PS. at the end of this section. [A.]

from the problem. Or rather: there is no problem; there are only solutions. Man's mind invents the problem afterward. He sees problems everywhere. It's screaming.[8]

Oh, would that my mind could let fall its dead ideas, as the tree does its withered leaves! And without too many regrets, if possible! Those from which the sap has withdrawn. But, good Lord, what beautiful colors!

Those ideas which one first thought one could not possibly do without. Whence great danger of basing one's moral comfort on false ideas. Let us check, let us verify first. Once the sun turned around the earth, which, as a fixed point, remained the center of the universe and focal point of God's attention. . . . And suddenly, no! It is the earth that turns. But then everything is upset! All is lost! . . . Yet nothing is changed but *the belief*. Man must learn to get along without it. First from one, then from another, he frees himself. Get along without Providence: man is weaned.

We have not reached this point. We have not yet reached this point. It requires much virtue to achieve that state of total atheism; even more to remain there. The "believer" will probably see in it nothing but an invitation to license. If this were so, hooray for God! Hooray for the sacred falsehood that would preserve humanity from collapse, from disaster. But cannot man learn to demand of himself, through virtue, what he believes demanded by God? Yet he must nevertheless get to this point; some, at least, must, to begin with; otherwise the game would be up. That strange game that we are playing on earth (unintentionally, unconsciously, and often unwillingly) will be won only if the idea of God, on withdrawing, yields to virtue, only if man's virtue, his dignity, supplants God. God has ceased to exist save by virtue of man. *Et eritis sicut dei.* (Thus it is that I want to understand that old word of the Tempter—who, like God, has existence only in our minds—and see in that offer, which has been characterized for us as fallacious, a possibility of salvation.)

• • •

[8] After using here the vulgar expression: "*C'est marrant,*" Gide adds this footnote: "This is the first time I have used this frightful word; do not even know how to spell it. . . . But it is the only one that fits."

God is virtue. But what do I mean by that? I should have to define; I cannot do so. I shall manage to do so only subsequently. But I shall already have accomplished much if I remove God from the altar and put man in his place. Provisionally I shall think that virtue is the best the individual can obtain from himself.

God lies ahead. I convince myself and constantly repeat to myself that: He depends on us. It is through us that God is achieved.

What rubbish all that literature is! And even were I to consider only the finest writings, what business have I, when life is here at hand, with these reflections, these carbon copies of life? The only thing that matters to me is what can lead me to modify my way of seeing and acting. Merely living calls for all my courage; merely living in this frightful world. And I know and feel that it is frightful; but I know also that it could be otherwise and that it is what we make it. If you point out the present horror in order to bring about a protest through indignation, through disgust, bravo! But if not, up and at the demoralizers!

There might very well be nothing; nor anyone. No one to notice that there is nothing, and to consider that natural.

But that there is something, and, whatever it may be, the strange thing! I shall never cease being amazed at this.

Something and not complete nonexistence. It required centuries of centuries to produce that something, to get that, whatever it may be, from chaos. Even more centuries to obtain the least life. And even more for that life to achieve consciousness. I have ceased to understand, and from its very beginning, that progress, that history. But more incomprehensible than all the rest: a disinterested feeling. Faced with that, I am amazed, I stand in awe. People are doubtless wrong in going into raptures over the maternal or conjugal or altruistic abnegation of animals; it is possible to explain it, to analyze it: there is really nothing disinterested in it; everything

follows its inclination and its pleasure. I grant this, but
only to admire all the more those sentiments when I
find them refined in man and capable of gratuitousness.
Before the least act of self-consecration, of self-sacrifice,
for others, for an abstract duty, for an idea, I get on
my knees. If it is to lead to this, all the rest of the
world is not useless: all the vast misery of men.

They do not recognize a serenity acquired outside of
their teaching. I am speaking here of the Catholics; any
doctrine that strays from their Church *must* lead to
despair.

"By speaking thus of that serenity on which you pride
yourself you put it on show; by putting it on show you
compromise it. It must be read in your features and in
your deeds, not in sentences that you do not know why
or for whom you are writing. . . ."

Get along without God. . . . I mean: get along without
the idea of God, without a belief in an attentive, tutelary,
and retributive Providence . . . not everyone can achieve
this.

The blinded bat is nevertheless able to avoid the wires
that have been strung in the room where it is now
flying without bumping anything. And probably it senses
at a distance, in the nocturnal air, the passage of this or
that insect on which it will feed. It does not fly at
random, and its gait, which strikes us as whimsical, is
motivated. Space is full of vibrations, of rays, that our
senses cannot perceive, but that are caught by the an-
tennæ of insects. What connection between our sensations
and their cause? Without a sensitive receiver, nature is
mute, colorless, odorless. It is in us, through us, thanks
to us, that number becomes harmony.

The wonderful thing is that man has been able to
construct instruments capable of making up for the insufficiency of his senses, of catching imperceptible waves
and unheard vibrations. With our senses we already
had enough to satisfy us; the rest is excess. But whether
or not we wish it, that rest is there. Man has rashly en-
larged his receptivity and immoderately increased his
power. A pity that he is not more up to it! He behaves

badly. Lack of habit perhaps (let us hope so); all this is so new! He trespasses and is overwhelmed.

When I had learned that little bows of ribbon were called rosettes (how old was I then? five or six . . .) I got hold of a large number of them, in my mother's workbasket; then, having closed myself in a room far from others' eyes which might have broken the charm, I laid out on the floor a whole flowerbed, a whole garden of them. Were they not flowers? The word said so. It was enough to believe so. And I strove to do so for a whole quarter of an hour. Did not succeed.

On a childish plane this marked the defeat of nominalism. And perhaps after all I lacked imagination. But above all I recall very well having said to myself: "What a fool I am! What is the meaning of this comedy? There is nothing there but bits of ribbon, that is all . . ." and I went and put them back in my mother's little basket.

The harshness of the epoch is such that we find it hard to imagine (or, rather, are unwilling to admit) that there could have been such a tragic one at any other moment in history. Better informed, we should perhaps get to the point of being convinced that, quite on the contrary, the exceptional was the long period of toleration in which we lived before the unleashing of the horrors (which decidedly feel *at home* on earth)—so natural seemed to us that intellectual freedom, so lamentably compromised today. Now a time is returning in which all will be traitors who do not think "properly."

Some, it is true, are still resisting; and they are the only ones who count. It matters little that they are not very numerous: it is in them that the idea of God has taken refuge.

But the temptation that it is hardest to resist, for youth, is that of "committing oneself," as they say. Everything urges them to do so, and the cleverest sophistries, the apparently noblest, the most urgent, motives. One would have accomplished much if one persuaded youth that it is through *carelessness* and laziness that it commits itself;

. . . if one persuaded youth that it is essential—not to be this or that, but—to be.

. . .

Take things, not for what they claim to be, but for what they are.

Play the game with the hand one has.

Insist upon oneself as one is.

This does not keep one from struggling against all the lies, falsifications, etc., that men have contributed to and imposed on a natural state of things, against which it is useless to revolt. There is the inevitable and the modifiable. Acceptance of the modifiable is in no wise included in *amor fati.*

This does not keep one, either, from demanding of oneself the best, after one has recognized it as such. For one does not make oneself any more *lifelike* by giving precedence to the less good.

PS.—It strikes me today, as I take out these pages again, that I was wrong to tear out those at the beginning of this notebook. However imperfect they were (I was recovering from an illness), they replied in advance to the remarks made me by a friend in whose wisdom I have great confidence; he never speaks uselessly and never says anything that is not sensible. He protests that these detached pages, which I have just given him to read, are much less subversive than I seemed to think at first; that even many eminent representatives of the Church of today would be willing to subscribe to them, and he cites a few names that I am careful not to reproduce. Already X. and Y. had told me this, maintaining that I didn't know very well the present state of the Church, the intelligent flexibility of its credo. I granted him that I was not at all "up to date" and that, for greater convenience doubtless, I confined myself to what Bossuet taught: that the moment *Variations* were involved, these could only be the *Variations of the Protestant Churches* (according to the title of his admirable work), from which the Catholic Church was distinguished by "its character of immutability in faith."

"To be sure," he continues; "yet it is constantly evolving. You would like to dry it up by making of it a perfectly finished thing; it is living and replies to new demands. Remember the fine pages by Chesteron that

Claudel had translated and that you yourself made me read in in the old *N.R.F.*[9] The Church, he said, is never motionless; and he compared it to a chariot hurtling at full speed on a narrow crest and constantly avoiding new dangers on both sides. "There is no doubt," my friend continues, "that enlightened Catholics would not be bothered at all by your recent assertions. What they call God you are free to name Virtue if you wish; simply a question of words; it is the same thing. The idea of God, the need for God, torments you; *they* ask nothing more in order to recognize you as one of theirs." And since, nevertheless, I protest that there is some mis-understanding, since I look for something that will make them reject me after all, I return to those opening pages, the first ones written in this notebook, those imperfect and torn-up pages: they concerned eternal life: a sort of premonitory instinct urged me to emphasize them, to speak of that first, and I now realize that it was indeed essential to begin with that.

That the life of the "soul" is prolonged beyond the dis-solution of the flesh seems to me inadmissible, unthink-able, and my reason protests against it, just as it does against the incessant multiplication of souls. (May 1948.)

[9] Claudel translated a few pages entitled "The Paradoxes of Christi-anity" from Chapter xii of Chesterton's *Orthodoxy*, which appeared in the August 1910 issue of the *Nouvelle Revue Française*.

1948

N̶ew plunge into Simenon; I have just read six in
a row.   *8 January*

And Sartre's *Réflexions sur la question juive*.[1] Altogether
somewhat disappointed after all the (perhaps excessive)
good that Pierre Herbart had said of it. The thesis
advanced here is the very one that my friend Schiffrin
defended: the characteristics of the Jews (I mean those
that you anti-Semites hold against them) are characteristics acquired through the centuries, which *you* have
forced them to acquire, etc. I recognize here certain
arguments of the long conversation I had with him,
which have ceased to shock me. Today that conversation
seems to me clever and specious rather than correct,
despite the deep and close affection I have always had,
and increasingly so, for Schiffrin, in whom, I must add,
I recognized but very few of what might be considered
Jewish *shortcomings,* but merely their good qualities.
Likewise in the case of Léon Blum, for whom my esteem
(and why not say my admiration?) has only increased
during the long time our friendship has lasted,[2] but
especially since tragic events have given him an opportunity to reveal his worth more amply. (I am thinking
particularly of the sinister—and for him glorious—Riom
trial.)

9 January

And it so happens that yesterday afternoon's mail
brought me a stirring letter from Blum. If this journal
is ever divulged, that surprising coincidence will seem
"faked" and the above paragraph written as an after-
thought. Nothing of the sort.

Our relations are very spaced out, yet without there

[1] This little book, published by Paul Morihien in 1946, was issued
in New York in 1948 by Schocken Books as *Anti-Semite and Jew* in a
translation by George J. Becker.
[2] Since the deaths of Valéry and of Marcel Drouin, he remains the
only surviving friend of my generation. [A.]

ever having been exactly any distance between us; but
we live and operate in different domains (or rather on
different planes), where tangent points are rare. After
all, he seems to me to have remained (for he always
was so) much more utopian and even mystical than I am
willing to be. Interesting to note that, between the Jew
and the Christian, it is on his side that Hope and Faith
are to be found. But I have rarely encountered in a
Christian such personal disinterestedness and such *nobility*. I am very grateful to him for not holding against
me the rather harsh passages of my *Journal* about the
Jews and about him (which, by the way, I cannot disown, for I continue to think them utterly correct). He
disregards them and has never spoken to me of them.
Just like all of us, he has, to be sure, his shortcomings;
and his seem to me most particularly to be Jewish shortcomings. But to what a degree his good qualities, even
(or especially) those that I believe specifically Jewish,
prevail! In my eyes he is an admirable representative both
of Semitism and of humanity; just as he managed to be,
in his official and political relations with foreign countries, an excellent representative of France (whatever the
nationalists may think of this) and for the greater honor
of our country.

I return to Sartre's book. However right certain of his
most important affirmations seem to me (for instance,
that "it is anti-Semitism that creates the Jew"), only
apparently paradoxical, it remains none the less true that
anti-Semitism is not (or not solely) an invention made
up out of whole cloth by hatred and the need of motivating and feeding hatred. Psychologically and histori-
cally, it has its *raison d'être,* on which Sartre, it seems
to me, does not throw sufficient light.

When I was in Tunis in '42, I had occasion to talk
with several *lycée* professors, "Aryans" themselves. Each
of them independently told me (and this would have to
be verified) that in each class and each subject the best
pupils were Jews. They were constantly at the head,
and over the head, of the others. Even though this does
not necessarily mean that the Jews have a better mind
than the "Aryans," but perhaps merely that the qualities
of the latter, more profound, develop and manifest them-

selves more slowly, I should be rather inclined to believe this and am very wary of precocity. . . . None the
less: the die is cast and now hearts are already sown with
the seed of fierce passions, which will merely await an
opportunity to come to the surface, even if need be in
violence, with that sort of permission and right to injustice which theoretical anti-Semitism provides them.

From Sartre's whole book, often pasty and diffuse, I
retain this excellent passage:

"The Jews are the mildest of men. They are passionately opposed to violence. And that obstinate mildness
they preserve amidst the most frightful persecutions, that
sense of justice and reason which they set up as their
sole defense against a hostile, brutal, and unjust society,
is perhaps the best of the message they hold for us and
the true mark of their greatness." Bravo, Sartre! I feel
cordially in agreement. But there is none the less a
"Jewish question," painful and obsessive, and far from
being settled.

19 *January*

However different Valéry, Proust, Suarès, Claudel, and
I were from one another, if I look for the way in which
we might be recognized to be of the same age, and I
was about to say of the same team, I think it is the
great scorn we had for the things of the moment. And
it was in this way that the more or less secret influence
of Mallarmé showed in us. Yes, even Proust in his depiction of what we used to call "the contingencies," and
Fargue, who of late has been writing in the newspapers
to earn a living, but still with a very clear conviction
that art operates in the eternal and debases itself by
trying to serve even the noblest causes. I wrote: "I call
journalism everything that will interest less tomorrow
than it does today." Consequently nothing seems to me
at once more absurd and more justified than the reproach
that is directed at me today of never having managed to
commit myself. Indeed! And it is in this regard that the
leaders of the new generation, who gauge a work according to its immediate efficacy, differ most from us. They
also aim for an immediate success, whereas we considered
it quite natural to remain unknown, unappreciated, and
disdained until after forty-five. We were banking on time,

concerned only with forming a lasting work like those we admired, on which time has but little hold and which aspire to seem as moving and timely tomorrow as today.

Nevertheless, when there was a need to *bear witness*, I did not at all fear to commit myself, and Sartre admitted this with complete good faith. But the *Souvenirs de la Cour d'Assises* have almost no relation to literature, any more than the campaign against the Great Concessionary Companies of the Congo or the *Retour de l'U.R.S.S.*

24 January

No shame as a result of facile sensual pleasures. Sort of vulgar paradise and communion through the basest in man. The important thing is not attributing any importance to them, or not thinking oneself debased by them: the mind is in no wise involved in them, any more than the soul, which does not pay much attention to them. But, in the adventure, an extraordinary amusement and pleasure accompany the joy of discovery and of novelty.

8 June

There is nothing to do but pick up the thread, without explanation and as if nothing had happened. Summer (after frigid days, now we have warm, glorious days . . .) helps me return to life. Yes, suddenly I caught myself enjoying life again. Last night, in a sort of joyous intoxication and new lease of life, I could not resign myself to going to bed until after midnight, and this morning I was awake before seven o'clock. I should have worked admirably if my whole morning (it is now half past twelve) had not been taken up by correspondence, like every day, or almost—and almost exclusively letters of refusal or excuse. That puts you in a sort of cantankerous state of mind, at least in a defensive state from which your friends run the risk of suffering. It wrinkles one's forehead and heart, and I am dreadfully sorry not to have been able to give a better welcome to Jef Last, who was considerably affected by my insufficiently cordial reception. He might have attributed it to some cooling of my friendship, whereas I was simply out of patience. How painful it is not to be able to *suffice*! I lack time and strength. I went through a long period of almost constant fatigue in which I longed to get out of the game; but impossible to *withdraw*. And just as in economics "bad money drives away the good," bores and intruders usurp and take over the field as masters; all that remains is theirs.

The worst is allowing people to think: "Yes, since the Nobel Prize, Gide has *become distant*." After that there remains nothing but to go and drown or hang oneself. And it so happens that since the warmth has returned, I have ceased to have any desire to do so. But before that, on certain days, I felt as if already completely detached; this, however, held me back: the impossibility of getting anyone to understand, to accept, the real reason for a suicide; at least, this way I shall be left alone and in peace. But go away on a trip . . . already on the steps of the train, what a relief to feel out of reach, liberated! But go where? I think of that little hotel that Alix told me about (I noted it down) in a fishing village on Lago di Garda. If only I were sure of finding room there. . . . Constantly called upon, I must put off from day to day; and constantly I hear the eldest of the Fates whispering in my ear; you haven't much time left.

3 September

These last days of life seem the most difficult to live through; but this must be an illusion, for one has only to leave it to time, and to gravity. . . . Valéry used to get angry at the fact that more importance is given to the last moments of a life than to all the rest; this in relation to last-minute conversions. I believe that not even he escaped the devotion of his family; but I have so much respect myself for the sentiments that, in such a case, motivate one's relatives that I prefer to beat a retreat, as perhaps Valéry did too. And what more would that prove than, most likely, a great conjugal love, which is certainly worth sacrificing something to; that something, after all, not having so much importance when it is given the lie by the entire work. But the use that is then made of it! The contradiction of the entire work that people try to see in it. . . . This is what must stiffen you.

An extraordinary, an insatiable need to love and be loved, I believe this is what dominated my life and urged me to write; an almost mystical need, moreover, since I consented to its not being satisfied during my lifetime.

Torri del Benaco, 7 September

I believe I am sincere in saying that death does not frighten me much (I am constantly thinking of it); but I see the summer go by with a sort of despair.

Never before had I seen such a long series of such beautiful, such splendid days.

Here since the 22nd of July, I believe; first with Marc (in the Hudson bought from Pierre, with a stop at Locarno and crossing of the Gothard), then with Pierre. In August, unbearable heat and suffocation. Besides: otitis and weakness of the heart. The heart is hardly any better, it seems to me (no pain, but insufficiency and a constant feeling of insecurity such as the skater experiences when venturing onto ice that he feels to be thin and ready to break under him).

Two wonderful and amazing storms:

Fluctibus et fremitu assurgens Benace marino.[3]

But since the beginning of September the air is light; the midday heat is no longer excessive; the mornings and evenings are cool. To the daily splendor is added a constant feeling of death near by which makes me keep repeating to myself that these fine days are the last for me. I am writing this without bitterness.

Paris, 15 December

Last words. . . . I do not see why one should try to pronounce them louder than the others. At least I do not feel the need of doing so.

[3] "You, Lake Benacus, surging up with waves and a roar like the sea," is from Virgil: *Georgics*, II, 160. Benacus is the modern Lago di Garda, on the shore of which stands Torri del Benaco.

1949

. . . **B**ut don't believe that. I recall having gone *30 January*
months, long series of months, without working, without being able to work at all. To such a degree as not to understand just why I did not utterly collapse. You see, what saved me was a certain obstinacy, a certain strength in clinging that kept me from letting go. Yet I have lived at least ten years of my life, if they were put end to end, in the belief that all was lost and that I should never again manage to say anything. Besides, on two occasions I tiresomely persisted on the wrong track. I spent as much time spoiling *L'Intérêt général* and then *Geneviève* (of which I destroyed almost everything) as in successfully completing *Les Faux-Monnayeurs*.[1] Everything that I wrote then, *invita Minerva,* remained unspeakably mediocre.

But doubtless it is not bad to find something to blush over in one's life, and without having to look very far.

15 May

Spiritualistic to an unbelievable degree, he never went to pray, or weep, or meditate over the tomb of his parents. For that goes far back, that disregard for matter which keeps it from holding his attention. It is as if he did not believe in it. I say "he," but that "he" is I. No logic in this; it is instinctive and spontaneous. I can find no better example of it than this: when at Cuverville I was present at the lugubrious delivery of my sister-in-law—I mean by this that I had to help the doctor in the dreadful operation to which he consented only after making sure that the baby's heart had stopped beating (he would have had to have recourse to a Cæsarean, but he did not have the surgical instruments)—I had to hold my sister-in-law's legs while he extracted what was already nothing but a corpse. . . . No, I cannot relate

---

[1] Neither the play *Robert or the Common Weal* (1944–5) nor the tale *Geneviève* (1939), which closes the cycle of *The School for Wives,* is generally considered among Gide's major works; whereas *The Counterfeiters* (1926) forms the cornerstone of his reputation.

that; nothing more painful can be imagined. And I recall that later on, in the night, the two of us alone and face to face beside that recumbent woman looked at each other. He was sweating. "We are assassins," he said. "But when the child has ceased to live, one tries to save the mother." (The pangs had lasted thirty hours.) Although she had not been put to sleep (it was still contrary to principles; there has been progress since), she was lying unconscious. Near her a jumbled mass of bloody, soiled remains. . . .

When the morning came, "Get that out of the way," I naïvely said to the gardener's wife when she at last came to see "how everything was." Could I suppose that those amorphous fragments, to which I pointed while turning away with disgust, could I suppose that in the eyes of the Church they already represented the human and sacred creature they were preparing to clothe? O mystery of the incarnation! What was my amazement, a few hours later, when I saw *it* again, which for me already had "no name in any language," cleaned up, dressed, bedecked with ribbons, lying in a little cradle in preparation for the ritual entombment. No one, fortunately, had been aware of the sacrilege I had been on the point of committing, had already committed in thought, when I had said: "Get that out of the way." Yes, quite happily that thoughtless command had been heard by no one. And I remained a long time lost in thought before *it;* before that little face with the broken forehead carefully hidden; before that innocent flesh which, if I had been alone, yielding to my first impulse, I should have thrown onto a manure pile near the afterbirth, and which now religious attentions had just saved from the abyss. . . . I told no one what I experienced then, what I am relating here. Was I to think that, for a few moments, a soul had inhabited this body? It has its tomb at Cuverville, in that cemetery to which I do not want to go back.

Half a century has passed. . . . I cannot say, to tell the truth, that I exactly still see that little face. No, what I recall precisely is my surprise, my sudden emotion before its extraordinary beauty. I had never before seen anything, I have not since seen anything, comparable.

The faces of the dead can be beautiful. Death often brings to our features a sort of calm and serenity in the renunciation of life. But that little corpse had not lived; its beauty remained utterly inexpressive. Some (some mothers especially) go about exclaiming over the beauty of the newborn. As for me, I do not believe I have ever seen a single other one that did not seem to me almost hideous, I confess, shriveled, grimacing, flushed. . . . This one (it was partly to this that he obviously owed his beauty) had not known the pangs of being born. And it was probably not enough that his features were beautiful (my sister-in-law was beautiful; my two other nephews and my niece were among the most beautiful children I have ever seen), but besides, altogether blood-less, the substance of which he was made did not seem like human flesh, but rather some ethereal substance, some translucent and nacreous paraffin, some immaterial pulp; it seemed like the flesh of a Eucharistic host. A bow of blue satin (it would have been pink, the garden-er's wife told me, if the baby had been a girl) on the right side of a delicate lace bonnet, as in the portrait of an infant by Sustermans (I believe), further emphasized the paleness of that face and of that uninhabited forehead. That little cranium had been emptied of the brain mat-ter, which had indeed been thrown on the manure pile with the scraps from that frightful operation, the mucus and the placenta.

This tale aims to prove what? That the soul is at a loss where to take refuge when its carnal support disappears? The Church provided for this when she enjoins us to believe in "the resurrection of the flesh."

As for the soul, it goes without saying that I believe in it! Why, of course I believe in the soul. I believe in it as in the glow of phosphorus. But I cannot imagine that glow without the phosphorus that produces it. In any case, I am not indulging in theories here. Theories and ratiocinations annoy me. *Animus, Animum, Anima.* . . . Such discriminations make me dizzy, for I have reached the point of not even distinguishing the soul from the body. I cannot conceive of one without the other. In writing this I am merely suggesting a personal attitude of mind that explains in my own eyes, without in any way justifying or excusing it, what I said earlier about the tomb of my parents; and this too: that I did not even dream of spending the night sitting by the bedside of my dead wife. It was all over. A telegram announcing her end had suddenly recalled me to Cuverville from Chitré in Poitou, where I was staying with a woman of my acquaintance. I had left my wife, a few days earlier, in a precarious state of health, to be sure, but not an alarming one, so that I had left her without fear. She was not only what I loved the most in the world; but it even seemed to me (it still seems to me today) that it was in relation to her that I lived, and that, really, I depended on her. Likewise I had been the tragic occupation of her life. And now it was over.

I can see her again on her deathbed. With no more of that smiling amenity left which always tempered her gravity, she seemed like a Jansenist painted by Philippe de Champaigne.

I left there those mortal remains. *"Et nunc manet in te,"* I said to myself; or at least (for I had not yet discovered these significant words in Virgil's *Culex*[2]) I felt urgently that henceforth *she* lived on only in my memory. And if I return now to that image of the phosphorus and its glow, it is to say that solely because of, and by virtue of, its glow the phosphorus matters to me, that solely the glow matters to me. . . . Oh, perhaps I should not speak in the same way if I had loved her carnally. And how explain that?—it was her soul that I loved, and yet I did not believe in that soul. I do not believe in the soul separated from the body. I believe that body and soul are one and the same thing, and that when life has withdrawn from the body, it is all over with both at once. That arbitrary, artificial distinction between the soul and the body—my reason protests against it: I believe (I cannot not believe) in their inevitable interdependence. So I may well say that the soul alone matters to me; but it cannot produce and manifest itself,

[2] "And now (she) remains in you" is found in line 269 of *The Culex* or *The Gnat*, a poem of doubtful authorship often attributed to Virgil's youth.

and I cannot understand and apprehend it save through the body. And it is through the body, despite all mysticism, that any manifestation of love becomes possible.

In writing this I am well aware that I am not throwing any light upon what remains the great mystery. But you do not throw any light whatever on it either by trying to give to the soul an existence distinct from that of the body. It even seems to me at times that it is because of you and your distinctions that I cannot understand anything about it, and that perhaps everything is simpler than you make it out. You shift and disperse the problem without solving it at all, and immediately you come up against many an impossibility.

Chanterez-vous quand serez vaporeuse? [3]

writes Valéry in an admirable sob, which is tantamount to saying: "Alas, great soul that I loved, I know that, without the vibrant body, the soul is absent." Now, that soul that I know to be unable to exist without the body, how could it then be immortal? I have already written, I don't recall where, that there is probably no word of the Gospel which I earlier or more completely adopted, subordinating my being to it and letting it dominate my thoughts: "My kingdom is not of this world." So that "this world," which, for the mass of human beings, alone exists—to tell the truth, I do not believe in it. I believe in the spiritual world, and all the rest is nothing to me. But that spiritual world, I believe that it has existence only through us, in us; that it depends on us, on that support which our body provides it. And when I write: "I believe that . . ." there is no question whatever of an act of faith. I say: "I believe" because there is no other way of expressing the establishment, by my reason, of that obvious fact. What have I to do with *revelations*? I want to appeal solely to my reason—which is the same and was the same at all times and for all men.

Beneath which sprawls at ease my constant sensuality.

I believe that there are not two separate worlds, the spiritual and the material, and that it is useless to oppose them. They are two aspects of one and the same universe;

[3] "Will you sing when you are vaporous?" is a line from *Le Cimetière marin* (*The Cemetery by the Sea*).

as it is useless to oppose the soul and the body. Useless is the torment of the mind that urges them to war. It is in their identification that I have found calm. And that the spiritual world prevails in sovereign importance is a notion of my mind, which depends intimately on my body; both conspire and agree in order to achieve harmony in me. I will not and cannot try to subject and subordinate one to the other, as the Christian ideal aims to do. I know by experience (for I long strove to do so) what it costs. On whichever side, body or soul, victory inclines, the victory is artificial and temporary and we have eventually to pay the expenses of the conflict.

27 May

Accumulation of days in the hospital; vague mass of more than a month; hesitating between better and worse. Succession of days filled almost solely with reading. Sort of desert morass with the daily oasis, charming beyond all hope, of the regular visits of the incomparable friend that, during this long period of purgatory, Roger Martin du Gard was for me. His mere presence already provided me a link with life; he forestalled all the needs of my mind and body; and however gloomy I might have been before his coming, I soon felt quite revived by his remarks and by the affectionate attention he paid to mine. I do not know whether I could ever have been more aware in the past of the ineffable blessing of friendship. And what an effacement (even excessive) of his own interest, of himself! No, no! Religion achieves nothing better, or so naturally.

The *Anthologie* so long awaited has finally appeared.[4] *Grosso modo*, very satisfied; and especially, perhaps, at not having made my personal taste, it seems to me, prevail unduly. I hope to have brought to light a number of exquisite little poems that deserved to be known and that I did not see quoted anywhere.

4 June

Some days it seems to me that if I had at hand a good pen, good ink, and good paper, I should without difficulty write a masterpiece.

[4] The printing of his *Anthology of French Poetry* was finally finished on 31 March 1949.

10 *June*

Hugo enjoys rhyming two diphthongs, one counting as two syllables, the other as one. I note in passing:

Qu'un vin pur fasse fête aux poulardes friandes!
Et que de cet amas de fricots et de viandes . . .[5]

I had noticed others.

Ces ~~dernières~~ lignes
insignifiantes
datent ou 12 juin 1949,

Tout m'invite à croire
qu'elles seront les
dernières de ce Journal.

André Gide.

25 janvier 1950. *

---

[5] Let a pure wine honor these dainty fowl!
     And of this mound of victuals and meats . . .

are lines spoken by Aïrolo in Hugo's comedy *Mangeront-ils?* (Will They Eat?), Act II, Scene iii.

* "These insignificant lines date from 12 June 1949 [sic]. Everything leads me to think that they will be the last of this *Journal.*— André Gide.—25 January 1950."

INDEX

THE TEXT of this book is set in Caledonia, a Linotype face that belongs to the family of printing types called "modern face" by printers—a term used to mark the change in style of type-letters that occurred about 1800. Caledonia borders on the general style of Scotch Modern, but is more freely drawn than that letter. The book was composed, printed, and bound by THE COLONIAL PRESS INC., *Clinton, Massachusetts. Paper manufactured by* S. D. WARREN COMPANY, *Boston, Massachusetts. Cover photograph by* DANIEL FILIPACCHI; *design by* HARRY FORD.